Class, State, and Power in the Third World

Other books by James F. Petras:

*Critical Perspectives on Imperialism and Social Class
    in the Third World*
*U.S. and Chile: Imperialism and the Overthrow of
    Allende* (co-author)
The Nationalization of Venezuelan Oil (co-author)
Puerto Rico and Puerto Ricans (co-editor)
Latin America: From Dependence to Revolution
Peasants in Revolt (co-author)
Politics and Social Structure in Latin America
*Cultivating Revolution: The United States and Agrarian Reform
    in Latin America* (co-author)
Fidel Castro Speaks (co-editor)
Politics and Social Forces in Chilean Development
Latin America: Reform or Revolution (co-editor)

Class, State, and Power in the Third World

with Case Studies on Class Conflict in Latin America

JAMES F. PETRAS

with MORRIS H. MORLEY, PETER DeWITT,
and A. EUGENE HAVENS

ALLANHELD, OSMUN   Montclair / LandMark Studies
ZED PRESS   London / Imperialism Series

ALLANHELD, OSMUN & PUBLISHERS, INC.

Published in the United States of America in 1981
by Allanheld, Osmun & Co. Publishers, Inc.
6 South Fullerton Avenue, Montclair, New Jersey 07042

ZED PRESS

Published in the United Kingdom in 1981 by Zed Press,
57 Caledonian Road, London N1 9DN

Library of Congress Cataloging in Publication Data

Petras, James F   1937–
    Class, state, and power in the Third World, with
case studies on class conflict in Latin America.

    (LandMark studies)
    Includes index.
    1. Social classes—Latin America—Addresses, essays,
lectures.   2.   Social conflict—Addresses, essays,
lectures.   3.   United States—Foreign economic relations
—Latin America—Addresses, essays, lectures.
4.   Socialism in Latin America—Addresses, essays,
lectures.   5.   Latin America—Foreign economic relations
—United States—Addresses, essays, lectures.
I.   Title.
HN110.5.Z9S66   1980   305.5   80–25938

(USA) ISBN 0-86598-018-7
        ISBN 0-86598-056-X (PBK)
(UK) ISBN 0-86232-096-8

Printed in the United States of America

Dedicated to the memory of Lelio Basso—
friend, scholar and fighter

Contents

Tables and Figures

Figure

Introduction

There is a great need to rethink many of the ideas and conceptions that informed much of the critical writing on the Third World in general and Latin America in particular. The demise of colonialism has been accompanied by the massive infusion of capital and significant penetration of the peripheral state. Greater flows of metropolitan capital have not led, in some cases, to mere "dependency and stagnation," but to rapid growth and socioeconomic transformation. The problems of "underdevelopment," in this context, have taken second place before the growing social polarities and class and regional conflicts that have recently emerged. Expanding capitalism has not led to greater stability, but to increasing class conflict and direct challenges to state power.

The changing forms of international domination also demonstrate the need for new thinking and analysis. Alongside commercial and investment exploitation, widespread financial penetration and lucrative licensing agreements have become increasingly important. Interest and rent payments are added to the traditional dividends and industrial profits that accrue to metropolitan corporate interests. Changes in the economic sphere have been accompanied by new forms of political rulership and interstate relationships, requiring a new analysis. The proliferation of all-pervasive dictatorial states linked to large-scale, long-term capital accumulation in the periphery, and the effort by the advanced capitalist countries to fashion a common political framework (trilateralism) in the face of increasing competition exemplify the need to recast political frameworks to account for new realities.

This book is essentially a *political* and *social* reading of contemporary developments in the Third World and its relationships with the advanced capitalist countries. The point of departure is an analysis of the process of class formation and conflict and their interrelationship. Class analysis, the perspective from which the book is written, thus encompasses more than simply an inventory or typology of classes; more basically, it refers to the interplay between productive systems, state and interstate relations, and classes. The book contains two parts: Part I includes an introductory theoretical and comparative-analytical section, including essays discussing the new mechanisms and patterns of economic and political domination; Part II contains a series of case studies discussing the social and political components of class conflict and socialist revolution.

The discussion of the relations between the United States and the Third World has been stymied by a conceptual roadblock. There has been no serious effort to go beyond the discussion of either the "capitalist state," rooted within a national unit, or the "colonial state," anchored in the previous forms of European domination. The notion of a postcolonial imperial state is introduced in the opening essay as a means of overcoming this theoretical and conceptual impasse. The capitalist state operates within a new set of boundaries that are essentially defined by the worldwide imperatives of capitalist expansion in an era of juridically independent nation-states. The concept of the imperial state focuses our attention on the political as well as economic dimension of imperialism by redefining the scope and nature of the state. In this conception, the illusion of state autonomy is highlighted. The analysis of the imperial state demonstrates the all-inclusive manner in which the decisionmakers are immersed in the symbols and substance of capitalist power. The imperial state is conceived of in terms of a dynamic reciprocal (dialectical) relation to the class struggle: It promotes "collaborator classes" and molds social structures of dominated formations as well as being shaped by dominant class forces.

The world economy is structured by the activities of imperialist capital, the framework for which is created by the imperial state. The framework is logically prior to the movement of private capital. This is the reverse of world-systems theory in which the state simply responds to the demands of capital and imperialism is seen as a purely economic phenomenon, autonomous of state action.

Methodologically, unlike modernization theorists, who take the nation-state as their point of departure, or the world-systems theorists, who operate with the idea of a world economy with component nation-states, our conception begins with the interstate system. Insofar as a world system is conceptualized, it emphasizes the political level. The imperial system is built on a complex set of class relations; the revolutionary rupture of those relations allows for a society to withdraw from the imperial system. A transformation in class relations sets in motion a contradictory situation in which a revolutionary society participates in a capitalist world market.

The second major issue that requires discussion is the transformation occurring in the Third World: The older notion of static, backward countries may be applicable in some areas, but it is precisely in the most dynamic Third World areas where the political and social action is occurring. Chapter 2, "Capitalist Expansion and Class Conflict in Advanced Third-World Countries," highlights a new conceptualization of revolution, emphasizing the links between capitalist expansion and class struggle. Working from a comparative-historical perspective, the chapter emphasizes that as capitalism grows in Brazil, Iran, and South Africa, so does class conflict and the probability of social revolution, given the political framework and social consequences that accompany rapid capitalist growth. It also emphasizes that in a number of "advanced" Third World countries the fundamental issue is *not* "underdevelopment," but class inequality and exploitation and social and political polarization, as necessary conditions and outcomes of rapid capitalist growth. The analysis points to the centrality of the advanced regions of the Third World as the epicenters of social revolution. From this perspective, social revolution is not a product of a *passing* moment of "modernization," but an *approaching* phase: Heightened class conflict accompanies capital maturity.

The chapters dealing with the political economy of advanced capitalist domination focus largely on Latin America. The analysis focuses on the interface of the imperial state and the multinational corporations and banks in shaping the world economy. Chapter 3, "U.S. Investment in Latin America," maps the various forms of surplus extraction and describes the shifts from agro-mineral to industrial and financial investments, regional concentration, and the new patterns of technological exploitation.

The accelerated growth of financial capital and the tendency for the former industrial states to become "rentier states" through the collection of interest payments is discussed in Chapter 5, "The Political Economy of International Debt." The political frameworks in the imperial and peripheral areas, which have been elaborated to contain the challenges from below and to promote worldwide expansion, are found in Chapter 4, "The Trilateral Commission and Latin America," and Chapter 5, "The Revival of Fascism." The former examines the attempt by the United States, Europe, and Japan to formulate a common framework to exploit the Third World and contain their increasingly conflicting and competitive interests. The latter analyzes the emergence of a species of peripheral state located in the intersection of externally induced capital expansion and rising class conflict. The conflict engendered between the two is resolved by an entity that frees markets and imprisons people.

Despite the significant changes and sometimes spectacular growth of productive forces in a number of Third World countries, the international economic order still reflects the patterns established in the colonial period. Chapter 6, "A New International Division of Labor?" criticizes a number of western writers who have overgeneralized from the industrial experiences of a few Third World countries and have overlooked the continuities with the past. The chapter points to the *unequal patterns of change* between regions and countries of the Third World and the continuing dependence of industrial growth on traditional exports and linkages to the metropolises.

The discussion of expanding U.S. capital and dictatorial peripheral regimes, however, fails to capture a new and increasingly important reality in the Third World: the tremendous growth of European (and Japanese) investment and trade and the concomitant growing political influence of European-backed Social Democratic movements. Chapter 8, "The Socialist International and Social Democracy in Latin America," examines this new option that has emerged in a number of countries and evaluates its viability as an alternative to the revolutionary socialist and fascist movements in these countries.

Part II, "Class Conflict and Revolution," emphasizes the centrality of class struggle in any understanding of the processes of long-term, large-scale change. The conceptualization of class is in terms of both structural development and political action. Chapter 9, "Socialist Revolutions and Their Class Components," emphasizes the linkages between class and political struggle. Socialist revolutions are analyzed as outcomes of particular forms and processes of capitalist expansion, embracing economic, military, political and cultural dimensions. The chapter reformulates and reinterprets the relative roles of workers, peasants, and intellectuals in the revolutionary process, highlighting the importance of the interrelationship of all three classes in different periods.

The country studies illustrate the class-analysis approach and concretely examine a number of issues pertaining to the issues of class struggle and state power. The relationship between class struggle and democratic institutions and procedures is considered in Chapter 10, "Political Opposition and the Rise of Neo-Fascism in Latin America." In periods of heightening class confrontation, democratic forms and procedures facilitating social change are shunted aside by propertied interests, and questions of force come to the fore. The case of Chile during the Allende period illustrates this point. The rise of fascist dictatorships, however, has to be viewed in a dynamic context—not as a set of durable institutions existing above the class structure. The chapter points to the growing and widespread opposition to these regimes as evidence of the new contradictions that are emerging in response to the new economic and political order.

The relationship between class struggle and economic development is examined in Chapter 11, "The Working Class and the Cuban Revolution." Through a historical overview of the period between 1933 and 1963, the chapter argues that the defeat of the working-class revolt of 1933 was only partial: The threat of a new uprising and the enduring tradition of struggle and organization were given institutional and juridicial expression to the point where they became a serious obstacle to capitalist accumulation. This historical institutional legacy forms the context for the political confrontation between the July 26th Movement and the Batista regime in the 1950s. The ultimate socialization of production between 1959 and 1963 is thus described not as a fortuitous phenomenon or reactive response to U.S. policy, but as linked to the general crisis of capitalist development engendered by the cumulative forces derived from the class struggle.

Chapter 12, "Peasant Movements and Social Change: Cooperatives in Peru," points to the decisive importance of class relations within the productive units and the class nature of the productive system as a whole in shaping the effectiveness of sectoral change—namely peasant receptivity to agrarian collectivization. Chapter 13, "Urban Radicalism in Peru," challenges the individualistic-incrementalist research methods that dominate urbanization studies and points to the growth of radical consciousness and collective political struggles among the slum settlers of Lima. Moreover, it demonstrates that greater urban-industrial development and integration—far from "moderating" political behavior—have a tendency to spur more radical electoral activity. By identifying long-term, large-scale structural patterns and emphasizing innovative political movements, the analysis moves beyond the narrow-focus limitations of survey research to the underlying forces informing radical squatter-settlement behavior.

Most discussion of class struggle and class politics has focused on national political organization and leaders and programmatic statements. Yet with the spread of dictatorial regimes, the absence of these national configurations has not been accompanied by the demise of working-class politics—at least in the case of Argentina. Chapter 14, "Terror and the Hydra: The Resurgence of the Argentine Working Class," points to the importance of microphenomena: how the family, the neighborhood, and the workshop sustain working-class culture. It is argued that informal associations provide the networks that buttress working-class solidarity and collective action in times of terror and severe repression.

The centrality of political organization, and the combining of a multiplicity of forms of political struggle, is evidenced in the successful outcome of the Sandanista-led Nicaraguan revolution. The outcome demonstrates the revolutionary potentialities among a number of oppressed groups and the possibility for class alliances. The process of class conflict, the tactical alliances with propertied groups, and the strategic consolidation of a revolutionary leadership are indicators of the maturation of the revolutionary process in Nicaragua. The question raised is whether this is an isolated phenomenon or whether it holds general lessons of great consequence not only to the people of Latin America and the Third World, but to all of us.

part one

THE IMPERIAL STATE AND THE WORLD ECONOMY

The U.S. Imperial State

by JAMES F. PETRAS and MORRIS H. MORLEY

The State in the Age of Imperialism

There remains a fundamental problem with most of the new writing on the state that has not been adequately dealt with: "The state" has been conceived within a national unit; the "national state" has been the point of departure for most discussion of classes and class struggle.[1] This notion is reproduced in the analysis of the "colonial state": the capitalist state transplanted to the colonial setting with its linkages to the metropolis.[2] The elaborations on the state have extended its domain of "function" from simple enforcer or repressive force to ideological and legitimating functions, the agent of economic promotion as well as coordinator of particular class interests, the latter seeming at times to carry with it a return to traditional liberal notions of the state as "broker."[3] Yet what is striking in the contemporary period is not the continued elaboration of internal functions, but the extended jurisdiction of the state as an imperial state far beyond its territorial borders. [Throughout this study, the terms "U.S. imperial state" and "imperial state" will be used interchangeably.] The imperial state, by its reach, is in effect setting up new rules of statehood *within* the interstate system. In due course these rules will serve to influence and shape the behavior of all other states on an ongoing basis.

Within the last decade even bourgeois writers have increasingly downplayed the operational distinction between "domestic" and "foreign" policy, and stressed the growing "interdependence" of the whole.[4] Is it not time that Marxists begin to understand the scope and nature of the interstate system in terms of the nature and scope of the central (i.e., imperial) state(s) as contrasted to the diminished sovereignty of all other imperialized states? To the extent that the former has become *more* of a "state," *to that extent* the latter has become less of a "state."

In discussing the United States today, we are not dealing with the "capitalist-state" or the "state in capitalist society," but with the imperial state. And it is time that we discard the notion that imperialism is an "economic phenomena" that can be analyzed by looking merely at the flow of capital and corporate behavior. The literature on the multinationals, as unsystematic and rich in detail as it may be, tends to forget the institution that created the universe in which they function: the imperial states.[5] Nor can any discussion of capital accumulation on a world scale become meaningful unless we understand the central role of the imperial state in creating the conditions for it. The imperial state does not function on the basis of some inner logic of its own but, on the contrary, responds to the interests and demands of capitalists seeking to *move capital abroad* in order to pursue accumulation activites on a global level. The U.S. state, as an imperial state shaped and controlled by "outward looking" capital, moves initially to create the conditions (e.g., "state building," infrastructure development) for long-term, large-scale multinational corporation (MNC) capital flows into the targeted (imperialized) countries. Furthermore, the efforts to analyze the postcolonial (imperialized) system have to be put in the context of the multiple activities of the U.S. imperial state (which included state formation, disintegration, and "reconstruction") designed to sustain the conditions for capital accumulation and expansion in the periphery of the capitalist world economy.

There is no sense in which the cumulative and multifarious activities of capitalism on a world scale—embodied in the notion of the world capitalist market—are adequately conceptualized by looking at imperialist relations vis-à-vis social formations.[6] In that view a simplistic notion of imperialism, with its site in particular social formations, can be taken into account. Metaphorical analogies to chains and links are a poor substitute for understanding the manner in which the totality of capitalist relations impinge upon the "chain," its "links" both metropolis and the dominated capitalist periphery.[7] The chain metaphor itself excludes the question of who makes the chain, since the metropolis is "part" of a key link. Was not the imperial state a prime forger of the chain?

The exploited classes seek to instrumentalize the state against imperialism as their ultimate weapon in the struggle. The locus of imperialism in the instrumentality of domination—so pervasive and decisive for exploitation in the dominated capitalist social formations—is obscured by the failure to recognize the centrality of the coercive role of the state in maintaining class domination and class rule, and to dilute the notion of class domination into a one-sided problem of "hegemony," i.e., presumably an ideological struggle with its emphasis primarily on education.[8] The notion of physical combat and struggle is relegated to the "exceptional state," a purposeful and deliberate academic effort to obfuscate the centrality of force in state power within bourgeois democracies.

To study the imperial state as opposed to the capitalist state, we must develop new conceptual thinking. The political, social, and economic context within which the "capitalist" state and the imperialist state function is radically different. Within the bounds of the nation-state, the capitalist state is the only source of sovereign authority. In contrast, the imperial state exercises its authority in a field of competing and aspiring sovereigns—competing imperialist states, regional powers, and local authorities. The competent authority is not clearly delimited in fact, if not in law.

In the setting of accumulation on a world-historical scale, the emergence of the United States as a competitive—and subsequently the dominant—imperial power within world capitalism is of relatively recent origin. Since the last decade of the nineteenth century, however, no movements of U.S. (proto) multinational capital have taken place without the sustained involvement of the U.S. imperial state, whether we talk about the entree, expansion, or survival of this capital in the states in which it has located. The centrality of imperial capital within the U.S. social formation defines the "domestic" and "external" structures and functions of the state as well as its policy. The roots of the state are anchored in the United States, and its branches span the globe: Its origins began in the national unit; its functions and operations grow in a multiplicity of societies and transnational organizations.

In the following discussion we will develop a theoretical framework in which to discuss the U.S. state, one that is anchored in the new realities of international domination and exploitation.

The U.S. imperial state can be defined as those executive bodies or agencies within the "government" that are charged with promoting and protecting the expansion of capital across state boundaries by the multinational corporate community headquartered in the imperial center. Some imperial agencies, such as the departments of Commerce and the Treasury, are more directly linked to the U.S. private corporate world than others, but the actions of all are directed toward the goal of facilitating U.S. capital accumulation and reproduction on a worldwide scale. The U.S. imperial state essentially exercises two major functions: one economic, the other coercive. Both the coercive and economic apparatuses operate to facilitate capital accumulation on a global basis. Although analytically distinct, these apparatuses perform interrelated functions at the operational level. The imperial state's cumulative economic pressures against the Cuban Revolution during 1959 and 1960, for example, served in part to create the basis for indirect military intervention in mid-1961 as a means of reconstituting the capitalist political-order (on one level, through the aegis of large-scale U.S. government economic assistance). In contrast to the failure in Cuba, however, the 1965 U.S. military invasion of the Dominican Republic successfully imposed a proimperial outcome on an internal social struggle that laid the groundwork for renewed U.S. "development" loans and credits from an assortment of public agencies (AID, Export-Import Bank). These flows of "infrastructure" capital functioned, in turn, to restore an appropriate and secure milieu for foreign capital accumulation. The activities of the U.S. capital state, concerned primarily with the perservation of internal order, are increasingly overshadowed by action directly addressed to the social order within the capitalist world as a whole. The duality of the state—guardian at home and instrument of expansion abroad—reflects distinct, as well as overlapping, jurisdictions of agencies. The Treasury Department, for example, controls the flow of currency inside the country and instructs its representatives in the "international banks" how to vote on loans regarding capitalist development abroad.

As more and more of the largest U.S. industrial and financial corporations have expanded abroad, and as a larger proportion of their total earnings are derived from their overseas operations,[9] the activities of the imperial state have become increasingly important for the maintenance of these "building blocks" of U.S. capitalist economy. The post-World War II imperial state apparatus preceded and initially grew much more rapidly than U.S. corporate capital.[10] While private funds began to advance abroad shortly after 1945, the networks and alliances fashioned by the much more voluminous state and public investments, in the form of foreign aid, were essential in creating the groundwork for the later acceleration of private capital investment.* For many writers who adopted a short-term view of these developments, the initial great excess in public expenditures and noneconomic activities over and against private investment and returns was an argument against the theory of imperialism. By emphasizing military organization and spending, they were given a false sense of "autonomy," and their growth was ascribed either to strategic thinking ("national security") or to the "imperatives of bureaucratic organization."[11]

The long-term global impact of massive military and nonmilitary expenditures and activities, however, were soon to be matched and surpass-

---

*In using the terms "public capital" to describe U.S. government funds and "private (corporate) capital" to describe U.S. corporate funds, we are of course cognizant that both are agencies "of capital" and that none of the "funds" at any time leaves the realm or circuits of capital. We make this distinction, however, to serve a very specific purpose, viz., to provide a basis to differentiate between state and society, between class and state. Otherwise, the particular relationship between state and (civil) society is fundamentally obscured, and, therefore, one cannot comprehend the nature of that relationship. Nor can one understand the basis on which the state as a product of class society and class struggle is, at the same time, not identical with that society.

ed by the massive flow and accumulation of private capital. From the latter phenomenon, a new group of writers began to assert the "autonomy" of "multinational" capital, forgetting the state's role in providing and sustaining the universe within which "multinational" capital operates.[12] These erroneous conceptions reflect the narrow interpretative focus of the research, which attempts to identify mechanical correlations between economic causes and political effects, or vice versa. The alternative approach is anchored in a wider world-historical analysis of the interplay between the political and economic forces within the capitalist state over time and across regions, emphasizing the role of the imperial state as the organizing force behind the process of world capitalist accumulation. The imperial state embodies the present and future collective interests of the most dynamic sector of capital.

The Imperial System and the Imperial State

The period of global military conflict from 1939 to 1945 produced irrevocable changes within world capitalism, above all the transition from an array of great and medium-size powers to a situation distinguished by the manifest absence of some of the most formidable imperial structures (e.g., British, French, Dutch) of the prewar era. Historically, the "notion" of "the imperial system" and its organizing center, "the imperial state," must be located within a set of processes that were central simultaneously to the emergence of U.S. hegemony ("imperial state") and capital accumulation (uneven development), both on a world scale. Together, these interrelated processes are equivalent to the imperial system, whose locus is formed entirely, at one moment in historical time, by the United States, whose government (or part of it) *thereby* becomes "the imperial state."

In the postcolonial period the U.S. imperial state, by necessity, functions through local intermediaries linked through military and economic alliances or through bilateral ties.[13] These linkages are sustained through reciprocal exchanges that mutually benefit the factions of ruling classes in each country. The conditional nature of imperial state domination is thus based on three sets of factors: the capacity to penetrate another nation's social structure, to create durable linkages, and to sustain collaborator classes.

The superimposition of imperial relations upon the class structure of a target society requires that political ties be matched by sociocultural linkages. The imperial state project requires the "throwing down" of roots into the *society* to create a social and cultural infrastructure to sustain the otherwise narrow and fragile base of external domination. Hence, the imperial state mobilizes social and cultural institutions within its own society to create a multiple series of linkages through which to transmit organizational and ideological instruments to reinforce imperial domination.[14] Insofar as there is a proliferation of relationships, which cover an array of spheres of society, we can begin to speak of "integration into the imperial system." The notion of integration, however, should be seen as a process, although one that is never completed. A subordinate state is never totally assimilated into the imperial system without political, social, and cultural conflicts. The process of integration itself is problematical because the basis for exchanges and exploitation varies, and because there are changes in the class structure, political regime, and legitimating ideology. Redefinitions in the world division of labor and the place that a state occupies within it will also affect the mode of integration.[15]

Hence, changes at various levels and conflicts within and between societies require specification of (1) the level of integration, (2) the type of global division of labor, and (3) the form of integration. For example, in colonial societies where "enclave" exploitation existed, there was a high level of integration between the enclave and the metropole, while the rest of society was only minimally affected, at least initially, and could continue, in some cases, with subsistence activities. Within the international division of labor, the colonies specialized in exports of agro-mineral goods, usually with a single hegemonic trading partner. The political form through which integration was elaborated was based on a state apparatus within which sovereign power was vested exclusively or primarily in externally appointed authorities from the metropole.

The pattern of integration within the imperial system becomes much more complex in the postcolonial period. On the one hand, postcolonial societies are more pervasively penetrated. The postcolonial period witnesses the extension of economic activities beyond the enclaves.[16] In one sense, this is cause and consequence of the multilayered forms and links that bind the society to the imperialist system. On the other hand, the political space engendered through formal independence and the juridical formulas that speak toward a national identity are occupied by endogenous political and cultural movements that strive to limit or eliminate imperial integration and to affirm the value of "internal" or national commitments.[17] This affirmation can take the form of seeking out precolonial antecedents, identifying with resistance movements of the past, and/or elaborating and projecting alternative ideologies that disintegrate the imperial relationships.[18]

In postcolonial societies there is a clear move to diversify economic activity and trading partners.[19] The growth of industry and the diversification of trading partners has caused changes in the world division of labor: Some former colonial countries are increasingly exporting industrial goods with a high labor component, usually from free-trade zones where imperial enterprises exercise quasi-sovereign control.[20] The industrializing Third World countries with free-trade zones thus combine features of the colonial period—special laws that provide exclusive privileges, prerogatives, and tax exemptions to the imperial firms (effectively granting them political autonomy)—with a new position in the world division of labor. Continuities reflected in the type of imperial integration (similar to the colonial period) are harnessed to a new position in the division of labor in which exchange is between high- and low-technology industrial countries. This form of imperial integration is, however, quite fragile, for the economic activity and exchanges are totally dependent on the political relationship: Third World export industries are dependent on maintaining substantial labor cost differentials, which, in turn, are sustained by repressive regimes.[21] The disequilibrium in power between working classes and regime—the favorable correlation in favor of the local ruling classes—sustains this redefinition of the division of labor.

This shift in the imperial system is only superficially the result of the "logic of capital" (capital moves toward low-wage areas to maximize profits).[22] At a deeper level, the shift is a result of the logic of class struggle: The low-wage areas are so defined by the ascendence of the local ruling class—class conflict that redefines the relationship will alter the cost of labor and effect the "logic" of capital. While the (relative) lack of class struggle politics is a necessary but not sufficient condition for the growth and expansion of capital in the periphery, its intensification serves both to inhibit the flow of capital "from the outside" and to accelerate the withdrawal (decapitalization) of capital "from the inside." Table 1.1, drawing on the experiences of selected Latin American countries during the 1968-75 period, underscores this tendency of capital accumulation to rise and decline in accordance with the level of class struggle in any particular country.

Table 1.1   Average Annual Growth of U.S. Direct Investment, 1968–75 (percent)[23]

	1968–71	Degree of class struggle	1972–75	Degree of class struggle
Argentina	5.3	Medium	-2.8	High
Bolivia	16.5	High	9.3	Low
Chile	-3.1	Medium-high	-17.2	High
Nicaragua	3.9	Low	1.4	Medium
Jamaica	10.5	Low	0.8	Medium-high

The imperial system is modified by the process of class differentiation, the growth of the working class and petty bourgeoisie, the conversion of merchants into industrialists, and the expansion of intermediary bureaucratic strata. Each laid specific claims for their class interests, and each impinges upon the functioning of the imperial system. New outlays of funds (foreign aid) and new liaison groups are generated within the imperial center to "accommodate" and contain these new actors. The different types of conflict engendered within the imperial system—from limited/negotiable to shifting accommodation/confrontation to systemic—reflects the demands of different participants and class forces. There exist first the negotiated conflicts between collaborative partners—the social classes in the periphery that accept the international division of labor and the role of multinational capital—who want to renegotiate the terms: the price of commodities, the terms of debt payment, the interest rate on loans.[24] These include large trading houses, big businessmen, industrialists, landowners, and so forth. At the other pole are the irreconcilable conflicts between the multinationals and the imperial state, on the one hand, and, on the other, the wage workers and peasants, whose conditions of exploitation facilitate worldwide accumulation and whose locus as "cheap labor" perpetuates the global division of labor.[25] Between the negotiated and irreconcilable conflicts are the intermediary conflicts that engage the national petite and medium-size bourgeoisie. These classes alternate between striking postures of confrontation and quiet negotiation, between proclaiming the need for structural changes and then adapting to the imperial system. They begin as a formidable critic, denouncing national subordination, and end as domesticated partners who in turn are subordinated to imperial interests.[26]

These multiple levels of conflict reflect the complex relations that converge within any social formation integral to the imperial system. More important, it is out of these class relationships and the power of the contending classes that the integration/disintegration of the imperial system originates.

Thus, while it is easy to identify the "structures" or "apparatuses" of the imperial "system," the fluidity of the ongoing class relations and class struggles that underlie the process of integration into the imperial system reflect a complexity that makes precision in specification difficult to establish.

The patterns of imperial integration—degree, level, position in the world division of labor—are all premised on high levels of exploitation of labor and cheap, readily accessible strategic materials. These conditions of exploitation/appropriation, moreover, occur in one social formation (periphery), whereas accumulation and elaboration occur in another. This disjuncture between producers and product and the overall adverse sociopolitical conditions that induce inward capital flows can be sustained only by repressive regimes. The coercive apparatus of the imperial state is a far more decisive actor in shaping the state in the periphery than in the metropolis.[27] In the conventional literature on the "capitalist state," coercion is viewed as a factor "in the last instance."[28] In the imperial system coercion is operative in the first instance—and it is sustained over time. The ideological dimensions of rulership so prominently discussed in the literature on the "capitalist state"[29]—meaning in the *metropolitan* capitalist countries—are secondary and subordinated to rule by force. Western-centered studies even speak of periods of repression as "state of exception,"[30] whereas this "exception" is the rule in the imperialized countries, thus vitiating any cognitive meaning in the term. The duality of the imperial system—ideologically induced consensus at home and coercively imposed control abroad—was noted some time ago by Franz Fanon.

The multiplicity of coercive regimes and their continual reproduction lead us to identify *force* as the central element in the imperial system—a position obscured by separating out, identifying, and comparing the political regimes of each nation-state. Against this approach, which fragments the notion of power and obscures the real, durable, and substantial linkages that bind the different social formations into one hierarchical unit, is the notion of the imperial system. An imperial system involves a multiplicity of nation-states linked through one or more capitalist states dominating others through exploitative relations sustained by collaborative classes and coordinated by the application of force through the coercive apparatuses of the imperial state. Thus the imperial system is based on a series of asymmetrical relationships that are organized at the state level, but whose roots are essentially located in the organization of production and distribution within the subordinated areas. The imperatives of imperial growth create a worldwide set of interests. Strategic interests are those that have long-term, large-scale importance to the overall operation of the systems. The pursuit of symbolic and tactical interests represents efforts to demonstrate superiority at the level of political or ideological appeal. Indo-China was an area of symbolic/tactical interest to the United States, whose total commitment to military victory and whose subsequent defeat weakened its capacity to intervene in two areas of strategic importance, Angola and Iran.[31] The development of imperial interests exceeded the capacity of the U.S. imperial state to defend those interests. The *social basis* of imperial mobilization within the imperial state was weakened in the struggle for symbolic gains; and the collaborator *classes* in strategic countries were unable to sustain the conditions for their domination. Thus the notion of imperial "state apparatuses" should be used with great care because it involves a mechanical metaphor (the machine), which belies the *social relations* that control the actual flow, operation, and application of the physical tools of repression.

If the imperial state is the central organizing unit of an imperial system, what is its relationship to the class struggle within metropolitan society? No area is more clearly removed from the everyday influences of the electorate and legislative bodies, which might reflect liberal democratic opinion, than the executive agencies that collectively fashion imperial policies. The socialization process and the screening, selection, and promotion procedures that accompany the recruitment of cadres for the permanent line and staff positions within imperial institutions are all guided by the need to defend the foundations and expand the growth of U.S. imperialism. The boundaries for political decisionmaking are constructed by the preexisting imperatives of the social system: the widest opportunity for access to markets, resources, and labor on a world scale. But the real world of imperial policymaking is never so easy to realize or so simple to formulate.

The complex contingency of competing imperial forces, internal class struggle, regional power bloc, and so forth, intervene in the formulation of policy and force the imperial policymakers to take account of their capacity to realize policies in *relationship* to the power configuration in each situation. Imperial state policymakers mediate the class interests of the ascendant groups within the ruling class in each configuration of forces. As such, they have *discretionary* power in the day-to-day tactical and conjunctural determinations. Questions that require short-term and immediate decisions affecting discrete sets of interests are largely resolved within the executive agencies in accordance with their estimation of their priorities and possibilities. The give and take of bureaucratic struggle, the interagency rivalries, and personality and opinion clashes between different sets of advisers all reflect the power struggles within the imperial state. While these struggles are of limited scope, they may have significant impact on the existing configuration of forces in any local or regional setting within the imperial system. Moreover, a series of decisions and results can have the cumulative outcome of defining a strategic set of interests.

Nonetheless, this "discretionary power" of the imperial state operates within a larger universe, defined by the organizing principles of the capitalist system: The process accumulation and reproduction and the defense of the class and state structure that conditions and facilitates this process constitute the strategic goals of the decisionmakers. When it comes to protecting the capitalist mode of production, especially in areas where their own imperial economic and military objectives are in question, there is a unity of purpose between the imperial state and classes. The more important the region or social formation to imperial expansion, the greater the coincidence of interest between capital and state, and the more directly will imperial state policy be an expression of class interests. In sum, the more centrally the class struggle affects the overall functioning of the imperial system, the more absolute dependence between state and class structure. The image of the imperial state standing above the class structure that organizes imperialist wars in fact disguises the greatest concentration of social power into the executive agencies of the imperial state and the subordination of civil society to the organized power of the imperial capitalist class.[32]

Within this framework differences among agencies and between the collective decisions of the state and the imperial classes are less a reflection of "autonomy"; rather, they reflect different manners of pursuing the same end. The policy instrumentalities vary, but the imperatives are constant and press upon the decisionmakers to decide in the most rational, direct manner how to maximize imperial interests. In crises, the decision-making process is permeated by the instrumental needs of imperial capital. To exaggerate the relative autonomy of the state is to miss the all-inclusive manner in which the decisionmakers are immersed in the symbols and substance of capitalist power.[33]

The juridical foundation of the state's past policies, the pressure of present interests, and the procedures, norms, and sanctions of existing institutional configurations dictate the boundaries of action. The illusion of autonomy is perpetuated when conflicts occur between the imperial state and class. Capitalists largely operate within the universe of their own firm; in the first instance, they make demands and seek redress from the state as their particular interests are affected.[34] Within the imperial classes a fraction articulates the general principles and policies that favor the opportunities for global capital accumulation for the whole class. Within this political class a smaller number is recruited, to form the executive leadership that formulates policy within the executive agencies that define the core of imperial strategy. Only in periods of crisis, when a wide array of capitalist forces are directly affected, does the imperial class act for itself. At other times, the political faction of the imperial class and the imperial state that represents the class formulate policies that incorporate its interests. The imperial state thus appears as the embodiment of the imperial class—with organized and continuing linkages with it.

Thus there are at least three levels of consciousness among the imperial class, ranging from enterprise to industry to class consciousness. *Enterprise-centered capitalists* respond overwhelmingly to policies that directly affect their firm. Threats of nationalization by a regime evoke in these entrepreneurs the demand for precipitous action by the imperial state; or it may entail an attempt to reach an individual settlement. *Industry-centered capitalists* attempt to coordinate activities across a range of firms sharing a common purpose (for example, mining enterprises) to develop a common policy and induce the state to act for their collective purposes. *Class-conscious capitalists* coordinate policy at the level of the imperial state in fashioning a timetable and agenda that not only takes account of the immediate needs being challenged but also of the feasibility of responding to that threat. The high degree of calculation in the pursuit of "rational self-interest" and the formulation of policy that encompasses a broad array of social forces and political circumstances are characteristic of class-conscious capitalists. For the most part, the calculations and decisions are taken within the imperial state. And in many cases it appears that the imperial state is "utilizing" the capitalist class to serve its policy ends. But this is a somewhat narrow interpretation. Rather, the collective needs of imperialism are mediated through the state, which then instrumentalizes, sacrifices, and defends individual firms and even industries in particular conjunctures in pursuit of historic goals. This overarching behavior of the imperial state in relation to the imperialist class reflects the broad division of labor between the narrower "tasks" of profitmaking (by classes) and the promotion of the broader chore of creating the conditions for profitmaking (state). Thus the apparent paradox that the consciousness of class interests of the imperialist classes are normally far more concentrated in the imperial state than in the individual class members themselves.

Among the imperial countries, the degree to which the imperial state has pursued military and/or economic functions varies. The Japanese and West German imperial states have concentrated on the economic problem of imperial capital, while the U.S. imperial state has shouldered the military burden and has been less effective economically in recent times than its competitors[35]—thus the demand by the United States that its imperial competitors shoulder the military costs of sustaining the empire as well as reaping the benefits.[36]

Postcolonial Imperialism Since World War II

The interrelationship between the U.S. imperial state and capital expansion has been crucial to the development of postcolonial imperialism since World War II. Essentially, we can identify three periods, determined largely by the predominance of three types of investment. In the period between 1945 and 1955 *imperial-state* investment predominated, largely directed toward rebuilding in Europe or constructing, in the Third World, capitalist state structures and economies. Technical aid, large-scale, long-term loans, infrastructure development, and, most of all, massive military spending were directed at forestalling social revolution, to give capital a chance to reemerge. Private investment was of lesser quantity and directed in Europe to industry and in the periphery to agro-mineral areas. Banking capital flows were limited and confined to financing trade and providing credit through isolated groupings.

In the second period, between 1955 and 1969, massive flows of *private investment* circulated throughout the globe—and the multinational conglomerate served as the major vehicle. This wave of investment was directed at all areas of society, but it was especially concentrated in industrial undertakings, both in Europe and in the Third World. Imperial state investments declined, relatively speaking, and were directed toward financing the power, communication, and transport systems, as well as new industrial facilities of advancing industrial capital. Finance capital was still in third position, but it was growing quickly to finance the new import requirements of the Third World, to organize capital markets, and to facilitate transactions among the multiplying capitals. These shifting investment trends are strikingly illustrated in Tables 1.2 and 1.3. These figures clearly illustrate the overall investment sequence as outlined above. The ratio of U.S. state overseas economic loans and grants to new U.S. direct private investment overseas declined from $5.7 to $1 billion between 1945 and 1954, to $1.44 to $1 billion between 1955 and 1964, to $0.63 to $1 billion between 1965 and 1974.

Table 1.2   **U.S. Direct Private Investment Overseas, 1945-74**
(in billions of dollars, approx.)

1945	8.4	1960	31.9
1946	8.9	1961	34.7
1947	10.0	1962	37.3
1948	11.2	1963	40.7
1949	12.5	1964	44.5
1950	11.8	1965	49.5
1951	13.0	1966	51.8
1952	14.7	1967	56.6
1953	16.3	1968	61.9
1954	17.6	1969	68.1
1955	19.4	1970	75.5
1956	22.5	1971	82.8
1957	25.4	1972	89.9
1958	27.4	1973	101.3
1959	29.8	1974	110.2

Source: Figures prepared by the Bureau of Economic Analysis, U.S. Department of Commerce; *International Transactions of the United States During the War 1940-1945* (Washington, D.C., 1948), p. 216; U.S. Department of Commerce, Bureau of Foreign and Domestic Commerce, Office of Business Economics, *Balance of Payments of the United States, 1949-1951* (Washington, D.C., 1972), p. 162; U.S. Department of Commerce, Bureau of Foreign and Domestic Commerce, Office of Business Economics, *Survey of Current Business* 31, no. 1, January 1951, p. 22; U.S. Department of Commerce, Office of Business Economics, *Survey of Current Business* 36, no. 8, August 1956, pp. 18-19; U.S. Department of Commerce, Office of Business Economics, *Balance of Payments Statistical Supplement, Revised Edition* (Washington, D.C., 1962), pp. 210-15; U.S. Department of Commerce, Bureau of Economic Analysis, *Selected Data on U.S. Direct Investment Abroad 1966-1976*, pp. 3-11.

The third period, from 1970 to the present, has witnessed the enormous growth of *finance capital*, the massive expansion of banking capital, and the accumulation of massive assets and extension of loans. Between 1960 and mid-1976 the total assets of the overseas branches of

U.S. private multinational banks increased from $3.5 billion to $181 billion.[37] By December 1976 the overall Third World external debt was estimated at around $200 billion, of which at least $75 billion was owed to private banks, including an estimated $50 billion of this latter amount to U.S. private banks. This new-found "global reach" of the American private banking community exacerbated an already rising debt service burden under which many peripheral governments labored, which necessitated further loans and an ever-spiraling debt problem. In some

Table 1.3 **U.S. Overseas Loans and Grants, 1946–74** (in billions of dollars, approx.)

	Total economic assistance	Total military assistance	Assistance from international organizations
1946–48	12.6	0.5	0.5
1949–52	18.6	3.3	0.8
1953–61	24.1	24.2	5.1
1962–69	33.4	19.3	14.5
1970	3.8	3.1	3.3
1971	3.4	4.6	3.9
1972	4.0	5.3	3.9
1973	4.1	5.3	5.4
1974	4.0	5.1	5.3

Source: U.S. Agency for International Development, Office of Program and Information Analysis Services. Statistics and Reports Division, *U.S. Overseas Loans and Grants and Assistance from International Organizations: Obligations and Loan Authorizations, July 1, 1945–September 30, 1976* (Washington, 1977), pp. 6, 177. The major multilateral financial lenders included in this table are the following: International Bank for Reconstruction and Development (World Bank); International Finance Corporation, International Development Corporation, Inter-American Development Bank, Asian Development Bank, and African Development Bank and African Development Fund.

cases (e.g., Peru), the ultimate outcome was direct U.S. private bank intervention in the economic decision-making process as a condition for further loans. A substantial proportion of these peripheral government debts to private foreign banks was located in Latin America, principally in the politically and/or economically strategic countries of Brazil, Mexico, and Peru. In 1976 approximately 20 percent of the Third World's total export earnings (an increase of 75 percent over 1973) went to pay the interest and amortization payments on the area's external debt.[38] Finance capital is intimately involved in all aspects of economic activity on a global level, diversifying its activities to all productive areas, and absorbing the huge oil surpluses and redirecting them into controlling far-flung activities. Industrial capital continues to expand, interpenetrating in the imperial centers and allying with the state for joint exploitation in the periphery.

Any extended definition of the U.S. imperial state would likely include the leading post-1945 multilateral financial institutions (World Bank, International Monetary Fund, Inter-American Development Bank), whose activities have both overlapped with and complemented the "peak" periods of private investment and finance capital flows on a worldwide basis. The period of greatest expansion of capital assistance from the international banking organizations coincided with the rise of independent states in the periphery of the capitalist world economy. These multilateral capital flows averaged less than $1 billion annually during the 1950s, rising to approximately $2 billion annually during the 1960s, and, as Table 1.3 shows, peaking in excess of $4 billion annually during the first half of the 1970s. The role this form of assistance has played has tended to be twofold: On the one hand, it has allowed all capitalist governments to assume some responsibility (on a consortium basis) for financing conditions for private capital expansion by all capitalist bloc countries; and, on the other, such loans and grants may, in particular conjunctures, have performed the important political function of politically neutralizing or defusing the close, ongoing relationship between U.S. state and private external capital flows.

Imperial state activity continues, in a less central role but an increasingly important source of funding for overextended debtors: The imperial state functions to bail out debtors and to cushion the adverse social consequences generated by industrial and finance capital's expansion. Thus imperial state activity focuses on "social needs," balance of payments problems, and military aid. Public development loans, however, are largely replaced by private ones. The logic of imperialism revealed by this historical succession is largely from imperial state investment to private industrial and finance capital. Massive imperial state activity was the necessary precondition for the development of "economic" imperialism. The development of industrial capital, in turn, was the necessary precondition for the extension of finance capital. The interrelatedness of overseas state-industrial-financial capital and the continuous interplay of all three, each with its specific and complementary functions, defines the contemporary imperial system.

The Imperial State: Specialization and Complexity

The imperial state can best be conceptualized as a complex web of interrelated but functionally specific sets of agencies coordinated at the top levels of the executive branch. The agencies can be subdivided into three major functional categories: (1) economic, (2) coercive, and (3) ideological. The economic agencies can, in turn, be divided into two sets: (a) those serving particular forms of capital (departments of Agriculture promoting agricultural exports), and (b) those performing specific tasks that cut across the different capitals (Treasury and Commerce departments), promoting foreign investment in general. Agencies tied to particular forms of overseas capital expansion develop especially close working relationships between those particular factions and work within the imperial state to maximize the interests of their "client." Similar behavior is evidenced with regard to the specific task-oriented agencies that develop ties within the United States and with their specific collaborator counterparts abroad. Commerce and Treasury department ties with the multinationals and big business abroad occasionally may lead to short-term conflicts with the State Deparment over policies that may conflict with the short-term interests of their clients.

The second major component of the imperial state, the coercive agencies, includes (1) the military (Defense Department); and (2) intelligence (Central Intelligence Agency, Defense Intelligence Agency, and the specialized groups within each branch of the military). The military operates in two capacities: (a) to promote and cultivate close relations within the military of target areas, through training schools, aid programs, overseas missions;[39] and (b) to intervene directly to forestall social revolution, through military invasions and occupations when their collaborative counterparts are incapable or unwilling to act in concert with U.S. interests. The intelligence agencies usually are heavily involved in recruiting liaisons (contacts for information within regimes and leaders within key organizations of a society) and organizing client groups to manipulate social forces for overt and covert action.[40] The activities of both groups usually are coordinated through agency heads, and their activities usually complement each, although jurisdictional disputes and conflicts over loyalties occasionally emerge.

The third component agency of the imperial state, the ideological, has two aspects: (1) the institutional activities directly tied to the state, and (2) the "subcontracted" activities related to the practices of unofficial groups drawn from imperial society and among collaborator groups. The U.S. Information Agency and the related propaganda arms of the state (Peace Corps, Fulbright-Hayes Program) create favorable images of U.S. imperial activity and denigrate revolutionary action; psychological warfare, including the creation of false consciousness, is a principal activity. In the postcolonial period, however, special importance in the ideological task of defending imperialism is taken on by societal forces—cultural, religious, educational, and so forth. Ideological use is made of their public image of possessing nonofficial status to give them the aura of "objectivity" and "independence," thus increasing the credibility of the propaganda message. These societal auxiliaries of the imperial state are usually "contracted" covertly by the intelligence agencies or overtly through other agencies, ostensibly for some apolitical purpose, i.e., "to promote cultural exchanges."[41] This illusory disjuncture between "state" and "society" obscures the convergence of purpose and allows the imperial state to pursue its ideological goals through a plurality of mutually compatible instrumentalities.

The forward and backward linkages of these agencies create specific ties; the close working relationships within the bureaucratic organization and with collaborator groups frequently leads to policy differences over which instrumentalities should be given priority in any specific circumstances. These and other conflicts are usually resolved within the imperial state and, if serious enough, at the executive level, within the boundaries established by imperial interests.

The Collaborator State

The "collaborator state" possesses several features that facilitate its subordination to the actions of imperial states.[42] First, it is a penetrated society: Political and military organization and cultural institutions contain leaders, formed and loyal to the ideas and definitions of reality formulated in the imperial centers. Crucial sectors of the economy are controlled or managed by multinational capital; thus the class structure is penetrated by imperial interests. State and societal *penetration* is matched by the organization and direction of the economy toward a *complementary role* within the imperial division of labor. Thus the *kind* of goods produced, the terms of exchange, and the direction of exchange all maximize gains to the imperial center and the principal classes and institutional members within the collaborator state.

Two sets of collaborator groups can be identified: the bureaucratic (political) strata and the socioeconomic classes. The bureaucratic-political strata, through their control over the state, receive part of the surplus generated through imperial exchanges and direct exploitation by the multinationals. Private wealth by "indirect relation" means that government officials who don't *own* the means of production appropriate wealth which they later convert to capital; membership on state boards of joint ventures becomes the basis of private entrepreneurship. The bureaucratic-political strata are rewarded by imperial capital for the invitation, insurance, and expeditor functions that they engage in within the exploited country.

Traditional collaborator classes, such as landowners and import-exporters, are now matched by local industrialists and businessmen, who develop joint ventures with the multinationals, become satellite subcontractors, rent technology or managerial skills, and combine and contract with world-marketing and shipping firms.[43] This "collaboration" usually does not reflect a total integration into the imperial system; rather it is a negotiated association subject to bargaining over terms, shifts in market demands, political power, and so forth. The important issue, however, is that postcolonial imperialism expands (and survives) with the growth and incorporation of collaborator groups. In fact, *the strength of the imperial system in large part rests on the influence and control exercised by the collaborative classes and strata within imperialized society.* There are various types of collaborator classes, ranging from those who share power to those who are clearly subordinated to imperial interests. Size, type, and scope of activity, as well as influence and control over the state, affect the relative standing of collaborator classes in relation to imperial classes. Large-scale industralists involved in production for the local market and with a powerful presence in the state are more likely to be *associate power-sharers* with imperial interests. Import-exporters tied to foreign markets, shipping, and credits are likely to be *dependent power-sharers.* Joint ventures, in which industrialists produce for foreign markets, drawing on foreign technology, capital, and management, and with little direct representation in the state, are likely to be *subordinate collaborators.*

The collaborator classes are oriented toward opening up markets, securing raw materials, and facilitating the recruitment of labor. Their main purpose is, however, *political*: to deal with the state and through their influence to handle "labor relations," repress class conflict, and negotiate labor contracts. Under the slogans of industrialization and development, the collaborator classes purport to "mix" foreign and local, state and private capital into a growth formula—the underlying condition for this growth being the appropriation of resources, the proletarianization of the labor force, and the subordination of the state within the imperial system. The essential policies pursued by collaborator class regimes are directed toward deepening these three processes, without being displaced by their more dynamic imperial partner.

The changes wrought in the society through collaborator-imperial-induced expansion create profound cleavages in society, while the state apparatus that facilitates this growth rests on a very fragile social base. The displacement of preimperial production and social relations erodes traditional bases of authority, evoking contradictions at two levels: (1) between the older social classes (petty-commodity producers) and political authorities being displaced, and (2) new social classes being exploited and effectively excluded from the state structures and political representation. The convergence of these two sets of divergent opposition forces (based on different social/political bases) is rooted in their common opposition to the collaborator-imperial-induced expansion. This alliance of forces presents a formidable challenge to collaborator domination and contains within it both the most advanced and the most backward forms of class struggle: mobilization to socialize capitalist production and efforts to return to petty-commodity production. For the very transformation in social relations and production is induced by the advanced firms from the most developed imperial centers. The organized worker opposition thus grows out of and reaches toward advanced forms of social control—the socialization of production and workers' control over the state.[44]

The uneven growth and importance among imperialized countries (a function of their size, resource base, and strategic location) result in a hierarchy within the imperial system. While cognizant that "hierarchy" as such among countries is not a function of external policymaking but, on the contrary, is a product and condition of the capitalist development of productive forces, we use the term here to denote the greater or lesser importance of countries relative to the primary, worldwide U.S. imperial state objectives. The more central a country is to the process of imperial capital accumulation, the greater is the role attributed to it within the imperial state network. The U.S. imperial agencies typically designate countries possessing large reserves of strategic raw materials and/or substantial markets for American exports as more critical to the accumulation process than countries with limited markets and few, if any, strategic resources. In certain contexts, however, it is possible to visualize the allocation of a priority role to certain regionally influential military powers (e.g., Iran under the Shah and Israel in the Middle East). Especially in the postcolonial period, the imperial centers, through their stronger collaborator states, have attempted to fashion a tier of "regional influentials" to whom they can delegate authority for policing a region. This sharing of regional power between imperial state and regional influentials is itself fraught with internal contradiction, for the outward demands can overextend the capacity of the collaborator classes and provoke their demise.

The "regional influentials" or subimperialist powers experience periods of high growth based on large-scale foreign financing and/or investment under the watchful eyes of repressive regimes. The regime, typically, further concentrates economic wealth at the top, expands the size of the wage labor force, and denies effective representation to the workers and petite-bourgeoisie. The delegation of regional powers reinforces and expands upon the coercive components of the regime, precisely when it lacks any substantial internal social support. Thus the regime's regional role occurs at a time when the internal contradictions—socialization of production and the accompanying concentration of wealth—lead to increasing internal polarization. External power, necessarily vulnerable to large-scale internal social upheavals that shift the locus of social power (and hence the allocation of funds) away from the coercive apparatus and the sustenance of the external linkages, thus becomes increasingly threatened. "Overcommitted" to the imperial system at the expense of internal linkages, the regime collapses, thus signaling the demise of an important link in the imperial chain. Other regional influentials have to be created, direct imperial military force has to be called upon, and the imperial system remains unstable in the area, subject to the internal dynamics of class forces in the region.*

The Imperial System in Crisis

The post-World War II, postcolonial imperial system has gone through two phases and is now entering a third. The first phase, roughly between 1945 and 1960, was the period in which the United States was the overwhelmingly dominant direct actor throughout the system: investor, military intervener, financier. In a word, the imperial system was *coterminus* with the imperial state of the United States: Power and decision were concentrated in the hands of Washington†; officials of imperialized states were informed of decisions or told what to do.

The second phase of the imperial system can be dated from the early 1960s and can be located approximately in the period between 1961 and 1976. In this period the growth of European and Japanese power and the growth of OPEC and, to a much lesser degree, other commodity producers forced the United States into a consultative relationship with "allies": While the United States still is "first among equals," it is increasingly obliged to accommodate the interests of other states and capitals. More important, the U.S. commitment in Vietnam drained resources from the economic to the coercive apparatus, improved the relative trade and investment position of Europe in relation to the United States, and created a flood of Eurodollars at a time when the U.S. productive base was unable to sustain them—thus threatening the U.S.-centered imperial financial system.[45] The inability of the United States to commit its allies in Vietnam was a consequence of their growing independence and had, as a further consequence, the result of strengthening their competitive position within the U.S. imperial umbrella. As this phase ended, the United States began its reach for means of delegating authority, of finding power surrogates ("regional influentials") in recognition of its limited capacity to defend the imperial system

---

*We recognize that the "collapse" or "demise" of any particular regime does not ipso facto weaken the imperial system. Coup d'etats are common in such "linkage" states, and, no less commonly, the "new" incumbents challenge not the "place " of the state in the imperial system but, at most, only the *terms* on which the *new* regime will continually reproduce that "place" through the existing, new, or altered relations. The "collapse" per se of a collaborator regime signals in itself nothing but its collapse. What becomes crucial in terms of the impact of this type of change on the imperial system are the processes and especially the opposition movements understood to be "responsible" for the collapse. Our concern is with large-scale sociopolitical struggles, with strong nationalist and anti-imperialist components, that bring the "demise" of collaborator regimes, e.g., the Shah's Iran.

†We do not here discuss the role of the dominant social class in the United States (owners and controllers of major corporations, banks, financial institutions) in the making of U.S. imperial state policy, but a central assumption that informs our analysis is that capitalist social forces are crucial to fashioning the boundaries within which the U.S. imperial state operates and to shaping the direction and goals of imperial state policy.

and its unwillingness to bear all the costs while its allies reap all the benefits.[46]

The third phase of the imperial system is highlighted by the steady erosion of the imperial system, both the outer fringes and inner fortresses: The defeat in Indo-China was followed by Angola, thus opening up southern Africa, and then the Middle Eastern regional power anchored in the Shah's regime.

At certain historical moments the imperial system is made vulnerable by a weakened capacity on the part of the imperial state to sustain a level of cohesion that the system requires. Between 1945 and 1965 the U.S. imperial state could count on a public opinion unified in support of its actions, an organized and mobilized military fighting force, and a high degree of cooperation from its allies in Western Europe, Japan, and the Third World. The U.S. involvement in Indo-China during the late 1960s and early 1970s substantially weakened the interventionary capacities of the imperial state consequent upon growing internal divisions among the populace at large, the decline of institutional solidarity and *esprit de corps* within the armed forces, and their increasing loss of legitimacy on the "home front," and widespread defections among allied opponents of the imperial state enterprise.*

In the post-Vietnam period the acceleration of national liberation and revolutionary struggles in the periphery of the capitalist world economy increasingly reflects the fact that the United States has lost its capacity to hold together the imperial system, while, at the same time, no other country has emerged to replace it. What we have is a series of state-by-state policy improvisations, unsuccessful annual trilateral meetings and the fragments of power, and the potent leftovers and linkages of the U.S. imperial state that still operate. Europe and Japan, imperial competitors, have been strong enough to weaken the United States but totally incapable of assuming the responsibility of creating the apparatuses and sustaining the universe in which competition and growth occur. They have operated under the mistaken assumption that: (a) the United States will bail them out in crisis circumstances; (b) their economic relations and "strength" are sufficient to guarantee favorable access in the operating environment; and (c) the existing state and class configurations

---

*At present, the U.S. imperial state is attempting to use the Soviet Union intervention in Afghanistan and its purported threat to Iran, Pakistan, and the Persian Gulf area in general as a pretext to create the basis for reconstructing the U.S. imperial capacity and mobilizing the population for future military interventions around the world. The multiple political-military response (reinstitution of the draft, massive increase in the military budget, expansion of the U.S. military forces abroad, creation of new regional, counterrevolutionary alliances with Egypt, Saudi Arabia, Pakistan, the application of enormous diplomatic pressures on Western Europe and Japan to "line up" with the U.S. position) cannot be understood in all its ramifications unless located in the context of previous U.S. imperial state vulnerabilities and the renewed efforts to reconstruct imperial capacities to a level appropriate to the desired operations of a U.S.-dominated imperial system.

that are functioning to their satisfaction are capable of enduring over time.

Recent events in Iran and Afghanistan, however, have generated a sustained U.S. effort to pressure West Germany, France, and Japan, in particular, to assume a greater share of the risks and costs inherent in fashioning a global, interventionary foreign-policy response for the imperial system as a whole. At the same time, Western Europe and Japan remain critically dependent on Middle East oil for the day-to-day operations of their economies, but their lack of military strength and limited economic leverage render them incapable of exercising any substantive control over OPEC pricing policies. Meanwhile, the overthrow of the Shah in Iran (a major capitalist-bloc petroleum supplier) has been followed by the appearance of fissures within the Saudi Arabian polity[47] and an overall increase in the level of economic and political instability throughout the Persian Gulf region. These new imperial rivals thus overestimate U.S. capability, underestimate the importance of imperial state linkages for sustaining "economic" dimensions of the imperial system, and miscalculate the sources of strength among collaborator classes in the Third World.

This profound misjudgment, however, is rooted in the structural constraints that have facilitated growth: The capacity to contain class struggle and promote capital growth has been based precisely on avoiding expenditures in sustaining coercive apparati and costly military intervention. For Western Europe and Japan to assume the political and military responsibilities commensurate with their expanded economic power would eventually result in a radical restructuring of the economic and political system with many unforeseen and dangerous consequences. It would, at minimum, require a redirection of national budget allocations away from economic development and toward increased military spending, which would likely presage a growing role for the political right in these countries and the emergence of the armed forces as a central actor in the political system. These events, in turn, could conceivably lead to the revival of militarism, territorial expansionist ambitions, and possible open military conflicts not only with the socialist bloc countries and the Third World, but with the United States as well.

In summary, the imperial system is in crisis. The capacity of the United States to hold together the imperial system and sustain its position as the dominant imperial power in the capitalist world economy has been severely strained, beginning with the recovery of its capitalist rivals in the early 1960s, deepening with the Vietnam War, and continuing in its aftermath. The subordinated allies in Europe and Asia, namely West Germany and Japan, who previously concentrated on internal rebuilding, have successfully branched out, capturing important markets and eagerly challenging U.S. economic domination.[48] Client-states have broken out of the imperial system, and a key regional influential base has been destroyed, increasing the cost of key energy resources and destabilizing regional hegemony. The close linkages between imperial state policies and the populace have been weakened, with the resultant constraints on the interventionary capacity of the coercive components of the state. Nonetheless, this process of declining U.S. imperial state capacities is not an irreversible one, as evidenced by the political-military propaganda campaign against the Soviet Union originating in the highest echelons of the Carter Administration as part of a concentrated effort to, at least temporarily, re-create the old bonds of the imperial system and reassert the preeminent role of the U.S. imperial state within that system.

The imperial state provided a protective nest within which U.S. capital operated in a manner *not* conducive to developing a competitive edge.[49] Tied foreign aid guaranteed U.S. sales until—imperial rivals could match the aid and underbid U.S. sellers. U.S. firms paid high dividends and ran down capital stock, while its competitors did the opposite. Military and political collaborators in client-states facilitated access to local markets for overpriced U.S. goods until changes in regime and/or personnel altered the balance toward alternative, more efficient sellers. Undisputed domination conditioned directors of U.S. multinationals to resist joint ventures where they held minority control, while their competitors eagerly seized the chance. In a word, the imperial system created a series of structural and sociopsychological conditions that *initially* greatly improved U.S. capital's position, but which later greatly reduced its competitive capability. Competition from Japan and West Germany, the equalization of exchange between petroleum and industrial goods established by OPEC, the internal constraints imposed by the class structure in the United States, and the revolutionary ferment in the Third World—beginning in Southeast Asia, continuing to southern and central Africa, and extending to the Middle East—have all created deepening fissures in the imperial system.

The relative decline of the United States, linchpin of the overall system, is manifest in the economic sphere by the relative deterioration in its share of world exports, production of industrial goods, and share of overseas investments, as well as by the relative increase in the cost of energy.[50] In the military sphere this relative decline has been manifested in the weakening in military interventionary capacity in southern and central Africa and the Middle East. Concomitantly, class struggle has weakened the role both of "old" (export-importers, landowners) and "new" (industrialists) collaborator classes in key areas. In Iran, Angola, and Afghanistan these classes have been overthrown. In Ethiopia and Rhodesia they are subject to substantial challenges, as is the case in Nicaragua and to a lesser degree in Brazil, Peru, Bolivia, El Salvador, Guyana, and Grenada. The network of economic and militarily strategic areas encompassing large and small countries, whose regimes collectively are an essential part of the imperial system, threatens to be torn asunder. This multiple challenge is both cause and consequence of the United States' declining capacity to intervene militarily. This illustrates the critical importance of the linkage between imperial state *and* internal classes in sustaining the imperial system. The declining global position of the United States, its internal manifestation, *and* the shift in class forces within the collaborator states combine to weaken the coercive apparatuses that sustain the imperial system.*

In the sociopolitical sphere the relative decline of the United States and the fissures in the imperial system have contributed to a decline in the standard of living for substantial sectors of the wage and salaried groups within the United States.[51] The combined effects of an inflation rate that exceeds wage increases and chronic high rates of underemployment and unemployment have highlighted the fact that the substantial improvements during the decades immediately after World War II were not outcomes inherent in "welfare capitalism"; rather, they were specific features resultant from the strength of the imperial system and the undisputed domination of the United States within that system. The internal manifestation of imperial crisis manifested itself in the contradiction between the decline of external opportunities and the socially defined high level of existence deemed necessary to reproduce labor.

The state's response is to impose a selective austerity plan to cushion the effects of the imperial crisis for capital by lowering the historic gains of wage and salaried workers.[52] The long-term accommodation and collaboration between imperial capital and the labor bureaucracy, based on external exploitation and internal reforms, begins to crumble. No longer able to provide improvements, and yet bureaucratized beyond the capacity to engage in sustained and all-encompassing struggles, the executive directorate of the trade unions is under increasing attack by the

---

*While increased "competition" among "states" within the interstate system does not, of course, bring the processes of capital accumulation and centralization to an abrupt halt, the weakened role of government as a cohesive factor does make the MNCs increasingly vulnerable—to the extent that they may be forced to more directly confront new anticapitalist antagonists (workers, peasants, and other adversaries), who embody a fundamental challenge to the accumulation process itself. Our principal concern, however, is with an evolving (dialectical) process that creates contradictions which are ultimately resolved in the confrontation of classes on a world scale, even though the particular locus of struggles are found in particular national political economies. The process of U.S. imperial state ascendence, challenge, and deterioration is located within a matrix of relationships whose component parts we seek to identify. The introduction of the notion of *capacity* implies that power is relative to those elements that are central to the exercise of power. Obviously, the qualitative demise of the imperial state would mean the heightening of contradictions that could lead to the destruction of capitalism. But this study is more immediately concerned with identifying the nature of the conflicts that condition the strengths and weaknesses of the U.S. imperial state; and to project some of the consequences through the identification of challenges emanating not only from competitive capitalist (corporate) sources, but from anticapitalist (social revolutionary) forces as well. In other words, this study is more concerned with the *process* (deterioration) than with the ultimate result of that process (e.g., an end to capitalist development of the world system), which is clearly much more problematical.

rank and file in major unions, including coal, steel, teamsters, and auto.[53] The consensus between the labor bureaucracy and imperial capital built during the heyday of the imperial system is beginning to break down—opening the possibility for the emergence of class politics.

Thus the military, economic, and socio-political foundations of the imperial system have begun to be affected, eroded but not undermined. While the crisis to imperialism is real, it should not be exaggerated: The military and intelligence networks still exist; traditional collaborator regimes are still strong in many areas (South Korea, Philippines, Thailand, Indonesia, Israel, South Africa, Zaire, Senegal, Kenya, Paraguay), and some additions have been added (Argentina, Egypt, Uruguay, Chile). Moreover, the growth of debt financing has strengthened the financial arms of the imperial system,* allowing the imperial states to restructure economies and societies through loans conditioned by meeting specific capital requirements. While the standard of living has declined in the United States, it has not been precipitous as yet, and, more important, it has been accompanied by a declining percentage of organized workers and the almost total absence of any class-based *political* challenge from among the militant trade unionists. Finally, while interimperial relations have led to increasing inroads by Europe and Japan on U.S. economic turf, they are still more dependent on the United States than vice versa.[54] And in a pinch the U.S. decisions still have a central importance to the performance of their economies.[55]

The Imperial State and "Imperial" Currency

The agreement reached at Bretton Woods in 1944 to create a new postwar international capitalist monetary system had as one of its central outcomes the decision to tie all national currencies to the dollar as the leading "imperial" currency. Thereafter, the U.S. imperial state began to supply dollars as a means of exchange to other capitalist countries for the purchase of the U.S.-manufactured goods. Nevertheless, throughout most of the 1950s the U.S. balance of payments remained in deficit to the tune of approximately $1 billion a year. Between 1958 and the mid-1970s, however, the average annual deficit climbed to around $3 billion to $4 billion.[56] This sustained balance of payments "problem" was attributable to three major factors: (1) the long-term, large-scale

---

*While it is conceivable that countries theoretically could raise the issue of debt repudiation, the almost certain likelihood of international pariah status within the capitalist world economy (in the areas of trade and financial resources) acts to circumscribe sharply the capacity of governments in these resource-scarce countries to contemplate seriously carrying through such an action. In the event that a country does possess alternative sources of trade and external funding, this type of threat may be useful, but only as a one-shot bargaining tool. Finally, with the exception of Brazil and perhaps a few other Third World countries, it is not clear that debt repudiation would have anything but a very minimal impact within the affected capitalist economies.

flow of dollars provided by the U.S. imperial state to finance the establishment and consolidation of a global political-economic network that would facilitate ongoing capital accumulation (investment and commerce); (2) a growing U.S. balance of trade crisis as the result of the reemergence of Western Europe and Japan as competitors for export markets on a world scale; and (3) the parallel refusal of American exporters to modernize their productive capacity, preferring instead to operate behind previously constructed high-tariff walls and concentrate their financial resources in the expansion of overseas branch plants. In other words, the large accumulations of dollars by allied capitalist countries were increasingly failing to serve their envisioned U.S. imperial state purpose—that of maintaining U.S. export competitiveness on a worldwide basis.

By the late 1960s the national economies of Western Europe and Japan had grown to the point where their own currencies were coming to be worth more than the dollar, creating a growing amount of surplus dollars in these countries. At the same time, the dollar costs of U.S.-produced goods continued to rise relative to the costs for comparable or superior goods available from other capitalist-bloc trading countries. The massive U.S. imperial state allocation of financial resources to prosecute the war in Indo-China failed to act as a stimulus to increased investment in U.S. export manufactures and, hence, did not generate any significant improvement in the competitive capacities of American exporters.

Between 1971 and 1973 the U.S. government sought to shift the burden of trade recovery onto its major competitors by forcing Western Europe and Japan to undertake an upward revaluation of their currencies and to accept fixed exchange rates to be decided upon by Washington. However, not even currency realignments or two dollar devaluations could halt speculation against the dollar. The amount of dollars held abroad rose from $53.3 billion in August 1971 to $82 billion in early 1973.[57] West Germany, possessing the strongest continental currency, was the primary recipient of unwanted U.S. dollars during this period. In an effort to bring some stability to the international monetary system, the European Economic Community finally decided in January 1974 to float their currencies against the dollar, which effectively ended the era of fixed exchange rates.[58]

Over time, it is clear that the dollar has been increasingly treated by other capitalist countries as a *store of value* rather than merely as a *medium of exchange* and that this, in essence, is the reason for the sustained U.S. "balance of payments" "problem." With little exaggeration, it might be argued that the "growth" and "decline" of the United States as "the" imperial state is traceable through the strength of the dollar. For the duration of the 1970s, as Figure 1.1 illustrates, the value of the dollar continued to decline relative to the other key capitalist bloc currencies.[59]

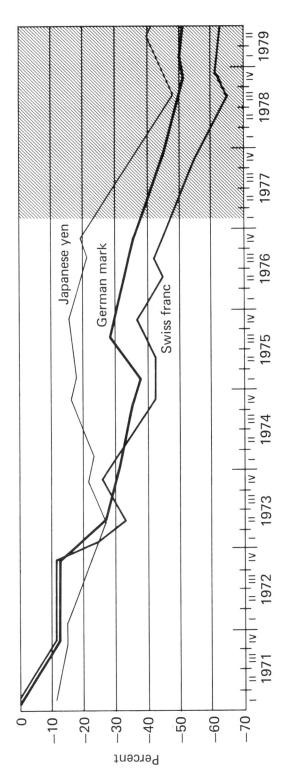

Figure 1.1 Comparative strength of the dollar to other currencies, 1971–79. *Source: Business Week*, August 6, 1979; p. 70.

27

Conclusion

While U.S. imperial state power continues to be formidable in relation to its main competitors within the imperial system, long-term structural and operational trends are countering that power. The long-term relative decline in productivity is an indicator of the weakening position of non-financial capital in the United States.[60] The incapacity of U.S. capital to sustain its competitive position is the result of investments and profit-taking decisions that hinder the continual rationalization and transformation of U.S. productive capacity to meet the terms of competition emerging from other capital. It is not labor, the loss of the work ethic, or wage levels that have been forced down productivity and weakened the U.S. market position, but the behavior and movement of capital.

The deterioration of the U.S. balance of trade, beginning in the late 1950s, was not solely a function of competition from the revitalized postwar economies of Western Europe and Japan. "The United States," as Fred Block reminds us, "had the resources—capital, skilled labor, technological sophistication, and entrepreneurial competence—to meet the competitive challenge directly and successfully."[61] What was lacking, however, was any substantial impulse toward modernization of local industry on the part of American exporters, who continued to operate behind protective high tariffs. Instead of concentrating on increased productive capacity at home to meet the new challenge, they began to invest in the setting up of overseas branch plants, principally in Western Europe. As a result, they suffered a long-term decline in their competitive position on a global scale. Between 1958 and 1964, for example, the U.S. balance of trade experienced an average annual surplus of $2.5 billion to $3 billion. Between 1968 and 1971 the U.S. trade figures spoke to an average annual deficit of approximately the same amount.[62]

The extent of the declining U.S. export competiveness is further revealed if we compare the changing patterns of U.S., Japanese, and West German exports of manufactured goods over the period 1963 to 1976:

World Trade Pattern[63]
(percentage distribution of manufactured exports)

	1963	1976
U.S.	17.24	13.55
Japan	5.98	11.38
West Germany	15.53	15.81

The United States experienced an absolute *and* a relative decline in its position vis-à-vis its major capitalist-bloc export competitors. While American exports as a percentage of the world total fell substantially, of even greater importance was that, whereas Japanese and West German exporters together sold approximately 30 percent more manufactured goods than their American counterparts in 1963, some thirteen years later they accounted for almost double the amount of manufactured goods entering the world market from U.S. sources.

While U.S. economic positions in world trade have declined, the costs of sustaining the political-military umbrella (the coercive components of the imperial state) have increased, leaving the U.S. political economy to pay the major share of the costs. Japanese and West German imperial policymakers concentrate almost exclusively on the economic functions of the imperial state, while U.S. policymakers divide their time and energies in coercive components. Thus while Washington tries to deal with problems of societal control and order ("stability and security"), Bonn and Tokyo concentrate on promoting capitalist development. The U.S. imperial state furnished stability, and its competitors exploit the development opportunities. This schism between expansion and maintenance of the imperial system, a costly imperial state and declining economic benefits, has its consequences: the growth of inflation and a declining standard of living.

This state of affairs presents U.S. imperial state policymakers with the following most likely choices: a combination of (1) exercise coercive and economic power to muscle out competitors in the periphery, as well as freezing out rivals dependent on U.S. markets; (2) pressure imperial competitors to share the cost of the coercive umbrella, thus vastly increasing their military commitments and intelligence networks; (3) increase the recruitment and responsibility of regional influentials among the collaborator regimes in the Third World, delegating costs and responsibilities for policing the imperial system; and (4) some combination of the above.

The policy of "exercising power" is a two-way street: Showing muscle invites similar responses elsewhere. Closing markets could lead to retaliatory measures and eventually to uncontrollable protectionism, cut-throat competition, and the demise of capitalist allies/rivals. Proponents of this "will to power" overlook the fact that U.S. economic interests are intertwined abroad with local and imperial competitors, and adversaries such as the Soviet Union, and many are fairly well entrenched and could effectively resist coercive efforts. In this circumstance, the degree of direct force and the ongoing control that would be required to displace and contain global and local rivals far exceeds U.S. capability at this time and in the foreseeable future.

The second, more modest proposal to pressure rivals to assume more of the costs of the maintenance of the imperial system is being applied, and some gains have been registered. Japan and West Germany are paying more but have hardly made a commitment commensurate to what the United States would like them to assume. In any case, this proposal does not directly affect the issue of competition (it tries to equalize the conditions for it), but rather institutionalizes the positions of all participants within the system. As such, it may strengthen the independence of the competitors, increase their challenge to U.S. hegemony, and raise their influence over collaborator regimes and classes in target countries.

With regard to the policy of promoting regional influentials, the Iranian experience points directly to the problems. The overextension of an internally vulnerable regime led not only to the demise of regional influence, but to the overthrow and transformation of a collaborator regime. Vast disproportions between expenditures on arms and social welfare and between the concentration of political power in the autocratic ruler and the lack of organs or popular representation combined to provoke a sociopolitical crisis that could not be contained by the regime. Apart from exacerbating the internal contradictions of collaborator regimes, the delegation of regional authority could whet their appetite for independent action, setting off a series of activities that could convert the subordinate collaborator into a competitive ally or at least threaten the security of neighboring collaborator regimes and classes.

Notes

1. E.g., Ralph Miliband, *The State in Capitalist Society* (New York: Basic Books, 1969); and Nicos Poulantzas, *Political Power and Social Classes* (London: New Left Books, 1973).

2. Colin Leys, *Underdevelopment in Kenya* (Berkeley: University of California Press, 1975).

3. Alan Wolfe, *The Limits of Legitimacy: Political Contradictions of Contemporary Capitalism* (New York: Free Press, 1977). See also Ralph Miliband, *Marxism and Politics* (London: Oxford University Press, 1979), pp. 90–106.

4. Susan Strange, "International Economics and International Relations: A Case of Mutual Neglect," *International Affairs* 46, April 1970, pp. 305–15; James N. Rosenau (ed.), *Linkage Politics: Essays on the Convergence of National and International Systems* (New York: Free Press, 1969); and Peter Katzenstein, "International Relations and Domestic Structures: Foreign Economic Policies of Advanced Industrial States," *International Organization* 30, no. 1, 1976, pp. 1–46.

5. Richard Barnet, *Intervention and Revolution: The U.S. in the Third World* (New York: World Publishing Co., 1968); and Raymond Vernon, *Sovereignty at Bay: The Multinational Spread of U.S. Enterprises* (New York: Basic Books, 1971).

6. Fernando Henrique Cardoso, *Dependencia y Desarrollo en America Latina* (Mexica: Siglo Veintiuno, 1976).

7. V. I. Lenin, *Imperialism: The Highest Stage of Capitalism* (New York: International Publishers, 1939). In justice to Lenin, in the introduction to his essay he refers to the omission of the political dimensions of the problem of imperialism to avoid the problem of censorship. It is inexcusable that subsequent writers follow the limited perspective outlined by Lenin when external constraints were no longer operative.

8. Santiago Carrillo, *Eurocommunism and the State* (London: Lawrence and Wishart, 1978); and Ernest Laclau, *Politics and Ideology in Marxist Theory* (London: New Left Books, 1977).

9. See Richard J. Barnet and Ronald E. Müller, *Global Reach* (New York: Simon and Schuster, 1974), pp. 16–17. A study prepared by Business International Corporation in 1972, for example, showed that 122 of the largest U.S. MNCs had a higher rate of profit from their overseas activities than from their domestic operations. See ibid. According to a report published by an influential Wall Street investment firm, interna-

tional earnings of the thirteen U.S. banks with the largest overseas operations rose from $177 million to $836 million between 1970 and 1975. Furthermore, the international assets of all U.S. banks represented nearly 21 percent of total assets at years end 1975, as compared with only 8.5 percent in 1970. See Salomon Brothers, *United States Multinational Banking: Current and Prospective Strategies* (New York: June 1976), p. 3. By 1976 the twelve or thirteen U.S. multinational banks that accounted for two-thirds of the overseas activities of all U.S. private banks on the average derived almost 50 percent of their total earnings from their foreign-based subsidiaries. International earnings, for example, accounted for 46 percent of Bank of America's total earnings, 72 percent of Citicorp, 78 percent of Chase Manhattan, 56 percent of Manufacturers Hanover, 53 percent of J. P. Morgan, 64 percent of Bankers Trust, and 44 percent of Chemical Bank. See U.S. Congress, Senate, Committee on Foreign Relations, Subcommittee on Foreign Economic Policy,*International Debt, The Banks, and U.S. Foreign Policy*, 95th Congress, 1st Session, Staff Report, Committee Print, August 1977 (Washington, D.C.; U.S. Government Printing Office, 1977, pp. 1, 9–10. See also Jonathan D. Aronson, *Money and Power: Banks and the World Monetary System* (Beverly Hills: Sage Publications, 1977), p. 47; and Barnet and Müller, *Global Reach*.

10. The costs of reestablishing profitability environments in the war-devastated economies of Western Europe in the immediate post-1945 period were largely borne by the U. S. imperial state:

> The obligation to take risks would be on the U.S. government, it was explicitly understood, especially if the United States were to assume the monumental tasks of dissolving the almost intact British trading bloc. As the familiar pattern of pre-war trade began to reemerge threatening the long-term American objective and it could no longer postpone action. . . . the United States in 1946 authorized $5.7 billion in the new foreign grants and credits—almost as much as the average for the next three years and fifth highest in post-war history.

In fact, only an estimated 15 percent of U.S. capital exports from 1945 to 1948 derived from private corporate sources. See Joyce Kolko and Gabriel Kolko, *The Limits of Power: The World and United States Foreign Policy, 1945-1955* (New York: Harper and Row, 1972), pp. 621-22, 26.

11. See, for example, Richard Barnet, *The Roots of War: Man and Institutions in U.S. Foreign Policy* (New York: Atheneum Books), pp. 76–133.

12. Barnet and Müller, *Global Reach*; and Vernon, *Sovereignty at Bay.*

13. Ronald Robinson, "Non-European Foundations of European Imperialism: Sketch for a Theory of Collaboration," in Roger Owen and Bob Sutcliffe (eds.), *Studies in the Theory of Imperialism* (London: Longmans, 1972), pp. 117–40.

14. Martin Carnoy, *Education as Cultural Imperialism* (New York: David McKay, 1974). During the 1960s *Ramparts Magazine* ran several exposé articles documenting the ties between a multiplicity of important cultural and social organizations and the CIA. See Hobart Spalding, "U.S. and Latin American Labor: The Dynamics of Imperial Control," in June Nash, et al., *Ideology and Social Change in Latin America* (New York: Gordon and Breach, 1977), pp. 55–91.

15. See Leon Trotsky, *The Permanent Revolution, and Results and Prospects* (New York: Merit Publishers, 1969); Samir Amin, *Accumulation on a World Scale* (New York: Monthly Review Press, 1974); and Immanuel Wallerstein, *The Modern World-System* (New York: Academic Press, 1976).

16. See Leys, *Underdevelopment in Kenya*; Gavan McCormack, "The South Korea Economy: GNP Versus the People," in Gavan McCormack and Mark Selden (eds.), *Korea North and South* (New York: Monthly Review Press, 1978), pp. 90–111; and James Petras, "State Capitalism in the Third World," in James Petras, *Critical Perspectives on Imperialism and Social Class* (New York: Monthly Review Press, 1979), pp. 84-102.

17. Mahmood Mamdani, *Politics and Class Formation in Uganda* (New York: Monthly Review Press, 1976); Issa G. Shivji, *Class Struggles in Tanzania* (New York: Monthly Review Press, 1976); and Samir Amin, *Neo-Colonialism in West Africa* (New York: Monthly Review Press, 1973).

18. Irving Markovitz, *Power and Class in Africa* (Englewood Cliffs, N.J.: Prentice-Hall, 1977).

19. In 1929 U.S. investment in Latin American agro-mining amounted to 44 percent of

the total regional investment, while manufacturing accounted for only 6 percent; in 1976 the former was less than 10 percent, while the latter accounted for 39 percent. See U.S. Department of Commerce, Office of Business Economics, *U.S. Business Investments in Foreign Countries* (Washington, D.C., 1960); and U.S. Department of Commerce, Bureau of Economic Analysis, *Selected Data on U.S. Direct Investment Abroad 1966-1976* (Washington, D.C., 1977). Latin America, Europe, and Japan combined have displaced the United States as the main trading partner of Brazil, Argentina, Paraguay, and Uruguay. See *Statistical Abstract of Latin America* (University of California at Los Angeles), vol. 18, 1977, p. 350.

20. Muto Ichiyo, "The Free Trade Zone and the Mystique of Export-Oriented Industrialization," in *Free Trade Zones and the Industrialization of Asia*, AMPO Japan Asia Quarterly Review, Summer 1977, pp. 9-32.

21. For a discussion of the "fragility" of externally-oriented industrialization in the Third World, see James Petras and Juan Manuel Carrion, "Contradictions of Colonial Industrialization and the Crisis in 'Commonwealth' Status: The Case of Puerto Rico," in Petras, *Critical Perspectives*, pp 751-70. See also Peter Evans, *Dependent Development* (Princeton: Princeton University Press, 1979).

22. Folker Frobel, Jurgen Heinrichs, and Otto Kreye, "The New International Division of Labor," *Social Science Information* 17, no. 1, pp. 123-42. See also by the same authors, "The Tendency Towards a New International Division of Labor," *Review* 1, no. 1, Summer 1977, pp. 73-88.

23. See Donald Castillo, "Caracteristicas Del Nuevo Modelo De Acumulacion De Capital En America Latina Con Ilustracion Del Caso CentroAmericano," *Estudios Sociales CentroAmericanos*, ano IX, numero 25, Enero-Abril 1980, pp. 164-65 (Table 1).

24. The proliferation of meetings and organization within which these lowest-common-denominator issues are discussed include North/South meetings, UNCTAD I, II, GATT, the meeting of the "77," and so forth.

25. James Petras, "Revolutions and the Working Class," *New Left Review* 111, September-October 1978, pp. 37-66. Ibid., "Toward a Theory of Twentieth Century Socialist Revolutions," *Journal of Contemporary Asis* 8, no. 2, 1978, pp. 167-95.

26. See James Petras, "State Capitalism in the Third World," in Petras, *Critical Perspectives*. John Saul, *The State and Revolution in Eastern Africa* (New York: Monthly Review Press, 1979); Anibal Quijano, *Nationalism and Capitalism in Peru* (New York: Monthly Review Press, 1971); and George D. F. Philip, *The Rise and Fall of the Peruvian Military Radicals 1968-1976* (University of London: Athlone Press, 1978).

27. Franz Fanon, *The Wretched of the Earth* (New York: Grove Press, 1963).

28. Poulantzas, *Political Power and Social Classes*.

29. Laclau, *Politics and Ideology in Marxist Theory*.

30. Poulantzas, *Political Power and Social Classes*.

31. On Angola, see Nathaniel Davis, "The Angola Decision of 1975: A Personal Memoir," *Foreign Affairs* 57, no. 1, Fall 1978, pp. 109-24. (Davis was an Assistant Secretary of State for African Affairs during the spring and summer of 1975 and played a central role in the policy-making debate over Angola that took place within the U.S. executive branch.) U.S. Congress, House, Select Committee on Intelligence, *CIA: The Pike Report* (London: Spokesman Books, 1977), pp. 198-218; and Seymour Hersh, "Angola-Aid Issue Opening Rifts in State Department," *New York Times*, December 14, 1975, pp. 1, 2.

On Iran, see Jim Hoagland, "U.S. Switches Effort to Post-Shah Regime," *Washington Post*, January 10, 1979, pp. A1, A12; Richard Burt, "U.S. Strategy on Iran Stirs a Fierce Debate," *New York Times*, January 12, 1979, p. 3; William Claiborne, "U.S. Seeks Khomeini Links," *Washington Post*, February 8, 1979, p. A10; Terence Smith, "Carter Says He's Prepared to Work With Tehran Leaders for Stability," *New York Times*, February 13, 1979, p. 10; Richard Burt, "A New U.S. Attitude on Iran," *New York Times*, February 13, 1979, p. 10; and U.S. Congress, House, Committee on Foreign Affairs, Subcommittee on Europe and the Middle East, *U.S. Policy toward Iran, January 1979*, 96th Congress, 1st Session, January 17, 1979 (Washington, D.C.: U.S. Government Printing Office, 1979).

32. Richard Neustadt, *Presidential Power* (New York: John Wiley and Sons, 1976); Edward Corwin, *The Presidency Today* (New York: New York University Press, 1956); and James William Fulbright, *The Arrogance of Power* (New York: Random House, 1966).

33. For an example of this type of "relative autonomy of the state" analysis, see Ellen Kay Trimberger, *Revolution From Above* (New Brunswick: Transaction Books, 1978).

34. See Morris Morley, *Toward a Theory of Imperial Politics* (Ph.D. dissertation, State University of New York at Binghamton, 1979); James Petras and Morris Morley, *The U.S. and Chile: Imperialism and the Overthrow of the Allende Government* (New York: Monthly Review Press, 1975).

35. In 1965, 7.9 percent of the U.S. GNP was spent on military, while Germany spent 4.3 percent and Japan 1 percent. By 1976 the figures were : U.S. 5 percent, Germany 3.4 percent, and Japan .9 percent. See also Seymour Melman, *The Permanent War Economy* (New York: Simon and Schuster, 1974), pp. 92 passim.

On Japanese and West German global economic expansion, see U.S. Congress, Senate, Committee on Foreign Relations, Subcommittee on East Asian and Pacific Affairs, *U.S./Japanese Relations,* 95th Congress, 2nd Session, April 28, 1978 (Washington, D.C.; U.S. Government Printing Office, 1978); Robert J. Samuelson, "U.S., Japan Find Old Relationships Have Unravelled," *National Journal* 11, no. 26, June 30, 1979, pp. 1068–79; and U.S. Congress, House, Committee on International Relations, Subcommittee on Europe and the Middle East, *Economic Conditions in the Federal Republic of Germany,* 95th Congress, 2nd Session, Committee Print, December 29, 1978. Report prepared by the Congressional Research Service of the Library of Congress (Washington, D.C.: U.S. Government Printing Office, 1978).

36. See, for example, U.S. Congress, Senate, Committee on Foreign Relations, *United States Foreign Policy Objectives and Overseas Military Installations,* 96th Congress, 1st Session, Committee Print, April 1979. Report prepared by the Congressional Research Service of the Library of Congress (Washington, D.C.: U.S. Government Printing Office, 1979).

37. See U.S. Congress, Senate, Committee on Foreign Relations, Subcommittee on Foreign Economic Policy, *International Debt, the Banks and U.S. Foreign Policy,* p. 1.

38. Ibid., pp. 51, 54. See also Aronson, *Money and Power,* pp. 161–84; and Barbara Stallings, "Peru and the U.S. Banks: Privatization of Financial Relations," in Richard R. Fagen (ed.), *Capitalism and the State in U.S.-Latin American Relations* (Stanford, Calif.: Stanford University Press, 1979), pp. 217–53. By mid-1977 U.S. private banking loans to peripheral governments totaled $52 billion. See "U.S. Prosperity and the Developing Countries," *GIST,* Bureau of Public Affairs, U.S. Department of State, August 1978. See also Robert A. Bennett, "Mountains of Debt Pile Up as Banks Push Foreign Loans," *New York Times,* May 15, 1977, pp. 1F, 13F; and Judith Miller, "Sounding Alarms on Foreign Debt," *New York Times,* September 18, 1977, pp. 1F, 4F.

39. See Miles D. Wolpin, *Military Aid and Counterrevolution in the Third World* (Lexington, Mass.: D. C. Heath and Co., 1972), pp. 11, 16, and passim; ibid., "External Political Socialization as a Source of Conservative Military Behavior in the Third World," in Kenneth Fidel (ed.), *Militarism in Developing Countries* (New Brunswick: Transaction Books, 1975), pp. 259–81; Michael Klare, *War Without End* (New York: Alfred A. Knopf, 1972), pp. 270–310; Richard Gott, "Canal Zone School Builds Brotherhood of Latin Generals," *Washington Post,* April 16, 1977, p. A10; and Jeffrey Stein, "Grad School for Juntas," *The Nation,* May 21, 1977, pp. 621–24.

40. See Philip Agee, *Inside the Company: CIA Diary* (New York: Stonehill, 1975); U.S. Congress, Senate, Select Committee on Intelligence, *Alleged Assassination Plots Involving Foreign Leaders,* 94th Congress, 1st Session, Report No. 94–465, November 20, 1975 (Washington, D.C.: U.S. Government Printing Office, 1975); and U.S. Congress, Senate, Select Committee on Intelligence, *Covert Action in Chile 1963–1973,* 94th Congress, 1st Session, December 18, 1975 (Washington, D.C.: U.S. Government Printing Office, 1975).

41. See, for example, Ronald Radosh, *American Labor and United States Foreign Policy* (New York: Random House, 1969).

42. The notion of "collaborating elites" is borrowed from Ronald Robinson, "Non-European Foundations of European Imperialism: Sketch for a Theory of Collaboration," in Roger Owen and Bob Sutcliffe (eds.), *Studies in the Theory of Imperialism,* pp. 116–42.

43. Barnet and Müller, *Global Reach,* chap. 7.

44. On the growth of worker militancy accompanying the expansion of multinational capital, see Fred Halliday, "The Economic Contradiction," *MERIP* Reports 69, pp. 9–18; "Brazil," *NACLA,* May–June 1979.

45. Harry Magdoff and Paul Sweezy, *The End of Prosperity: The American Economy in the 1970's* (New York: Monthly Review Press, 1977). The size of the Eurodollar market grew from $100 billion in mid-1970 to more than $900 billion by mid-1979. See Larry

Kramer, "Rapid Eurocurrency Growth Worrying Global Economists," *Washington Post*, September 9, 1979, p. F1. On the West European and Japanese export expansion between 1960 and 1977, see U.S. Central Intelligence Agency, *Handbook of Economic Statistics, 1978*, p. 53. According to the U.S. Department of Commerce, overall foreign investment in the United States increased by $5.7 billion in 1978, as compared to an increase of $2.5 billion in 1974. See "Neo-Mercantilism in the '80's: The Worldwide Scramble to Shift Capital," *Business Week*, July 9, 1979, p. 52.

46. National Security Council adviser Zbigniew Brzezinski outlined the key Carter Administration foreign-policy goals in a memorandum to Cabinet members on May 8, 1978:

> We seek wider cooperation with our key allies and a more cooperative world system. Close collaboration with Japan and Western Europe has long been the point of departure for American's global involvement. Responding to changes over the past 15 to 20 years in the global distribution of power, we are seeking to broaden these patterns of cooperation. This means developing new and wider relationships with such regionally influential nations as Nigeria, Indonesia, India, Saudi Arabia, Iran, Venezuela, and Brazil.

"Memorandum for Members of the Cabinet," from Zbigniew Brzezinski, May 3, 1978, reprinted in *The Nation*, June 24, 1978, p. 749.

47. See, for example, "New Data Link Mecca Takeover With Islamic Political Discontent," *New York Times*, February 25, 1980, pp. 1, 10.

48. The quadrupling of oil prices by the OPEC countries in 1974 and the emerging global energy crisis had a visible negative impact on the more highly export-dependent economies of Western Europe and Japan (and on their industrial growth rates) of greater magnitude than was experienced by the territorially defined U.S. political-economy. In 1977, for example, U.S. imports rose by 13 percent as compared to a 3.5 percent growth for Japanese and West German imports. In the area of industrial production, there was a severe decline in growth rates during the mid- and late 1970s. However, Western Europe and Japan evidenced a greater decline than did the United States:

Average Annual Growth of Industrial Production (percent)

	Western Europe	Japan	United States
1963–1973	5.6	10.5	5.4
1974/75–1978	1.1	3.9	2.5

See "New World Economic Order," *Business Week*, July 24, 1978, p. 70; "Neo-Mercantilism in the 80's: The Worldwide Scramble to Shift Capital," *Business Week*, July 9, 1979, p. 52. Parenthetically, because units of the U.S. economy also operate on a global scale, it is possible that while trade deficits, spiraling inflation, and so forth, may have had a direct adverse effect on the territorially defined U.S. political economy during this period, other units within the U.S. global economy (private multinational banks, multinational oil companies) may have actually experienced substantial growth and soaring profits (e.g., recycling of petrodollars into U.S. branch banks in Western Europe).

These essentially conjunctural shifts and changes, however, should not be confused with the overall trend toward a relative decline in the U.S. position within the capitalist world economy—evidenced, in part, by the sustained fall in the value of the dollar vis-à-vis other major capitalist-bloc currencies during the 1960s and 1970s. "G. William Miller: Carter's Agent to Prop up the Dollar and Win the 1980 Election," *Business Week*, August 6, 1979, pp. 68–74. On the decline of the U.S. dollar in international money markets, see Ann Crittenden, "A New World Disorder," *New York Times International Economy Survey*, Section 12, February 4, 1979, pp. 1, 38–39; and Jeremy Morse, "The Dollar as a Reserve Currency," *International Affairs* 55, no. 3, July 1979, pp. 36–63. Between 1960 and 1977, for example, the U.S. dollar lost more than half its value in terms of the German mark. See U.S. Congress, House, *Economic Conditions in the Federal Republic of Germany*, p. 14.

Recent export trends among the major capitalist countries suggest that this trend is continuing. A substantial resurgence of Japanese and West German exports to Iran and Saudi Arabia in payment for increasingly costly large-scale petroleum imports has acted to limit the outflow, and thereby sustained the strength, of the yen and the mark. By contrast, U.S. export sales have been insufficient to prevent an ongoing extensive dollar outflow for needed oil imports. See Eliot Janeway, "The Oil Shortage is a Malthusian Myth," *New York Times*, February 24, 1980, p. F16; and Paul Lewis, "A New Monetarism Sweeps the West," *New York Times International Economic Survey*, section 12, February 3, 1980, pp. 9, 14.

49. The declining competitive position of the United States and its growing deficits in trade are discussed in length in Melman, *The Permanent War Economy*, chap. 14; and Fred Block, *The Origins of International Economic Disorder* (Berkeley and Los Angeles: University of California Press, 1977), pp. 109–202.

50. U.S. productivity (output per hour) between 1961 and 1972 was 3.3, while in West Germany it was 5.2, and in Japan 9.8. U.S. Central Intelligence Agency, *Handbook of Economic Statistics, 1978*, p. 23. In 1953 the United States accounted for 47 percent of Latin America's exports; in 1976 this figure had fallen to 36 percent. See *U.N. Statistical Yearbook* (New York) 1965, 1973, 1977.

51. Although current dollar weekly earnings of full-time wage and salary workers rose each year between 1967 and 1978, as Figure 1.2 shows, earnings in real, or constant, dollars (May 1967 equals 100) peaked in 1973. The real median weekly earnings for full-time workers in May 1978 was the same as it had been in May 1977 *and approximately 3 percent below the 1973 level.*

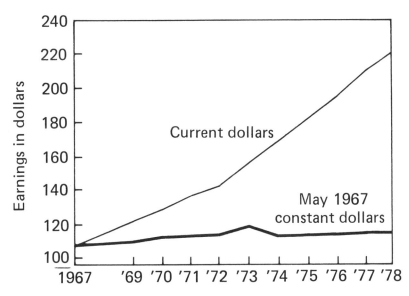

Figure 1.2 Median usual weekly earnings of wage and salary workers who usually work full time, in current dollars and in May 1967 constant dollars, May 1967–May 1978. *Note*: Constant dollars, shown here in comparison with current dollars, were calculated using the Consumer Price Index (admusted to May 1967 = 100).

Janice Neipert Hedges and Earl F. Mellor, "Weekly and Hourly Earnings of U.S. Workers, 1967–1978," *Monthly Labor Review* 102, no. 8, August 1979, pp. 31–33. See also Harry Magdoff and Paul Sweezy, "Productive Slowdown: A False Alarm," *Monthly Review* 31, no. 2, June 1979, pp. 2–5.

52. For example, in mid-1978 the Carter Administration's Chairman of the Council on

Wage and Price Stability, Alfred E. Kahn, warned of an inevitable "deep, deep recession" or mandatory wage-price controls if the government's voluntary inflation program proved unable to curb rising prices. Quotes in Steven Rattner, "Kahn Cautions on Depression," *New York Times*, November 16, 1978, p. D1.

53. Burton Hall, *Autocracy and Insurgency in Organized Labor* (New Brunswick: Transaction Books, 1972); See also *Labor Notes* (published in Detroit) for fortnightly reports.

54. The following observation is appropriate: "The American [investment/capital] presence in Europe is so immense—and so profitable—that even five years of steady decline of the dollar, world recession and heightened competition have not diminished its dimensions." Murray Seeger, "Competitive Balance Shifting in Europe," *Washington Post*, January 14, 1979, p. K4.

55. Prior to the economic summit meeting of seven capitalist-bloc countries in Bonn, West Germany, in July 1978, to take an instance, the host leader, Chancellor Helmut Schmidt, declared that U.S. actions would be decisive to any improvement in the capitalist world's economic problems: "Let's assume theoretically that America would see no possibility to succeed in the aforementioned field of oil and inflation, then I would be afraid that others would have difficulties to overcome their domestic obstacles as well and to compromise their interests." French and Japanese participants similarly maintained that American actions would determine the outcome of the summit consultations. Quoted in John Vinocur, "Schmidt Says U.S. Holds Key to Economic Accord," *New York Times*, July 14, 1978, p. 3.

56. Block, *The Origins of International Economic Disorder*, p. 135.

57. Magdoff and Sweezy, *The End of Prosperity*, p. 5.

58. For the most comprehensive analysis of the post-World War II international capitalist monetary system, and the place of the dollar within that system, see Block, *The Origins of International Economic Disorder*.

59. "G. William Miller: Carter's Agent to Prop up the Dollar and Win the 1980 Election," *Business Week*, August 6, 1979, p. 70. According to the International Monetary Fund, the percentage of dollars held in official foreign-exchange reserves of countries declined from four-fifths in 1976 to almost three-quarters in 1979. These funds moved largely into German marks, Swiss francs, and Japanese yen. See Robert J. Samuelson, "An Exercise in Economic Diplomacy," *National Journal* 11, no. 39, September 29, 1979, p. 1613.

60. See Harry Magdoff and Paul Sweezy, "Productive Slowdown: A False Alarm," *Monthly Review*, June 1979, pp. 1–12.

61. Block, *The Origins of International Economic Disorder*, p. 146. As regards the 1970s, see also Harry Magdoff and Paul Sweezy, "Capital Shortage: Fact and Fancy," *Monthly Review* 27, no. 11, April 1976, pp. 1–19.

62. Block. *The Origins of International Economic Disorder,* p. 159.

63. See Robert J. Samuelson, "U.S., Japan Find Old Relationships Have Unravelled," *National Journal*, June 30, 1979, p. 1071. By the 1970s Japan had replaced the United States as the major trading partner of a number of Asian nations and, in particular, now "dominate(d) the trade patterns of Southeast Asia." Mark Seldon, "Global Enterprise: The American Record in Asia," *Peace and Change* VI, no. 1, Fall 1976, p. 22 and passim. See also ibid., "American Global Enterprise and Asia," *Bulletin of Concerned Asian Scholars* 7, no. 2, April-June 1975, pp. 15–33.

2

Capitalist Expansion and Class Conflict in Advanced Third World Countries

by JAMES F. PETRAS and MORRIS H. MORLEY

International Political Economy: A Class Analysis

Capital accumulation and expansion on a world scale, notwithstanding periodically recurring crises (recessions, depressions, and fluctuations), have been characteristic of our epoch. Hence, this study contends, the critical problem for analysis is not that of stagnation and underdevelopment, but one of examining the conditions under which the process of capital accumulation takes place and its impact on the class structure. Class relations are viewed as a point of departure within which to locate the problem of capital accumulation and expansion.

The conditions under which accumulation takes place include: (a) the nature of the state (and state policy); and (b) class relations (process of surplus extraction, intensity of exploitation, level of class struggle, concentration of the work force). The impact of capital accumulation on class structure includes: (a) class formation/conversion (small proprietor to proletarian, or kulak, rural proletarian to urban subproletarian, landlord to merchant, merchant to industrialist, national industrialist to branch plant manager of a multinational corporation); (b) income distribution (concentration, redistribution, reconcentration of income); and (c) social relations, including labor market relations ("free" wage, trade union bargaining), semicoercive (market and political/social controls), and coercive (slave, debt peonage).

As production expands, growth occurs in cyclical patterns, largely as a function of external decisions (foreign investors, importers, and financiers) and internal conditions (externally linked classes, alienated state, repressed social movements). Accumulation is characterized by uneven development, reflected in the particular product areas integrated to the external world and sharp income inequalities derived from the external class linkages, control over state revenues, and coercive controls over working class and peasantry (Amin, 1974). Unlike dependency studies, which center on the growth of productive forces and how the external ties block growth, the focus on conditions of accumulation and its impact on class relations allows us to focus more concretely on the nature of the state ultimately involved in both accumulation and class formation, as well as internal class relations as they emerge from, as well as shape, capitalist development.[1]

The postindependence national regime can choose among at least three strategies or types of class alliances for capital accumulation. In the first instance, it can join with imperial firms and regimes in intensifying surplus extraction from the labor force through a variety of postindependence working relationships outlined under the rubric of dependent neocolonialism. An alternative strategy for the national regime involves extracting the surplus from the labor force and limiting or eliminating the share going to the imperial firms, thus concentrating it in the hands of state and/or private national entrepreneurs. This approach, which can be referred to as a national developmentalism without redistribution, leads to concentration of income at the top of the national class hierarchy.

A third alternative is for the national regime to ally itself with the laboring population, extend the areas of national control (through nationalization), reinvest the surplus of the national economy, or promote a redistribution of income within the national class structure.

The type of class alliance on which the national regime rests and the strategy for capital accumulation directly affect the distribution of income. Capital accumulation "from above and outside," or what can be called the "neocolonial" model results in an income structure that resembles an inverted pyramid—with wealth and power concentrated in the hands of foreign capital. The national bourgeois development approach, which capitalizes on the foreign elite and the national labor force, concentrates income among the intermediary strata (in the form of the governing elite of the periphery), leading to income distribution along the shape of a diamond. The alliance between national intermediaries and the labor force, or a "national-popular" strategy, leads to a broader-based society in which income is more diversified, spreading downward and taking the shape of a pyramid.

As the above indicates, the struggle against imperial domination is now mediated through a class structure that itself contains contradictions, i.e., is itself a source of exploitation. The pattern of exploitative relations varies from one development strategy to another. In the neocolonial model, the national bourgeoisie serves as a means of heightening imperial exploitation in order to extract a share of the surplus for itself; examples of this regime include Brazil, Chile, Indonesia, Iran, Taiwan, South Korea, and South Vietnam. Policy is characterized by coercion and a demobilized population, open access to raw materials, and tax and other incentives to foreign investors. The forms of joint exploitation vary greatly, expressing the differences in bargaining power between the national and imperial bourgeoisie. Under conditions of total foreign control of the economy, the national bourgeoisie obtains tax revenue. Under conditions of partnership in which majority ownership and management prerogatives are in foreign hands, the national bourgeoisie obtains a minority share of earnings plus tax revenues. Whatever the specifics, the foreign component is clearly dominant in internal, as well as external, relations.

The major impetus to class formation, mainly externally directed capital accumulation based on simple surplus extraction, gave way to a more complex process where an internal ruling class with its own state apparatus emerged to mediate the process of exploitation and accumulation. Capital accumulation in the periphery has had a varied experience: The least durable and expansive regimes have been the most popular and nationalist; the least popular have been the most expansive and least national; and the regimes that have been national but not popular have eventually evolved into one of the other two approaches.

Recent historical experience suggests that among capitalist countries in the periphery the most effective instrument of capital accumulation and growth is precisely the least national and most exploitative model, the neocolonial, or "from above and outside," approach. The historical conditions, more specifically the political preconditions, for this growth have in fact been nonpopular, externally oriented regimes resting largely on alliances between military elites and property classes, whose incapacity to accumulate capital leads them to rely on foreign capital.

Subimperialism: Regional and Global Linkages

Three major subimperialist powers—Iran, Brazil, and South Africa—are experiencing major political crises that could eventually lead to fundamental societal and economic changes. Shifts in power, regime, and social system have already, or may, occur[ed] within these and other countries, whose economies are, or have been, among the fastest growing in the Third World. Moreover, changes within these countries, described by the Carter Administration as "regionally influential nations" (Brzezinski, 1978:749), will have a profound effect throughout the surrounding areas, as well as within the major imperial centers of world capitalism. Unlike the Vietnamese, Cambodian, Cuban, Mozambican, or Nicaraguan revolutions, which had only limited impacts beyond their territorial boundaries, revolutions in the subimperialist countries will inevitably lead to a drastic shift in the balance of forces within the regions.

Iran, Brazil, and South Africa exercise economic, military, and political power in adjoining areas that serve to limit the scope and possibilities for politico-economic transformations within smaller and weaker states. The Shah's Iran participated directly (military forces) or indirectly (bases, weapons, equipment, training) in support of right-wing and reactionary regimes in North Yemen, Oman, Pakistan, Northern Iraq, South Vietnam, Morocco, Jordan, Zaire, and Somalia (Halliday, 1979:271–72). Within the Middle East region, it also supplied Israel with oil and provided diplomatic support for initiatives authored by Saudi Arabia, Egypt, and other conservative regimes. The Brazilian military dictatorship lent soldiers to the U.S. military occupation of the Dominican Republic in 1965–66, provided training and support to Chilean counterrevolutionaries, who overthrew the democratic socialist government of Salvador Allende in 1973, exerted pressures on the armed forces in Uruguay to clamp down on the political left and urban guerrilla forces in the early 1970s, and penetrated the neighboring economies of Bolivia and Paraguay. The apartheid regime in South Africa, which has emerged as the main pillar of white supremacy in southern Africa, has promulgated a strategy of economic "outreach" into several adjoining states (Zambia, Botswana, Lesotho, Swaziland, and Mozambique) in the pursuit of new markets, raw materials, minerals, labor exploitation, and investment opportunities (Seidman and Seidman, 1978:137–41, 162–91); and it has posed a military threat to other states in the region, as the Angolan invasion of late 1975 most dramatically illustrated. Moreover, the concentration of capital and the development of the productive forces within these countries provide the key to developing the productive forces within other countries in the region. The transformation and integration of the former subimperialist countries will tremendously accelerate developments within the region. Otherwise in isolation, each of the revolutionary changes in the more underdeveloped countries will encounter severe obstacles, as well as pressures and distortion from their participation in the world market.

The significance of the growing mass and guerrilla struggles in southern Africa, the nationwide popular upheaval in Iran, which culminated in the overthrow of the Pahlavi dictatorship, and large-scale economic strikes and the resurgence of political opposition in Brazil affect strategically placed countries whose position in the world capitalist system and geographic location have multiple effects on a whole series of other countries: Herein, the domino theory has real applicability. Fundamental political changes in large semi-industrialized countries can loosen the military-police controls in regions where revolutionary forces have been kept in check and beyond that, can provide active support for new initiatives.

As important and direct as their impact is within the immediate continents and region, perhaps even more crucial from the long-range perspective is their collective impact on the capitalist world economy as a whole and specifically on the imperial centers of the East and West. The oil links between Iran and the core capitalist countries are extensive and of great strategic consequences to their overall economic expansion (See Table 2.1).

Table 2.1 Oil Imports from Iran as a Percentage of Total Oil Imports, January–June 1978

United States	10.0
Japan	17.9
Great Britain	17.0
France	8.0
Italy	14.0
West Germany	18.0
Denmark	35.6
Holland	22.7
Belgium	22.3
Israel	65.0
South Africa	90.0

Source: Merip Reports, 1979:17.

Moreover, because of its importance in OPEC, Iran plays a crucial role in shaping policy of all oil producers in relation to the imperial centers (New York Times, October 16, 1979:1).

Iran also provided a massive market for military and consumer goods from the United States, Europe, and Japan, in addition to imports of machinery and civilian and military technicians during the Shah's reign (U.S. Congress, 1976). In 1972 the Nixon Administration decided to sell Iran the F-14 and F-15 aircrafts, "and, in general, to let Iran buy [any military equipment] it wanted, effectively exempt[ing] Iran from arms sales review processes in the State and Defense Departments" (U.S. Congress, 1976 : viii–ix). Between 1972 and 1976 Iran purchased $10.4 billion worth of military supplies from the Pentagon, making it Washington's largest single customer in this area (U.S. Congress, 1976 : vii). In concert with its "regional influentials" strategy, the Carter White House saw fit to sustain the Nixon-Ford military supply "pipeline" to Iran despite the President's self-imposed ceiling on overseas arms sales. In one instance, the administration neatly circumvented this "constraint" in order to provide the Shah with a number of costly armed frigates. The tactic employed was one of allowing allied European countries to assume the major cost burden of building the ships, for which the United States then supplied the less expensive weaponry necessary to make them effective (*Washington Post*, August 19, 1978 : A1, A6). Within six months of the Shah's overthrow, some $7.7 billion out of an estimated $12.6 billion worth of pending military equipment contracts had been cancelled by the successor regime (*New York Times*, July 29, 1979 : 1, 18; U.S. General Accounting Office, 1979; U.S. Congress, 1979 : 5)

Iran was also an important export market for capitalist bloc countries, especially West Germany, Japan, and the United States. The latter provided about $6 billion in goods and commodities to Tehran during 1978 (*New York Times*, February 27, 1979 : D13). Between March 1977 and March 1978 the Iranian economy purchased an additional $5.8 billion in services from foreign multinationals, approximately one-third of which was forthcoming from American firms (*Wall Street Journal*, March 8, 1979 : 1). Capitalist-bloc MNC investments in Iran and Iranian financial holdings in Western banks provided further massive sources of earnings and capital that generated growth in the advanced industrialized countries, especially in times of industrial stagnation and balance of payments difficulties. The overall economic importance of Iranian expenditures (military and nonmilitary) to the American economy may be gauged from the fact that in 1977 alone the United States took in about $6 billion from these sources and paid out $3.5 billion, mainly in oil purchase requirements (*New York Times*, July 9, 1978 : 1, 10). At the end of 1978 the U.S. Department of Commerce estimated that the combined Iranian state and private enterprise commitments from U.S. firms were in the vicinity of $20 billion (*Wall Street Journal*, March 8, 1979 : 1).

While Iranian petrodollars found their way into the branches of U.S. and European private multinational banks, these financial institutions, in turn, extended large-scale credits to sustain the capitalist industrialization program promoted by the Shah state. The country's foreign debt rose to $5 billion over the duration of the Shah's rule, of which approximately $2 billion was owed to U.S. banks, principally Chase Manhattan and Citibank (*New York Times*, January 9, 1979 : D1, D9). Iran was also the recipient of approximately $1.5 billion in U.S. government economic assistance between 1962 and 1975, and more than $1 billion in credits from the major international capitalist financial organizations during the same period (U.S. Agency for International Development, 1979 : 17, 207). In 1977 and 1978 Tehran entered the Eurodollar money market and successfully syndicated loans totaling $2.6 billion (*New York Times*, January 9, 1979 : D1, D9).

The national popular upheaval that overthrew the Shah produced a regime whose rhetoric spoke to the re-allocation of priorities away from armaments, luxury goods, and overseas bank deposits and toward national development, social investments, and redistributive measures. The initial actions taken by the Khomeini-dominated government drastically curtailed the role of foreign multinationals within the Iranian economy, who, according the the *London Financial Times*, suffered combined overall losses totaling close to $80 billion (*Manchester Guardian Weekly*, August 26, 1979 : 11). The new regime's decision to join the international oil boycott of Israel severely complicated the latter's supply problems in the short run, increasing the burden on U.S. efforts to sustain the level of economic activity. The net effect of these developments is likely to be a new round of external-accounts deficits in the advanced capitalist countries at a time when they have yet to emerge from a period of global economic recession ("stagflation"), encouraging further "austerity" measures and heightening internal class tensions. (*New York Times*, February 27, 1979 : D13; June 13, 1979 : D5). Conceivably, this process could begin to erode and dissipate the parliamentary consensus in the imperial centers.

South Africa also has great significance for the advanced capitalist countries. Gold provides an important basis for stabilizing currencies, especially in times of increasing Western currency fluctuations and the general weakening of the dollar on international money markets. Large-scale investments and loans for South Africa provided by most of the biggest multinational corporations and banking institutions, as well as by multilateral financial organizations, generate a substantial proportion of earnings for specific firms and countries in the core areas of the capitalist world economy. In particular, the United Kingdom's investment, financial, and commercial linkages are especially important, and a sharp turnabout would have grave consequences, spreading from the financial and industrial centers to the rest of the economy and society. Although England accounted for approximately half of the almost $12 billion in direct foreign investment in South Africa in 1972 and was that country's leading capitalist-bloc trade partner up through the early 1970s (Seidman and Seidman, 1978 : 74; Johnson, 1977 : 290), the most rapid expansion during this period was experienced by American investments and commerce. Between 1968, when the Nixon Administration linked "constructive change" on the African continent to the persistence of white minority-dominated governments (National Security Council Memorandum No. 39), and 1973, U.S. investments in South Africa increased in value from $692 million to approximately $1.24 billion. This latter figure, however, did not include investments made through U.S.-controlled British subsidiaries or Western European firms located there. In 1973 the United States, Western Europe, and Japan accounted for 80 percent of South Africa's import needs. By 1976 total U.S. trade with Pretoria surpassed that of all other capitalist countries, including the U.K., in value ($1.3 billion). At the same time, the book value of American direct corporate investment in the country had risen to $1.67 billion, which was 37.3 percent of total U.S. direct investment in the continent as a whole. This total investment figure was divided among more than 250 U.S. multinationals active in the South African economy (Seidman and Seidman, 1978 : 74–77, 150–58; U.S. Congress, 1978 : 7–8; Milkman, 1979 : 275).

South Africa has likewise been the recipient of increasingly large amounts of financial capital from the private multinational banking community, in addition to consistent infusions of International Monetary Fund (IMF) short-term funds to alleviate a chronic balance of payments problem. In December 1976 the South African foreign debt stood at $7.6 billion, primarily owed to private commercial banks and investment banking houses in the United States ($2.2 billion) and Western Europe ($5.4 billion) (U.S. Congress, 1978 : 7). Increasingly, however, the trend has been in the direction of a greater proportion of external credits supplied by American banking sources. In addition, Pretoria received $205.4 million in U.S. government Export-Import Bank loans between 1972 and 1976, and it was successful in obtaining a further $1.5 billion in international credits by year's end in 1976, in the form of $1.0 billion from outstanding bond issues and an IMF grant of credits totaling $366 million (U.S. Congress, 1978 : 7, 21). In December 1977, with the forceful backing of American and British representatives, the IMF increased its original allocation to $464 million (Morrell and Gisselquist, 1978). Between 1974 and 1976 external credits rose from 15 percent to an estimated 32 percent of total foreign investment (U.S. Congress, 1978 : 21–22). These international lines of credit offered critical supports in the area of economic infrastructure development and acted to limit government budget deficits brought about by increased costs of petroleum and military equipment imports, whose combined expenditures catapulted from approximately $400 million in 1973 to an estimated $2 billion in 1976. The South African government's access to short-term borrowings in the capitalist money markets, during a period when gold, its major foreign exchange earner, was falling in price, was crucial to its ability to cover the large oil-defense-related increase in the current accounts deficit (U.S. Congress, 1978 : 21–22).

The expanding U.S. investment-banking-financial network in South Africa in recent years has been complemented by a massive expansion of arms sales, in contravention of the United Nations voluntary embargo on arms transfers to that country. While there is no hard evidence to suggest illegal sales to Pretoria under the auspices of the U.S. government's military procurement program, the fact that U.S. corporations and their subsidiaries have channeled millions of dollars worth of military equipment to the white supremacist regime is at best indicative of a serious breakdown in Washington's export control operations (Gervasi, 1978; Klare, 1979; *Washington Post*, August 5, 1979 : B1, B2). The Western European military "connection" with South Africa has been promoted largely through the vehicle of NATO and, to a lesser extent, through such activities as joint naval maneuvers. Richard Johnson notes that since 1972, and perhaps earlier, NATO has been a major contributor of sophisticated electronic equipment for Project Advocate—"a comprehensive surveillance, monitoring and communications programme"—whose center of operations is located just outside of Simonstown, South Africa (Johnson, 1977 : 214).

Notwithstanding these developments, the growth of guerrilla warfare and urban-based struggles could, in the immediate future, limit the profits that currently accrue to Western countries, forcing the withdrawal of funds at a time when alternative investment regions are also closing up or requiring massive, long-term financial outlays.

Brazil has similarly been the target of a massive flow of financial and investment capital. Since the mid-1960s an array of multinationals from the advanced capitalist countries have made large-scale, long-term investments in consumer durables, manufacturing, and so forth. By the end of 1972 total direct U.S. private investment in Brazil exceeded $2 billion, although increasing Japanese and Western European investments began to make inroads into the dominant U.S. position during the 1970s (U.S. Department of Commerce, 1973:9, *Business Latin America*, March 8, 1973:75, October 24, 1973:33738, January 16, 1974:18, April 10, 1974:113-15). While foreign capital investment in Brazil grew by 25 percent between 1970 and 1978, the overall American share declined from 45 percent to 32 percent, whereas that of West Germany, Japan, and Switzerland rose to 12 percent, 11 percent, and 10 percent, respectively. Much of this external capital went into the most dynamic and "modern" industrial sectors of the economy, such as automobiles (99.8 percent foreign control), pharmaceuticals (100 percent foreign control), and electronic equipment (74 percent foreign control) (*Le Monde Diplomatique*, January, 1979 : 14). Some of the major corporations, like Volkswagen, were increasingly dependent upon earnings in Brazil to sustain a substantial part of the entire international operations. Paralleling and to a considerable degree laying the groundwork for these external capital investment flows has been the extraordinary financial largess displayed by the U.S. government and the U.S.-influenced international financial institutions toward opponents of the nationalist Goulart Government (1962–64) and, subsequently, to the military dictatorship that succeeded it. Between 1962 and 1976 Washington's combined economic and military assistance to Brazil totaled approximately $4.2 billion. During the same period the multilateral banks contributed another $4.7 billion, in the interests of facilitating a profitable environment for multinational capital to operate and flourish (U.S. Agency for International Development 1979 : 42, 212).

As with investment capital, finance capital also assumed a growing stake in the Brazilian economy. Between December 1973 and December 1978 the country's foreign debt skyrocketed from about $12.6 billion to approximately $40 billion, and it is expected to exceed $50 billion by

December 1979 (Economist Intelligence Unit, 1978 : 16, 1979 : 18; *Latin American Economic Report*, July 20, 1979: 220; *New York Times*, October 7, 1979 : E3). According to a U.S. congressional study, American private banks were Brazil's major creditors as of December 1976, to the tune of $13 billion (U.S. Congress, 1977 : 56). A breakdown of the country's principal creditors as of March 1978, when the foreign debt stood at $36.4 billion, shows that while the American share may have marginally declined, the overall rise in Brazilian indebtedness to the international capitalist banking community continued apace: United Kindom ($7.8 billion); United States ($5.6 billion); Bahamas ($5.5 billion); Japan ($2.3 billion); West Germany ($2.2 billion); France ($1.7 billion); and the Inter-American Development Bank ($0.6 billion) (Economist Intelligence Unit, 1979 : 18). The debt-service ratio as a percentage of the value of merchandise exports rose from approximately 35 percent in 1973 to 66 to 67 percent in 1978 ($8 billion) (Economist Intelligence Unit, 1979: 18; *Le Monde Diplomatique*, January 1979 : 14).

Despite this trend, private multinational bankers continue to express limited concern over Brazil's growing debt, preferring to cite its sustained industrial growth during the 1970s—especially its ability to recover quickly from the effects of the 1974–75 global economic recession—as sufficient guarantee of its capacity to service the debt adequately. Furthermore, the residual concerns that remain over the spiraling debt are quickly assuaged by the persistant high level of profits accruing to Brazil's major financial creditors. In 1976, for example, U.S. Citicorp's estimated $2.5 billion worth of claims on Brazil generated some 13 percent of its $405 million consolidated aftertax earnings "and were the largest single overseas source of revenue [during that twelve-month period)" (*Business Week*, December 5, 1977 : 72–73). In 1978 alone it has been calculated that approximately half of the total external capital inflow of between $12 billion and $13 billion derived from private capitalist banking sources. These "exterior" financial borrowings contributed substantially to an estimated fivefold to sixfold increase in Brazil's overall balance of payments surplus over 1977 (from $630 million to approximately $3.5 to $4.5 billion) (Economist Intelligence Unit, 1979 : 18).

Therefore, at a time when a very large proportion of the earnings of the major capitalist-bloc multinational banks is derived from overseas holdings, a major political shift in regime could lead to serious financial crises within these banking institutions. The vast pipeline of loans to the Brazilian dictatorship from Citibank, Chase Manhattan, and other multinational banks could redound to their disadvantage, with ramifications throughout the national and international financial communities.

Given these substantial linkages, it is clear that consequential shifts in power within these key countries can have a significant effect on the economies and societies of the advanced capitalist countries.

Dictatorial Regimes and Economic Growth

Throughout many areas of the Third World, highly repressive regimes have become firmly ensconced as part of the "permanent" scenery, one might say.[2] For some observers, this phenomenon is generally associated with the general problem of "backward areas" or, more politely, underdeveloped countries: Lacking the political experience and traditions of the West, the dictatorial regime is the best that can be expected (Huntington, 1968). For others, the current regimes are merely continuations of past "authoritarian traditions"—more organized (bureaucratized) perhaps, but firmly wedded to a past in which government by the few was the norm (Pike and Stritch, 1974). Both of these approaches emphasize: (1) the *internal* factors that lead to the repressive structures, and (2) the *continuation* with the past, i.e., more repression by the same type of regime. First, these views of the recent wave of repressive regimes are fundamentally wrong: The origins and proliferation of repressive regimes are not products of internal developments, but responses to demands that originate primarily on a global level. Second, the organization and functioning of the state and its relationship to economic processes and social structures are vastly different from the dictatorial state of the past.

The term that best expresses the *character* of this new state, and its relationship to the class structure and economic system, is "neo-fascist." Fundamentally, the state exists through the permanent and pervasive direct use of force, coercion being the key element that binds the varying classes together in productive relations. The ideological element in rulership is clearly secondary and restricted to the few. "Authority" is embodied by the figures of force. There is little sense in which authority is freely recognized as a source of legitimacy. The submission of the citizens to the state is not based on the recognition of legitimate authority, but on the *fear* generated by the use or threat of force. Hence, the "authoritarian" tradition is subsumed within a larger universe of *violence*, which pervades all of society and affects all areas of social life.

The organization of the state is permeated by the forces of violence. The proliferation of government by military officials involves the all-pervasive penetration of political and economic life by the instrumentalities of violence: Education and labor relations are dictated and enforced by the official whose direct contact is with repressive forces, either military or police. That the officials of violence became involved in bureaucratic roles and routines within bureaucratic structures says little about the dynamic linkages that allow them to draw upon the tools of violence, to circumvent the procedures and lines of authority of bureaucratic organization, and to engage in extrabureaucratic modes of repression. In some ways, the bureaucratic structure is a facade—an alibi that disguises the multiple forms of repression and the arbitrary nature of the state. In this sense, the notion of bureaucratic authoritarianism itself is an ideology that serves to mystify the violent and arbitrary nature of the state (O'Donnell, 1973).[3]

The neo-fascist state in the initial period is essentially a repressive state: an apparatus geared toward destroying the organizations of mass mobilization, annihilating militants, and, in a specific sense, systematically demobilizing the masses. But this initial function does not exhaust the historic characteristics of the neo-fascist state. Rather, this "revolution," as its supporters refer to it, is the basis for "reconstruction"—that is, the creation of policies, institutions, and conditions for a particular type of socioeconomic development. The neo-fascist state hence has the second essential function of creating the conditions of large-scale, long-term economic expansion based on the promotion of multinational capital (Petras and Morley, 1975 : 165–66). Thus the very process of demobilization of the masses flows into a policy of creating optimal conditions for capitalist development: The process of repressing the left is directly linked to "disciplining" the labor force for capitalist production; the elaboration of infrastructure projects through the growth of state firms is linked with the growth of foreign investment in manufacturing, minerals, and agriculture. The neo-fascist state, through the extension of a multiplicity of state activity, inserts itself as a complementary force promoting foreign growth.

During the 1960s and 1970s Brazil, Iran, and South Africa experienced rapid industrial growth and the incorporation of large amounts of foreign capital. The reasons are apparent: These countries possess raw materials of great value to the industrial countries, they have substantial earnings generating a substantial market for exports, and they are ruled by regimes that facilitate the inward and outward flows of capital and contain labor and nationalist discontent. In the past several years, as the industrial processes in the advanced countries have become more sophisticated, there has been a need to increase the flow and efficient production of raw materials that feed into this process. Hence, there has been a growth in the level of technological development in the extraction, processing, and transportation of raw materials. This new investment has been accompanied by the growth of satellite industries and increasing local consumption, in addition to far-reaching state investments in joint ventures and complementary activities. While the rates of industrial growth have been high, and while there has been a substantial increase in the size and importance of social strata tied to the new industries, the changes have been concentrated in particular regions and have accentuated socioeconomic differences. The new growth served to erode previous forms of production, marginalizing their producers, without creating a new base of support within the new industrial project.

Phases of the Development Model

The early stages of this socioeconomic process were initiated under the strict rule of harsh dictatorial regimes, which systematically excluded the economic producers from any form of political representation. This form of domination—approaching total control—served to reconcentrate income in the property-owning classes, as well as to attract international financial and corporate groups interested in large-scale, long-term investments in a politically secure environment. The compression of salaries and wages in South Africa and Brazil was sustained through the elaboration of an immense repressive apparatus that permeated civil society and prevented the emergence of mediating groups. This process of capitalist growth "from above and outside" circumscribed the activities of preexisting social, political, and economic groups, limiting their influence without incorporating many in the new types of political-economic process. Small property owners were overwhelmed by the rise in urban land prices; unable to sustain operations in the city, they moved to the periphery. Imported cheap finished goods undermined local producers, the small handicraft workshops. The growth of power in state authorities in Iran, for example, undermined the influence of traditional religious and cultural figures: The increasing monopolization by the state of education and other instruments of value-formation forced the traditional right to react against the advance of dictatorial capitalism through appeals to the displaced and downwardly mobile social strata.

This first stage of political-economic growth is characterized by the forceful uprooting of previous sociopolitical representative organizations and the efforts to *implant* the conditions for economic concentration and growth. The regime is characterized by massive and savage assaults on the left, followed by the consolidation of a regime of permanent repression.

The second stage is characterized by large-scale economic expansion (following the groundwork laid down earlier), the institutionalization of regimes (accompanied by a modernized police force), and the attempt to foster collaborative social and political association among the producers. Within this expansive period, the incorporation of large new contingents of workers and technicians takes place. Rural migrants and the new middle class "take their place" in society without *great* resistance, accepting the conditions of domination as the price for incorporation into the stable labor force. Labor conflicts are limited and harshly repressed; street riots by students and marginal urban producers are isolated from the mass of modern productive facilities.

The third stage involves the continual reproduction of capital, the extension and deepening of the process of industrialization, and the "acculturation" of the industrial labor force and middle class in an industrial class-divided society. The changes are not only in terms of the size and scope of the modern industrial and service sector, but in the quality of the participants: The demands and frame of reference are no longer in terms of the past agro-feudal society, but in terms of the current condition of urban industrial society. The proletarianization process obliterates notions of relative improvement evidenced among the earlier rural migrants turned laborers. Likewise, the economic costs and sociopolitical constraints that daily affect the educated middle class employed in the services devalorize the status achievements and consumer goods that were so important during the earlier phase.

In a word, the nature of the political regime—the primitive exclusionary and dictatorial forms of domination—comes into conflict with the demands of the modern working and middle class "in place" within the urban-industrial centers. The very process of *class transformation* unleashed by the industrial expansion comes into conflict with the ongoing framework of political control, which incubated both. The demands to decompress controls over wages involve direct attempts in collective organization, which in turn generate demands for political representation *independently* of the regime. The notion of political autonomy from the state resonates far beyond the confines of the political and social strata within the capitalist vortex, however, and accompanies all those petty-commodity producers, marginalized masses, and traditional cultural figures who have been displaced, bypassed, or adversely affected by the dynamics of accumulation and reproduction of capital. The convergence of modern working and middle classes within capitalist production and petty-commodity producers and traditional leaders outside generates a society wide protest that threatens the foundations of regime domination. The erosion of the regime from among the older propertied groups and within the new propertyless groups isolates the repressive apparatus and undermines its ideological appeals: Since the opposition incorporates property, the struggle cannot be waged on the property/propertyless division; since the struggle includes workers and employees, it cannot be presented as a struggle between "modernity" and "traditionalism." The repressive apparatus stands nakedly exposed, without passive acquiescence of the masses, without ideological legitimacy, and subject to political and social pressures from all sides, generating internal divisions that could, in the final analysis, tumble the regime.

Brazil

The period 1964 to 1966 in Brazil represented a transition from an industrial capitalist development strategy based on wage increases, controls on foreign capital flows, and limited state investments in the most dynamic sectors of the economy to one based on the depression of wage levels, the formation of an internal market based on the bourgeoisie, and a new incentive mechanism geared to facilitate long-term, large-scale foreign capital penetration. The shift was from a priority emphasis on redistributive measures to a process based on the concentration of political power and the reconcentration of income and capital. The military regime promoted the state and foreign capital as "cofinanciers" of the new industrial project, developing a series of financial enterprises to expedite this integration strategy.

This economic transformation involved major demographic shifts, with resultant changes in the class structure attendant upon the growing importance of industrial wage labor. During its initial phase the dictatorial state expanded its own orientation (new agencies) and simultaneously began to incorporate new workers (peasants) into the urban work force. Accelerated capitalist industrialization was based on the exploitation of labor in the modern sector and the margination of older economic groups (inefficient industries and small businesses, old landowners), who at the same time were weakened as potent political forces in society. The reconcentration of wealth in the bourgeoisie, based on the exacerbation of class and regional inequalities, served to create an expanding internal market anchored in the increased purchasing power of the upper 20 percent of the population (Tavares and Serra, 1973 : 61–140).

Repressive capitalist development "from above and outside" was rooted in the assumption of complementary responsibilities by the state and foreign capital: The military dictatorship provided the security guarantees and a controlled, low-paid labor; and the multinationals provided the advanced technology and skilled managerial and technical personnel necessary to meet the goals of the industrialization program. The state repressive apparatus ushered in a period of limited conflicts in society—with the minor exception of the 1967–68 student movement, which was swiftly crushed. Meanwhile, the incorporation of imported technology and other new production techniques generated a process of uneven development in which highly developed forms of production (modern factories) coexisted side by side with primitive forms of agricultural enterprise. One consequence of the way in which technology was inserted into the development process was an increasingly segmented work force as less productive/competitive enterprises were gradually pushed down, thus extending the gap between employees and workers in growth and declining industries (Schlagheck, 1977 : 41).

Between 1967/68 and 1974 the average annual rate of industrial production in Brazil was 13 percent, exceeding the average annual rate of growth of the country's GDP during the same period (World Bank, 1979 : 43; Baer and Kerstenetzky, 1972 : 107-8). This "economic miracle" was stoked by massive infusions of foreign capital, directed primarily into the most dynamic and "modern" sectors of the economy (electrical equipment, automobiles, tractors, pharmaceuticals), as well as large-scale state investments in the less profitable intermediary and infrastructure sectors (oil, mining, steel). By the mid-1970s the state held 23 percent of the total net assets of the 2,500 companies located in Brazil with assets of $1 million or more (Schlagheck, 1977 : 16). The industrialization program was largely concentrated in the São Paulo–Rio de Janiero–Belo Horizonte region. As the site of approximately 80 percent of all manufacturing plants, São Paulo has been a magnet for hundreds of thousands of impoverished rural laborers, experiencing a 5.5 percent-annual population growth between 1960 and 1976 (*Le Monde Diplomatique*, January 1979 : 4).

After 1974 the limitations of this type of industrialization strategy, based on the primacy of durable (export) consumer-goods expansion over the growth of basic consumer-goods production—and on a sustained decline in proletarian wage levels and increasing external financial dependence—became more and more manifest under the combined weight of internal and global factors. During 1974–75 the overall economic growth rate declined significantly as a result of the impact of a recession in the advanced industrialised countries and the 1973 OPEC decision to quadruple the world market price of oil. Brazil imported approximately 80 percent of its total oil requirements, and the actions of the major producer nations had a singularly negative effect on an already fragile balance of payments situation. By December 1975, however, industrial activity had rebounded, and the economy experienced a 9 percent growth rate during 1976, notwithstanding the burden of oil imports costing nearly $4 billion and representing 31 percent of total imports (International Monetary Fund, 1976; Anderson, 1978 : 65). This growth rate was slashed by almost half in 1977, largely as the result of a decline in industrial production. While manufacturing output expanded by almost 13 percent in 1976, it rose by a mere 2 percent to 3 percent in 1977, consequent on a fall in the production of textiles, rubber, machinery, and motor vehicles, and a slowdown in the rate of growth of output of electrical products (*Latin American Economic Report*, October 27, 1978 : 332; International Monetary Fund, 1978 : 1–2). During 1978 the economic growth rate hovered at around 5 percent, while the industrial growth rate revived to around 6 percent or 7 percent. This upswing, however, failed to impact significantly on the chronic unemployment problem, generating only a small increase in the number of new jobs in the São Paulo area (Economist Intelligence Unit, 1979 : 7; *Latin American Economic Report*, October 27, 1978 : 332).

Despite an expected growth rate of between 5 percent and 6 percent in 1979, on the basis of gains in the industrial sector, government officials estimate that annual export earnings ($14.7 billion) will only be sufficient to pay for the increased cost of oil imports ($7.0 to $7.5 billion) and service the approximately $50 billion foreign debt and other invisibles ($8.5

billion), thereby further exacerbating the already serious balance of payments problem. These developments are expected to increase Brazil's current account deficit from $6 billion in 1978 to $10 billion in 1980. In addition, another portion of the enormous foreign debt has to be renegotiated between 1980 and 1982 (*Latin American Economic Report*, July 20, 1979 : 220; *New York Times*, October 7, 1979 : E3; *Business Latin America*, July 4, 1979 : 212; *Business Week*, October 22, 1979 : 95.

Paralleling this increasing dependence on finance capitalists located in the imperial centers has been a striking incapacity on the part of the military rulers to control inflation in the midst of a continued economic growth-rate pattern. Largely under the impact of oil price increases, the 17 percent average annual rate of inflation between 1971 and 1973 skyrocketed to 34.5 percent in 1974, sustained its upward course to 46.3 percent in 1976, and then declined marginally to around 45 percent in 1978 (although it was estimated at approximately 60 percent for basic mass-consumption goods) (Morgan Guaranty Trust Company, 1975 : 2; *Latin American Economist Report*, October 27, 1978 : 332; *Le Monde Diplomatique*, January 1979 : 14). In Rio de Janiero the cost of living index increased by 41.9 percent during 1976, and by 43.7 percent in the following year (Economist Intelligence Unit, 1978 : 13). During 1979 rising oil import costs have contributed to an inflation rate that was expected to approach 60 percent by year's end (*New York Times*, October 7, 1979 : E3; *Business Week*, October 22, 1979 : 95; *Latin American Economic Report*, August 10, 1979 : 242).

The process of capitalist industrialization in Brazil has been based, in part, on a sustained decompression of wage levels and contraction of overall socioeconomic conditions of life for the majority of the country's working class. Tables 2.2, 2.3, and 2.4 present graphic illustrations of the increasing maldistribution of income and the declining purchasing power of the masses, which have gone hand in hand with Brazil's emergence as one of the most advanced industrial countries in the semiperiphery of the capitalist world economy.

Table 2.2 Income Concentration in Brazil, 1960, 1970, and 1976 (percent)

Division of active population	1960	1970	1976
Poorest 50 percent	17.7	14.9	11.8
Following 30 percent	27.9	22.8	21.2
Upper-middle class 15 percent	26.7	27.4	28.0
Upper-class 5 percent	27.7	34.9	39.0

Source: *Le Monde Diplomatique*, January 1979 : 14.

Table 2.3 Decline of the Minimum Salary in Brazil

	Nominal minimum salary (in cruzeiros)	*Sum necessary to maintain purchasing power at 1959 level*
1964	42.00	53.00
1968	129.00	254.31
1972	268.00	587.81
1974	376.80	1,162.25
1978	1,560.00	3,520.00

Source: *Le Monde Diplomatique*, January 1979 : 14.

Table 2.4 Measures of Equity in Semi-Industrialized Countries

	Percentage in absolute poverty	*Income share of poorest 40 percent*	
Egypt	20		n.a.
Philippines	33	1970–71	11.9
Colombia	19	1974	14.3
Korea	8	1976	16.9
Turkey	14	1973	11.4
Republics of China			
and Korea	5	1971	21.9
Mexico	14	1977	10.3
Brazil	15	1972	7.0
Argentina	5	1970	14.1
Yugoslavia	5	1973	18.4
Spain	n.a.	1974	17.8

Source: World Bank, 1979 : 10.

The reconcentration of income in favor of the bourgeoisie, combined with a precipitous decline in the real value of the minimum wage, has ejected the majority of Brazilian workers to the margins of economic existence. On a comparative basis, Brazil has one of the most unequal income-distribution patterns of all the semi-industrialized countries for which data are available. In mid-1978 one authoritative study concluded that at least 70 percent of the population lived below the officially deemed economic survival level. If the persistent high level of inflation is taken into account, even this figure may underestimate the actual extent of impoverishment among the masses (*Latin American Economic Report*, September 22, 1978 : 296). The state-decreed minimum wages and wage adjustments over the duration of the "economic miracle" have remained substantially behind inflation levels, not only reducing the workers' purchasing power but also resulting in large-scale additions to the unemployed and underemployed. In 1977, for example, at least 100,000 workers in the construction and automobile sectors alone were laid off from their jobs (Anderson, 1978 : 65).

The Brazilian government's wage and other economic policies detonated a new cycle of proletarian opposition in 1977, centered in the industrial (automobile, metallurgical) and service sectors of the economy, and characterized by a groundswell of support for autonomous labor organizations. By mid-1978 "the new industrial militancy [had] spread well beyond São Paulo, where it first appeared, and there have been strikes in most cities in the interior" (*Latin American Economic Report*, August 18, 1978 : 256). Confronted by a wave of strikes, which involved thousands of industrial workers and began to incorporate public-sector employees (teachers), the state enacted new labor legislation intended to contain and, if necessary, repress the spreading labor unrest (*Latin American Economic Report*, September 22, 1978 : 296). Increasing discontent over the government's wage policies, as well as its constraints on political activity, also enveloped sectors of the middle class, and it was manifest through the opposition political party of the national bourgeoisie, the Movimiento Democratico Brasiliero (MDB). In the November 1978 congressional elections, the MDB, whose participation was sanctioned by the military, easily defeated the proregime Arena Party in both the Senate and the Chamber of Deputies, by votes of 18.5 million to 13.6 million and 16.5 million to 14.9 million, respectively (*Le Monde Diplomatique*, January 1979 : 15). The loci of MDB support were the industrialized southern areas of the country (*Latin American Political Report*, November 24, 1978 : 361).

Throughout 1979 the strategic industrial centers of the economy—São Paulo, Rio de Janiero, and Belo Horizonte—witnessed continued strikes against the regime's wage and labor policies, as hundreds of thousands of wage workers (metalworkers, state employees, electricity and construction workers, bank clerks, school teachers, taxi-drivers) pressed the new government of General João Baptista Figueiredo for acceptance of their demands (*Latin American Economic Report*, March 23, 1979 : 96, March 30, 1979 : 97, July 20, 1979 : 224, September 21, 1979 : 289; *Latin American Political Report*, April 27, 1979 : 121-22, May 4, 1979 : 134-35, July 20, 1979 : 221-22, September 21, 1979 : 292). Figueiredo's "liberalization" policy, which dictated a less than maximum use of force against the strikers and the granting of limited wage concessions (increase in the minimum wage), failed to defuse this sustained antiregime economic offensive by Brazilian workers, who saw their standard of living being constantly eroded by spiraling inflation (*Latin American Political Report*, May 4, 1979 : 134-35; *Latin American Economic Report*, September 28, 1979 : 304).

In the present conjuncture, the forces pushing for change in Brazil go beyond the workers and national bourgeoisie and extend into the reaches of the state apparatus itself. Sectors of the military are openly calling for a return to "democracy," decrying the political corruption and economic giveaways to the multinationals. In addition, the Church, especially the bishops' councils, have repeatedly and pointedly denounced the "social costs" of the economic development process for the labor force. This challenge has created deepening fissures within Brazilian society, increasing the political pressure on the Figueiredo Administration to "democratize" the political system—*a demand that, if realized, will only further accelerate the process of social change, accompanying the political reforms.*

South Africa

The South African economy has experienced alternating periods of (relative) stagnation and expansion since the late 1940s. The average annual rate of economic growth between 1946 and 1966 was 8.3 percent, although within that time frame can be identified a high growth-rate period (1947–54) and a relatively lower, average growth-rate period (1955-62). The yearly economic growth rate increased to approximately 10 percent between 1967 and 1972, only to level off significantly during the subsequent five-year period (Innes, 1975 : 111–12; *Business International*, September 22, 1978 : 303).[4]

Changes in South African state policy, beginning in 1948, underwrote a transformation from a primarily agro-mining economy to one based on large-scale industrialization. The provision of a coerced and exploitable labor force and substantial infrastructure investments reflected the "motor" role of the state in this shifting emphasis. Between 1947–51 and 1967–71 the manufacturing and construction sectors of the economy increased their contribution to the GDP from 19.6 percent to 26.6 percent (Innes, 1975 : 113). Furthermore, through most of this period the manufacturing sector grew at an average annual rate in excess of the growth rate of the economy as a whole. While the total number of manufacturing enterprises experienced a marginal decline from 1955 to 1971 (13,275 to 13,121), an increasingly socialized productive process generated a fourfold and nineteenfold growth in terms of labor and capital, respectively. By 1971 the private manufacturing sector was the largest individual source of South Africa's national income (31 percent) (Houghton, 1976 : 128–29, 286). One distinctive feature of this process of industrial development has been its concentrated location within and around the major urban population centers of the Witwatersrand (Johannesburg, Pretoria), Cape Town, Durban, and Port Elizabeth.

The role of imperial capital in promoting capitalist industrialization in South Africa has been a critical one. The first decade of Afrikaner rule (1948-58) was characterized by overall economic stagnation, while at the same time the state authorized large-scale expenditures in infrastructure development (transportation, power facilities). In 1958 the new Verwoerd Government initiated a policy that increasingly linked economic growth, rapid industrialization, and "separate development" to foreign capital investment.

Between 1959 and 1964 South Africa remained a net exporter of capital. After 1964, with the introduction of exchange controls, together with rapid economic rates based on foreign capital investment, the country was transformed into a massive net importer of capital. Multinational capital increased its share of new investment in industry from 24.4 percent in 1956 to 33.7 percent in 1970. Studies commissioned by government and private sources have concluded that around 40 percent of South African industry is directly controlled by foreign capital, and that an additional 40 percent of industrial production is indirectly controlled "from the outside" (Rogers, 1976 : 96–97). The external capital dependence has largely been tied to the immediate requirements of the industrialization program, principally the importation of sophisticated and up-to-date technological equipment and expertise, and Pretoria's failure to develop a locally competitive technological base. Ruth Milkman (1979 : 273, 277) points out that the country's sustained dependence on primary-product exports since 1948—raw materials, for example, accounted for 60 percent of all exports in 1972—and the confinement of competitive manufacturing exports to the African continent is essentially an outgrowth of its technological plight. "Without foreign investment," she writes, "South Africa's industrial sector would be almost nonexistent."

The massive inflow of investments and loans during the decade after 1964 contributed mightily to ameliorating the persistent trade deficits, especially in a context where the major "financier" of the country's imports—gold—was accounting for a declining percentage of its import needs. The ratio of gold exports to total imports steadily declined from 56 percent in 1961 to only 32 percent in 1971 (Innes, 1975 : 124). This lowered capacity of gold earnings to finance imports was largely the result of the import demands of the industrialization program and only secondarily to a gradual fall in the rate of gold production. Between 1974 and 1976 gold experienced a period of volatile downward price movements in the international capitalist market, as its percentage share of merchandise exports fell to 30 percent (U.S. Congress, 1978 : 47). The result was a deepening of South Africa's foreign financial dependence in order to offset an increasing trade deficit brought about by global capitalist recession (decline in new capital investment) and rising oil prices. The decline in the price of gold from an average of $165 per ounce in 1975 to $114 per ounce in mid-1976 was reversed during 1977, contributing to an improved balance of payments situation (Milkman, 1979 : 275-76).

The 1976 Soweto insurrection played a major contributing role in shifting South Africa back to a net exporter of capital. Between 1976 and 1978 the net capital outflow continued at an increasing rate. During the first nine months of 1977 approximately $820 million in short-term capital left the country. For the same period in 1978 this figure reached nearly $900 million, in addition to a further $300 million in long-term capital outflows, which pushed the total loss for this second nine-month period to around $1.2 billion (*New York Times*, International Economic Survey, February 4, 1979 : 74). To a significant degree, however, this trend has been offset by a fortuitous rise in the world price of gold to $225 per ounce in December 1978, peaking at around $400 per ounce in late 1979. Additionally, these gold earnings of $4.5 billion in 1978, and an estimated $6 billion in 1979, have played a crucial role in financing increased oil costs and covering a large portion of the debt repayment schedule (*World Business Weekly*, September 17, 1979 : 23). Nonetheless, an accumulation of factors in the recent period have joined forces to provide the basis for another period of economic stagnation: worsening inflation; long-term income concentration; a 1.5 million black unemployment, and an incapacity to generate a growth rate capable of absorbing the approximately 260,000 black workers added each year to the economically active population; the continued dependence on external sources of financing, especially in a period when foreign multinationals are engaging in the large-scale export of capital. (*World Business Weekly*, September 17, 1979 : 24; *New York Times*, July 13, 1979 : 13).

The process of rapid industrial expansion has been dependent upon an exploitative capitalist development strategy based on the massive incorporation of black wage labor. The development of industrial capitalism in South Africa prior to, and following, the beginning of Afrikaner political rule in 1948 was linked to the elaboration of a migratory labor system, which formed the basis of apartheid policy. In 1946 nonwhites comprised 64 percent of the total work force; by 1970 this figure had risen to approximately 80 percent of all workers (Rogers, 1976 : 38–43; Houghton, 1976 : 102). During the 1950s the governing Nationalist Party sought to coordinate and regulate more effectively the movement of the native African population through the extension of legislation already in force and through the application of new "separate development" measures—principally in the form of black "homelands," or Bantustans (Legassick, 1974 : 24–26; Davenport, 1978 : 331-52). [5]

The maintenance of a highly repressive labor-control system was also accompanied, especially during the 1960s, by a strictly enforced ban on working-class political organization.

Between 1967 and 1970 the Vorster Administration vastly accelerated the uprooting and resettlement of rural blacks on the basis of myriad new legislative and regulatory actions (Legassick, 1974 : 24–26). Between 1960 and 1970 some three million nonwhites were relocated in "homelands" that served as "a chain of labour reservoirs where people were held in a state of compulsory unemployment until the white economy wants them" (Johnson, 1977 : 179, 184). Recent estimates suggest that this process has accounted for approximately half of all presently employed black laborers in the industrial centers (Rogers, 1976 : 48). These black urban wage workers are predominant within virtually every major industrial sector of the economy. While the manufacturing and construction sectors expanded their overall work force from 1 million in 1960 to 1.5 million in 1970 to 1.8 million in 1975, the percentage of white workers employed in these sectors declined from 31 percent to 22 percent to 21 percent, respectively (Houghton, 1976 : 164). These demographic changes, however, have not been accompanied by any contraction in income differentials between black and white workers. On the contrary, the absolute gap had been steadily increasing, both in industry and mining. This trend was not halted by the provision of larger-percentage wage increases for black miners and industrial workers in the 1970–75 period (Houghton, 1976 : 167–70; Brotz, 1977 : 87–91; Rogers, 1976 : 32–38).

The first major instance of labor resistance to the racial and economic policies promulgated by successive South African governments since 1948 took place in 1960, in opposition to the "pass laws," and culminated in the Sharpville Massacre. Between 1961 and 1964 opposition to government policies manifested itself in a variety of forms (sabotage actions, protest marches, boycotts, strikes, civil disobedience), but it failed to generate any political crisis of consequence (Van den Berghe, 1965 : 162–66). By the late 1960s, however, the exploitative industrialization strategy began to serve as the basis for a resurgence of strike actions by urban wage workers in pursuit of social and economic demands. Between 1969 and 1974 thousands of workers took part in hundreds of industrial strikes that affected the operations of the most strategic sectors (mines, communications, transportation) of the South African economy (Horner, 1975 : iv). In the first three months of 1973 alone, Natal was the center of more than 100 strikes involving some 100,000 workers (Rogers, 1976 : 78).

This period of renewed labor militancy was fueled by the increasing rate of decline of the standard of living of the South African masses. Between 1970 and 1974 food prices more than doubled, as compared with a rate of inflation during the 1960s that averaged around 3.3 percent annually. Approximately 60,000 industrial workers participated in strikes in and around Durban beginning in October 1972, and these were only settled (in February 1973) in return for wage increases of from 15 percent to 18 percent. Within weeks, however, Durban was again the center of industrial unrest over economic and legislative issues, this time spreading to the area around Natal and into the Transvaal. During late 1973 a further wave of strikes was detonated, principally by miners, textile, and automobile workers, which extended through March 1974 (Johnson, 1977 : 85–86).

In early 1976, against the background of an economic downturn occasioned largely by the 1975-76 fluctuations in the world market price of gold, wage increases that failed to keep pace with the increases in the rate of inflation growing unemployment problem, which bore most heavily on those leaving school to enter the work force, and the ramifications of a nationalist-socialist government in Angola, the most serious challenge to the apartheid system in two decades was mounted in the black Johannesburg township of Soweto. The initial uprising was the result of repeated government efforts to enforce the use of Afrikaans as a 50 percent teaching medium in the African schools of the southern Transvaal, over the entrenched opposition of black parents, teachers, and pupils. In May the struggle against the imposition of this alien medium of instruction was transformed into an active resistance by the school students of Soweto. Their actions provided the catalyst for a major urban insurrection, which occasioned a massive display of government firepower and repression. In mid-June a demonstration of 15,000 students had a ripple effect in other areas around Johannesburg and, indeed, in townships throughout the Transvaal. In August, Soweto was the scene of a successful three-day strike, followed in mid-September by a student-initiated strike supported by 500,000 workers across the Witwatersrand (Johnson, 1977 : 176, 191-93).

Although the apartheid state was able to contain this conjunctural challenge to its authority with the help of its vast repressive apparatus, the massive urban insurrection in Soweto, the increasing activity of guerrilla forces, and the sporadic conflicts in industry and in white centers suggest that the crises of the regime is just beginning to unfold, in part, because the white supremacy regime still retains a cohesive basis of support within the racially segmented labor force. Nevertheless, the growth of black industrial labor and the very racial divisions that sustain the regime combine to create *homogenous* class-race segments (without mediating institutions) whose *cumulative* grievances likely can lead to more fundamental changes in the totality of society. As industrialization has accelerated, the South African regime has been forced to incorporate new layers of the black proletariat, while sustaining the same system of exclusive political domination. As labor becomes proletarianized under conditions of social production and political exclusion, the basis for radical class-race consciousness emerges: The struggle for economic gains becomes immediately transformed into a struggle against the state. The politicization taking place within South Africa among the black industrial proletariat is underwritten by the deep and profound changes in social relations generated by the dynamics of capitalist economic growth in the framework of a tightly repressive and exclusionary political system.

Iran

Between 1965 and 1975 Iran experienced a period of accelerated capitalist industrialization, with its locus in and around the capital city of Tehran. The heavy geographical concentration was reflected in this region's role as the site of more than half of all manufactured goods produced, of the primary nonoil adjunct industries (automobiles), and of an industrial work force that represented 22 percent of the total laboring population (Graham, 1978 : 24). In addition, the large-scale insertion of imported technology into the economy to facilitate this transformation process contributed to the highly uneven pattern of development, overwhelmingly confined to Tehran and a handful of provincial cities. The Iranian state, as well as foreign capital, played a central role in financing the industrialization project, largely as a result of soaring government revenues, beginning with the quadrupling of world oil prices in 1973. Petrodollar profits increased from $817 million in 1968 to $2.25 billion in 1972-73 to $19.6 billion in 1975-76 (Halliday, 1979 : 139). During 1973-74 output in the industrial and mining sectors increased by 18 percent, the number of new companies registered in the large population centers almost doubled, total capitalization rose almost threefold, and per capita income climbed from $501 to $821 (Graham, 1978 : 83). Between 1973 and 1976 the manufacturing sector increased its output each year by 17 percent (Halliday, 1979 : 138). By 1977 state expenditures accounted for 60 percent of all industrial investments in Iran (Halliday, 1979 : 149). The state was also crucial for the participation of the urban bourgeoisie in the new economic program through the provision of financial credits to this class, even though the latter's areas of economic activity were mainly confined to trade and investments in housing and light industry.

This process of state-directed industrialization was accompanied by a major demographic shift in the form of an increasingly urbanized population, as unemployed rural laborers were incorporated into the booming manufacturing and construction sectors of the economy. The agricultural work force declined from 75 percent of the total economically active population in 1945 to less than 50 percent in 1966 to approximately 33 percent by the late 1970s (Halliday, 1979 : 173). High levels of unemployment in the agricultural sector were, in large part, a result of the state's decision to promote a capitalist transformation in the countryside during the 1960s, through the aegis of a multiphased agrarian reform program. The reforms created a rural bourgeoisie, who were the beneficiaries of substantial amounts of economic and technical assistance from government agencies. At the same time, approximately 40 percent of the rural population received no land whatsoever under the program. Between 1956 and 1966 those landless rural workers, who moved to the urban areas in search of employment, accounted for 80 percent of the decline in the agricultural labor force during this period (Bharier, 1971 : 140-41). By 1977 the growing importance of industrial wage labor in the Iranian economy had become evident: Out of an economically active population totaling 10.4 million, an estimated 2.5 million were employed in the approximately 250,000 manufacturing firms, while another 1 million found job opportunities in the construction sector (Halliday, 1979 : 15, 173).

As with the Brazilian experience, the economic transformation toward an industrial capitalist society in Iran was based on the exploitation of labor in the "modern" sectors, the margination of traditional economic forces (petty-commodity producers, precapitalist, commercial, and religious groups), and the intensification of class and regional inequalities. In the search for a monopoly of power, the Shah's regime preferred the application of a repressive strategy that indiscriminately affected all opposition forces. As a result, it failed to harness traditional social relations to capitalist modernization, as reflected in the refusal to delegate a sphere of influence over social policy, with its accompanying prestige, to the religious (Islamic) community.

Newly established state banking and financial institutions, and trading companies, began to displace the traditional commercial/moneylending centers presided over by the *bazaaris* (small merchants and traders), generating growing discontent within this class over its economic position in society. Although the massive oil profits of 1973–74 temporarily assuaged the hostility of the bazaar entrepreneurs to increased government intervention in the economy, it soon resurfaced in the context of ongoing corrupt practices within the state structure and the incapacity of the regime to control inflation. Their lingering resentment of government policy was exacerbated by the 1975 "antiprofiteering" campaign, during which more than 250,000 businesses were briefly closed, more than 8,000 shopkeepers were jailed, and another 23,000 shopkeepers and merchants were sentenced to deportation (later rescinded) to remote areas of the country (*New York Times Magazine*, December 17, 1978 : 134–35). This burgeoning opposition of the mosque and the bazaar to the Shah's rule was also reinforced by historic interlocking ties: Prior to the state's intervention in the education system, the sons of the *bazaaris* were educated by the religious leaders (*mullahs*), who, in turn, received large-scale financial support from the bazaar community.

Meanwhile, the new workers incorporated into the urban labor force—but not fully integrated into the capitalist productive process during the first stage of industrialization—were, in this second or "peak" phase, proletarianized, to the extent that the earlier emphasis on the relative improvement in living standards vis-à-vis agriculture was completely obliterated. Income disparities between skilled and unskilled industrial wage laborers, as well as between urban and rural workers, continued to widen with each passing year (Looney, 1975 : 97; Schulz, 1977 : 15–18, 38). The wage increases gained during 1973–75 were barely sufficient to keep pace with the rate of inflation, which was fueled by the bottlenecks and shortages created by inadequate communications, port and power facilities, an increased dependence on food imports (from $32 million in 1973 to $1.5 billion in 1978), and large-scale military expenditures (*Business Week*, November 27, 1978 : 55). The real rate of inflation hovered at around 50 percent for the three-year period 1975 to 1977, eroding the per capita income rises and thereby depressing the purchasing power not only of the working class, but of the bourgeoisie as well (*New York Times*, January 14, 1979 : 2E; January 17, 1979 : 9; *Manchester Guardian Weekly*, January 21, 1979 : 20).

By late 1977 a repressive and corrupt ruling class was forced to confront the manifest problems associated with its oil-financed industrialization project: the lack of competent administrators, bureaucrats, and skilled manpower; insufficient energy sources and an inadequate communications infrastructure; rising food prices and housing costs; faulty economic planning; a massive waste of resources; spiraling inflation, and growing regional-class socioeconomic inequalities (Graham, 1978 : 105-6, 129-51; Halliday, 1979 : 78-80; *Washington Post*, May 9, 1977 : A1, A7, January 17, 1979 : A1, A16; *Le Monde Diplomatique*, December 1978 : 12). In August the government acted to clamp down on inflation through the imposition of credit controls, which signaled a deceleration of the industrialization program. The consequences of this strategy were threefold: (1) the construction industry, a major source of employment for unskilled rural labor, underwent a severe contraction, while rural migrants as a whole suffered the greatest decline in living standards because of inflation, food shortages, and the need to use a large portion of their income for rents; (2) the bazaar merchants, dependent on state credits to finance many of their activities, and affected by inflation, came to feel their economic role in society increasingly threatened by the pattern of capitalist development, which narrowed their possibilities for private capital accumulation and upward social mobility; and (3) local industrialists, joined by the merchants, expressed their opposition to price controls, antiprofiteering campaigns, and a plethora of government decrees placing limits on capital accumulation and expansion.

Increasingly, the locus of opposition to the Shah shifted to the Islamic religious centers, which alone remained independent of the government's "reach," despite the state's erosion of their economic independence (property losses) and its takeover of social-civil functions (control of law and education), which traditionally had been the responsibility of the mosques. "With growing popular resentment to the regime's social and political policies after 1973," writes one authority, "the mosque found itself the focus of opposition, the only institution able to give voice to popular discontent in a situation where every political activity was prohibited (Halliday, 1979 : 19). This new phase of the resistance struggle against the Pahlavi dynasty was organizationally enhanced by the inclusion of the bazaars and the mosques with their interlinked national communications networks.

The low-level and fragmented nature of the opposition forces prior to 1973 was now gradually transformed as a variety of social-class forces exploited and/or excluded by the industrialization process (old property groups, new propertyless groups, national bourgeoisie, petty bourgeois), or opposed to the closed and repressive nature of the political system (intellectuals, students), formed a loosely structured but increasingly massive movement to seek the Shah's overthrow. The resurgent struggle, initially centered in the mosques in the provincial cities, swiftly shifted to the large urban areas, principally in and around Tehran, as the *bazaaris* and proletarian forces became active participants in the antidictatorial struggle (Halliday, 1979 : 290–97; Abrahamian, 1978 : 4). As the struggle progressed, there was a growing tendency for divisions within the society at large to be reflected in the Shah's repressive military-police apparatus. There were numerous instances of conscripted soldiers refusing to fire on antiregime protesters or deserting the armed forces under the pull of social-class ties:

A wide gulf between officers and soldiers appears to be one of the chief sources of tension. Officers, 80 percent of whom are regulars, live a life apart. They are pampered and privileged, with high salaries, personal servants, free medical care and special low-priced stores. . . . Privates and corporals, on the other hand, are usually conscripts. Drawn from the same strata of society that produce many of the demonstrating crowd, they are subject to the same religious and political influences. Although well-fed, they are ill-paid, with starting pay of about $1.50 a month. And there is almost no chance for an enlisted man to win a commission. [*New York Times*, December 19, 1978 : 1]

If the mosque had emerged as the epicenter of this new phase of the process of struggle against the Shah's dictatorship, it was the industrial working class, specifically the oil workers, who played the pivotal role in hastening the demise of the regime. The value of Iran's oil exports during the late 1970s amounted to between $22 billion and $23 billion annually, as this primary foreign-exchange earner continued to play a critical role in financing the process of capitalist industrialization. Hence, the antiregime oil-field strikes during September-December 1978, involving some 67,000 workers, who pumped, refined, and shipped the countries petroleum resources, struck at the very core of the economy's lifeline (*New York Times*, December 31, 1978 : 1E).

The catalytic nature of the oil workers' actions manifested themselves politically in two major respects: They qualitatively, as well as quantitatively, strengthened the forces pushing for the overthrow of the Shah; and they exerted a lever that served to weaken the regime's international support, especially among Iran's capitalist-bloc petroleum customers. In mid-October a strike of 35,000 oil workers and administrative personnel over economic *and* political demands (wage increases, dismantling of Savak, the state security apparatus, release of political prisoners, an end to martial law, and the punishment of corrupt officials) forced oil production down from an average 5.3 million barrels daily to a low of 800,000 barrels daily within a month. Only after the government had threatened, and then acted, to arrest strike organizers and dismiss workers from their jobs did approximately 60 percent of the oil workers return to their posts. At the world's largest petroleum complex in Abadan, the armed forces arrested all twelve members of the strike committee. The regime also offered substantial increases (and bonuses) in pay raises previously offered to the striking workers. This played an important role in the decision of the workers' representatives to call for a return to work (*Washington Post*, November 1, 1978 : A1, November 10, 1978 : A1, A16, November 13, 1978 : A1; *New York Times*, November 14, 1978 : 1, 9, November 15, 1978 : 1).

In early December industrywide strikes and work stoppages again became the order of the day, such that by the end of the month the country's oil production had plummeted to around 600,000 to 700,000 a day, compared to a peak capacity of 6 million barrels a day and a daily local consumption (in quiescent periods) of approximately 700,000 barrels. The military prime minister failed to intimidate the workers and break the strike by threatening the offenders with incarceration and legal prosecution before a military court (*New York Times*, December 5, 1978 : 1, 11, December 27, 1978 : 1, 9; *Washington Post*, December 17, 1978 : A1). The subsequent arrest of strike leaders only deepened the workers' resolve to continue the struggle. A government attempt to "bribe" them to return to the oil fields, in the form of proposed pay raises of 60 percent to 100 percent, also failed to achieve its desired purpose (*New York Times*, December 31, 1978 : 1E). By year's end the alliance of reactionary and "modern" groups had brought the Shah's rule to an end. The strategic location of the oil workers in the economy and the key role played by the working class as a whole, however, must be viewed within a context in which the class was at no point able to hegemonize the leadership of the opposition movement. Organizational preeminence remained with the right-wing religious forces, who were essentially able to define the terms of the struggle on the basis of their prestige among, and influence over, the Iranian masses.

Of the three countries examined in this study, Iran under the Shah reflected the contradictions of capitalist development most acutely. Here, prolonged dictatorial rule reigned during a period of massive economic and demographic change. Sustained urban expansion and the multibillion-dollar investments were accompanied by the growth of a modern working and middle class in and around the petroleum and derivative industries and state services. Older traditional religious and cultural leaders were marginalized from official positions, while, in some cases, agrarian reforms transferred land from religious notables to commercial farmers. The post-1973 influx of petrodollars led to speculative fever, skyrocketing prices, and a relative decline in living standards for many. The oil boom exacerbated all of the contradictions inherent in the pattern of uneven development, and it increasingly affected the employed salaried, and wage-earning classes as well as those on the periphery of the "growth sectors."

The tensions between the autocratic dictatorship and the increasingly socially differentiated population were, for a time, attenuated by the pervasive penetration of civil society by the secret police. The only arena where organization and activity withstood police "blanketing" was in the precapitalist religious bodies, which maintained a semblance of independence, a network for mobilization, and a set of simmering grievances resulting from the onslaught of capitalist expansion. The absence of alternative political arenas forced all political grievances to be channeled initially through the only "legitimate" organizations—the traditional religious leaders searching to recuperate political autonomy and their economic base. Thus the "religious" riots became the *starting* point for a set of struggles that, over time, moved far beyond the original "reactionary" core to embrace broad strata of the population, whose purpose was to democratize the social as well as political system and to nationalize the economy, as well as to liberalize the basis of political representation.

The inclusive nature of the emerging protest movement was indicative of the varied groups and classes that have been subject to the processes of exploitation, exclusion, and domination. The enormous cost of urban-industrial growth and the vast inequalities that were generated through the Shah's collaborative efforts with Western European and Japanese capital produced as its counterpart an irresistible wave of opposition, embracing a broad array of classes, ranging from petty-commodity producers, industrial workers, and intellectuals to engineers, managers, and other professionals. The convergence of classes and groups making claims for political changes within the industrial/urban sector with those seeking to recover political and economic power reflecting past positions created a broad movement that limited the capacity of the dictatorship to launch a massive wave of terror and purges. This movement succeeded in ousting the Shah, only to confront a new set of conflicts over how the new dominant social bloc would be reconstituted.

Conclusion

The question arises: Why do the contradictions take such an acute form in these "subimperialist," semi-industrialized countries within the world capitalist system at this time? At the level of the social formation we discussed, the contradiction is between the "primitive" repressive state—standing isolated from the social forces emerging from the economic process, a static reactive force, and the dynamic process of class formation. At a deeper level, however, the process of *transition* from an agro-mineral dependency to a semi-industrial subimperialist power has been nurtured by the simultaneous flow of capital from both the imperial center and the dependent periphery. The convergence of capital from both directions—the one in search of higher profits through the exploitation of labor, raw materials, and markets; the other through exchange relations and exploitative productive relations in the less developed areas—has provided these countries with a special dynamic, which accentuates the disjuncture between the old repressive state and the proliferating social forces emanating from accelerated capital expansion. The specific role of these regimes as policemen within their respective regions has led to the overdevelopment of their repressive apparatus at the expense of the elaboration of representative institutions: Domestic policy is an extension of foreign policy, and vice versa. The connection between the internal control and external police function reinforces or "overdetermines" the repressive aspects of the state, accentuating the dictatorial character of the state.

The process of capital accumulation and industrial expansion combined extremely high levels of capital investment and the latest techniques of production in the development of the productive forces with the most coercive forms of social relations derived from typical "peripheral" societies of the past. The contrast between the dynamic development of the productive forces and static conditions of labor has led to an explosive social situation. Where the dictatorial state lacks political "reserves" to cushion the conflict (i.e., no recognized and legitimate social democratic opposition to draw into a "cabinet of national unity"), as in Iran, the struggle accelerates into a massive confrontation with the regime.

The general crisis of capitalist expansion—the stagnation in the periphery and the overcapacity in the core—has focused capital and labor flows into the dynamic subimperialist centers. The channeling of capitalist energies within these societies, however, in the frantic search for profits, has disrupted the previous patterns of domination, reorganized society without altering the old state apparatus. The machinery of repression blocks all mechanisms for selective social incorporation and elite representation. Moreover, the high growth (and inflation) engendered by the flow of imperial capital has increased the costs of labor subsistence while displacing the supplementary sources of income characteristic of the periphery—thus proletarianizing and pauperizing labor while it becomes increasingly part of the social division of labor. In this authoritarian context, class formation occurs without "bureaucratization"—bringing in its wake the possibility of direct expression of class interests—in conflict with the state through direct action.

The political economy of the periphery is moving in a new direction that involves redefining the problematic, reformulating key concepts, and developing a more dynamic and inclusive analytical framework. The previous problematic, which focused on development, abstracted from the social relations of production and emphasized to a great degree the extension and increase in productive forces. The result has been to downgrade the degree to which labor is the creator of value and the source of wealth. The focus on social relations of production allows us to examine the issue of exploitation and the forms and techniques by which labor is degraded, as well as to understand the forms by which exploitative relations of production can be transformed.

By redefining the problematic of political economy from development to exploitation, we thus are required to reformulate the key concepts with which we analyze the new problematics. Notions such as dependence and modernization, which operate to explain or discuss development, are inappropriate. Rather, our focus should be on the class relationships, both at the internal as well as the international level, and within the class structure of peripheral societies and its relationship to the peripheral state and dominant classes. The implication here is that class cleavages are less confined to national boundaries and more involve class units that cut across national boundaries.

Thus this approach locates the process of capital accumulation within the framework of class/state relationships. It is within this schema, based on the determination of class coalitions and hegemonic influence, that studies of income distribution and types of regimes could be fruitfully analyzed.

Notes

1. By using a class analysis approach, we are able to view the process of a capitalist development in terms of social dynamics (expansion-contradictions-crisis-conflict). Alternative approaches such as dependency, modernization, and world systems, on the other hand, tend to see this process in much more linear terms (growth vs. stagnation, modernization vs. underdevelopment), and to locate societal conflicts within these contexts (Baran, 1957; Gunder Frank, 1967, 1969; Dos Santos, 1971; Cardoso, 1977; Huntington, 1968; Wallerstein, 1974, 1976). The world systems approach operates largely at the level of relations between systems and nations and, thereby, fails to take account of the importance of internal classes and the processes of class formation and class conflict, whcih shapes relations between countries as much as it is shaped by intersystem relations (Wallerstein, 1974, 1976). In contrast to these *general theories*, the use of the *concept* of "bureaucratic-authoritarian" to describe regime development essentially freezes class relationships in that it seeks to locate the problem of regime crisis at the level of the economic system (obstacles to industrialization) (Malloy, 1977). Eschewing such overly economistic interpretations, this study locates industrialization within a more inclusive framework, which also includes state organizations and class relations.

2. For a résumé of some aspects of repression in the Third World, see the annual reports of Amnesty International (1977, 1979).

3. The approach understates the kind and quality of repression, exaggerates the autonomy of the bureaucracy vis-à-vis the class structure, understates the role of imperialism, and confuses the "technocratic" posture of middle-level functionaries and the important ideological elements in the running of the regime. Finally, this view sees its "bureaucratic-authoritarianism" as a mechanism for "deepening" industrialization rather than as a product of the push of capital flows from the outside *and* the class conflicts within a country. The approach too narrowly conceives of the economic dimension (tying it to a

particular phase of industrial expansion, ignoring developments on a world scale and the emergence of fascism prior, during, and after the "deepening" process) and understates the singular importance of class conflict, which creates the "need" for the deepening . . . of repression (De Riz).

4. Ehrensaft (1976) provides a stimulating historical overview of capitalist industrialization in South Africa between 1948 and 1974, as well as some comparisons with the Brazilian experience.

5. Davenport (1978) presents a cogent historical discussion of apartheid and "separate development."

References

Abrahamian, Ervand. 1978. "Iran: The Political Crisis Intensifies." *MERIP Reports* 8 : 3–6.

Amin, Samir. 1974. *Accumulation on a World Scale*. New York: Monthly Review Press.

Amnesty International. 1977. *Report*. London: Amnesty International Publications.

———. 1978. *Report*. London: Amnesty International Publications.

Anderson, Robin L. 1978. "Brazil's Military Regime Under Fire." *Current History* 74 : 61–65, 87.

Baer, Werner, and Isaac Kerstenetzky. 1972. "The Brazilian Economy." In Riordon Roett, ed., *Brazil in the Sixties*. Nashville: Vanderbilt University Press.

Baharier, Julian. 1971. *Economic Development in Iran 1900–1970*. London: Oxford University Press.

Baran, Paul. 1957. *The Political Economy of Growth*. New York: Monthly Review Press.

Brotz, Howard. 1977. *The Politics of South Africa*. London and New York: Oxford University Press.

Brzezinski, Zbigniew. 1978. "Memorandum for Members of the Cabinet, May 8." *The Nation* 228 : 749.

Cardoso, Fernando. 1977. "The Consumption of Dependency: Theory in the United States." *Latin American Research Review* 12 : 7–24.

Davenport, T. R. H. 1978. *South Africa: A Modern History*. Toronto and Buffalo: University of Toronto Press.

De Riz, Liliana. 1977. "Formas de Estado y desarrollo del capitalismo en America Latina." *Revista Mexicana de Sociologia* 39.

Documents. 1979. "Documents: The Oil Workers' Strike: *MERIP Reports* 9 : 17.

Dos Santos, Teotonio. 1971. "The Structure of Dependence." In K. T. Fann and Donald C. Hodges (eds.), *Readings in U.S. Imperialism*. Boston: Porter Sargent.

Economist Intelligence Unit. 1978. *Quarterly Economic Review of Brazil*. Annual Supplement.

———. 1979. *Quarterly Economic Review of Brazil*. No. 1.

Ehrensaft, Philip. 1976. "Polarized Accumulation and the Theory of Economic Dependence: The Implications of South African Semi-Industrial Capitalism." In Pete C. W. Gutkind and Immanuel Wallerstein (eds.), *The Political Economy of Contemporary Africa*. Beverly Hills: Sage Publications.

Gervasi, Sean. 1978. *The United States and the Arms Embargo Against South Africa: Evidence, Denial, and Refutation*. State University of New York at Binghamton: Fernand Braudel Center.

Graham, Robert. 1978. *Iran: The Illusion of Power*. New York: St. Martin's Press.

Frank, Andre Gunder. 1967. *Capitalism and Underdevelopment in Latin America*. New York: Monthly Review Press.

———. 1969. *Latin America: Underdevelopment or Revolution*. New York: Monthly Review Press.

Halliday, Fred. 1979. *Iran: Dictatorship and Development*. Great Britain: Penguin Books.

Horner, D. B. (ed.). 1975. *Labor Organization and the African Worker*. Johannesburg: South African Institute of Race Relations.

Houghton, D. Hobart. 1976. *The South African Economy*. Cape Town: Oxford University Press.

Huntington, Samuel. 1968. *Political Order in Changing Societies*. New Haven: Yale University Press.

Innes, A. Duncan. 1975. "The Role of Foreign Trade and Industrial Development in South Africa." In *Foreign Investment in South Africa: The Economic Factor.* Uppsala, Sweden: Africa Trust Publications.

International Monetary Fund. 1976. *Brazil—Recent Economic Developments.* Confidential Report, SM/76/111.

———. 1969. *Latin America: Underdevelopment or Revolution.* New York: Monthly *Parties to the GATT.* Confidential Report, SM/78/113.

Johnson, Richard W. 1977. *How Long Will South Africa Survive?* New York: Oxford University Press.

Klare, Michael T. 1979. "South Africa's U.S. Weapons Connection." *The Nation* 229 : 75–78.

Legassick, Martin. 1974. "Legislation, Ideology and Economy in Post-1948 South Africa." *Journal of Southern African Studies* 1 : 5–35.

Looney, Robert E. 1975. *Income Distribution Policies and Economic Growth in Semi-Industrialized Countries.* New York: Praeger Publishers.

Malloy, James M. (ed.). 1977. *Authoritarianism and Corporatism in Latin America.* Pittsburgh: University of Pittsburgh Press.

Milkman, Ruth. 1979. "Contradictions of Semi-Peripheral Development: The South African Case." In Walter L. Goldfrank (ed.), *The World System of Capitalism: Past and Present.* Beverly Hills: Sage Publications.

Morrall, James, and David Gisselquist. 1978. *How the IMF Slipped $464 Million to South Africa.* Washington, D.C.: Center for International Policy.

O'Donnell, Guillermo. 1973. *Modernization and Bureaucratic-Authoritarianism: Studies in South American Politics.* Berkeley: University of California, Institute of International Studies.

Petras, James, and Morris Morley. 1975. *The United States and Chile.* New York: Monthly Review Press.

Pike, Frederick, and Thomas Stritch (eds.). 1974. *The New Corporatism.* Notre Dame: University of Notre Dame Press.

Rogers, Barbara. 1976. *White Wealth and Black Poverty.* Wesport, Conn.: Greenwood Press.

Schlagheck, James L. 1977. *The Political, Economic, and Labor Climate in Brazil.* Philadelphia: University of Pennsylvania, The Wharton School.

Schulz, Ann T. 1977. "Iran's New Industrial State." *Current History* 72 : 15–18, 38.

Seidman, Ann, and Seidman, Neva. 1978. *South Africa and U.S. Multinational Corporations*, Westport, Conn.: Lawrence Hill.

Tavares, M. C., and J. Serra. 1973. "Beyond Stagnation: A Discussion on the Nature of Recent Development in Brazil." In James Petras (ed.), *Latin America: From Dependence to Revolution.* New York: John Wiley and Sons.

U.S. Congress. 1976. *U.S. Military Sales to Iran.* Report. Senate Foreign Relations Committee. Washington: U.S. Government Printing Office.

———. 1977. *International Debt, the Banks, and U.S. Foreign Policy.* Report. Senate Foreign Relations Committee. Washington: U.S. Government Printing Office.

———. 1978. *U.S. Corporate Interests in Africa.* Report. Senate Foreign Relations Committee. Washington: U.S. Government Printing Office.

———. 1979. *Prospects for Multilateral Arms Export Restraint.* Report. Senate Foreign Relations Committee. Washington: U.S. Government Printing Office.

U.S. Department of Commerce. 1973. *Foreign Economic Trends—Brazil.*

U.S. General Accounting Agency. 1979. *Financial and Legal Implications of Iran's Cancellation of Arms Purchase Agreements.* B-174901, FGMS)D 79-47.

Van Den Berghe, Pierre L. 1965. *South Africa: A Study in Conflict.* Middletown, Conn.: Wesleyan University Press.

Wallerstein, Immanuel. 1974. "The Rise and Demise of the World Capitalist System." *Comparative Studies in Society and History* 16 : 387–415.

———. 1976. *The Modern World-System.* New York: Academic Press.

World Bank. 1979. *Growth and Equity in Semi-Industrialized Countries.* Staff Working Paper. No. 351.

3

U.S. Investment in Latin America

Imperialism has become the central feature of the postwar U.S. economy. The massive sustained growth of U.S. corporate-controlled productive forces throughout the globe is the central issue of our epoch. Even more so than in the time of Lenin, U.S. corporate growth is premised on its capacity to exploit foreign labor, markets, and raw materials. Rather than see a "decline in imperialism," as some pundits would have it, we have witnessed a spectacular growth in U.S. overseas investment and trade: From 1945 to 1975 U.S. foreign investment grew from $7 billion to $133 billion, and foreign subsidiaries of U.S. firms produce four times the dollar value of U.S. exports. The process of accumulation of capital through the exploitation of wage labor on a world scale and the need to realize profit have produced an inexorable cycle of expansion, which, in the final analysis, defines the logic of imperialism. Colonial, postcolonial, industrializing, and agricultural "underdeveloped" and developed societies have all been targets of the outward advance, shaped and adapted in varying degrees to the imperatives of the accumulation logic. Whether the regimes are formal democracies or outright dictatorships depends on their capacities to modify the class struggle to the logic of capital expansion.

Today, most major U.S. corporations and banks depend on foreign earnings for a decisive proportion of their earnings. Practically every growth industry—manufacturing or financial—has far-reaching links abroad. It is inconceivable to think of U.S. corporate capitalism surviving without its massive overseas empire: The initial drive for higher profit margins has been transformed into a drive for a vital proportion of overall profits. This neverending quest takes place in a world in which labor is increasingly becoming conscious of its exploitative conditions.

71

The class struggle emerges with the exploitative conditions. The class struggle emerges with the exploitation accompanying the advance of imperial capitalism, not as a response to backwardness or underdevelopment. It is in the conflict between the imperatives of accumulation and the increasing growth of popular mobilization where dictatorial regimes emerge to re-create favorable conditions for the private accumulation of capital.

The patterns of imperialist growth are nowhere better illustrated than in Latin America: the growth, diversification, and concentration of investment; the combined forms of investment and technological forms of exploitation; the repressive political and exploitative social conditions that accompany rapid and comprehensive growth; the centrality of the imperial state, which links the private banks and multinationals to the "international" banks and dictatorial states.

The Growth and Changing Nature of U.S. Investment

Since the early 1940s, U.S. investment in Latin America has increased almost tenfold; from the mid-1960s to the mid-1970s, it has more than doubled. In 1976 Latin America accounted for 17 percent of all U.S. investment abroad and 81 percent of the total U.S. investment in the Third World. (See Table 3.1.) Latin America, which accounts for 18 percent of all U.S. income earned abroad, is a significant area of U.S. global expansion, especially within the Third World. Since the early 1970s, the proportion of U.S. investment in Latin America to the rest of the world has been holding steady and even showing a slight increase, reversing the post–World War II decline.

There has been a shift from mainly agro-mineral and public utilities to manufacturing, petroleum, finance, and trade. Investments are not confined to "enclaves" but permeate the whole society, exploiting labor throughout society and capturing a substantial part of the internal market.

In 1929 agriculture and public utilities accounted for more than 48 percent of U.S. investments, while in 1966 they registered only about 8 percent of the total. Conversely, in 1929 manufacturing took 6 percent of U.S. investment, while in 1976 it accounted for 39 percent. (See Table 3.2.) A number of factors account for these changes. First, during the Depression and World War II numerous protective tariff barriers were established in Latin America to encourage local industry and to limit the entry of finished goods from the metropolitan counties. This led to an expansion of the internal market. Hence, in order to continue to penetrate local markets, U.S. corporations began to establish subsidiaries within Latin America, hopping over the tariff walls.

The decline of U.S. investment in agricultural production merely reflects the shift away from farming to the more lucrative and secure agro-manufacturing fields, which supply the farm inputs (farm machinery, fertilizers, seeds) and process and sell farm products (canneries, mills). The growth of U.S. investments in finance reflects largely the movement of capital to tax-havens—the Bahamas and Bermuda account for more than 60 percent of the total. The growth of a massive free trade zone in Panama accounts for a substantial proportion of the growth of U.S. investment in trade. The overall decline in investment in petroleum is accounted for by Venezuela's nationalization of petroleum

Table 3.1 Growth of U.S. Foreign Investment in Latin America (in millions of dollars)

1929	3,519
1936	2,847
1943	2,798
1950	4,576
1957	8,052
1966	9,752
1976	23,536

Source: *U.S. Business Investment in Foreign Countries*, Department of Commerce, Office of Business Economics, 1960. *Selected Data on U.S. Direct Investment Abroad, 1966–76*, U.S. Department of Commerce, Bureau of Economic Analysis.

in 1976. New investments in oil, however, are underway in Chile, Argentina, Brazil, and Peru under the auspices of dictatorial regimes linked with the multinationals.

The growth of large-scale diversified investments had led to demands by U.S. investors for more comprehensive controls over labor and nationalist movements under the euphemism of "political stability." As industry has expanded and concentrated—workers in large-scale productive units, facilitating communication and organization of labor—the class struggle has emerged. The growth of multinational capital and their demands for control in the face of growing class-struggle politics have been the basis for the rise of the neofascist states in Latin America. The biggest jump in manufacturing investment (between 1966–75, a threefold increase) coincides with the rise of dictatorial regimes and the defeats of the labor movement, especially the Brazilian turnaround.

U.S. Investment, Industrialization, and Authoritarianism

U.S. manufacturing investment has been concentrated in the countries with the largest internal market, the most repressive regimes, and those with policies that provide the greatest incentives to capital.

Clearly authoritarian, Brazil has been the greatest area of U.S. foreign

Table 3.2 Changing Patterns of U.S. Investment in Latin America (in millions of dollars)

	Total Invest- ment	Agro	Percent	Mining	Percent	Pub Util	Percent	Petro	Percent	Mfg	Percent	Finance	Percent	Trade	Percent
1929	3,519	817	23.3	732	21	887	25	617	18	231	6	n.a.		n.a.	
1936	2,847	400	14.1	708	25	937	33	453	16	192	7	n.a.		n.a.	
1943	2,798	385	13.8	405	14	875	31	618	22	325	12	n.a.		n.a.	
1950	4,576	523	11.4	666	15	942	21	1303	28	781	17	n.a.		n.a.	
1957	8,053	571	7.0	1232	15	1049	13	2998	37	1280	16	n.a.		n.a.	
1966	9,752	232	2.4	1340	14	542	6	2454	25	2973	30	957	10	1135	12
1976	23,536	n.a.	n.a.	1600	7	285	1	1653	7	9242	39	5478	23	2404	10

Source: U.S. Business Investment in Foreign Countries, Department of Commerce, Office of Business Economics, 1962, p. 93.

74

investment (manufacturing investment increased six times between 1966 and 1976), followed by Mexico, which more than doubled its investment but declined in percentage terms because of massive flows into Brazil, and Argentina. In 1966 two-thirds of all U.S. investment was concentrated in these three countries, and by 1976 it rose to about three-fourths, as shown in Table 3.3.

All areas of Latin America, with a few exceptions, such as Panama, have manufacturing as the primary area of U.S. foreign investment.

Table 3.3   **Pattern of U.S. Manufacturing Investment** (in millions of dollars)

	1966	Percent		1976	Percent	
Total mfg. invest.						
(Latin America)	2973	100		9242	100	
Brazil	574	19		3667	40	
Mexico	924	31	67%	2223	24	74%
Argentina	510	17		895	10	

Source: *Selected Data on U.S. Direct Investment Abroad, 1966–76.* U.S. Department of Commerce, Bureau of Economic Analysis.

Even in Central America one-third of all U.S. investment is in manufacturing.

While it is clear that U.S. investment has focused on capturing the markets of the larger Latin American countries, within this category Brazil, the country with the most stringent controls over trade unions and nationalist and democratic parties, has been by far the favorite area of corporate investors, over and against Argentina, which possessed, during the same time span, a militant, well-organized working-class movement. Between 1966 and 1976, $3.1 billion in U.S. investment entered Brazil, while only $385 million went to Argentina. Since 1976 the Argentine military dictatorship has been making a concerted effort to attract U.S. investors, through the destruction of the labor movement and by dismantling the nationalist enterprises and policies established over the previous thirty years.

U.S. Decapitalization of Latin America

While U.S. investment has flowed *into* Latin American industry, a large percentage of earnings have flowed out of Latin America, creating balance of payments problems and depleting the area of capital, as well as depleting funds for financing basic services and needs for the great majority of the population.

Between 1966 and 1976, dividends, interest, fees, and royalties flowing *out* of Latin America to the United States exceeded capital flows from the United States by $2.5 billion; while $7.5 billion was transferred to Latin America, more than $10 billion was taken out. (See Table 3.4.) This transfer of funds limits the potential growth of the economy and increases social tension by lessening the surplus for redistribution within Latin American society.

Table 3.4   Capital Flows to and from The United States and Latin America
(in millions of dollars)

	Net capital flow from United States	Reinvested earnings	Interest dividend remitted to United States	Fees and royalties
1966	303	309	708	175
1967	311	202	918	211
1968	708	361	825	247
1969	385	331	906	267
1970	579	453	514	274
1971	696	373	688	269
1972	272	645	270	259
1973	645	991	529	269
1974	2,208	1,109	927	341
1975	1,215	1,621	-21	376
1976	145	1,302	796	299
1966–76 Total	7,476	7,697	7,061	2,987

Source: Selected Data on U.S. Direct Investment Abroad, 1966–76. U.S. Department of Commerce, Bureau of Economic Analysis.

The bulk of U.S. investment in Latin America does not come from *outside* but from within Latin America: the reinvested earnings extracted from the exploitation of Latin American labor. Reinvested earnings account for 51 percent of total investments in Latin America. Moreover, the great bulk of the funds invested in Latin America that are not derived from reinvested earnings are derived from "external sources," including loans from Latin banks, hence, in fact, exploiting internal resources. (See Table 3.5.)

More than 80 percent of the capital financing U.S. majority-owned affiliates is derived from "foreign sources" (non-U.S. sources)—including the savings of countries to be exploited. The bulk of U.S. investment thus is not the result of transfer of capital from the advanced country to the underdeveloped Latin American country, but it is based largely on the exploitation of Latin funding sources. This is a major reason why U.S. multinational corporations invest in Latin America.

Table 3.5   Sources of Investment Funding[a] (in millions of dollars)

	United States sources	Foreign sources
1966	4	105
1967	-54	27
1968	-99	549
1969	185	496
1970	19	816
1971	81	552
1972	466	596
Total	755	3141

[a]From a sample.

Source: *Aspects of International Investment*, U.S. Department of Commerce, Bureau of Economic Analysis.

The Rising Importance of Technological Exploitation

The growth of multinational affiliates abroad, as well as national capitalists, has generated an increasingly important new area for U.S. imperial capital domination: the sale and rental of technology. Because of high dividend payments, profit remittances, and investments in high-profit nonproductive activities, Latin America's bourgeoisies devote little, if any, investment to basic research and development, preferring to depend on foreign technology, especially from the United States. A substantial proportion of Latin America's so-called national bourgeoisie is dependent on U.S. technological agreements.

Earnings transferred from Latin America are increasingly derived from technological exploitation rather than from direct investment exploitation. (See Table 3.6.) Between 1967 and 1971 royalties and fees accounted for 25 percent of transferred earnings, while between 1972 and

Table 3.6   Remittances to the United States from Latin America (in millions of dollars)

	Interest, dividends, etc.	Royalties and fees
1967–71	3,851	1,268
1972–76	2,501	1,544

Source: *Selected Data on U.S. Direct Investment Abroad, 1966–76*. U.S. Department of Commerce, Bureau of Economic Analysis, 1978.

1976 royalties and fees accounted for 38 percent of remitted earnings. Control over technology and its sale to Latin America is becoming the fastest growth source for decapitalizing the area.

U.S. Multinational Corporations Sales

The U.S. multinational corporations are oriented toward capturing markets in the Third World, not in capturing world trade and earning foreign exchange. In 1976 total sales by majority-owned Latin American affiliates of U.S. companies totaled $60.6 billion. Of this, $42.1 billion was in local sales (within Latin America), $6.4 billion in export sales were to the United States, and $12.1 billion in export sales were to other foreign countries. Approximately 70 percent of all U.S. multinational corporation sales were directed toward the internal market.

Among majority-owned Latin American *manufacturing* affiliates of U.S. companies, the pattern is even more accentuated: Local sales accounted for 94 percent of the total manufactured goods sold. (See Table 3.7.)

If we examine what is sold and where it is sold, we discover a clear division of products. The multinational corporations are oriented toward capturing the local market for manufactured goods, while selling minerals and petroleum back to the industrialized capitalist countries. (See Table 3.8.)

The multinationals allow the metropolitan countries to capture Latin American markets for finished goods and to extract the raw materials that are needed. More than 90 percent of multinational corporations' manufactured goods are sold locally, while 56 percent of mineral and petroleum goods are sold to the U.S. and elsewhere. *Thus, while the multinational corporations participate in the industrialization of Latin America, they perpetuate the international division of labor whereby Latin America remains essentially a raw-material export area.*

Table 3.7   Sales by Latin American Manufacturing Affiliates of U.S. Companies by Destination (in millions of dollars)

	1974	Percent	1975	Percent	1976	Percent
Local sales	19.400	93	22.600	94	24.600	94
Exports to United States	.509	3	.486	2	.633	2
Exports to other countries	.912	4	.971	4	1.043	4
Total sales	20.900	100	24.100	100	26.300	100

Source: Aspects of International Investment, U.S. Department of Commerce, Bureau of Economic Analysis, 1978.

Table 3.8   **Sales by Majority-Owned Latin American Affiliates of U.S. Companies by Destination, 1976** (in millions of dollars)

	Local Sales	Percent	Exports to United States	Percent	Exports to other foreign countries	Percent
Mining and Smelting	632	43	484	33	369	24
Petroleum	10,458	45	4,576	19	8,595	36
Manufacturing	24,575	93	633	2.7	1,043	4.3

Source: *Aspects of International Investment*, U.S. Department of Commerce, Bureau of Economic Analysis, 1978.

The Political and Social Consequences of Imperialism

The growth of U.S. industrial investment has been conditioned by particular types of regimes pursuing specific policies: police-states and military regimes repressing labor. The authoritarian regime is based on an alliance of state bureaucrats, technocrats, international banks, and multinational corporations against trade unions/working class, peasants, and petty-bourgeois/small-medium national capitalists. Their policies include: (1) destruction of an independent labor movement; (2) outlawing left-wing, Marxist, Nationalist, and Populist parties that represent masses; (3) restricting income, with concentration on upper-income groups (Mexico, Brazil, Chile, Argentina); (4) freeing prices, and raising profits; (5) eliminating profit controls, facilitating transfers to parent firms in the metropole; (6) lowering tariff barriers, permitting multinational corporations to undermine local producers; and (7) easy access to credit, with loans favoring multinational corporations.

Promotion of industrial/financial capital on a large-scale, long-term basis requires the creation of durable and long-term authoritarian regimes to provide guarantees: Brazil has experienced fifteen years of repression; Pinochet announces that the dictatorship will continue until 1990. Uruguay and Argentina also have indicated indefinite military rule.

The growth of multinational capital, conditioned by the repressive policies of authoritarian and dictatorial states, has led to the exacerbation of existing social and geographical inequalities. In Brazil, working-class inomes plummeted by 50 percent as U.S. capital increased seven-fold. Likewise in Mexico, the growth of U.S. investment has, at best, perpetuated income inequalities and, at worst, increased the gap between classes. At the same time that the multinational corporations, with their modern technology, are increasing the size of the product output, their impact on employment has been minimal. The modern manufacturing sector employs only 17.5 percent of industrial workers but accounts for 62.5 percent of the product. In agriculture similar patterns prevail: The technologically modern sector is substantially composed of agro-business, owned or linked with U.S. multinational corporations. And here 6.8 percent of the agricultural workers account for 47.5 percent of the product, while the technologically backward, locally owned sector employs 65.5 percent of the labor force but accounts for only 19.3 percent of the product. In each sector multinational corporations have polarized society and concentrated wealth, producing a large surplus army of under- and unemployed that varies from 40 percent to 60 percent in the countryside and cities of Latin America.

The Role of International Banks

The World Bank has been an important instrument in promoting overseas U.S. investment. Its loans have contributed to the growth of roads and transportation networks that have facilitated the extraction of raw material from Latin America; their loans have exploited energy resources to promote cheap power for large-scale industrial enterprises. These and other financial transactions have been conditioned by the political nature of the regimes: Populist and socialist governments that attempted to redistribute income and nationalize production were shut off from assistance. The World Bank did not provide the Allende government in Chile with a single loan up to the coup; subsequently, under the Pinochet dictatorship the spigot has been opened, and $126.9 million in World Bank loans have flowed into the dictatorship coffers between 1974 and 1977. (See Table 3.9.)

The same pattern occurred earlier in Brazil: The World Bank refused to loan funds to the populist Goulart government (1962–63) and then subsequently provided almost $3 billion to the military dictatorship that has ruled since. The same pattern occurred in Bolivia: fifteen years of populism without a loan, while the right-wing regime received $195 million. The World Bank has served as an instrument of U.S. investment policy, contributing to the destabilization of popularly based nationalist regimes while providing financial support to right-wing military regimes that open their doors to multinational corporate exploitation.

The World Bank, of course, is not alone. The Inter-American Development Bank and the International Monetary Fund (IMF) pursue similar policies, imposing their political economic criteria through the offering and withdrawal of loans. The IMF "recommendations" to countries applying for loans usually require increasing prices and freezing salaries and wages, leading to precipitous declines in the standard of living for the masses, while their proposals to lower protective barriers and to sell off public enterprises leads to the takeover by the multinational

Table 3.9 World Bank Loans and Political Regimes (in millions of dollars)

Country	Type of regime	Time period	Amount lent	Average lent per year
	National developmental	1953–61	149.5	16.6
Brazil	National Populist	1962–63	0.0	0.0
	Right-wing military	1964–77	2,961.5	211.5
	National populist	1952–64	0.0	0.0
Bolivia		1969–70		
	Right-wing military	1970–77	195.0	24.4
	Christian Democrat (Nat. Dev.)	1965–70	98.0	16.3
Chile	Democratic Socialist	1971–73	0.0	0.0
	Right-wing military	1974–77	126.9	31.7

Source: Data computed from tables in *U.S. Overseas Loans and Grants, July 1, 1945–September 30, 1977* (AID: Office of Programming and Information Analysis Service). *U.S. Overseas Loans and Grants and Assistance from International Organizations, July 1, 1945–June 30, 1972* (AID Statistical and Reports Division, 1973).

corporations of local markets and enterprises.

The policies of the World Bank and IMF result in widespread poverty and social discontent, creating a political threat to the status quo. Here the liberals in the World Bank propose "basic human needs" programs to cushion the worst effects caused by the evolving structures that they are fashioning. These programs channel loans to sustain impoverished subsistence farmers and a labor force for future exploitation; cooperatives financed and directed from above are organized to *undercut* horizontal solidarity between peasants and workers and to promote vertical linkages between reactionary regimes and client groups. Thus under the guise of human needs programs, the World Bank attempts to fragment segments of the lower classes adversely affected by its larger development programs and to deflect their activity away from class struggles toward integration into market activities.

The Role of U.S. Financial Capital

The "debt crisis" in the Third World has served as a major lever through which international capital is restructuring societies, economies, and states. Throughout the Third World in the post–World War II period, state promoted and protected productive enterprises have increasingly been coming under the influence or control of multinational capital. The whole ensemble of "national development" policies has come under attack and is being undermined. Protective tariffs, state subsidies, foreign exchange controls, restrictions on profit remittances, limitations on foreign investment, and so forth, have been eroded by the

IMF-banks as part of their debt-financing. This massive transformation over the past several years involves the privatization of state enterprise, the denationalization of national firms, and the respecialization of Third World countries into a new international division of labor. Thus, while most commentators have focused on the issues of debt payments, default, and the monetary crisis, the real issue that seems to be unfolding is the role of the banks in the *restructuration* of Third World economies and societies to facilitate the free flow of international capital. Through the levers of debt payments, the banks are in effect reversing the "nationalist-statist" development trends of the last several decades and creating a new neomercantilist world order. This process has advanced unevenly, but it appears to be the historic direction in which the global push of bank policies are directed. The bankers' vision of a world "free enterprise" system is setting in motion opposition at all levels of national societies: Disruption and disorder lurk behind each freezing of prices, bankruptcy and industrial stagnation behind each lowering of tariffs, hunger and unemployment behind each austerity measure. The radical transformations wrought by the bankers in pursuit of their global neomercantile vision is engendering an equally radical adversary within the Third World.

Conclusion

The multinational corporations and banks supported by the World Bank have changed and are changing Latin America. But the more it changes, the more it stays the same. Industry is growing, yet so is economic and technological dependency, and the international division of labor remains. The gross national product is growing, and so are the socioeconomic inequalities. Exports are expanding, but the foreign debt financing that expansion is growing even faster. Commodity booms in coffee, sugar, and minerals are followed by resounding busts, destabilizing economies, governments, and planning. State activity is increasing, but foreign penetration of that state is even more pervasive through ubiquitous loans from international banking agencies and their advisory missions. National capital grows, but so does foreign dependence on patents and licenses. The growing inflow of capital is followed by a greater outflow. The concentration of capital and the exploitation of labor have led to the creation of a large wage-earning class, concentrated in the big cities, increasingly conscious of their interests, as against capital, it struggles against the autocratic regimes and its state controlled trade unions. In Córdoba, Argentina, 12,000 auto workers walked out, despite the fact that 30 persons are "disappeared" by the regime every month. In Rio de Janeiro and São Paulo, 200,000 metallurgical workers struck and forced an agreement, despite the jailing of 1,200 workers.

And in Chile thousands of workers prepare to march on May Day in defiance of the Pinochet regime, in solidarity with 30,000 comrades who have been killed over the past six years.

The struggle continues.

4

The Trilateral Commission and Latin American Economic Development

In order to understand the formation and policies of the Trilateral Commission, we must understand the context from which it developed. Several large-scale, long-term developments over the past quarter of a century have been crucial determinants of Trilateral thinking. First has been the notion of a "world social economic order," the scope of concern today extending far beyond the conventional concerns of individual capitalist states and social formations. Trilateralism is first and foremost an effort at *global* conceptualization—an effort to fashion a world order in which the fundamental interests of the major imperial countries are safeguarded against social revolutionary and nationalist capitalist forces in the Third World, and to a much lesser extent against the competitive interests of the communist countries. Within this overall concern, a second issue is the effort to resolve the problems resulting from the growing global competition and conflict among the imperial countries and regions; namely the United States, Europe, and Japan. The third issue that has focused attention among the Trilateralists is the recognition that the old imperial structure centered on U.S. power and dominance is no longer viable, that problems of unemployment and inflation are chronic and global in nature, and that no single power can resolve the problem, let alone impose a solution.

We will outline the material basis for the emergence of the Trilateral Commission by examining the growth of international capital. First, we will detail the global nature of U.S. expansion, as well as its growth in

Latin America, and second, the increasing challenge by European and Japanese capital. We will then examine the structure, function, and purpose of the Trilateral Commission, its overall achievements and limitations, and the particular impact it has in relation to Latin American development.

The Global Nature of U.S. Expansion

Between 1945 and 1977 U.S. foreign investment grew from $7 billion to $148 billion.[1] Within Latin America, U.S. investment grew from $2.8 billion in 1943 to $27.7 billion in 1977. Sales by majority-owned foreign affiliates of U.S. companies have also been growing at an astronomical rate. In 1967 they accounted for $108.5 billion in sales, while in 1976 their sales rose to $514.7 billion.[2] Finally, if we look at U.S.-owned multinational banks, we find the same inexorable growth—and the decisive importance that overseas expansion has for sustaining these operations. In 1970 the thirteen leading U.S. banks earned $177 million overseas, accounting for 16.7 percent of their total earnings, while in 1976 they earned $886.2 million, amounting to 49 percent of their total earnings.[3] The compound annual growth rate between 1970 and 1975 for overseas earnings was 36.4 percent, compared to .7 percent for domestic activity.

The growing importance of private finance capital during the 1970s was noted in a recent report in the *New York Times*, which indicated that the bulk of oil earnings were recycled by private banks:

Just how much of the recycling job has been handled by the private banks is revealed in figures put together by the Chase Manhattan Bank. These show that of the total $185.1 billion OPEC current account surplus from the beginning of 1974 to mid-1978, only $37 billion went directly to developing nations and $10.25 billion to international financial institutions. The bulk of the remaining funds, about 75 percent of the total, went to Western financial-intermediaries, and much of that was then lent to borrowers in deficit countries.[4]

Yet, as finance capital has spread throughout the globe, it has created the conditions for its own downfall:

Private recycling has been so thorough that a vast, symbiotic, and increasingly precarious relationship between the banks and the debtor nations has been created. Loosening that web of interlocking interests, as some private banks now seem to want to do, will be fraught with peril for both debtors and creditors. As some see it, then, pointing to the successful recycling of the past is to point out the dangers of the future.[5]

Within this overall process of expansion, Latin America continues to play a vital role: 18 percent of *all* U.S. direct investments in 1977 were found in Latin America, while 82 percent of all U.S. investments in the Third World were located there. In the area of sales, in 1976 U.S.-owned multinationals based in Latin America accounted for $60.6 billion worth of business, or 12 percent of the world total. The decisive importance of this economic expansion for the survival of U.S. capitalism required the initiation and continuance of a massive program of public economic and military aid to sustain the relationship with collaborator states and classes in the Third World: Between 1955 and 1977 the United States provided $50.2 billion in military aid[6]; between 1946 and 1977, $94.3 billion in economic aid went to Third World collaborators.[7]

The massive, long-term public and private, economic and military investments of the United States define its profound involvement in the world economic order and its need to sustain its control and involvement.

The European and Japanese Challenge

While the U.S. involvement in the world economy, the Third World, and Latin America has grown precipitously, it has been increasingly challenged by the growing power of European and Japanese capital. This challenge is manifested by a number of indicators, which strongly suggest that while the U.S. continues to grow in absolute terms, in relative terms its position is declining. In 1960 the U.S. gross national product accounted for 43.5 percent of that of developed countries, while the European Economic Community (EEC) and Japan represented 42.5 percent.[8] In 1977, however, U.S. gross national product was 38 percent, and the EEC and Japan accounted for 45.5 percent of the product of the developed capitalist countries. In terms of the growth of per capita GNP, Japan and the EEC experienced substantially higher growth rates than the United States in the 1960s, until the crisis of the 1970s lowered the rate for all of them.[9] In the area of exports in 1960, the United States accounted for 23 percent of total OECD exports, while the EEC accounted for 50 percent and Japan five percent. In 1977 the United States accounted for 17 percent, the EEC 53 percent, and Japan 11 percent.[10] In the area of productivity (output per hour), the average annual rate of growth between 1961 and 1972 was: United States 3.3 percent, Japan 9.8 percent, and West Germany 5.2 percent.[11] In 1977, the figures were, respectively, 2.6 percent, 6.1 percent and 4.2 percent.

Clearly, Europe and Japan are narrowing the gap that existed in the first two decades after World War II. The growing importance of European and Japanese expansion is evidenced in the rapid growth of investment in the United States, jumping from $27.6 billion in 1975 to $34.1 billion in 1977.[12] From all directions, it is clear that in the past decade European and Japanese capital have emerged as major forces in shaping the world capitalist economy and, in some cases, are seriously challenging U.S. industrial and trade positions. Even in Latin America, Europe and Japan have begun to make significant inroads on U.S. dominance, displacing the latter as the main trading partner (among advanced capitalist economies) of Brazil, Argentina, Cuba, Paraguay, and Uruguay, as well as exceeding the United States in importing goods from Chile, El Salvador, Nicaragua, and Peru.[13]

The overall decline in U.S. control over Latin American export trade is demonstrated by the fact that in 1953 it accounted for 47 percent, while in 1976 it represented 36 percent. While the combined European and Japanese percentage of Latin American exports also declined, they did so at a lower rate (from 30 percent to 27 percent) during the same period, reducing the difference between their relative shares.[14] Meanwhile, Japanese investment in Latin America has grown from $329 million in 1968 to $2,877 million in 1976—from 3 percent to 12 percent of U.S. investment in the region.[15]

The Emergence of Trilateralism: The New Realities

It stands to reason that some effort would be made to recognize the growing influence and importance of European and Japanese capital in shaping the world capitalist system. One principal reason for the emergence of the Trilateral commission was the need for an institutional structure that could accommodate the shift from absolute U.S. dominance to shared power with the new rising imperial powers. Another reason was the need to increase the involvement of the European and Japanese powers in the common effort to beat back the economic and political challenge emanating from the Third World.

U.S. policymakers, following the defeat in Vietnam, recognized that the United States was not capable of sustaining alone the military-political-economic networks necessary to maintain the imperial system in the Third World. Moreover, the United States was shouldering a disproportionate share of the military costs, while Europe and Japan were pouring state investments in productive activity, thus increasing their competitive advantages. In 1970 the United States was spending 8 percent of its gross national product on defense expenditures, whereas Japan expended .8 percent, or one-tenth of the amount.[16] In 1976 the wide disparities between the United States, Germany, and Japan persisted: U.S. military outlays were 5 percent of the GNP, with Japan .9 percent and West Germany 3.4 percent. The same pattern was evident in the area of grants and loans to collaborator regimes in the periphery: Between 1954 and 1976 the United States supplied $156.7 billion, West Germany $13.7 billion, and Japan $11.2 billion.[17] Clearly, the United States was footing the bill to maintain the structures of domination in the Third World, while Japan and Europe were reaping the benefits. Thus, trilateralism was an attempt to involve Japan and Europe into sharing their costs of the maintenance of the system and deflecting some of their capital away from the productive side of empire building.

The third reason for the rise of the Trilateral Commission was the incapacity of the United States to confront the challenge from the Third World—a challenge that now increasingly affects European and Japanese imperialism also. The defeat in Vietnam was followed by upheavals in Angola, Iran, Afghanistan, and Ethiopia, which threaten to spread to Central (Nicaragua, El Salvador, Guatemala) and South America (Brazil, Peru, Bolivia). In addition, the organization of commodity producers, especially OPEC, has cut into the profits of the imperial countries and, in some cases, it has accumulated surpluses that provide new centers for economic and political influence in the global capitalist market place.

The old system of undisputed U.S. power within the capitalist world is being seriously eroded, even as the United States remains the single most powerful capitalist country. Yet no other single country is in a position to replace the United States as the organizing force within the global system. Hence, the Trilateral Commission must be seen as an effort to create a collective leadership to coordinate and synchronize policies among the capitalist powers as a way of minimizing internal friction and maximizing gains in the Third World.

The Trilateral Commission: Its Function and Purpose

The Trilateral Commission, founded in 1973, is composed of 200 members drawn from European, U.S., and Japanese big business, banking, mass media, political, and academic circles: The Commission meets once a year to discuss working papers prepared by research teams around issues of importance to its members. Between meetings, most business is handled by an executive committee and director. The initiative to organize the Commission came from David Rockefeller and Zbigniew Brzezinski. Faced with the growing fissures within the imperial system, the Commission seeks to achieve several goals: (1) to coordinate the interests of the major capitalist groups located in different countries, especially the corporate and banking firms involved in international trade, finance, and investment; (2) to create a collective leadership from among the major capitalist countries to develop a common front against challenges from Third World social revolutionaries and OPEC, as well as to negotiate common positions vis-à-vis the Communist countries; (3) to promote more authoritative and effective supranational bodies to synchronize their economic policies (common positions on inflation, growth, unemployment); (4) to develop common policies and procedures guiding the relationship between multinational corporations (MNC) and the state, including measures to protect the multinationals from Third World nationalization; and (5) to elaborate policies and agreements that promote multilateral trade (and undermine protectionist policies) and develop agreements that stabilize income for collaborator-producers in the Third World.

The need to coordinate interests is rooted in the profound interdependence that has developed between capitalist interests. Of all U.S. foreign investment, 73 percent was located in the advanced capitalist countries, and 63 percent of all U.S. exports went to the OECD countries in 1977. In 1976, 65 percent of all the sales of majority-owned foreign affiliates of U.S. companies took place within the "developed countries." On the other side, 48 percent of Japanese exports went to the OECD countries, while 74 percent of German exports went to the same group. In addition, between 1975 and 1977 foreign investment in the United States from the advanced capitalist countries jumped from $24.5 billion to $30.4 billion. Clearly, the growth of integrated networks of capitalist groups between countries parallels their increasing competition. The problem of "coordination" thus involves attempts to balance the areas of common interest against those of conflicting interests. The latter problem emerges most clearly in the competition between "capitals" located in different nations over scarce energy resources, resulting in bidding up the spot-market oil price, in some cases to $40 a barrel. Thus the frequent summit meetings of heads of state of the imperial countries that convene to search for a way to contain the competition undermining each economy. The periodic meetings serve as a substitute for the absence of any transnational political authority capable of executing a common policy.

Trilateral Achievements and Limitations

It is obvious that the Trilateral Commission has achieved few concrete results. The idea of an international ruling class capable of coordinating and synchronizing the policies of capital on a global scale has remained more on paper than manifested in practice.

The limitations of Trilateralism were aptly summed up recently on the financial pages of the *New York Times*:

Fresh on the heels of still another OPEC price rise, expected at Geneva on Tuesday, leaders of the West's seven leading industrial nations are meeting in Tokyo on Thursday to try to regain control of their economies.

But, on the record of small accomplishments in the four-year history of Western economic summitry, their chances appear less than brilliant. Agreement will not come easily to President Carter and the six other politically diverse leaders, each bringing differing degrees of governmental experience and differing fears and preoccupations.[18]

Summarizing the meager results of previous meetings by Trilateral powers, the *Times*' economic analyst noted the major shortcomings:

As they look back to their past four annual economic conclaves, the leaders will find small grounds for optimism. Attempting to regain control of a world economy knocked into a tailspin by the fourfold oil price hike of 1974, their first two meetings were wasted trying to repair the international monetary system undermined by President Nixon's decision to reverse United States willingness to exchange gold for dollars and thrown into confusion by ensuing huge United States deficits. Now the world monetary system is in tatters as President Carter struggles to defend the dollar in the face of a heavy trade deficit (despite the improvement reported last week, which many experts say will again be reversed by rising oil prices) and double-digit inflation. After a four-month period of recovery, the dollar was sliding again last week.

In later meetings, the seven leaders switched their efforts to spending their way out of the downswing without rekindling inflation. But these recovery hopes have been squashed by a new world-wide inflationary upsurge, aggravated by sharply rising oil prices. At Tokyo, the seven must face the fact that five years after the first big oil price hike, they still have not taught their economies to run on less oil.

In 1977, they endorsed the optimism of an international panel of economists chaired by former White House adviser Paul McCracken, which concluded that "a period of sustained increase in real incomes and employment is a reasonable prospect" if they pledged 5.5 percent annual expansion between 1975 and 1980. But last week White House economic adviser Charles L. Schultze conceded that growth was unlikely to top 3 percent this year, a figure many American analysts consider optimistic, and probably would be less in 1980.[19]

Noting the deepening crisis confronting the Trilateral countries, the *Times*' analyst points to the continuing problems and the unlikely prospects for common future action, given the competitive disadvantages all seem to encounter:

In the longer run, the seven leaders must struggle to prevent the dreary low-growth phase they are now re-entering from becoming self-perpetuating, as governments protect and subsidize their ailing industries, building inefficiency into their economic systems. In theory, everyone agrees that inefficient industries should be eased out of business and the free trade commitments in the new Tokyo Round General Trade Agreement respected.

But all this is much easier when displaced workers have new jobs to go to, and much harder when they may not. Amid the unsatisfying fruit of the first four Western economic leadership conclaves, therefore, the seven leaders must face the fact that promises must be translated into painful action. It is not so much on what they agree that will interest the world this week, but whether they can carry it out.[20]

The influence of the Trilateral Commission is manifest in several areas: (a) regular meetings of permanent operating committees involving top U.S., European, and Japanese officials have been set up to deal with managing world capitalist economy; (b) committees of finance ministries from twenty of the leading nonsocialist states have been set up to handle monetary and financial issues; (c) the International Monetary Fund has established a new system of capitalist currency and financial relations;

(d) five summit meetings by heads of state from the Trilateral countries perhaps reflects the Commission's influence; and (e) some influence from the Commission may be operating at recent gatherings on international economic cooperation and in the hardening position of the Trilateral countries in the North/South negotiations over tariff and trade—the GATT meetings.

The limitations of the Trilateral Commission are abundantly in evidence: (a) increased investment competition between Trilateral countries, evidenced in the increasing pressure by the United States to "open up" Japan, the growth of foreign investment in the United States, and the continued expansion of Europe and Japan in areas previously under U.S. domination; (b) growing trade competition, especially over oil and other scarce raw materials, evidenced in efforts by each Trilateral country to secure access through bilateral agreements; (c) interimperial trade restrictions, evidenced in European constraints on U.S. agricultural goods, U.S. restrictions on Japanese steel, textiles, and so forth; and (d) declining capacity of the United States to intervene to prevent the demise of collaborator regimes (Angola, Iran, and Nicaragua) and the unwillingness or incapacity of the Trilateral "partners" to make any effort to assist. The only exceptions were: (1) Zaire, where the Belgian regime mobilized troops and the French found surrogate supporters in Morocco, and (2) Turkey and Peru, where a consortium acted to prevent collapse and the immediate loss of economic stakes by multinationals from the involved countries.

The most dismal failure thus far has been the effort to break or weaken OPEC. The efforts to reinvest Arab funds have reached the saturation point—overextending the Trilateral banks, involving them in high-risk loans to unstable Third World areas overburdened with debts.

Commenting on the growing limitations of Trilateral banks to recycle petrodollars, one financial writer pointed to the immediate problems emerging from the oil price increases of 1979:

The price increase will widen the already expanding trade deficits of the developing countries by some $35- to $40 billion, at a time when banks are showing clear signs of uneasiness with more balance of payments loans. The current account deficit of the developing countries already amounts to a staggering $238 billion, and more than one-half of that is owed to commercial banks.

One expert who is concerned is David Rockefeller, chairman of the Chase Manhattan Bank, who warned in a recent interview that "the commercial banks are unlikely to play the predominant role in recycling that they did last time," largely because of the already astronomical levels of foreign debt piled up by the developing world. . . .

The consensus at a recent international bankers conference in London was that the commercial banks had almost had enough of this kind of business. Chase itself, according to Mr. Rockefeller, is no longer making the kind of huge balance-of-payments loans it made in 1973 and 1974.[21]

The U.S. ties to the Israeli clerical-colonial regime have forced Saudi Arabia toward a more accommodationist position within OPEC. The EEC and Japan, in opposition to U.S.-Israeli alliances, have been ineffectual in courting the Saudis, for they can offer no effective means to counter Israeli colonial occupation policies. What is striking about the Trilateral Commission thus far is its inability to become the "executive arm of international capital."

The differences among the Trilateral powers were evident prior to the latest economic summit meeting in June 1979. On policies toward the energy crisis, France, which previously refused to join the newly created International Energy Agency, is disposed to coordinated policy among the Trilateral powers. However, West Germany believes that higher oil prices will ration supplies—knowing well that since the German economy is the richest and has the largest trade surpluses in Europe, it can afford the higher prices. Japan is pushing for a "consumer's cartel" to match OPEC—a toughening of policy in the direction of greater coordination. Major differences between these oil-dependent countries and almost self-sufficient Great Britain and Canada are sure to weaken common action and fronts.[22]

The competition and conflicts persist, and the absence of an overall political military police force is obvious. The lack of coordination in the area of inflation, trade, and monetary problems is continuous. Trilateralism has been less than a great success in dealing with the relations between the member countries. But how has it fared in relation to Latin America and the Third World?

Trilateralism and Latin America

Little has been published that reflects the conscious, coordinated efforts of the Commission in relation to Latin America. What emerges from the general position of the Commission is a view that favors the *joint* exploitation of Latin America through the espousal of policies that promote "free-market" economics (minimal restrictions on trade, flows of capital, profit remittances). This position, which is advocated in Latin America, however, contradicts some of the policies and trends among Trilateral countries: thus while free-market economics is promoted abroad, increasing protectionism is encouraged at home, causing considerable consternation among the economic ministers in the Southern Core (i.e., Argentina, Uruguay, and Chile).

The major impact of Trilateral behavior on Latin America has been the growth in industrial investment, the diversification of trading partners, and the *maintenance* of the traditional international division of labor. The competition for markets and raw material, the drive to invest accumulated capital, and the demand for industrial growth in Latin America have led to the massive growth of industrial and financial investments: 62 percent of U.S. investments in Latin America in 1976 were in those two areas; 62 percent of Japanese investments were located in manufacturing, finance, and insurance in the same year. If we examine the sales of their major overseas subsidiaries, however, we will find that most manufacturing sales are directed toward the *local* market, and most enterprises operating in the raw material field are directed toward *overseas* markets, i.e., back to the imperial metropole. Thus external rivalries among Trilateral countries for markets and raw materials have contributed simultaneously to diversifying Latin America's trading partners, industrializing the country, *and* maintaining their position in the international division of labor. Even when there is Trilateral cooperation—joint investments and joint efforts to refinance financially troubled countries (most of Latin America)—the internal protectionist forces within the imperialist countries have limited the scale and scope of imports from Latin America. Moreover, the systemic crisis evidenced in the chronic and recurring recession among Trilateral countries has limited the demand for Latin exports and constrained the banks and multinationals from undertaking massive new commitments. Finally, the upsurge of the class struggle spearheaded by a new, radicalized wage-earning class in the cities, a product of the large-scale industrialization process, may also serve as a further check in the growth of Trilateral capital movements. All these constraints on Trilateral initiatives operate to confine its policy successes to those regimes who continue to espouse the free-market rhetoric, namely Chile, Argentina, and Uruguay, and decreasingly in Brazil.

The centrality of oil in Mexico and Venezuela provides the regimes in these countries with a limited amount of leverage in diversifying their trading partners and increasing the role of national capital in the industrial process, although the results thus far are not overwhelming. The competition between France and the United States over Mexican oil was highlighted by the recent visits of their respective heads of state. Clearly what is occurring is that where common interests are affected in specific contexts, the Trilateral governments and firms act in concert, i.e., financing of "free-market" economies, avoiding bankruptcy in Peru, joint ventures in Brazil, and so forth. Where competing interests are involved over scarce opportunities involving long-standing interests, Trilateralism has broken down and each power has tried to maximize its advantages at the expense of the others. The notion of the Trilateral Commission as an omnipotent power, coordinating the interests of international capital and imposing a new, rational and coherent international order, is far from the realities of continuing internal contradiction, inter-imperialist competition, systemic crisis, and social and national revolutions.

Even the proposals by the Commission to establish "new international rules to check the effort of national governments to seize for their own countries a disproportionate share of the benefits generated by foreign direct investment'' has been something less than a success. While European capital was expropriated in Angola, U.S. Gulf Oil continued to pump out petrol. While U.S. interests were adversely affected with the downfall of the Shah, the French attempted to develop ties with the Ayatollah. As U.S.-supported military regimes in Latin America began to weaken, European Social Democrats increased their activity among opposition groups.

Conclusion

Thus, while the Trilateral Commission has been successful in identifying problem areas, each of the Trilateral countries has been unable to subordinate the immediate interests of its major economic components for the historic interests of the whole. While the Commission has been successful in formulating an outlook that encompasses the major capitalist countries, that ideology has not been the operative basis of policies. The Commission's influence is manifest in the frequent summit meetings, but the decisive decisions that shape the course of each country are taken elsewhere. Finally, and most fundamental of all, the Trilateral Commission has not been able to contain social and national revolution—to put the Third World in its place. The demands of the newly aroused mass movements far exceed the bounds compatible with static regimes. The scheme of so-called viable democracies is neither viable nor democratic in any popular sense. The export-oriented free-market economies and industrialization from outside and above, promoted by the Trilateralists, will be the first to succumb as these popular forces move from opposition to power. Let us make no mistake, the present crisis of the Trilateral countries is just beginning.

Notes

1. *Survey of Current Business*, August 1978, p. 16.

2. Ibid., March 1978, p. 32.

3. U.S. Senate (1977), Subcommittee on Foreign Economic Policy of the Committee on Foreign Relations, *International Debt: The Banks and U.S. Foreign Policy* (Washington, D.C.: U.S. Government Printing Office).

4. *New York Times*, June 24, 1979, p. 5.

5. Ibid.

6. CIA, *Handbook of Economic Statistics*, 1978, p. 72.

7. Ibid., P. 71.

8. Ibid., p. 17.

9. Ibid., p. 21.

10. Ibid., p. 53.

11. Ibid., p. 23.

12. *Survey of Current Business*, August 1978, p. 40.

13. *Statistical Abstract of Latin America*, University of California, Los Angeles, vol. 18, 1977. p. 350.

14. *U.N. Statistical Yearbook*, 1965, 1973, 1977.
15. *Business International*, February 18, 1977, p. 54, 55.
16. CIA, *Handbook of Economic Statistics*, 1978, p. 31.
17. Ibid., p. 69.
18. *New York Times*, June 24, 1979, p. E1.
19. Ibid.
20. Ibid.
21. *New York Times*, Financial section, June 24, 1970, p. 1.
22. *New York Times*, June 17, 1979, pp. F1, 9.

5

The Political Economy of International Debt

by PETER DeWITT and JAMES F. PETRAS

The Dynamics of Finance Capital

As Marx brilliantly observed, one of the central features in the development of the capitalist system has been the growing tendency toward greater concentration and centralization of capital. Today, that phenomenon has been extended on a world scale, increasingly involving all nations, regions, and productive systems. The fastest growing aspect of this process of Western-centered accumulation has been, first, the growth of multinational corporations and commercial enterprises and, since the 1960s, multinational banking. In the earlier phases of overseas expansion, the growth of industrial and commercial capital was facilitated by public loans: Public loans were, in large part, export subsidies for Western manufacturers and instruments for financing multinational corporate investments. The cumulative consequences of externally oriented development were to heighten dependence. Unequal terms of exchange, fluctuating prices, and massive transfers of earnings created severe balance of payments problems, most of which preceded the so-called oil crisis, which greatly exacerbated the problem. The growth of long-term, large-scale movements of finance capital thus must be seen as part of a larger picture of externally controlled industrial and commercial investments linked to public finance; the debt crisis is only one aspect of a larger crisis of world capitalist development.

During the last decade and a half, major banks have been emulating the giant corporations by going multinational. The lion's share of this expansion has been by the U.S. banking system, which has followed the multinational corporations abroad, establishing a complex global network of branches, subsidiaries, and other offshore affiliates. In 1960 only eight U.S. banks had branches abroad with assets of $3.5 billion. By mid-1976, however, U.S. bank assets abroad had increased to $181 billion, with more than a hundred banks and branches overseas.[1] A recent study by Andrew Beveridge and Philip Wellons revealed the extent of U.S. commercial bank activity abroad, noting that in 1975 the Eurocurrency market for developing countries was dominated by two North American nations, namely the United States (44 percent) and Canada (18 percent). Indeed, they found that the Bank of America alone in 1975 was involved fully in 42 percent of all loans.[2] Other studies have also provided strong evidence of the dominance of private U.S. banking institutions in world capital markets. A 1977 study by the Subcommittee on Foreign Economic Policy of the Senate Committee on Foreign Relations noted that financing in private capital markets is not only concentrated in a few countries but also in a few large multinational banks. For instance, 66 percent of all non-OPEC private bank debt is owed to U.S. banks. A survey by the Subcommittee on Multinational Corporations indicates furthermore that two-thirds of all U.S. private bank lending to the twenty-five developing countries studied was done by six banks.[3]

The growth of private bank lending by U.S. banks has been precipitous in recent years, particularly since the credit crunch caused by the now sixfold increase in the price of petroleum has created a dramatic demand for loans, especially to nonoil-producing, less developed countries. The amount of debt outstanding to private multinational banks at the end of 1976 equaled $130.83 billion from some selected borrowers, as illustrated in Table 5.1.

This very substantial private debt is compounded by the fact that recent estimates of long-term public debt of eighty-six less developed countries (including undisbursed amounts) exceeded $200 billion at the end of 1976. The outstanding public and private debt obligations of the selected nations alone exceeded $330 billion at the end of 1976. These figures are generally 20 to 25 percent higher than those for 1975, and it is estimated that international debt has been expanding at this rate since the oil crisis in 1973.[4] Of the private debt of the selected countries, $69.30 billion is owed to U.S. commercial banks, or more than one-half of the outstanding private debt.

A 1976 study by Saloman Brothers, an investment and financial house, demonstrated the international lending bonanza for the thirteen largest U.S. multinational banks. As illustrated in Fig. 5.1, their earnings rose from $177 million in 1970 to $836 million in 1975. The study revealed that U.S. domestic banking operations have been relatively less productive, increasing from $884 million in 1970 to only $918 million in 1975. Therefore, international banking operations for the thirteen largest U.S. multinational banks produced a dramatic 95-percent increase in the total earnings during this five-year period.[5] As a group, U.S. private banks presently derive about 50 percent of their income from overseas operations. And for some, as Table 5.2 indicates, the international share of total earnings is even higher.

That movement of finance capital abroad was largely a necessary result of the relative decline in profits in the metropolitan centers: The need to maintain higher rates of profits in the face of accumulating reserves forced the banks to become multinational. If the oil crisis did

---

Table 5.1 Bank Claims on Selected Countries, 1976 (in billions of dollars)

	All banks	U.S. banks	Non-U.S. banks
Non-OPEC LDCs	76.83	52.03	24.85
Brazil	21.22	13.86	7.36
Mexico	17.85	13.00	4.85
Korea	3.90	3.23	.67
Argentina	3.40	2.34	1.05
Peru	2.83	1.92	.91
Philippines	2.61	2.29	.32
Taiwan	2.56	2.56	
Turkey	2.06	1.27	.79
Colombia	1.03	1.34	.29
Thailand	1.43	.82	.61
Chile	1.09	.81	.25
Others	16.25	8.51	7.70
OPEC countries	24.80	12.08	11.82
Venezuela	6.86	4.37	2.49
Indonesia	3.44	2.22	1.22
Others	11.50	6.30	8.11
Eastern Europe	29.20	4.29	24.91
U.S.S.R.	10.35	1.51	8.84
Others	18.95	2.78	16.07
Total	130.83	69.30	81.53

Source: Morgan Guaranty, *World Financial Markets*, June 1977.

---

not exist, it would have had to have been invented. For the cumulated problems facing the banks were resolved through movements abroad, thus heightening and extending the contradictions within the Third World. Bank loans neither aided nor ameliorated the development problems; rather, they further exacerbated the balance of payments problem, generally hindered productive activity by capturing local savings, and provoked a deepening of dependency by appropriating local productive facilities as assets. The internationalization of finance capital, the merger of finance capital with industrial capital, and the appropriation of local savings and industry through purchases of financially troubled local firms set the stage for a crucial development: The survival of the largest banks in the West has become increasingly dependent on the profits that are accrued in the Third World. Thus, while in the early 1970s internationalization of capital became a necessary outlet for surplus loan capital, in the 1980s the profits from those commitments have become an essential element in the overall operation of the banks.

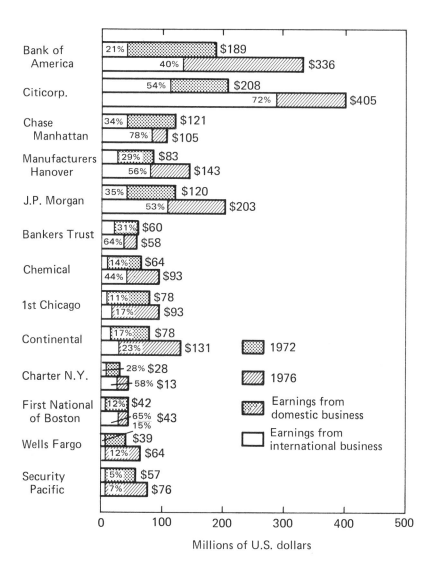

Figure 5.1 Total international and domestic earnings of thirteen large U.S. banks for 1972 and 1976. *Source*: U.S. Senate, Subcommittee on Foreign Economic Policy of the Committee on Foreign Relations, *International Debt, the Banks and U.S. Foreign Policy* (Washington, D.C.: U.S. Government Printing Office, August 1977), p. 10.

Recognizing this, the capitalist state has become increasingly in-volved—directly or through their representatives in the so-called interna-tional banks—in attempts to restructure political power and economic systems in the Third World, while assuming greater direct involvement in the operations of the banks within these societies. In this context, "default" is not a real issue: Rather, the state and the banks are manipulating regimes (and changing them when necessary) to foster con-ditions that (1) allow or force the labor forces of the Third World to pay, (2) allow the banks to appropriate income to pay debts before anyone else, and (3) promote the massive appropriation of resources and strategic goods. The "debt threat" to the banks thus has been transformed into an instrument for threatening the livelihood of Third World labor and, indeed, the sovereignty of nations, as recent developments in Zaire and Peru graphically illustrate.[6] The capitalist world economic system is not threatened by debt so long as the multinational banks and their state receive payments through neocolonial regimes that continue to exploit labor (austerity) and resources. The debt problem will become a threat to world capitalist stability when mass-movement-based regimes refuse to follow the dictates of the banks and nationalize their holdings, thus preventing them from collecting their debts. Western intervention in Zaire had more to do with bankers and corporate interests than with sav-ing white-expatriate lives.

Dynamics of International Debt Peonage

For years, bank officials and academics partial to banking interests argued that "creditworthiness" was the key criterion for loans. The term itself, however, was so nebulous in practical terms that it was rather useless as a guide to bank-loan behavior. For example, Chile after 1973, Argentina after the spring of 1976, and Brazil after 1964 experienced severe recessions and monstrous inflation and yet still received massive financial support.[7] Clearly, other factors were involved aside from the rather vacuous concept of creditworthiness.

A cluster of factors that help identify which regimes get loans include: (1) a deep commitment to an open-door policy to foreign flows of capital (of all sorts); (2) strategic resources and policies which promote easy ac-cess to raw materials; (3) large internal markets with little hindrance to foreign penetration; and (4) substantial surplus labor pools and a will-ingness to promote export platforms for foreign capital. Indeed, most of the easy terms of loans are intimately tied with Third World regimes that facilitate the internationalization of capital. The "model" most likely to be financed is one based on "growth from above and outside." Finance capital both promotes and deepens this approach. In some cases (South Korea, Hong Kong, Formosa), external finance has led to extended growth based on export industries exploiting cheap labor. In other cases, loans either have led local investors to transfer capital to nonproductive sectors (construction, speculation) or states to increase military spending. Or the loans to productive sectors have failed to generate the surplus to pay back the loans, especially loans to finance the exploitation of raw materials that have suffered on the world market (copper) or failed to materialize (oil exploration).[8] In other cases, Third World export-oriented industrialization has suffered from the recession in the metropoles and the protectionist measures that have been adapted, as in Mexico and Brazil. Finally, in some cases, externally funded industrialization may lead to rising wage levels, which could cause capitalists to pick up their assembly plants and move to new lower-wage areas within the third World, leaving the country with the debt and declining revenues. Puerto Rico is illustrative.[9]

Externally financed economic expansion is a precarious undertaking that contains within it numerous possibilities of falling into the "debt trap."[10] Regimes that loyally pursue the model of "growth from above and outside" periodically enter into crisis for any one of the above political or economic reasons. Several structural features of dependency contribute to the growth of indebtedness and the growing centrality of finance capital. Third World growth based on the expansion of multinational capital carries with it the massive remittance of profits, payments for licenses, patents, and so forth. In addition, most multinational corporations have an unfavorable balance of payment, importing far more goods than they sell abroad—as Brazilian authorities have recently noted.[11] Further, the terms of exchange have, overall, been unfavorable for a number of Third World countries specializing in a limited number of raw materials, hence leading to declining income and severe balance of payments problems. Both investment and trade policies premised on growth through dependency produce imbalances in payments that are covered by loans. As the imbalance deepens during cyclical downturns, debts increase and the regime intensifies its debt position.

The dynamics of international debt peonage are intimately tied to the dependent structures of Third World productive systems. As the crisis deepens, the terms of loans become more onerous. Local entrepreneurs become bankrupt, state firms are sold, and foreign capital gains greater concessions; in some cases, the banks themselves take over enterprises. Hence, the rise of regimes oriented toward dependent growth leads to greater concentration of ownership by foreign capital (not homogenization or leveling between countries), greater internal inequalities, and the intensification of exploitation of labor to pay for the "recovery," and therefore greater regime repression to sustain the overall effort.[12]

Since 1973–74, when the oil crisis hit and world recession began to take hold, nonoil-producing, less developed countries were caught in a credit squeeze. Private banks, however—not public international lending agencies like the World Bank or International Monetary Fund (IMF)—have underwritten most of the massive debt buildup that has occurred in the less developed countries since 1973. The demand for credit to meet the increased cost of petroleum in the nonoil-producing Third World provided one incentive for commercial banks lending abroad, and this was heightened by a decline in domestic bank earnings, a result of the impact of the world recession on the developed world economies. This rapid buildup of debt in the less developed countries is illustrated in Table 5.2. The statistics illustrate the extensive nature of debt in the developing world.[13]

Analyzing this debt over time, Table 5.3 illustrates that the net foreign indebtedness of the sixteen nonoil-producing, less-developed countries that have done most of the borrowing has increased at an annual rate of 15 percent in real terms, allowing for inflation. In this period, these same countries' combined real gross national product grew about 4.5 percent per year. Thus, clearly, external indebtedness has been growing faster than the capacity of these economies to carry it.

In the stampede to meet the burgeoning demand for credit in the nonoil-producing developing world, commercial banks, and particularly U.S. private banks, may have overextended themselves. A 1977 study by the Overseas Development Council of predictions or rescheduling and major defaults for 1970, 1976, and 1977, as shown in Table 5.4, indicated that at least ten of the countries selected for study had a high probability of default or the need to reschedule their external debt. The twenty-four debtor nations included accounted for more than three-fourths of the total debt outstanding at the end of 1974. In 1977, of the twenty-four debtor nations, at least seven, including Mexico, would face situations that would have brought defaults in the past. These seven are responsible for about 26 percent of the long-term public debt outstanding. In addition, Zambia, Uruguay, Bangladesh, and Brazil were also flagged as potential problem countries for 1977. Default by Brazil especially could raise substantially the percentage of the long-term public debt held by these high-risk nations. Clearly, these are not hard and fast predictions, but recently several of these countries have faced real debt crises. Zaire, for instance, defaulted on some of its obligations to Citibank and has experienced a formal rescheduling of certain debts, while Peru and Argentina have suffered debt crises that were resolved without rescheduling.[14] A default by either Brazil or Mexico, because of their concentration of debt, could rock the international banking system. A recent study by the World Bank estimates that at the end of 1976 Brazil and Mexico accounted for 44 percent of identified gross outstanding debt to banks by nonoil-exporting countries and 86 percent of the net bank debt.[15]

While the predictions raised in Table 5.4 do not guarantee default or rescheduling, they do indicate that more countries are reaching the point

Table 5.2 External Debt of 85 Developing Countries, December 31, 1976 (in billions of dollars)

Income groups[a] (per capita income)	Total medium and long-term external debt	Public and publicly guaranteed debt[b]	Private nonguaranteed debt[c]		Private debt as a percentage of public debt
			Estimated value	(possible range)	
All countries	202.5	157.0	45.5	39.9–57.6	25–37
High-income (over $2,500)	30.2	18.2	12.0	10.7–15.1	59–83
Upper-middle-income ($1,136 to $2,500)	48.4	29.4	19.0	17.2–21.0	59–71
Intermediate-middle-income ($551 to $1,135)	62.1	53.2	8.9	7.4–15.0	14–28
Lower-middle-income ($281 to $550)	15.7	12.4	3.3	3.0– 3.6	24–29
Low-income ($280 or less)	46.1	43.8	2.3	1.7– 3.0	4– 7

Note: Components may not add to totals because rounding amounts outstanding are shown on a "disbursed only" basis. Debts included are those with an original and extended maturity of more than one year.

[a] Gross national product per capita for 1976, expressed in 1976 dollars. See World Bank, *World Economic and Social Indicators*, January 1978, for the country composition of these income groups.

[b] Preliminary data, as published in *World Economic and Social Indicators*, January 1978.

[c] Figures are in part World Bank staff estimates.

Source: IMF Survey, June 5, 1978, p. 176.

Table 5.3   Total Long-Term Public and Publicly Guaranteed External Debts of Selected Developing Countries[a] (in billions of dollars)

	End 1973		End 1974		End 1975		End 1976
Non-OPEC LDCs	Total debt	Owed banks	Total debt	Owed banks	Total debt	Owed banks	Total debt
Latin America							
Argentina	2.89	.66	3.35	.63	3.16	.52	4.20
Brazil	6.92	2.60	9.30	4.40	11.50	5.80	15.00
Chile	3.04	.51	3.73	.55	4.00	.50	4.20
Colombia	1.94	.22	2.12	.26	2.36	.37	2.70
Mexico	5.42	2.36	8.08	4.24	11.25	6.66	14.00
Peru	1.44	.56	2.07	.95	2.67	1.34	3.30
Asia							
Korea	3.20	.31	3.98	.64	5.23	1.00	6.20
India	10.40	.03	11.24	.01	11.88	.02	12.20
Pakistan	4.30	.06	4.52	.08	4.89	.11	5.50
Philippines	.81	.22	1.03	.28	1.28	.32	1.80
Taiwan	.96	.05	1.16	.14	1.69	.42	1.90
Thailand	.44	.01	.51	.02	.62	.05	.80
Africa							
Egypt	1.73	.19	3.89	1.08	6.31	1.21	7.30
Tanzania	.46	.02	.61	.02	.79	.01	.96
Zaire	.89	.41	1.31	.66	1.68	.89	1.90
Zambia	.57	.23	.68	.21	.95	.35	1.20
Total above	45.41	8.44	57.58	14.17	70.26	19.57	83.66
Others	11.89	1.21	15.82	3.03	20.24	4.53	26.34
Total, 71 Non-OPEC LDCs	57.30	9.65	73.40	17.20	90.50	24.10	110.00

[a]Debt contracted by the public sector of the borrowing country or by a private borrower with an original or ex-tended maturity of more than one year, repayable in foreign currency, goods, or services. Such debt encompasses the bulk of a country's external debt, but not all of it. By definition, it excludes all short-term credits and all long-term nonguaranteed private borrowings. Adding these credits to long-term external public debt brings the total debt of seventy-one nonoil producing, less developed countries outstanding at the end of 1976 to somewhere around $160 million. Data on public and publicly guaranteed debt are collected and published by the World Bank. Unfortunately, the data on the other types of debt are neither as reliable nor as comprehensive as those of the World Bank and are therefore of only limited value.

Source: World Bank and Citibank estimates, as cited by Harold Van B. Cleveland and W. H. Brittain, "Are the LDC's in Over Their Heads?" Foreign Affairs 56 (July 1977) : 734.

Table 5.4   Predictions of Reschedulings and Major Defaults, 1970, 1976, and 1977
(Frank-Cline Quadratic Function)

	1970	*1976*	*1977*
Argentina	No	No	No
Bangladesh	n.a.	No	Yes
Bolivia	No	Yes	Yes
Brazil[a]	Yes (public debt)	No (public debt)	No (public debt)
		Yes (all debt)	Yes (all debt)
Chile	Yes	Yes	Yes
Colombia	No	No	No
Ghana	No	No	No
India	Yes	No	No
Indonesia	No	No	No
Kenya	No	No	No
Korea	Yes	No	No
Malaysia	No	No	No
Mexico	No	Yes	Yes
Pakistan	Yes	Yes	Yes
Peru	No	Yes	Yes
Philippines	Yes	No	No
Morocco	No	No	No
Singapore	No	No	No
Sudan	No	Yes	Yes
Taiwan	No	No	No
Tanzania	No	No	No
Thailand	No	No	No
Uruguay	No	Yes	Yes
Zaire	No	Yes	Yes
Zambia	No	No	No

[a]Approximately 40 percent of Brazil's medium- and long-term debt is not public or publicly guaranteed.

Source: See Gordon W. Smith, *The External Debt Prospects of the Non-Oil Exporting Countries* (Washington, D.C.: Overseas Development Council, October 1977), pp. 12-19, for an explanation of the methodology employed in their predictions.

where the cost of prompt debt servicing may begin to outweigh those at- tached to default. This scenario is even more likely if private bank credit begins to dry up, making it impossible for debtor nations to "roll over" loans, and if recovery in the industrial countries does not proceed as ex- pected. Another indication of the high cost of debt to less developed countries is illustrated in a study by American Express, which estimates that one out of every four dollars borrowed abroad by less developed countries in 1977 will go for debt servicing. By 1980 it is estimated that one out of every two dollars will be used to repay old debts.[16] These figures seem to indicate that less developed countries generally are becoming more debt-dependent, and it is perhaps only a matter of time for many less developed countries until the cost of default and rescheduling will be less than to continue to service their debt. What impact such an eventuality would have on the entire international economic system and on host and sponsoring nations alike is an issue of widespread concern.

For the developing countries the debt burden has a cumulative impact on the overall structure of dependency between the less developed countries and their creditors. One issue, of course, is the size of the debt, which estimates define as in excess of $300 billion, up nearly seven times from the level of debt in 1967. For the critical countries, as outlined in Table 5.4, the servicing of this debt is weakening their economic development capacity and lowering their national standards of living as the interest on the debt consumes between 20 and 50 percent of foreign-exchange earnings on exports.

Another important factor to Third World debtor nations is that an increasing proportion of loans received by less developed countries are from private rather than public sources. Private debt typically carries a higher rate of interest and a shorter repayment period. The stiffer terms of the commercial banks have placed new economic burdens on the less developed countries. Increasingly, the commercial banks are using the offices of the International Monetary Fund to impose conditions on the less developed countries. This not only increases economic hardship but also places increasing demands on the stability of the political system, because the governments of the less developed countries are forced to impose austerity programs to ensure repayment.

The shorter loan terms are illustrated by the following. For example, according to the World Bank, only 31 percent of the debt owed by less developed countries to international organizations is due in five years, compared with 79 percent of the debt owed to private sources that matures in five years. In 1971 the average maturity for all loans, both public and private, was thirty-two years for low-income, less developed countries. By 1974 the average maturity to those same countries had dropped by eight years.[17]

As the maturity date over time has been shortened, the interest rates have increased, as is illustrated in Table 5.5, thus intensifying the debt burden to the less developed countries.

Another illustration of the increasing debt burden on the less developed countries is the increase in debt outstanding as a percentage of gross national product from 1969 to 1975. For example, Somali, 42.3–77.5 percent; Zaire, 16.9–76.4 percent; Guyana, 27.9–50.6 percent; and Chile, 24.1–49.1 percent.[18] These conditions have increased the debt burden of the less developed countries, as well as their structural dependence on the developed economies and particularly the commercial banks.

In theory at least, the relationship between the banks and the less developed countries is one of mutual benefit. In fact, however, the beneficiaries have been largely the multinational banks, who have profited from the credit squeeze placed on the less developed countries by their historically dependent position. This was heightened by the recent increases in the cost of petroleum. Most less developed countries are not borrowing for development reasons but rather to resolve balance of payment problems or to maintain a national standard of living. The latter has certainly been the case for Brazil and Mexico, two of the largest borrowers of the less developed countries.[19]

The structural basis of growth through debt, however, poses some serious problems for both the developed and developing nations. Lending in the developed world has been on reserve requirements of, let us say, 10 percent. However, the unregulated nature of offshore lending in, for instance, the Eurodollar market has allowed multinational banks to be more flexible in the reserve requirements for lending to less developed countries, which has the effect of artificially creating money. The ag-

Table 5.5   Average Interest Rates on Loan Commitments, Selected Countries (percent)

	1967–70	1971–72	1974	1975
Afghanistan	2.1	2.2	1.7	1.3
Argentina	6.0	7.8	7.0	6.6
Bangladesh	n.a.	1.9[a]	2.6	1.7
Costa Rica	5.7	6.9	8.0	7.8
Ecuador	5.7	6.0	5.5	6.4
Ethiopia	3.7	2.2	0.7	1.4
Indonesia	2.6	3.4	4.9	7.6
Ivory Coast	5.4	6.5	7.1	7.9
Jamaica	6.2	6.4	10.5	8.8
Korea	4.6	4.6	7.7	6.6
Malaysia	5.0	5.8	5.8	8.5
Paraguay	4.2	5.4	5.9	3.9
Philippines	5.9	5.2	6.1	6.4
Singapore	3.8	5.8	6.3	7.8
Sri Lanka	3.2	2.4	5.0	2.9
Sudan	4.1	2.6	6.4	4.2
Taiwan	5.4	6.3	7.2	8.3
Thailand	5.7	6.2	5.7	7.6
Turkey	3.2	4.4	5.6	7.4
Uruguay	6.0	7.5	9.0	8.8
Zaire	4.5	6.4	7.2	6.6
Zambia	4.3	4.7	4.6	5.8

[a]1972 only.

Note: All countries for which 1975 numbers were available that had at least $400 million in debt outstanding and disbursed by December 31, 1975, were included.

Source: See Gordon W. Smith, *The External Debt Prospects of the Non-oil Exporting Countries* (Washington, D.C.: Overseas Development Council, October 1977), pp. 12–19, for an explanation of the methodology employed in their predictions.

gregate amounts of offshore deposits have been estimated at more than $300 billion, and it may be safe to assume that the amount created by off-shore banks runs into the tens of billions.[20]

The consequences and implications of this unprecedented explosion in multinational banking in the last ten years is far reaching. First, so far as the commercial bank is concerned, it has meant an enormous increase in profits from their overseas operations, as Figure 5.1 illustrated. This process has important effects in both the developing and developed world. For one, the artificial creation of money by the offshore bank is a factor in generating inflation on a global scale. Second, this situation holds the potential of several types of crises: (a) of borrowing countries that are forced to reschedule or default on loans and are faced with a national crisis as a result of their inability to continue to import supplies on which they have become heavily dependent; (b) political instability in less developed countries as a result of austerity conditions imposed on the debtor nation by public and private international lenders; and (c) the crisis of the multinational banks themselves, threatened by the default of borrowers which, in conjunction with other factors, such as a decline in world economic growth, holds the potential of undermining the international monetary system.

The Impact of Bank Capital on Third World Countries

The political dimensions of finance capital expansion are essential: The type of regime, its policies, class character, and its willingness to use force to sustain its international obligation are major considerations in discussing the impact of bank capital on Third World societies. The Third World countries are not undifferentiated entities embracing a common interest; rather, they are likely to be highly polarized societies with conflicting interests. Hence, it is a serious error to overlook the differential interests of these conflictive classes and their relations to multinational banks, corporations, and metropolitan states.

As was mentioned above, bank capital has been channeled predominantly toward regimes with a favorable orientation toward international capital. Most of these regimes, with very rare exceptions, have been authoritarian and/or highly repressive. This triangle—bank loans, open-door regimes, repressive policies—has been found in sufficient numbers to warrant some comment. First, bankers are less concerned with human rights than they are with the "bottom line"; more important, insofar as repression is selectively applied to class-conscious social forces and economic nationalist political groups, it has been positively supported by bank officials. The president of the First National City Bank recently reassured Brazilian authorities of the bank's concern: "The problem of human rights has nothing to do with the loan policies adopted by the large international banking organizations. Brazil's debt to Citibank is about 2,000 million United States dollars and we still are not imposing any restrictions."[21]

The pursuit of policies that encourage the flow of foreign capital precludes regimes from securing the support of popular majorities through welfare ideological appeals. At best, paternalistic measures (job security) and horizontal mobility (rural to urban movements) complement the use of force. The bulk of the loans are concentrated among three groups: multinational corporations, local monopoly capital (rural or urban based), and the state. Most of the latter's investments are used to promote low-cost infrastructure facilities that enhance the spread of private activity. Hence, the prime beneficiaries of private bank loans are the economically powerful who control productive state or financial resources. In such cases, the bank loans serve to strengthen their social, economic, and political power and contribute to widening the inequalities within society. Studies of societies as varied as Brazil, Chile, Argentina, and Zaire—all major recipients of large-scale, long-term loans—have shown that bank capital, while not necessarily contributing to the growth of production resources, has exacerbated the inequalities.[22]

While the loans are specifically channeled into particular classes and groups, the foreign currency used to repay those debts is earned or squeezed from the population at large. Thus regardless whether the loans went into urban real-estate speculation, someone's Swiss bank account, or into building a factory, the debt payments are assumed by the society at large. When the private banks or the International Monetary Fund demand "austerity" (cutbacks in public spending, wage freezes, credit squeezes) and price freedom as a condition for loans to deal with past debts, the burden is borne by the classes that least benefit from the initial loans.[23] Thus the banks reinforce a political system in which the loan beneficiaries and debt payers are distinct and opposing classes. While in the economic-sphere bank capital contributes to economic dependency, in the social structure it leads to a reconcentration of income at the top; and in the political sphere its policies contribute to increasingly authoritarian practices. One of the crucial elements in interpreting and understanding the dynamics of indebtedness and repayment is to demystify the relations by going beyond "national" units and identifying the class actors who play the game.

The effect of the application of private-bank and IMF-dictated austerity measures on the populace of Peru is illustrated in Table 5.6, which gives figures on protein and caloric intake by class. These figures demonstrate a substantial decline between January and March 1977 and January and March 1978, without taking into account the massive price increases of May 1978, which further accelerated the decline. Table 5.7 shows that real salaries have declined by almost one-third between 1973 and June 1978.

Most discussion of bank demands on Third World countries focus on policies, specifically economic policies that facilitate loans, rescheduling of payments, or debt financing. But the recommendations of the private banks and, more specifically, of the IMF, have major consequences for the structure of society and economy, as well as on the political orientation of the state. Bank demands for cutbacks in public spending and salaries adversely affect salaried and wage groups, as well as those sectors of national capital tied to public contracts, i.e., construction. The constraints on wages lead regimes to impose constraints on unions, thus

Table 5.6   Protein and Caloric Intake in Metropolitan Lima by Income Strata

Socioeconomic strata	1977				1978
	January/ March	April/ June	July/ September	October/ December	January/ March
Proteins (grams)					
Middle	58.6	53.1	49.4	49.0	51.5
Lower	57.9	53.2	52.9	50.9	45.2
Calories					
Middle	1,835	1,570	1,505	1,480	1,578
Lower	1,862	1,657	1,633	1,646	1,490

Note: Minimum level recommended by FAO: calories: 2,400; proteins: 56.2.

Source: Ministerior de Alimentacion.

Table 5.7   Average Salaries (Sueldo) and Monthly Salaries—Nominal and Real—in Metropolitan Lima (1973 = 100)

	Sueldo Nominal/Real				Monthly Salary Nominal/Real [a]			
	Soles	Indice	Soles	Indice	Soles	Indice	Soles	Indice [a]
1973	10,338	100	10,312	100	5,150	100	5,137	100
1974	11,088	107	9,389	91	5,670	110	4,801	93
October 1975	13,962	135	9,052	88	8,460	164	5,485	107
September 1967	16,926	164	7,905	77	10,607	206	4,954	96
June 1977	19,177	186	7,176	70	11,361	221	4,252	83
December 1977	19,886	192	6,690	65	12,070	234	4,061	79
June 1978	22,608	219	5,416	53	14,792	287	3,544	69

[a]Deflated price consumer index.

Source: BCR.

strengthening the power of employers; increases in prices raise profits for property owners at the expense of nonproperty owners. The net effect of bank policy is to alter the distribution of income and power in society toward propertied groups and classes.[24]

In the economic sphere the emphasis on "market" criteria—the "lowering of productive costs" through the elimination of tariff barriers—adversely affects national industries, both private and state, in favor of the multinationals. State enterprises are transferred toward the private sector, and previously subsidized national capital goes bankrupt, increasing the economic importance of private foreign capital. In essence, the measures lead to a restructuring of the economy, a shift in the basis of production.

Finally, bank policies are not only "recommended" but in periods of crisis are imposed: Regimes in severe financial difficulties who refuse to abide by these measures are denied loans and are pressured to meet all their obligations. Frequently, internal conflicts are generated through these pressures and impositions: One result is a shift in governing personnel. Those who lack the "confidence" of the banks because of their previous association with nationalist/populist policies or unwillingness to follow all the demands of the banks are pushed aside or replaced. New officials emerge who, by background or ties, are willing to collaborate with the banks in the execution of their class-biased stabilization programs. Thus bank policies are linked to societal, structural, and governmental changes that go far beyond the areas of simple financial, transactions and encompass the nature and orientation of the political economy as a whole. The technocratic posturing and apolitical rhetoric of bank officials is a mask for far-reaching actions that are, first and foremost, political in the broad sense of the term.

The underlying basis for this crisis in international debt management lies in the deteriorating international economic position of the Third World, traceable to both rising import prices and relative falling export earnings. To deal with this situation, two sets of solutions have been proposed—one by the less developed countries and the other by the developed economies. The less developed countries have proposed a number of measures that would either alleviate the debt directly (through rescheduling or debt moratorium) or redistribute wealth by means of commodity-price agreements on exports. The developed countries, on the other hand, see the debt crisis in the Third World as the result of the oil crisis and the less developed countries' failure to deflate their economies and reduce import demand in reaction to the recent world recession.

The proposals advocated by the developed capitalist countries, therefore, have called for debt management through a belt-tightening process, the imposition of which is having an important impact on regimes, development policy, and political stability in the third World. Economic austerity is being imposed from within by less developed countries' governments and externally by international agencies, such as the

IMF, to deal with the debt repayment of the less developed countries. These austerity measures involve programs to reduce the consumption standards of the populations of the less developed countries through the following means: restrictive monetary and fiscal policies that deflate their economies; restriction on labor's right to strike as a means to hold down wage increases; income policies aimed at reducing real wages; and import controls and tariffs on imports.[25]

The political consequences of these policies have been riots, strikes, and the falling of governments from power. Often, less developed countries' governments have become more repressive in order to impose austerity measures, which reduce the standard of living of a recalcitrant population already living at a subsistence level. Riots in Egypt, civil war in Zaire, and strikes and the fall of several ministers of finance in Peru are recent examples. The developed countries, and particularly the commercial banks who recently have underwritten most of the less developed countries' debt burdens, are the real beneficiaries of this development strategy through austerity. This strategy is now being institutionalized and assisted by governments in the developed nations to the benefit of the private multinational banks.

U.S. Policy Toward Third-World Debts and Finance Capital

Having entered the Third World largely on commercial criteria, the multinational banks have become increasingly concerned about the problem of repayment and are continuing to encourage internal policy changes within the less developed countries. The multinational banks no longer see themselves as direct policymakers in the less developed countries, as was the case in Peru.[26] Instead, they are encouraging support for an expanded IMF lending capacity and a greater role for the IMF in the strict enforcement of austerity programs. In May 1977 U.S. Treasury Secretary, W. Michael Blumenthal, proposed that more formal links be established between the IMF and private banks in dealing with debtor countries: "It seems to me important, therefore, to give careful study to the possibilities of developing closer interaction, a smoother transition, between financing through the private market and official financing through the International Monetary Fund."[27]

Increasingly, private U.S. multinational banks are looking to the government to bail them out by providing public monies through foreign assistance programs to the less developed debtor countries, who can, in turn, use these public monies to pay off their private bank debt.[28] In this regard, the Carter Administration has recently encouraged an expansion of the IMF's lending capacity from its present $45 billion to $90 billion.[29] The linkage between the IMF and the U.S. government is supportive of the private banks' position. President Carter, in his March 25, 1977, press conference, echoed the strong support the government has shown for U.S. commercial-bank lending in the Third World, stating that, "I'm not in favor of a debt moratorium."[30] The United States would rather take a case-by-case approach to debt relief, which enables the state to employ the debt question as an instrument of U.S. foreign policy. Thus it can exert pressure directly or indirectly through the IMF or other multilateral or bilateral foreign assistance agencies to influence the internal policies and development strategy of particular less developed countries. This approach, of course, helps to ensure continuous repayment of the less developed countries' debt to the private banks.

The U.S. government is also concerned with the role of the commercial banks in the Third World because of the threat that they may pose to international monetary stability: If enough Third World countries default on their loans, the whole international monetary system may collapse. Concern for the stability of the international banking system and its linkage to the international monetary structure has been intensified by a number of recent bank failures in Europe and the United States and by some recent defaults and near defaults by debtor nations. These problems of international debt have been orchestrated in a number of publications, which illustrate the growing awareness of the seriousness of the debt situation.[31]

Of the bank failures, the first occurred in June 1974, with the closing of Bankhaus I.D. Herstatt of Cologne, one of West Germany's largest private banks. Herstatt had lost more than $200 million in foreign-exchange dealings. In October 1974 the most spectacular failure came when Franklin National Bank of New York, the twentieth largest bank in the United States, declared itself insolvent, even though the Federal Reserve Bank of New York had pumped $1.75 billion in emergency low-interest loans to help cover Franklin's foreign-exchange losses. This was the single largest bank failure in the history of the United States.

While the failure of Herstatt and Franklin National serve perhaps to dramatize the problem, they are not the only banks that have failed recently.[32] Furthermore, individual bank failures cannot be viewed as being isolated from other components of the international banking system. These individual bank crises have had an impact on other banks in the system because much of the current international bank activity is in interbank transactions. When a bank fails, it affects other banks doing business with that institution. For instance, in the wake of the Herstatt failure, two U.S. banks stood to lose more than $30 million in unpaid foreign-exchange commitments to Herstatt. Most of the recent losses appear to be the result of foreign-exchange speculation, which has become extremely volatile since 1971, when fixed-exchange rates broke down and not the result of default on debt. These losses, however, do illustrate the interdependence of American multinational banking and its counterparts throughout the world and how bank failures because of interbank linkages can create instability in the international banking system.

The recent concern about bank failures has been heightened by the defaults and potential defaults of debtor nations, whose outstanding obligations to U.S. multinational commercial banks are in the hundreds of millions and billions of dollars, which could have a far-reaching impact in destabilizing the entire banking system. The Basel Agreement of July 1974, in which the Board of Governors of the Bank for International Settlements (the central bankers' central bank) agreed that each nation's central bank should make good the losses of its branches, suggests that the central bankers do give credence to the domino theory of international banking—that several bank failures could set off a chain reaction throughout the interbank network and perhaps bring the whole system down.

Because of this Cassandra-like prediction, the U.S. government is now encouraging the creation of the IMF's Witteveen facility to provide financing, over the next two or three years, of $25 billion to help offset the burden of the less developed countries' debt.[33] While this facility has not been established in theory to bail out private banks that have lent unwisely or excessively, the banks will certainly benefit directly from its establishment. On January 23, 1978, the House Banking, Finance, and Urban Affairs Committee approved the U.S. contribution to the Witteveen facility of $10 billion.[34] This public bail out of the commercial bank is not new for the IMF, as was reported in a recent *Washington Post* article: "A study released yesterday charges that a substantial amount of money the International Monetary Fund funnels to developing countries now goes to repaying old, high interest loans made by private multinational banks, rather than to development projects."[35]

The relationship between the state and the international lending institutions is clearly procommercial bank and probusiness.[36] Professor Albert Fishlow of the Department of Economics, University of California, Berkeley, in testimony before the Senate Foreign Relations Committee in September 1977, provided some definition to the symbiotic relationship among business, the state, and the international lending institutions:

For every dollar that went out in debt to the developing countries, about one and one-half dollars has been estimated to have come back in increased demand for exports from the industrialized countries. So one does have a very tightly connected system here between the nature of the debt and the industrialized countries in the real sense and not merely the financial.[37]

The relationship between the banks and the state in the industrialized countries is seen as one of mutual benefit and provides support for the IMF's Witteveen facility. The risk, assuming the capacity of the developed state is vis-à-vis the commercial banks, is on the increase, given the enormity of the debt problems in the less developed countries and the negative impact that they may have on the stability of the international financial system. Recent testimony before the Senate Foreign Relations Committee in 1977 suggests that international agencies (World Bank, Export-Import Bank) and the regional multilateral development agencies (Inter-American Development Bank, Asian Development Bank, or African Developmnt Bank) also should come to the assistance of the commercial banks. What has been suggested is a rather significant swap between the private commercial banks and the officials banks. For example, it has been proposed that the World Bank would issue its bonds to private commercial banks and, in turn, would accept some of the portfolio loans to developing countries that the commercial banks currently have outstanding.[38]

The commercial banks and the state therefore have been employing the leverage of the looming international financial crisis from international debt as a bargaining tool to shift the burden of debt to public institutions. Whether or not the crisis is real is difficult to evaluate. However, for most less developed countries, default is almost a nonalternative because of the consequences. Although austerity is difficult for the lower classes to absorb, the resulting impact of default could mean economic and political chaos for the ruling classes, including a precipitous drop in essential imports. The weakening of the import capacity in many less developed countries could also damage continued growth of multinationals from the advanced economies. Thus it seems that default is not a real possibility for most less developed countries, and that developed states such as the United States and their commercial banks will continue the process of international indebtedness, so long as the commercial bank can continue to make profits and so long as the labor force of both developed and underdeveloped countries can be made to absorb the cost.

Notes

1. U.S. Senate, Subcommittee on Foreign Economic Policy of the Committee on Foreign Relations, *International Debt, the Banks and U.S. Foreign Policy* (Washington, D.C.: U.S. Government Printing Office, August 1977), p. 1.

2. Andrew A. Beveridge and Philip Wellons, "Societal Effects of International Bank Lending," unpublished, 1977, pp. 29-32.

3. Ibid., p. 56.

4. David O. Beim, "Rescuing the LDC's," *Foreign Affairs*, vol. 54, July 1977, p. 1.

5. *International Debt, the Banks and U.S. Foreign Policy*, pp. 9-10.

6. See "Two LDC Borrowers Justify the Worries," *Business Week*, June 5, 1978, p. 58; *Latin American Economic Report*, vol. VI, no. 15, April 21, 1978, p. 113; *Latin Ameican Economic Report*, vol. VI, no. 20, May 26, 1978, p. 154; *Latin American Economic Report*, vol. VI, no. 19, May 19, 1978, p. 146; *New York Times*, April 27, 1977, p. A5, and April 5, 1976, pp. 51 and 53. Also see the exchange between A.C. Weed of the World Bank and James Petras and Robert LaPorte in *Foreign Policy*, no. 8, Fall 1972, pp. 159-165.

7. See "Bankers Put Welcome Mat Out for Argentina," *Latin American Economic Report*, vol. VI, no. 13, April 7, 1978, p. 97; "Chile Returns to Favour with Foreign Bankers," *Latin American Economic Report*, vol. V, no. 25, July 1, 1977, p. 98; James Petras and Morris Morley, *The United States and Chile* (New York: Monthly Review Press, 1975), pp. 43-78; "The Brazilian Gamble," *Business Week*, December 5, 1977, pp. 72-81;

and "Latin America Opens Door to Foreign Investment Again," *Business Week*, August 9, 1976, pp. 34–38.

8. See "Even before Zaire the Outlook Was Bleak," *Business Week*, June 5, 1978, p. 69.

9. See James Petras and Juan Manuel Carrion, "Contradictions of Colonial Industrialization and the Crises in 'Commonwealth' Status," unpublished, 1977.

10. See Cheryl Payer, *The Debt Trap* (New York: Monthly Review Press, 1975).

11. See "Brazil Takes Harder Line on Transnationals," *Latin American Economic Report*, vol. VI, no. 15, April 21, 1978, p. 114; and Richard J. Barnet and Ronald E. Müller, *Global Reach* (New York: Simon and Schuster, 1974), pp. 152–53.

12. Barnet and Müller, *Global Reach*, pp. 153–55.

13. It should be noted that some countries have no restrictions at all on capital outflows, making data on private nonguaranteed debt from such countries more difficult to obtain. The only source of such data is a direct survey of individual private enterprises, which is difficult.

14. U.S. House, Committee on International Relations, 95th Congress, First Session, July 26–27, 1977, *Dollars, Diplomacy and Development* (Washington, D.C.: U.S. Government Printing Office, 1977), pp. 37–38.

15. *International Debt, the Banks and U.S. Foreign Policy*, pp. 53–54.

16. Ibid., p. 51.

17. Howard M. Wachtel, *The New Gnomes: Multinational Banks in the Third World* (Washington, D.C.: Transnational Institute, 1977), pp. 20–21.

18. See World Bank, *World Debt Tables*, vol. I, September 2, 1977, p. 221, for an appreciation of the extent of this problem.

19. U.S. Senate, Report to the Subcommittee on Foreign Economic Policy of the committee on Foreign Relations, *Market Power and Profitability of Multinational Corporations in Brazil and Mexico* (Washington, D.C.: U.S. Government Printing Office, 1977).

20. Paul M. Sweezy, "Multinational Corporations and Banks," *Monthly Review*, vol. 29, no. 8, January 1978, pp. 8–9.

21. *Latin American Economic Report*, vol. V, no. 13, April 1, 1977, p. 51.

22. See Payer, *The Debt Trap*; Jose Serra, "The Brazilian 'Economic Miracle,' " in James Petras, *Latin America from Dependence to Revolution* (New York: John Wiley and Sons, 1973); and Irma Adelman and Cynthia Taft Morris, *Economic Growth and Social Equity in Developing Countries* (Stanford, Calif.: Stanford University Press, 1973).

23. See Wachtel, *Multinational Banks in the Third World* (Washington, D.C.: Transnational Institute, 1977), pp. 23–37.

24. See *Latin American Economic Report*, vol. V, no. 25, July 1, 1977, p. 99; and *New York Times*, March 21, 1976, p. 3.

25. Wachtel, *Multinational Banks*, pp. 28–29.

26. *Dollars, Diplomacy and Development*, p. 85.

27. Remarks by W. Michael Blumenthal, Secretary of the Treasury, International monetary Fund Conference, Tokyo, May 24, 1977.

28. Cheryl Payer, "Will the Government Have to Bail Out the Banks?" *The Banker's Magazine*, vol. 16, no. 2, Spring 1977, pp. 86–87.

29. Bernard D. Nossiter, "U.S. Urging Allies to Join 16 Billion Dollar Expansion of the IMF," *Washington Post*, April 1, 1977, p. D11.

30. Wachtel, *Multinational Banks*, p. 38.

31. See Emma Rothschild, "Banks. The Coming Crisis," *The New York Review of Books*, May 27, 1976, pp. 11–22; P. A. Wellons, *Borrowing By Developing Countries on the Eurocurrency Market* (Paris, 1977); and Gordon W. Smith, *The External Debt Prospects of the Non-Oil Exporting Developing Countries* (Washington, D.C.: Overseas Development Council, October 1977).

21. In October 1974 several other major international banks announced major losses on foreign-exchange trading: Banque de Bruxelles admitted losses of $25 to 79 million; Union Bank of Switzerland lost $47.3 million; and the Lugano Branch of Lloyds of London lost $79.2 million.

33. U.S. Senate, Subcommittee on Foreign Economic Policy of the Committee on Foreign Relations, *The Witteveen Facility and the OPEC Surpluses* (Washington, D.C.: U.S. Government Printing Office, 1978), pp. 25–26.

34. Howard M. Wachtel and Michael Moffitt, "Bailing Out Banks that Strait Jacket the Third World," *Washington Star*, February 12, 1978, pp. D1–D4.

35. Dan Morgan, "Much IMF Help Goes to Repay Commercial Loans, Study Finds," *Washington Post*, June 25, 1977, p. 1.

36. See, for example, R. Peter DeWitt, *The Inter-American Development Bank and Political Influence* (New York: Praeger, 1977) and James F. Petras and Moris Morley, *The United States and Chile* (New York: Monthly Review Press, 1975) for a more detailed analysis of the U.S. probusiness influence in international lending institutions.

37. *The Witteveen Facility and the OPEC Surpluses*, p. 57.

38. Ibid., pp. 61–63.

6

A New International
Division of Labor?

A number of theorists have called into being a "new international division of labor," in which the old colonial division of labor involving Third World exports of raw materials and importation of finished goods has been transcended.[1] According to this new division, Third World countries have been industrialized to produce cheap labor-intensive manufacturing goods to be exported to the core capitalist countries for more advanced capital-intensive goods. The proponents of the new division of labor argue that the accompanying industrialization of the Third World reflects the new, world capitalist rationality and logic.

In order to assess these assertions, we will examine forty-seven countries drawn from a World Bank study, which has data for both 1960 and 1976. In 1976 in 85 percent of selected Third World countries, primary commodities accounted for 70 percent or more of exports. Furthermore, in half of these countries primary commodities accounted for upward of 90 percent of their exports. (See Table 6.1.)

What is striking about these results is the *continuity* in the pattern of the world division of labor twenty years after most countries have achieved formal independence. Despite the growth of industrial production in many areas of the Third World, the main role of Third World countries in the capitalist world economy is still as suppliers of primary commodities. It is clear that trade diversification and the growth of industrial exports were not greatly influenced by the political changes accompanying independence. It appears that the continuing socioeconomic links with the markets and classes within the core capitalist countries are stronger than changes in political leadership.

The evidence thus far does not substantiate the claim by the advocates of a new international division of labor (NIDL): the overwhelming majority of Third World countries are still predominantly exporters of primary producers.

The NIDL argument might take the form of arguing that as Third World countries become more "developed," they will begin to modify their position in the world division of labor. If we consider their level of income (again using World Bank measures) and divide them into low-

Table 6.1 Country Groupings by Percentage of Total Exports Accounted for by Primary Exports (N = 47)

Percentage of exports primary commodities	Percentage of countries	
100 to 90	42.6	
89 to 80	21.4	85.4
79 to 70	21.4	
69 to 60	2.4	
59 to 50	2.4	
below 50	16.7	

Source: World Bank Development Report 1979 (Washington: World Bank, 1979).

income/middle-income countries, we find that over four-fifths of the middle-income countries are predominantly primary goods exporters (70 percent or more), compared to less than three-quarters of the low-income countries. (See Tables 6.2 and 6.3.)

Clearly, the level of development in the national economy is not a good indicator of any propensity among Third World countries to shift their role within the international division of labor. In low-income countries like Pakistan and India, the great unevenness in development manifests itself in the growing industrial-export sector side by side with typical Asiatic poverty. In the middle-income countries, the huge labor pools, massive infusions of outside funding (initially, at least), and products of politico-military strategic interests have led to industrial exports in the three leading countries (South Korea, Hong Kong, and Taiwan).

It is clear that the simple growth of income within Third World countries is not incompatible with a continuing dependence on primary-commodity exports. In fact, the industrialization for export patterns seems to be more attracted toward the lowest-income countries, rather than the higher-income countries.

While the old division of labor still defines the global relationship between Third World and core capitalist countries, there is a *trend* away from this pattern. Almost two-thirds of the selected countries show a

Table 6.2   Percentage Share of Primary Commodities by Level of Income

	1960	1976	Percentage Difference 1960–76
Low-income countries			
Ethiopia	100	98	+ 2
Mali	96	99	− 3
Burma	99	99	0
Malawi		96	
India	55	47	+ 8
Pakistan	73	43	+ 30
Tanzania	87	91	− 4
Sri Lanka	99	86	+ 13
Haiti	100	49	+ 51
Central African Republic	98	82	+ 16
Kenya	88	88	0
Uganda	100	100	0
Indonesia	100	98	+ 2
Middle-income countries			
Egypt	88	73	+ 15
Cameroon	96	90	+ 6
Ghana	90	99	− 9
Honduras	98	90	+ 8
Nigeria	97	99	− 2
Thailand	98	81	+ 17
Yemen Arab Republic		87	
Philippines	96	76	+ 20
Congo Peoples Republic	91	87	+ 4
Papua/New Guinea	92	99	− 7
Morocco	92	84	+ 8
Ivory Coast	99	92	+ 7
Jordan	96	79	+ 17
Colombia	98	78	+ 20
Ecuador	99	98	+ 1
Republic of Korea	96	12	+ 74
Nicaragua	98	84	+ 14
Tunisia	90	74	+ 16
Syrian Arab Republic	81	90	− 9
Malaysia	94	84	+ 10
Algeria	93	99	− 6
Turkey	97	76	+ 19
Mexico	88	69	+ 19
Jamaica	95	44	+ 51
Chile	96	95	+ 1
Republic of China (Taiwan)		15	
Costa Rica	95	71	+ 24
Brazil	97	75	+ 22
Iraq	100	100	0
Argentina	96	75	+ 21
Iran	97	99	− 2
Trinidad and Tobago	96	94	+ 2
Hong Kong	20	3	+ 17
Singapore	74	54	+ 20

shift in exports toward nonprimary goods between 1960 and 1976. (See Table 6.4.) The claims of the NIDL are grossly exaggerated, but there is some basis for examining *modifications* of exchange within the global marketplace. However, the general trend of diversification still has a long way to go, and almost one-quarter of the countries show no changes or are *increasingly* dependent on primary-product exports. Moreover, in analyzing this trend it is important to examine the rate of change. We examined thirty-two countries from the World Bank sample, for which we have data for a sixteen-year period. (See Table 6.5.)

Table 6.3 Comparison of Low-Income and Middle-Income Third-World Countries and the Percentage of Exports Accounted for by Primary Products, 1976 (N = 47)

Level of income	Percentage of countries with 70 percent primary exports or over	Percentage of countries with less than 70 percent primary exports
Low	72	23
Middle	82	18

Table 6.4 Comparison of Percentage Exports of Primary Commodities among Selected Third-World Countries, 1960–76

Third-world countries decreasing percentage of primary commodities in exports	63.8
Third-world countries increasing percentage of primary commodities in exports	17.0
Third-world countries maintaining percentage of primary commodities in exports	8.5
No data	6.4

Table 6.5 Percentage Increase of Nonprimary Exports among Industrializing Countries, 1960–76 (N = 32)

Percentage increase		Percentage of countries	
Less than 5	18.8	low	37.6
5–10	18.8		
11–20	40.6	medium	40.6
over 20	21.9	high	21.9

The actual growth of industrial exports indicates a very diverse pattern: More than three-quarters of the selected countries evidenced low to moderate growth, while only slightly more than one-fifth demonstrated substantial growth. In evaluating these growth figures, one should also remember that most Third World countries started with very low base figures, and the subsequent striking gains still leave many heavily dependent on primary commodities. Of the twenty countries showing substantial increases of nonprimary exports, thirteen, or 65 percent, still were heavily dependent (70 percent or more) on primary-product exports. In fact, in only seven countries do nonprimary products account for more than 50 percent of the total (Hong Kong, India, Pakistan, South Korea, Taiwan, Haiti, and Jamaica).

By focusing on these exceptional seven cases, NIDL advocates have attempted to theorize about the Third World while overlooking the particular strategic military *political* positions that some of these countries occupied in the global confrontation between capitalist and socialist countries (namely, Hong Kong, South Korea, and Taiwan) and the historical roots of *national* industrial development (India).

Moreover, in part, industrial growth and diversification of exports have been stimulated by exports to nonmetropolitan countries, quite the opposite of what NIDL theorists propose. For many of the more dynamic industrializing Third World countries, regional expansion is becoming much more central to their growth patterns.

The trade patterns of the past are only partly evidenced in the destination of the exports. Among the low-income Third World countries, exports to nonmetropolitan areas account for 37 percent and 34 percent in 1960 and 1976. Among the middle-income Third World countries, there has been a shift upward from 29 percent to 33 percent in the proportion of industrial exports to nonmetropolitan areas.

It is within this context, in which most countries continue to depend on primary commodities and only a very few have achieved industrial diversification, that a limited trend toward "a new international division of labor" should be discussed. By 1976 about 52 percent of the low-income manufacturing exports and 64 percent of the middle-income exports were going to the core capitalist countries. Among the more industrialized Third World countries, textiles and clothing accounted for 20 percent of Indian, 32 percent of Pakistani, 36 percent of South Korean, 30 percent of Taiwanese, and 44 percent of Hong Kong's industrial exports. The predominance of textiles and clothing suggests the fragile and limited nature of the industrial push, even in these, the most dynamic third World countries. Essentially, the availability of cheap labor for labor-intensive manufacturing is a major consideration in the advance of industry, but it is hardly a basis for sweeping assertions concerning a new international division of labor.

The NIDL theorists have obscured many of the fundamental issues that confront the Third World. Rather than seeing the growth of a new division of labor growing from the logic of industrial capital in the metropolitan countries, the real issue is the very limited opening of industrial markets in the metropole, the constraints on industrial financing, the construction of barriers to the transfer of technology, and so forth. The intellectual bankruptcy of the NIDL theorists reflects their incapacity to analyze the class forces that shape state policy in the metropole and the real behavior of the multinational corporations. Operating from an abstract deductive model of capitalism, haphazardly selecting illustrative "cases" to buttress their arguments, they have failed to consider that more than 90 percent of multinational industrial production in the major countries of Latin America is geared toward capturing the internal market.[2] Fixated by the Hong Kong–South Korea–Taiwan experience, they fail to come to grips with the major conflicts between North and South precisely over the *incapacity* of the Third World countries to break into new markets and the intransigence of the metropolitan countries in resisting the creation of a new international division of labor. What industrial exports there have been is mainly a result of the combined pressures of bourgeois Third World countries and limited sectors of metropolitan competitive capitalism (electronics, clothing and so forth). The NIDL theorists have been largely taken in by the rhetoric of Trilateral Commission position papers, which are *not* the operating basis on which the economic policies of the member nations are formulated.

The very terms with which the NIDL arguments are framed are suspect. The notion of "industrialization" means different things in different settings.[3] In the metropolitan countries it refers to the routinization of innovative large-scale research and development, elaboration of machinery, processing, assembly, sales, and shipping. In the periphery "industrialization" refers to only elements: All of the technology is imported, as is much of the machinery and sales. Moreover, in many countries the location of industries is contingent on a specific set of social factors—low wages, no taxes, no strikes—which, on the one hand, limit the "spread effects" of industrial development and, on the other, could lead industry to pack up and abandon a country if their conditions changed.[4] Both the historical and contemporary experiences should lead to the rejection of the simplistic notions that Western "industrialization" is the "mirror" of the East.

A closer look at the nature of Third World industrialization shows that much of it is assembly plants, involving little industrial training and investment. Moreover, the growth of free-trade zones in Southeast Asia, Mexico, Central America, and the Caribbean, in which the corporations, for all intents and purposes, exercise sovereignty in the areas of production means that the production is "national" only in the most vacuous, juridicial sense: The territory is "national," but the operations, laws, and production are in fact run by foreign nationals. Moreover, the fragmented nature of industrial production in most Third World countries suggests that we are not dealing with integrated processes of production, but with partial and limited production controlled and dependent on metropolitan forces.

Clearly, capitalism is transforming more and more of the Third World. Primary products are being subjected to mechanization, transportation and commercial expansion are being promoted by the capitalist state, and industrial processing of agro-mineral products is clearly on the ascent. Within the national political economy, industry is growing and primary-goods production is declining. Proletarianization is accompanied and exceeded by the growth of a mass of semiproletarian rural and urban labor pools with temporary and seasonal employment. Yet this industrial growth is overwhelmingly dependent on the continued growth of traditional exports to finance and sustain it.

Moreover, the most dynamic growth sectors of industry are not only internal, but are largely directed to the purchasers of durable goods, namely the 20 percent of the population found in the affluent middle and upper classes. The *lack* of a new international division of labor, and the dismal prospects of Third World countries achieving even 15 percent of world industrial exports by 1990, heightens the internal contradictions between a growing industrial capacity and an ever-increasing surplus labor force uprooted from primary production. Rather than looking for a new division of labor, we can expect a new round of Third World labor-based social revolutions.

Notes

1. See Folker Frobel, Jurgen Heinrichs, Otto Kreye, "The New International Division of Labor: Origins, Manifestations and Consequences," (Mimeographed); and Bill Warren, "Imperialism and Capitalist Industrialization," *New Left Review* (September/October 1973). See also Martin Landsberg, "Export-Led Industrialization in the Third World: Manufacturing Imperialism," *The Review of Radical Political Economics* 2, no. 4, pp. 50–63.

2. See James Petras, "Comment l'Amerique latine alimente la prosperite des Etats-Unis," *Le Monde Diplomatique*, August 1979, p. 3.

3. Philip McMichael, James Petras, and Robert Rhodes, "Industrialization in the Third World," in James Petras, *Critical Perspectives on Imperialism and Social Class in the Third World* (New York: Monthly Review Press, 1979), pp. 103–36.

4. James Petras and Juan Manuel Carrion, "Contradictions of Colonial Industrialization and the Crises in Commonwealth Status: The Case of Puerto Rico," in Petras, *Critical Perspectives on Imperialism and Social Class in the Third World*," pp. 253–70.

7

The Revival of Fascism

Throughout many areas of the Third World, highly repressive regimes have become firmly ensconced as part of the "permanent" scenery, one might say.[1] For some observers this phenomena is associated with the general problem of "backward areas" or, more politely, underdeveloped countries: Lacking the political experience and traditions of the West, the dictatorial regime is the best that can be expected.[2] For others, the current regimes are merely continuations of past "authoritarian traditions"—more organized (bureaucratized) perhaps, but firmly wedded to a past in which government by the few was the norm.[3] Both of these approaches emphasize (1) the *internal* factors that lead to the repressive structures, and (2) the *continuation* with the past, i.e., more repression by the same type of regime.

These views of the recent wave of repressive regimes are fundamentally wrong. First, the origins and proliferation of repressive regimes are not products of internal developments, but responses to demands that originate primarily on a global level. Second, the organization and functioning of the state and its relationship to economic processes and social structures is vastly different from the dictatorial state of the past. The term that best expresses the *character* of this new state and its relationship to the class structure and economic system is "neo-fascist."[4] Fundamentally, the state exists through the permanent and pervasive direct use of force, coercion being the key element that binds the varying classes together in productive relations. The ideological element in rulership is clearly secondary and restricted to the few. "Authority" is embodied by the figures of force.

There is little sense in which authority is freely recognized as a source of legitimacy. The submission of the citizens to the state is not based on the recognition of legitimate authority, but on the *fear* generated by the use or threat of force. Hence, the "authoritarian" tradition is subsumed within a larger universe of *violence*, which pervades all of society and affects all areas of social life. The proliferation of government by military officials does not result in their transformation into political and economic functionaries. Rather it reflects the penetration of political and economic life by the instrumentalities of violence. Education and labor relations are dictated and enforced by the official whose direct contact is with repressive forces, whether military or police. That the officials of violence become involved in bureaucratic roles and routines within bureaucratic structures says little about the dynamic linkages that allows them to draw upon the tools of violence, to circumvent the procedures and lines of authority of bureaucratic organization, and to engage in extrabureaucratic modes of repression. In some ways, the bureaucratic structure is a facade, an alibi that disguises the multiple forms of repression and the arbitrary nature of the state. In this sense, the notion of bureaucratic authoritarianism itself is an ideology that serves to mystify the violent and arbitrary nature of the state.[5]

This analysis of the neo-fascist state will proceed through a discussion of its organization, economic role, and ideological rationale, and then proceed to compare and contrast Third World neo-fascism and European fascism.

Defining the Neo-Fascist State

Several features that characterize the neo-fascist state are found in other types of states, but it is their combination that distinguishes one from the other. The formation of the neo-fascist state reflects its "alienated" character. The origin, maintenance, and defense of the neo-fascist state are strongly dependent on the activities of the metropolitan state. This factor accounts for the disproportionate power of the state over the rest of civil society, as well as its relative autonomy from particular pressures and demands within the society. The organization of the neo-fascist state is substantially the result of the insertion of part of the metropolitan state apparatus within Third World politics and the promotion of an ensemble of state apparatuses—notably the military and police bureaucracies.[6] The sustenance of these apparati by the advanced capitalist countries leads to their technological development and staffing far in advance of the rest of society. The "overdeveloped" features of the neo-fascist state offer a prime example of the external alliance that nurtures it.

The second feature of the neo-fascist state is the permeation of society by the forces of order and violence: Terror and purges, recurring activities, vary in intensity and scope.[7] The growth of paramilitary forces from the "regular" police and military forces complements and attempts to disguise the direct involvement of the highest levels of government in the processes of physical coercion. The routinization of repression (including the widespread use of torture, assassination, and kidnapping) is thus accompanied by the absence of regular juridical procedures; arbitrariness is the norm, and each "norm" (including those previously established by the regime) can be preemptorily rescinded. These methods of rulership are based on the concentration and centralization of power within the executive branch—a structure that completely subordinates all "representative" organs of civil society to the mandates of the dictatorial executive. The scale and scope of physical coercion (and the organization of the state to engage in its systematic application) are central ingredients of the neo-fascist state, but cannot be considered apart from its socioeconomic and ideological components.

The neo-fascist state in the initial period is essentially repressive: an apparatus geared toward destroying the organizations of mass mobilization, annihilating militants, or, in a specific sense, systematic mass demobilization. But this initial function does not exhaust its historic characteristics. Rather, this "revolution," as its supporters refer to it, is the basis for "reconstruction"—that is, the creation of policies, institutions, and conditions for a particular type of socioeconomic development. The neo-fascist state hence has the second essential function of creating the conditions of large-scale, long-term economic expansion based on the promotion of multinational capital.[8]

Thus the very process of demobilization of the masses flows into a policy of creating optimal conditions for capitalist development: The process of repressing the left is directly linked to "disciplining" the labor force for capitalist production; the elaboration of infrastructure projects through the growth of state firms is linked with the growth of foreign investment in manufacturing, minerals, and agriculture. The neo-fascist state, through the extension of a multiplicity of state activities, inserts itself as a complementary force promoting foreign growth. Nevertheless, the centralization of state power, the command of the state over internal resources, and the growth of state firms produce a "nationalist" component within the neo-fascist regime that conflicts with foreign capital on a series of issues within their common economic development project. Absolute political control creates, in some factions of the neo-fascist regime, a desire to extend the power of the state into the economic sphere, competing and displacing foreign capital.[9] This national fascist element is held back by the long-term dependence established within civil society and the state, and by the fact that it has little independent basis outside of the military and within the neo-fascist institutional arrangement.

In rejecting the "nationalists," the mainstream neo-fascist currents in the regime embrace several other ideological strands: the doctrine of national security, anti-Communism, traditional revivalism, and economic modernization. Depending on the particular history, culture, and region, the ideological rationale of neo-fascism has varied. What all these ideological doctrines possess, however, is a rejection of a class definition of society as a means for defining instruments for repressing class conflict. National security doctrine allows the regime to promote itself above the class structure as the guardian of the "national interest," defined as the existing class hierarchy.

Beginning in the 1960s, more and more neo-fascist regimes began to legitimate their rule through the doctrine of national security: The abolition of parties, elections, and trade unions was justified by the neo-fascists under this doctrine. As a corollary, the notion of "internal war" was developed in place of international confrontation. The subordination of civil society to the regime was a logical outcome. In the Third World it served to atomize the working class and subordinate the national bourgeoisie to international capital. Nevertheless, the contradiction between the neo-fascist espousal of the political doctrine of *national* security and their economic subordination to foreign capital has weakened the appeals and effectiveness of the doctrine, except within the confines of the state-multinational complex, where it has taken on the character of a holy writ. Policies and measures are defined in terms of their contribution to national security.

The doctrine of national security frequently has been coupled with strident attacks on "Communist" opponents, who are portrayed as enemies of national security and representatives of foreign powers. Anti-Communism and the demonology associated with it are used by the regime to focus attention away from the issues of inequality and dependence and to ally itself with all of the most retrograde groups in the society and to subordinate itself to Western powers. The appeals of anti-Communism are usually tied to traditional revivalist evocations: the promotion of religious moralistic authority. These appeals together, however, are complemented by the idea of economic modernization. Borrowing a page from Western social-science literature (and, earlier, European fascist sloganeering), the neo-fascists justify their regime through economic growth figures—the growth of industry, exports, total income, and so forth. The "modernization" rhetoric conveniently cloaks the levels of exploitation, concentration of income, and living conditions of the labor force.

Thus the ideology of neo-fascism attempts to harness traditional reactionary beliefs and authorities to the dynamic of externally induced capitalist expansion. Ideological appeals vary by strata: for the elite, the doctrine of national security; for the masses, anti-Communism and traditional morality. The neo-fascist regime produces its own ideological synthesis—importing and combining "modernization" with "traditionalism" as instruments for ideological domination—while applying the doctrine of "national security" and "anti-Communism" to legitimate physical repression.

European Fascism and Third-World Neo-Fascism

Contemporary Third World neo-fascism shares with its earlier European counterpart a number of features. Both regimes rely heavily on terror and repression to sustain capitalist socioeconomic order and to promote its development. In both cases, ideology has been a major component within the regime, defining objectives and adversaries and exalting the regime. In both, the organization of the state permeates civil society and subordinates all social organization. Past and present versions of fascism concentrate power far beyond traditional authoritarian and democratic states and provide no checks on the degree and kind of coercion. This configuration is what defines the essential fascistic nature of the regimes. Yet the variations and differences within this common framework are substantial and consequential for the evolution of the regimes and in the kinds of contradictions that can emerge. The differences involve economic development patterns, ideological elements, and the social basis of support.

Classical fascism was strongly oriented toward internally based national economic development: The state and the national bourgeoisie were the twin engines for organizing and mobilizing resources and investment for expansion.[10] The firm bonds between the national bourgeoisie and the fascist state gave some substance to its claims to being a "movement of national revival." In contrast, the neo-fascist state funtions essentially within and as an instrument of dependent development: External finance and investment, export markets, and so forth, are the lifeblood of the regimes' economic strategy. The contours of policy are essentially based on "external linkages." The appeals of the regime and its sources of support may originally be directed toward a broad array of forces, but over time the evolving economic decisions concentrate increasingly on an alliance of the neo-fascist state and the multinationals.

These differing economic strategies reflect the different social bases that increasingly define the variations in trajectory of fascism in the dependent and advanced capitalist countries. In the initial moment of the fascist seizure of power, especially in moments of crises and polarization, there is the possibility of securing a mass base of support. This mass base is very heterogeneous and contains classes with contradictory interests. Nevertheless, given the expansive and national character of classical fascism, its full employment policies are able to sustain substantial support beyond the initial seizure of power. In the case of neo-fascism, given its dependent character and the lack of any commitment to mass employment, the support of the national middle classes and lower-income groups that may have been attracted initially by its ideological appeals begins to dissolve. The disintegration of the amorphous base of support is accelerated by the economic model that shunts the national bourgeoisie to a secondary role. The growth of state power and the expansion of the multinationals limit the space within which national capital can function. The depression of salaries undermines the local market, further eroding the basis of middle-class support. The lack of mass support, in turn, precludes the formation of mass parties and organizations, features that are prominent in European fascist and corporative experience. The military remains the vertebrae of the movement: The bureaucracy becomes the "shell" out of which the fascist regime operates, rather than the mass party.[11]

With these differences in social base and economic strategy, there emerge differences in ideological appeals: The classical fascist emphasis on mass appeals of nationalism and social-imperialism is translated by the neo-fascist in appeals to "national security," directed toward an elite constituency. Some neo-fascists engage in expansionist forays (Indonesia in East Timor and Brazil's continental visions), but they are lacking in mass appeal and support and operate within the sphere of influence of great powers. While both promote rabid anti-Communist campaigns, the neo-fascists generally omit the explicit racist and anti-Semitic ideas found in the earlier version of fascism.

Instead, contemporary fascists are more directly concerned with the *class* content of the opposition: anti-Communism without anti-Semitism leads to a more distilled, concentrated attack on the class basis of anticapitalist politics. Rather than the old, irrational appeals to "blood," the new appeals are to "modernization"—through the blood and sweat of the labor force. Large masses of cheap labor pools that are available for exploitation within and outside the "export platforms" cement the bonds between the neo-fascist regimes and the multinationals, just as scapegoating of Jews served to create bonds between the fascist state and the petty bourgeoisie.

The pillaging of labor in the name of development is no more rational under the Brazilian, Indonesian, or Korean neo-fascist regimes than European fascism's destruction of so-called inferior races was in the name of the greater fatherland.

The differences between fascism and neo-fascism have important consequences for the development of contradictions. The demise of classical fascism was essentially a result of external expansion that conflicted with the established powers, leading to rivalries, war, and defeat. Neo-fascism based on internal exploitation has intensified a series of vertical and horizontal conflicts involving labor and the middle classes against the regime and the multinationals. The tension between a narrowing economic base and the erosion of ideological appeals and mass support, on the one hand, and the constant search for an institutional formula to stabilize and legitimate rule, on the other, has led the neo-fascists to seek means of disguising the fascist content of the regime through cosmetic changes (controlled and rigged elections, amnesty). On a more sophisticated level, ideologues attempt to emphasize the rational/technical side of the regime, selecting for emphasis the developmental elements and the formal structure of power. Hence, neo-fascism becomes transformed into "bureaucratic authoritarianism," in which capitalist class rule is "replaced" by various notions of bureaucratic domination, and authority is replaced by terror.[12] That the neo-fascist state exacts a price for meeting the demands of the capitalist class in no way subtracts from the essence of the situation: The operations of accumulation and profit-taking are greased by the hands of the gendarmes and technicians of the fascist state.

Neo-Fascism and Accumulation on a World Scale

The emergence of neo-fascism in Third World countries of disparate historical backgrounds and internal social structures suggests that a common *external* factor operates along with internal processes. The emergence of neo-fascism in Chile, Brazil, Uruguay, Argentina, Indonesia, South Korea, and Iran under the Shah and the tendency for regimes to develop policies that evolve in the same direction among a larger number of countries suggest that we are dealing with a world-historical phenomenon.

The process of neo-fascist formation is not, however, a product of a whole society moving inexorably toward a common goal. Rather, it is the product—indeed the direct result—of conflicting classes (and even at times competing segments within the same class) operating within a social formation but drawing support and being informed by social forces acting at the global level. The central fact that informs the emergence of neo-fascism on a worldwide basis is the growth of the accumulation of capital on a world scale. This singular "coincidence" of course is not fortuitous, as we will demonstrate.

Since World War II, U.S. investment and assets abroad have multiplied severalfold, whether in direct investment, loans, or the capture of local savings through bank subsidiaries.[13] Moreover, a growing proportion of trade between Third World countries is actually exchanges between subsidiaries and home corporations—accounting for 35 percent of total trade in Latin America.[14] The expansion of imperial capital has gone far beyond the enclave plantation-mining systems of the past. Today, it embraces the totality of economic activities covering the whole country: manufacturing, services, communications, finance. The extent of control and the earnings through management contracts, technology, and sales have mounted tremendously in recent years. Alongside this global process of accumulation, select countries have emerged as specific targets for large-scale, long-term investments—countries whose policies and practices facilitate the unimpeded growth of capital with a maximum of political guarantees. In most cases, these are neo-fascist regimes or those that most approximate the model. It is fairly clear that neo-fascist regimes have been most effective in creating an investment climate conducive to large-scale, long-term external flows of capital.

Although the process of capital accumulation and reproduction follows from the logic of the capitalist mode of production, the decisions concerning the choice of areas of expansion, and "risks" accompanying expansion are largely political questions.[15] The appropriation of surplus value has always been accompanied by conflict between labor and capital. The problem for capital is to locate in areas and economic activities where the level of conflict is compatible with optimal rates of profit. The specific problem facing imperial capital in the 1960s and 1970s was that huge capital surpluses needing to expand into new areas of high profits confronted an increasingly mobilized labor force, which was intensifying the constraints on the mobility of capital, its rates of exploitation, and its very possibilities to exist.

The problem for expanding capital, then, was that its global perspective was coming into conflict with the particular social forces emerging within specific social formations that offered the most lucrative prospects for expansion—namely, Brazil, Argentina, and Indonesia, among others. The type of political solution that was fashioned had to respond to several imperialist imperatives:

1. The regime had to develop *comprehensive controls* over the entire labor force and political spectrum, for capital's new sweep embraced the whole society, not just the "enclaves."
2. The regime had to retain control *indefinitely* and not be a mere caretaker regime, for mature capital was not interested in speculative adventures, but in long-term investments—thus necessitating long-term guarantees of stability.

The neo-fascist formula fit both requirements. The regime's permeation of society and its sense of "historical mission" have served to provide the guarantees that corporate capital has required. The resolution of inner conflicts through "reversion" to violence, purges, and arrests has highlighted the constant need to renew the commitments to capital, lest political situations emerge that violate the guarantees to investment.

Massive inflow of capital, substantial industrial growth rates, and the high levels of absolute and relative exploitation accompanying neo-fascism promoted foreign capital development. The neo-fascist "alternative" to class conflict and national development based on social revolution is the large-scale capitalist transformation of society, encompassing massive inequalities, social rigidities, huge surplus labor pools, and forms of recolonization, i.e., the establishment of export platforms in which the multinationals, for all intents and purposes, possess territorial sovereignty.[16]

Neo-fascism emerges as stimulus for and consequence of capital accumulation on a world scale. Blocked by nationalist or militant working-class organizations, the multinationals join with reactionary military officers, local businessmen, and conservative petty bourgeois to overthrow populist regimes and massively purge civil society of opposition, establishing in its stead the neo-fascist state. In many cases, the evolution to neo-fascism is facilitated by the presence of multinational capital and its demands for tighter controls and expansion. The specific policies pursued by the regime to optimize conditions for capital expansion include:

1. *Control over labor*: imposition of labor bureaucrats; restrictions or abolition of strikes, meetings, elections; wages fixed at low levels to maximize profit; job security weakened, giving employers absolute freedom to change the composition of the labor force and intensify exploitation.
2. *Freedom from fiscal obligation*: low tax rates; tax holidays; exemptions on exports; import of machinery.
3. *Public subsidies*: land grants free; industrial parks constructed and leased at little or no cost; infrastructure constructed (ports, railroads, communications); loans provided at low interest; access to local savings.
4. *Guarantees against expropriation*: nationalization partial or for expedience is accompanied by market-value compensation.
5. *State development complements development of private enterprise*: no risk of competition or absorption by state.

The effective implementation of these conditions by neo-fascist regimes has resulted in large-scale flows of capital and extensive investment in a variety of areas, including raw materials, light and heavy manufacturing and assembly, and services (tourist, shipping). The industrial growth rates in Brazil, South Korea, Taiwan, Singapore, and Malaysia attest to the capacity of the regimes to fashion the requisite conditions for foreign capital exploitation. In this context, high growth rates are an index of the high rates of exploitation and repression. The extraordinary growth of exports similarly attests to the absolute freedom of corporate capital to function in relation to world demand and the constraints imposed on the demands of the local labor force (i.e., the internal market). The class basis of neo-fascist development policy is evident in the contrast between large-scale foreign flows of funds—loans and investments—high industrial growth rates, growing export markets for capital on the one hand, and, on the other hand, by low levels of social participation, declining or stagnant standards of living, and increasing costs of food and essentials for the mass of labor. These contrasts, which in a democratic society would lead to explosive conflicts, are held in check by the sustained and pervasive use of force, which characterizes neo-fascist rule.

Neo-Fascism: The All-Purpose State

Two final points should be made. First, neo-fascist regimes are not merely concerned with "economic" questions; they are also concerned with political and strategic issues in the global confrontation of classes and nations. Moreover, internal classes and institutions play an essential role in carrying out and sustaining the regime and share in the benefits. Second, neo-fascism confronts severe pressures, both internally and externally, that have a constant tendency to erode its base of control.

The neo-fascist state, in addition to its economic role, serves functions at the national and international level that buttress Western capitalist interests. Contrary to those writers who focus on and contrast "Western democratic values" and neo-fascist behavior, the predominant relation between the Western democratic capitalist regimes and Third World neo-fascism is complementary and not conflictive, although specific conflicts certainly emerge from time to time.

Politically, the neo-fascist regimes sustain military and police ties that serve to provide the Western countries with support in containing local and regional revolutionary forces: For example, Thailand and South Korea were prime examples of support and collaboration during the United States' effort to suppress the revolution in Vietnam; Morocco's troop deployments were valuable to the French in Zaire; and Brazil's funneling of funds to Chile against Allende aided United States' efforts. At the international level, at forums and in efforts to create regional blocs, the neo-fascist states have functioned effectively to weaken or undermine Third World solidarity. For example, Chile withdrew and weakened the nationalist impulse within the Andean Pact.[17] Neo-fascism, with its strident anti-Communism, reinforces and supports Western positions against revolutionary states in such international forums as the United Nations. Nevertheless, tensions develop between the immediate needs of neo-fascist regimes to consolidate their power through terror and the Western governments' dependence on democratic norms to maintain legitimacy. Other conflicts develop over the tendency for the neo-fascist state to enrich its supporters and the needs of the corporation for an efficient administration that sustains services.[18]

The "costs" of the expansion of the state apparatus and the impositions upon the corporation are also areas of contention. The activation and expansion of state enterprises can lead to areas of conflict and negotiation between neo-fascist regimes and the corporations. Finally, the aggressive pursuit of exports through state subsidies by the neo-fascists can lead to conflicts with the metropolitan state, especially in times of high unemployment.[19] In this context, metropolitan states may toy with the idea of "democratizing the state," essentially a reshuffling of the regime to weaken the statist push, cover the criticism from the "human rights side," and weaken the competitive trade position of the regime.

The neo-fascist state thus, in pursuing its short- and long-term positions, creates tensions—between its need for a repressive machine and its need to convert the state into an instrument for economic development, requiring a minimum flow of ideas, external exchanges, and recruitment of skilled labor. The state in neo-fascist society faces the task of sustaining a position of "strength" (repression) against labor and a position of permeability and accessibility toward the multinationals, combining both selectively with rival cliques of national capital. The process of institution-building involves creating elaborate state structures of control over labor/populace without jeopardizing the sense of "freedom" essential for capital growth. The regime must be internally dynamic, providing a variety of measures to promote extensive/intensive exploitation, and externally dependent, looking to outside sources to promote trade, investments, and technology. Neo-fascism embodies the principles of a politically closed and economically open community.

In conclusion, the appearance of neo-fascism in Asia and Latin America is linked with a common process of economic development from the "center." There is a necessary interrelationship between long-term, large-scale capitalist development from the outside and fascism, *given* high levels of class and nationalist conflict *prior* to the initiation of the process. In this sense, repressive regimes are not merely a function of an economic development strategy or a phase of industrialization, but rather an outcome of a combination of political, social, and economic processes that emerge at both the national and international level.

Notes

1. For a résumé of some aspects of repression in the Third World (although not exclusively of the Third World); see *Amnesty International Report: 1977* (London: Amnesty International Publications, 1977).

2. Samuel Hintington, *Political Order in Changing Societies* (New Haven: Yale University Press, 1968).

3. The articles by Stritch, Wiarda, and Pike are especially relevant in Frederick Pike and Thomas Stritch, (eds.), *The New Corporatism* (Notre Dame: University of Notre Dame Press, 1974).

4. For a discussion of fascism in Latin America, see Marcos Kaplan, "Hacia un Fascismo Latinoamericano?" *Nuevo Politica* (Mexico), no. 5-6, April–September 1977. See also his *Estado y Sociedad* (Mexico: UNAM, 1977). See also *Revista Mexicana de Sociologia*, vol. 39, nos. 1 and 2; both issues are devoted to the "State and Political Process."

5. For a general statement of this perspective, see Guillermo O'Donnell, *Modernization and Bureaucratic-Authoritarianism: Studies in South American Politics* Berkeley: Institute of International Studies, University of California at Berkeley, 1973). The approach grossly understates the kind and quality of repression, exaggerates the autonomy of the bureaucracy vis-à-vis the class structure, understates the role of imperialism, and confuses the "technocratic" posture of middle-level functionaries and the important ideological elements in the running of the regime. Finally, this view sees its "bureaucratic authoritarianism" as a mechanism for "deepening" industrialization, rather than as a product of the push of capital flows from the outside *and* the class conflicts within a country. The approach too narrowly conceives of the economic dimension (tying it to a particular phase of industrial expansion, ignoring developments on a world scale and the emergence of fascism prior, during and after the "deepening" process) and the singular importance of class conflict, which create the "need" for the deepening of repression. See Liliana de Riz,

"Formas de Estado y desarrollo del capitalismo en America Latina," *Revista Mexicana de Sociologia*, vol. 39, no. 2, April–June 1977.

6. Michael Klare, *Exporting Repression* (Washington, D.C.: Center for International Studies, 1977).

7. The number of deaths, jailings, and exiles run into the hundreds of thousands and, in some cases, higher: In Indonesia about 500,000 were killed after the 1965 fascist coup, and hundreds of thousands of others were jailed; in Chile the total approaches 25,000, and in Argentina 15,000 to 30,000; Uruguay has similar figures. See *Reports of Bertrand Russell Tribunal on Repression in Latin America 1974–1976* (Rome, 1976).

8. Comparisons of the flow of financial aid before and after the fascist coups in Brazil and Chile bear this out. See James Petras and Morris Morley, *United States and Chile* (New York: Monthly Review Press, 1975), pp. 165–66; for a further discussion of Chile, see Orlando Letelier, *Chile: Economic Freedom and Political Repression* (Washington, D.C.: T.N.I. Publications, 1976).

9. Brazil is a prime case of efforts to project a national-independent course out of a period of extreme dependence. Unfortunately, this nationalist effort has been greatly exaggerated by some writers, who focus on specific policies in particular conjunctures and overlook the larger financial technological dependence.

10. Franz Neumann, *Behemoth: The Structure and Practice of National Socialism 1937–1944* (New York: Octagon Books, 1963).

11. In Latin America the centrality of class politics over the bureaucracy is shown by the shifts and adjustment in military personnel and politics as a result of class pressures from the imperial center; in Chile the chief of the secret police is pushed out and "amnesty" is declared (including the criminals in the police force). In Brazil efforts by the state bureaucrats to control oil exploration and expand at the expense of the multinational corporations is attacked. See *Business Latin America*, March 15, 1978, pp. 86–87; *Latin America Economic Report*, vol. VI, no. 19, May 19, 1978, p. 151. The tug and pulling between state bureaucrats and the multinationals over the terms of exploitation can be seen over the issue of the cost of technology. See *Latin America Economic Report*, vol. VI, no. 9, March 3, 1978, p. 66.

12. Candido Mendes, *Beyond Populism* (Albany, N.Y.: Graduate School of Public Affairs, SUNY/Albany, 1977).

13. Richard J. Barnet and Ronald E. Müller, *Global Reach* (New York: Simon and Schuster, 1974), pt. II, pp. 123–212.

14. *Transnational Corporations in World Development: A Reexamination*, United Nations Center on Transnationals, April 1978, Sales No. # 78 IIA5.

15. On the role of the imperial state, see Petras and Morley, *op cit*, Preface.

16. Tsuchiya Takeo, "Free Trade Zones in Southeast Asia," *Monthly Review*, vol. 29, no. 9, February 1978, pp. 29–41.

17. James Petras and Morris Morley, "Comment le pacte andin fut vide de sa substance," *Le Monde Diplomatique*, April 1978.

18. Edouard Bustin, "The Problem in Zaire: A Corrupt Regime," *Christian Science Monitor*, May 26, 1978.

19. "United States Attacks Brazil's Trade Policy," *Latin America Economic Report*, vol. VI, no. 21, June 2, 1978, p. 166.

8

The Socialist International and Social Democracy in Latin America

The Scope of Social Democratic Growth

In the past few years Latin America has witnessed a veritable explosion of activity by the European Social Democratic parties and the Socialist International. Conferences, meetings, and visits between party leaders and prospective and actual members have been accompanied by funding for research, leadership training, political organizing, and even for guerrilla warfare (in Nicaragua). There is hardly a country in Latin America that does not contain at least one party (and, in some cases, two or more) or movement that is not associated with or in contact with the European Social Democratic movement. Operating through Party organizations, as well as through foundations such as the Frederich Ebert Foundation, European Social Democrats have developed a solid and growing base among the nationalist and populist parties, as well as among labor-based parties.

In Latin America, Frederich Ebert Foundation's most important operation is CEDAL (Centro de Estudios Democraticos sobre America Latina), a conference center and training facility located twenty minutes from San José, Costa Rica. "La Catalina," the center's more familiar name, regularly hosts regional youth-leadership training courses, election campaigning courses, "think-tank" strategy sessions, and political meetings. The latter range from political gatherings of Costa Rica's Partido de Liberación Nacional (PLN) to solidarity meetings. Moreover, Social Democratic ideological influence has spread beyond its formal membership, as evidenced by the renewed emphasis on popular-front coalitions, stage theories of revolution, and classless democracy found in many of the political pronouncements of Latin American political leaders and intellectuals.

The advances of Social Democracy are evidenced in the fact that at least two governments are under their control (Dominican Republic and Jamaica), while in at least two other cases (El Salvador and Nicaragua) they participated in mixed juntas. Beyond that, they have a strong presence in Venezuela, until recently controlling the government and still in command of the trade union apparatus, and they are a growing influence in Bolivia (Movement of the Revolutionary Left, or MIR) and Brazil (Brazilian Labor Party, or PTB).

Many of these linkages were forged during Latin America's long period of exile, when the European Social Democrats provided a haven to leaders fleeing the dictatorial onslaught of the 1960s and early 1970s. More than 400 Latin American political refugees, the majority from left-wing political parties, have scholarships from the International University Exchange Fund (IUEF; FIIU in Spanish), which is based in Geneva. The bulk of IUEF's funding for its Latin American Program comes from Western European government aid agencies. IUEF is very close to the Socialist International (SI) networks in England, Sweden, and Germany especially. This external material support and, presumably, the arguments put forth by the Social Democratic leaders convinced some of the Latin Americans that their future lay with the evolutionary rather than with the revolutionary paths of the past.

The ideological attraction of Social Democracy lay in its willingness to countenance movements that expressed "socialist" goals, criticized U.S. imperialism and intervention, and opposed the extreme right-wing dictatorships dominant in the region—*and* avoid the label of being a Communist subversive. The formula of being a *left oppositionist with Western legitimacy* seemed to provide the protective umbrella that would allow the exiles to return to mass organizing. Membership in the Socialist International would allow Latin American oppositionists to draw on European support in periods of "emergency": the threat of economic sanctions, diplomatic pressure, and political isolation by European Social Democratic governments or opposition could stay the hand of repression. Thus economic resources, political legitimacy, and organizational support have been the principal factors that have revitalized Social Democracy in Latin America.

As will be discussed later, some of these very "assets" in refloating Social Democracy as a political movement of opposition are historic liabilities in tackling the area's long-standing problems. There are several reasons why some Latin American leaders have turned toward the Social Democrats, but why have the Social Democrats taken such a widespread and deepening interest in Latin America? In recent years Europe and Japan have made significant inroads on U.S. dominance, displacing the latter as the main trading partner of Brazil, Argentina, Paraguay, and Uruguay, as well as exceeding the United States in importing goods from Chile, El Salvador, Nicaragua, and Peru. The overall decline in U.S. control over Latin America's export trade is demonstrated by difference in trade shares between the United States and Europe and Japan, which declined from 17 percent in 1953 to 9 percent in 1976. The same pattern appears to be true on the investment side.

It is hard to avoid completely the conclusion that the pink flag of Social Democracy may be following the green mark of German capital. An additional important incentive for European Social Democratic Third World expansion was the Europeans' recognition, following the 1973 oil crisis, of their "dependence" on Third World for raw materials trade. Much of the leadership for the SI in developing better Third World ties came from Willy Brandt following his May 1974 resignation as German chancellor. The growth of overseas European expansion and especially in certain areas of Latin America is indeed one of the salient characteristics in recent years. Large-scale, long-term investments and trade relations require close working relations with governmental and nongovernmental political leaders to facilitate contracts and licensing agreements, tax and labor arrangements, and so forth. While the Europeans have been able to work well with the incumbent military regimes, they have not felt altogether comfortable with them for several reasons: (1) the military has long-standing previous ties with U.S. business interests and, in some cases, was brought to power with U.S. assistance, thus lessening European access and influence; (2) the Europeans are wary of the stability of these regimes and avoid the kind of experience that the United States recently had in Iran; and (3) European labor movements have directly experienced fascist and dictatorial movements and are less sanguine about supporting them in Latin America than their counterparts in the AFL-CIO, hence there exists a strong pressure within the labor and left to limit economic relations with the dictatorial right.

The Social Democratic unions throughout Europe are mostly all members of the International Confederation of Free Trade Unions. The ICFTU has had relatively little direct influence among Latin American trade unionists because the AFL-CIO (which left the ICFTU in 1969) has always retained membership in the ICFTU's regional organization ORIT (Organización Regional Inter-Americana de Trabajo). In fact, the AFL-CIO dominated the "international" relationships of ORIT's Latin American affiliates either directly or through the American Institute for Free Labor Development (AIFLD). The Europeans and Canadians (Canadian Labour Congress, or CLC) are now involved in a struggle to dislodge the Americans from their hegemonic position within ORIT. For example, in order to sidestep the AFL-CIO's opposition to boycotts (especially those that did not include Cuba), the CLC hosted an ICFTU meeting to inaugurate its Subcommittee for the Defense of Trade Union and Human Rights in Latin America. Being an ICFTU, not ORIT, meeting the Americans were not present. It was following the subcommittee's second meeting (in Caracas, July 23-27, 1979) that the ICFTU's General Secretary and several other members traveled to Nicaragua and helped to establish an emergency aid program. The Latin Americans who identify themselves as "socialist" trade unionists line up with the Europeans and Canadians, while the hardline "anti-Communists" stand close to the AFL-CIO. The "socialist" line is fighting an uphill battle because of the persuasive influence of the Americans as a result of their funding programs. European and Canadian funding for various "trade union" courses is now beginning to match that of the Americans.

Other indications of growing SI-oriented influence includes: the substitution of ORIT's General Secretary, Julio Etcheverry, by Juan José Del Piño. Not as closely identified with the U.S. trade union movement as Etcheverry, Del Piño was previously the head of the Venezuelan Petroleum Workers Federation and was nominated to ORIT executive as a CTV (Confederación de Trabajadores de Venezuela) representative. The CTV is known to represent the Social Democratic "left" within the ORIT. As well, both Del Piño and ORIT's press officer, Javier Sandoval, were special delegates at the SI Congress held in 1978 in Vancouver.

A further erosion of AFL-CIO influence was seen when three centrals, which are particularly close to it, and AIFLD were expelled from the ICFTU at its World Congress, held in Madrid on November 19-23, 1979. The centrals were charged with "having been accomplices in the oppression and violation of human rights in their respective countries." At the same World Congress, two Latin Americans were elected to the ICFTU who are not closely identified with the AFL-CIO: Mañuel Penalver from Venezuela's CTV and Fidel Velázquez from Mexico's CTM.

Although SI-oriented influence does not completely dominate the membership of ICFTU/ORIT, what is significant is the shift that has occurred over the last five years (U.S. influence in ORIT was one of the major tensions dominating the discussion at the ICFTU's World Congress in 1975, held in Mexico City). It is also important to keep in mind that in many countries the centrals affiliated to CLAT (Latin American Workers Central—Christian Democrat; in turn, part of the World Confederation of Labor, or WCL) have a more progressive Social Democratic stance than the ICFTU affiliates. This is true in Honduras (where CLAT's Central General de los Trabajadores is more militant than ICFTU-ORIT's Confederación de Trabajadores de Honduras) and Nicaragua (CLAT's Central de Trabajadores de Nicaragua versus CUS [United Trade Union Center—pro-U.S.]).

These objective interests—economic, political, and ideological—have operated within the *European context* to generate an interest in Latin American Social Democracy. This orientation converges with several objective factors operating in Latin America. Latin America has been experiencing relatively high levels of industrial growth, accompanied by the expansion of commercial agriculture. The combined economic processes of industrialization and commercialization have greatly increased the absolute, if not relative, size of the wage-labor force. However, the political conditions facilitating this economic growth have been largely defined by autocratic states that have merely attempted to harness the labor forces to the needs of capitalist accumulation through pseudorepresentative, state-controlled "corporatist" organs. Large-scale inflows of overseas capital responded to the capacity of the dictatorial state to contain class conflict. The great concentration of labor, an outcome of capital growth, has led, however, to "illegal" or semilegal parallel organizations to those set up by the state. The lack of representation of the officials organs, the exploitative conditions accompanying capitalist expansion, and the lack of political autonomy of the workers' movement became the basis for new struggles and organizations. Because the severe state repression that preceded and accompanied the process of growth was especially directed at the revolutionary left, it was not and is not in a postion to capitalize on the growth of mass discontent. Many of its militants were killed and its activities continue to be severely circumscribed, limiting its ability to reach out publicly to the vast new strata in motion. Moreover, much of the mass opposition has as its immediate preoccupation the recovery of living standards and elementary political rights—demands that are not incompatible with the program and leadership of consequential Social Democrats.

This burgeoning popular movement has little interest in the regional organizational vehicles floated by the American AFL-CIO. Historically linked to U.S. intelligence agencies, corporate interests, and right-wing movements, U.S. trade unions and liberal political groups have little appeal in Latin America. Moreover, the issues that are being contested in Latin America involve a combined political and trade union struggle that exceeds the narrow boundaries set forth by the business unionist leadership of the AFL-CIO. Thus a "vast space" exists in Latin America for European Social Democracy. The growth and scope of the working class in the region lends itself to the "labor-based" movements in Europe; the dictatorial nature of the developmental regimes allowed the Social Democrats to play the role of consequential fighters for democracy; and, finally, the weakening of the revolutionary left and the bankruptcy of the AFL-CIO provide few competitive challenges, at least in the short run in some countries.

New Orientations of Social Democracy

For many years social democracy was dormant and something of a joke in Latin America. European Social Democratic parties concentrated almost exclusively on promoting capitalism and welfare provisions within each of their nation-states and developing ties largely within the European context. In Latin America, parties describing themselves as "social democratic," such as APRA in Peru, Acción Democratica (AD) in Venezuela, and the National Liberation Party in Costa Rica, had long ceased to be innovative reform parties. Indeed, they had turned into conservative bureaucratic apparatuses linked to foreign and domestic business groups, promoting policies that had little to do with their populist-nationalist rhetoric.

Although at least two of these parties remain in the "socialist fold," the resurgence of popular movements in the region has required the Socialist International to move beyond the crusty anti-Communist rhetoric and programmatic confines of these older members to a more "radical" adaptation to the new members that they have recruited or are seeking to draw into the fold. The shift from the older, more conservative Social Democrats to the new forces is clearly evident in the efforts to win over major elements of the Sandinista Movement in Nicaragua—especially the more moderate elements, Brizola and the Brazilian Labor Party, the New Jewel Movement in Grenada, and so forth. In addition, the trade unionists and some sectors of the leadership of the Dominican Revolutionary Party (PRD), the nationalists, populists, and democratic socialists in Jamaica's People's National Party (PNP), sections of the Radical and Socialist Party of Chile, and the Nationalist Revolutionary Party of El Salvador all reflect the "new reformism" *within* the Latin American sections of Social Democracy. Altogether, ten Latin American parties are members of the Socialist International.

The recent attempt to widen and deepen the influence of Social Democracy began in April 1976 in Caracas, when a meeting was held to discuss the new oppotunities opening on the continent. Under the sponsorship of Venezuela's AD, then the governing party, the basis was laid for expanding contacts and connecting up with new forces emerging in the area. In March 1978 Mario Soares, the Portuguese socialist responsible for containing the mass revolutionary upsurge of the mid-1970s and known within the Socialist International as the "German's man," headed a delegation to Mexico, the Dominican Republic, Venezuela, Jamaica, and Costa Rica. The delegation established further contacts with groups and individuals from Brazil, Bolivia, Ecuador, Uruguay.

The results of this organizing drive and the successful electoral efforts of the PRD in the Dominican Republic had a snowball effect—evidenced by the presence of twenty-nine Latin American organizations at the SI Congress in November 1978, including the Puerto Rican Independence Party and the FSLN of Nicaragua. A special working group on Latin America was established, through Swedish initiative, headed by Michael Manley of Jamaica with Peña Gómez of the PRD as secretary. In addition, the Congress named four Latin Americans as vice-presidents: Manley of Jamaica, Oduber of Costa Rica, Gonzalo Bárrios of Venezuela, and Anselmo Sule of Chile.

The elections and appointments reflect the jockeying for position within the Socialist International between the more reformist Swedish section and the more capital-oriented German section. Barrios and Oduber reflected the old-guard conservative business-oriented Social Democrats that the German SPD favors, while Sule, Peña Gómez and Manley represent the new, more populist, nationalist groups favored by the Swedes. German strength within the SI was expressed by Willy Brandt's role as initiator of SI's reinvigorated "internationalism," his role as its president, and the fact that the SPD contributes 60 percent of the SI's total budget. It would seem that the SI is willing to accept the FSLN's radicalism and grant it international support in exchange for the SI's own identification with the Sandinistas—a valuable political commodity for a growing movement with continental aspirations.

While it would be a mistake to exaggerate the differences among the European Social Democrats and underestimate their cooperation and common purposes, it is important to note the different context in which they operate and the different nuances in their approach. The German Social Democrats operate within a context of massive growth of overseas capital and growing trade ties in Latin America, staunchly promoted by the policies of the Schmidt Government. The links between the Ebert Foundation, Social Democratic research funding agencies, and German big business are intimate and closely monitored. The proposition that German Social Democracy is oriented toward creating a political base for German capital in Latin America is generally accepted in European circles. The orientation of the Swedish Social Democrats in Latin America is less directly tied to capital. Swedish overseas capital is less prominent and dynamic. Also, the interests of Swedish trade unions, especially the metalworkers, is more concerned with preventing the flight of Swedish capital to low-wage areas and, hence, are more interested in monitoring working conditions of Latin American workers employed by Swedish multinational capital. The less direct linkages between Swedish Social Democracy and capital thus allows them greater flexibility and more options in dealing with new radical and leftist forces in Latin America. Having said that, however, it should be clear that the Swedish Party still is part of the Socialist International and still operates out of a capitalist system, thus limiting its anticapitalist options. What it does mean is that the Swedes have a greater tactical flexibility and capacity to penetrate areas that their German counterparts would find difficult.

Fluctuating Fortunes of Latin American Social Democracy

The experience of the past five years is sufficient for us to attempt to evaluate the recent experiences of Social Democratic movements in opposition and in power. Two major patterns seem to recur: (1) in opposition to right-wing military or civilian regimes, the Social Democratic movements have been able to gather broad support and even, in a number of cases, to take control over the government; (2) in power, the Social Democrats have failed to implement their programs, sustain mass support, and retain political power; and (3) sharp divisions between the political leadership administering the state and the mass-based organizational apparatus lead to protracted internal struggles and occasional splits to the right and left.

In recent years two Social Democratic parties held office and eventually were ousted (AD in Venezuela and PLN on Costa Rica) and two parties have recently won elections (PRD in the Dominican Republic and PNP in Jamaica). In all four cases, maximum strength of the parties is derived from their national-populist-reformist programs *before* they are elected to office. In the case of Venezuela, despite enormous oil revenues, the gap between the Social Democratic promise and the developmental-capitalist reality was so great as to erode substantial sectors of the electoral base. The same process was evident in Costa Rica. The concentration of resources in promoting capitalist development, the linkages between party leaders and business, the lack of any comprehensive redistributive program, and the increasing polarization of wealth implicit in the model of capital accumulation certainly left nothing but "patronage" prebendary practices as the only forms of reward to the masses. The result was that the bourgeois–working-class alliances to welfare capitalism, championed by the parties, turned out to be more bourgeois than working class, more capitalist than welfare.

A similar process is occurring with the two remaining Social Democratic governments in the Caribbean. In Jamaica the Manley Government, which began with radical-reform programs of nationalizing foreign enterprise, mass mobilization, and income redistribution, has been turned into a regime whose economic and social policies are dictated by the International Monetary Fund, the policies of which have reduced living standards of wage workers by 20 to 30 percent. The mass demonstrations organized by the Jamaica Labor Party, the proliferating strikes, and the general discontent visible throughout the island suggest that Manley's Democratic Socialist government is well on its way out of office. The massive enthusiastic popular majorities of the recent past have been replaced by the angry, sullen faces of the unemployed crowding the slums of Kingston.

In the Dominican Republic a similar scenario is starting to unfold. The Guzman regime, elected by a mass popular landslide, has been increasingly hostile to the demands from the working class and even from its own trade union members—pursuing the same capitalist development policies of its predecessor, Joaquin Balaguér. Beyond their narrow electoral and civil liberties commitments, the Social Democrats have little to offer. No effort is made to alter the fundamental property, class, and state relations that perpetuate inequalities. Moreover, because of their dependence on private capital—both foreign and private—they are limited as to the kinds of income policies they can pursue.

Efforts to reform capital that conflict with the conditions for the accumulation of capital lead to flight and stagnation. Efforts to secure external finance bring in their wake the overt forms of intervention in governmental policymaking: The Social Democrats are forced to become the instruments for restructuring public spending, social services, and wage levels. These practices lead to divisions within the parties, further weaken their organizational capacity, and inevitably lead to the party's electoral demise. The very forces that facilitated victory in opposition—the alliances with capital, the "classless democracy," the welfare capitalist model—are the same ones that prevent comprehensive and consequential changes. The links to the Social Democrats that facilitate loans from the World Bank and the International Monetary Fund provide the occasion for these very same banks to liquidate the reform aspirations of their mass supporters. Our reading of recent history suggests that in Latin America, Social Democracy as a comprehensive and consequential social reform movement capable of sustaining popular support has been a dismal failure. Yet it is not dead in Latin America; on the contrary, in many areas it is *growing and will continue to grow*, given the conditions existing in Latin America and given the limited options that the masses have to choose from.

The Growth of Social Democracy in Latin America

In line with the previous discussion, in those areas *where social democracy is in opposition*, especially to military or dictatorial regimes, it will be able to enlist mass support on the basis of its democratic welfare program and the energetic financial and organizational support of the Socialist International.

In Brazil the return of Brizola and the formation of the Brazilian Labor Party should provide an organizing pole for the Social Democrats in the southern cities. Parallel efforts are being conducted to coopt the union leadership, especially among the metallurgical workers; the widespread discontent evidenced in the growing strike wave of public employees, construction, and metallurgical workers suggests that substantial gains can be made in the immediate period. In Bolivia the shaky alliance between the Siles Zuazo MNR and MIR (the Social Democratic forces), which recently won the election but were prevented from taking power, remains the major electoral force—although marginally influential over the bulk of the union movement. In Nicaragua the Social Democrats established a major beachhead through their connections with the group of professionals known as Los Doce and with segments of the FSLN. The enormous devastation and destruction wrought by the Somoza regime has left the regime in very dire straits—thus necessitating outside support, to which the Swedish Party has responded. The reticence of the rest of the SI is, in part, evidence of its concern with the revolutionary tendencies within the movement and its desire to secure their limitations. Toward the end of November the Germans finally agreed to provide $17 million in assistance, a meager contribution considering the needs of the Nicaraguans.

In El Salvador the National Revolutionary Movement broke ranks with the left-revolutionary opposition and joined a junta of self-styled reformist colonels and liberal businessmen. The "centrist" position of the Social Democrats is clearly illustrated: "Oppositionist" against the right-wing military, "counter-revolutionary" against the revolutionary left. Allied with the left against the fascist right, they become the allies of the bourgeoisie against the left in the postdictatorial period. When the regime was unable to carry out minimum reforms, and the left continued to grow, the Social Democrats abandoned the coalition, having accomplished nothing.

There are other examples of growing SI influence. In Panama General Torrijos has been attempting to institutionalize his power base through the creation of a mass-bureaucratic political party. The party, Partido Revolucionario Democratico, or PRD, was established with guidance from Costa Rica's Partido de Liberación Nacional (especially Alberto Monge's section), and PRD militants were sent to Spain to be trained by Felipe González's Socialist Party of Spain (PSOE) (González himself has been a frequent visitor to Panama). When the registration for political parties formally ended in July 1979, the PRD had 154,145 "signatures." The next runner-up was the Liberal Party (47,797), with the Broad Popular Front (an "opposition" grouping that is pro-Torrijos) claiming 34,693 signatures. No other parties gained the minimum 30,000 signatures, but Arnulfo Arias's Panameñista Party boycotted the registration. The PRD seems content to accept the organizational support of some SI parties without seeking formal membership itself. Association and not membership with the SI also means that PRD can claim not to be "controlled" from outside the country, a charge often directed at the Partido del Pueblo (pro-Moscow CP).

In Guatemala, although no party is officially a member of the SI, several are closely identified with it. The Partido Revolucionario (PR) at one time did characterize itself as Social Democratic and maintained some ties with the SI. The PR moved to the right and today participates as a member of General Romero Lucas's Government. One section of the PR that split off formed the Democratic Socialist Party (PSD) under the leadership of Alberto Fuentes Mohr. (Mohr was assassinated in January 1979, just as his party was being legalized). Another Social

Democratic grouping is the United Revolutionary Front (FUR), which under the leadership of Mañuel Colum Argueta gave tacit political support to the Lucas slate during the 1978 Presidential elections. The predecessor to the FUR was the Revolutionary Democratic Party (URD), founded by Colom Argueta, Adolfo Mijangos, and Francisco Villagran Kramer. Today Villagran Kramer is the vice-president of Guatemala. Colom Argueta was assassinated in March 1979.

While these groups remain in opposition, we can expect them to gain new forces, combining efforts with both the left and the liberal bourgeoisie. These political gains, however, will be short-lived once they assume responsibility for the state and have to choose policies that favor capital or labor. The "internal" demands of the wage earners for redistribution measures will come into conflict with the "external" demands of financial capital for wage constraints, free markets, and reductions in public spending. Capitalist members of the Social Democratic coalition will demand measures promoting growth and imposition of labor discipline, thus limiting any comprehensive working-class-supported reforms. In the end the contradictions of Social Democracy will produce the same fluctuating patterns among the new emerging groups that we have witnessed among their more established cothinkers. The logic of class struggle in Latin America cannot be encapsulated within the democratic class collaborationist formulas developed in Western Europe.

U.S.–Social Democratic Relations: A Final Note

At one level we can describe the emergence of the conflicts between Latin American Social Democracy and the military regimes as part and parcel of a conflict between U.S. capital and European capital. Longstanding U.S. capital is tied to the existing politico-military machines, trained and financed by the Pentagon. Newly emerging European capital, seeking to establish its place within Latin America, is tying its fortunes with the conservative and reformist civilian opposition forces seeking to diversify sources of finance, trading partners, and greater political independence from the United States.

From this perspective, the rival political forces are proxies for different variants of capitalist development, in which the democratic struggle against the dictatorships loses a great deal of its mass egalitarian character. While this perspective may overstate the importance of external ties in shaping the policies of movements and regimes, it nevertheless highlights the internal and external contradictions that face any attempt to impose reformist solutions in Latin America. No doubt the reformist movements have a substantial degree of autonomy, vis-à-vis their international benefactors, and they can take initiatives that go beyond those prescribed and practiced in Europe—as in some cases they will have to do to retain the minimum degree of popular support, i.e., nationalize property, expropriate selective landed estates, denounce U.S. intervention. Nevertheless, the framework of sectoral changes, class collaboration, and capitalist accumulation taken over from their European counterparts will define the overall pattern of development. The ideological competition between U.S.-based conservative "free enterprisers" and European-backed Social Democrats will continue and may, at times, take on the appearance of fundamental conflict. Nevertheless, it should be kept in mind that in the final analysis, faced by a socialist revolution, both Social Democrats and conservatives will bury their differences and cooperate in an attempt to isolate and defeat the revolution—as was recently the case in El Salvador, where the Social Democrats joined Church liberals, businessmen, and the military against the mass-led Popular Bloc Forces. In a revolutionary crisis, even the United States can find a use for Social Democracy.

APPENDIX

A Partial Listing of ICFTU Affiliates
in Latin America and the Caribbean*
(*These unions are also members of ORIT*)

Mexico	Confederación de Trabajadores Mexicanos (CTM), completely identified with PRI
Dominican Republic	CONATRAL (National Confederation of Free Workers), later CNTD (National Confederation of Dominican Workers).
	However, because the CNTD is closely identified with the United States and "yellow trade unionism," the new PRD government has been promoting a new central, UGTD (General Union of Dominican Workers). (ICFTU?)
Honduras	Confederación de Trabajadores de Honduras (CTH)
Panama	Confederación de Trabajadores de la Republica de Panama (CTRP)
Costa Rica	Confederación Costarricense de Trabajadores Democraticos (CCTD)
Nicaragua	Consejo de Unificación Sindical (CUS)
Guatemala	Expelled
El Salvador	Expelled
Paraguay	Expelled

*The AFL-CIO is *not* a member of ICFTU, but it is a member of ORIT (Inter-American Regional Organization of Workers). Presumably the three expelled members of ICFTU have retained their membership in ORIT (Central de Trabajadores Federados, CFT, Guatemala; Central General de Sindicatos, CGS, El Salvador; and Central Paraguaya de Trabajadores, CPT).

Venezuela	Confederación de Trabajadores de Venezuela (CTV)
Colombia	Union de Trabajadores de Colombia (UTC)
Peru	Confederación de Trabajadores de Peru (CTP)
Argentina	CATE and CGEC
Bolivia	CNTCB
Brazil	CNTC, CONTCOP, and CNTTT
Guyana	CGTU
Puerto Rico	FTPR
Trinidad	TTLC
Uruguay	CGTU
Ecuador	CEOSL

Note: Also an ICFTU and ORIT affiliate is Canada's Canadian Labour Congress (CLC).

Membership of the Socialist International:
(Latin America and the Caribbean)

Full-member parties

Argentina	Partido Socialista Popular (PSP, Popular Socialist Party)
Barbados	Barbados Labour Party (BLP)
Chile	Partido Radical (PR, Radical Party)
Costa Rica	Partido de Liberación Nacional (PLN, National Liberation Party)
Dominican Republic	Partido Revolucionario Dominicano (PRD), Dominican Revolutionary Party)
El Salvador	Movimiento Nacionalista Revolucionario (MNR, National Revolutionary Movement)
Jamaica	People's National Party (PNP)

Consultative parties

| Venezuela | Acción Democratica (AD, Democratic Action) Movimiento Electoral del Pueblo (MEP, People's Electoral Movement) |
| Paraguay | Partido Febrerista Revolucionario (PFR, Febrerista Revolutionary Party) |

Parties Informally Linked to the Socialist International†

| Bolivia | Movimiento Nacionalista Revolucionario de Izquierda (MNRI, Nationalist Revolutionary Movement of the Left) |
| | Movimiento de Izquierda Revolucionario (MIR, Left Revolutionary Movment) |

†These parties have participated at conferences held by the Socialist International or have sought SI support as a result of domestic repression.

Grenada	New Jewel Movement (NJM)
Uruguay	Frente Amplio (FA)
Guatemala	Frente Unido de la Revolucion (FUR, United Revolutionary Front). The PSD's National Director, Mario Solorzano Martinez, also participates on the International Committee for Latin America and the Caribbean.
	Partido Socialista Democratico (PSD, Democratic Socialist Party)
Nicaragua	Group of Twelve (Grupo de los Doce)
	Frente Sandinista de Liberación Nacional (FSLN, Sandinista National Liberation Front)
Mexico	Partido Revolucionario Institucional (PRI, Revolutionary Institutional Party)
Argentina	Union Civica Radical (UCR, Radical Civic Union)
	Movimiento Peronista Montonero (MPM, Montonero Peronist Movement)
Brazil	Partido Trabalhista Brasileiro (PTB, Brazilian Labor Party)
Chile	Partido Socialista (Socialist Party)
Ecuador	Partido de Izquierda Democratico (PID, Left Democratic Party)
Panama	Partido Revolucionario Democratico (PRD, Revolutionary Democratic Party)
	Partido Socialdemocrata (PS, Social Democratic Party
	Movimiento Independiente Democratico (MID, Democratic Independent Movement). PS and MID are competing for recognition by SI.
Peru	Alianza Popular Revolucionario Americana (APRA, American Popular Revolutionary Alliance)

part two

CLASS CONFLICT AND REVOLUTION

9

Socialist Revolutions and Their Class Components

Any attempt to theorize socialist revolution must start at the point where conditions of exploitation are converted into the practice of class struggle. Socialist revolutions in the twentieth century have unfolded as complex processes decisively dependent on the emergence and growth of a revolutionary political organization. The central political organization (party or movement) passes through several crucial interrelated phases, *each* of which provides a unique contribution to the ultimate success of the whole enterprise. The sequence leading to the revolutionary transformation begins with the formative period, involving the organization and ideology of the party. This is followed by class and political struggles, in which forces are accumulated, roots are put down among the masses, a mass membership is won, and, finally, power is seized. Subsequently, the socialist revolutionary process includes the establishment of a government, reorganization of the state, and efforts to transform social relations.

The Origins of Revolutionary Organization

While later influences play an important part in shaping the form and content of the revolutionary process, the origins and initial organization of the revolutionary party play perhaps the key role. Critical to an understanding of the embryonic revolutionary organization is the political culture in which it is embedded—the degree to which class struggle and social mobilization have occurred. The insertion of the embryonic

153

revolutionary party into an ascending mass movement or within a politicized population is crucial in the creation of the collective experiences within which the cadres will frame their revolutionary programs. The cadres are the distillation of class struggles and the bridges between past struggles and the future revolution. As carriers of the early formative class experiences, they play a decisive role in determining the ultimate direction of the revolutionary process and in weaving its specific organizational forms, leadership, and ideology. But the cadres themselves, and the struggles they lead, are reflections of broader historic conflicts that provide the parameters within which particular actions and movements occur.

In Russia the events of 1905—the uprising of the working class and the formation of Soviets—propelled the Bolshevik Party forward, strengthening the socialist component in its ideological armory, creating cadres, and providing a historical reference for the social transformation in October 1917. In China the early workers' struggle provided the organizational and ideological direction that sustained the Communist Party on a socialist path, despite the shift of activity toward rural petty-commodity producers. The continuity of the revolutionary movement in China must be stressed against all those who attempt to submerge China's socialist revolution in a host of special features and events related to China's rebellious peasantry, the strategic wisdom of Mao, the nature of guerrilla war, the Japanese invasion (peasant nationalism)—all of which fail to explain the *particular moment* of revolutionary mobilization, or the *substantive changes* that took place after the revolution. China's socialist revolution did not take place during centuries of rebellious peasant movements; nor did it occur during more than a half century of imperialist invasions and guerrilla warfare; nor was the socialist orientation a product of Mao Tse-tung alone. The peasantry moved towards socialist revolution only after the worker-based Communist Party inserted itself in the country and after the peasants uprooted by Japanese imperial capital found an ideological and organizational expression in the Communist Party—and in no other party or army. Finally, Mao's own strategic orientation toward the class-struggle road to socialism, and even his fundamental tactical commitment toward maintaining an autonomous army/party, were products of the experiences of the 1921-27 period (although drawing lessons from the negative experiences of subordination to the Kuo Ming Tang).

If we conceptualize the revolution as a protracted and complex process, we capture the historical importance of the formative period: the qualitative ideological and organizational factors that enabled the party to gain the allegiance of the great mass of exploited Chinese and ultimately to succeed in revolutionary combat. Any periodization of the revolution that focuses exclusively on the "Yenan period" (Mark Selden), the Japanese invasion (Chalmers Johnson), or the postwar disintegration of the KMT fails to explain the politics of each period.[1]

For each account presents particular features of an environmental setting (rural areas, peasantry; war-induced conditions, nationalism) as the basic determinants of the policy and direction of the revolutionary struggle. Yet these features affected all tendencies and political groupings within the political system, while only one—the Communist Party—was able to fashion a program and accumulate forces capable of taking it to ultimate success. The basis of this success was not conjunctural, but the result of a painstaking and continuous effort to create the human political resources needed to formulate tactics, strategies, and organizational structures through each conjuncture.

The central notions of class struggle, combining social and democratic revolution, derived from Marx and Lenin and embodied in the Chinese Communist cadre, contributed immensely to establishing a revolutionary strategic direction. The adaptions and nuances of application in the surrounding agrarian areas by Mao and his colleagues were innovations at the level of applied theory. The particular forms that armed struggle took—efforts to destroy the state—were based on classical Marxist-Leninist notions of the class character of the state. The same can be said concerning the politics of the revolutionary forces vis-à-vis the national bourgeoisie, although here Mao's analysis at times ran counter to his organizational practice: While arguing that such classes existed, he never allowed the party to become enmeshed in a subordinated alliance.

The party, founded on the principles of class struggle, baptized in the fire of mass urban struggles, proceeded to the countryside and reeducated a whole generation of rural laborers, petty-commodity producers, and their uprooted brethren in the ideology of class struggle and class politics. The fundamental politics of Yenan originated in the 1920s, as did the anti-imperialism that brought forth the anti-Japanese alliance. Without the basic cadre formed in the earlier phase, the mighty waves of peasant masses might have broken before the onslaught of the organized Japanese or KMT forces, leaving little long-term, large-scale change in the society. Thus the study of revolution as a process requires that the continuity and interrelatedness of each period be emphasized. Particular events mark historical moments, with particular configurations of forces. But without an understanding of the preceding sequence, the molecular processes of accumulation of forces, the end product of successful revolution, cannot be grasped. Each differential moment in the revolutionary process contributes to the understanding of the whole. The issue, in determining the final outcome, is to understand the relationship between each sequence.

Periodization and Ideology

The second basic requirement for a theory of socialist revolution is to differentiate correctly the periods in which different classes enter the revolutionary process. In periods of profound societal crises, classes enter into political and social combat unevenly, and in many cases political parties are not present to provide the organizational mechanisms through which they can act. Moreover, the moment of entry of a class—especially during a massive and tumultuous eruption—can bend the direction and orientation of the revolutionary movement. For example, in the case of the Cuban revolution the petite bourgeoisie and bourgeoisie entered the revolutionary movement in the late 1950s: that is, after the early founders of the 26 July Movement, but before the mass of workers and peasants who joined early in 1959. Thus these bourgeois, antisocialist forces neither held the organizational leadership nor had ties with newly awakened rural and urban workers. The prior presence of the Castro leadership—shaped ideologically by the earlier workers' struggles of the 1930s—ensured that the key posts and measures would not be controlled by bourgeois forces. The subsequent entry of the working class into the revolutionary movement, facilitating (and reflecting) the transformation in state power, undermined the position of bourgeois representatives in the government. The urban/rural workers became the dominant force in the revolutionary process after the uprising that overthrew Batista. The latter was merely one moment in the revolutionary struggle, whose crucial significance was that it facilitated the massive *arming of the working class*, which in turn was the critical factor permitting the overthrow of class relations.

The importance of periodizing the entry of different classes into the revolutionary process is highlighted by the fact that many writers, in seeking to identify the class character of a party, adopt an excessively numerical approach, which downplays the determination by specific social forces. In the case of China, for example, many scholars write off the relative importance of the working class because of the rural setting of much of the fighting and the fact that the revolutionary movement was predominantly composed of peasants. In the case of Cuba the same writers emphasize the presence of middle-class participants in the mid- to late 1950s as the central characteristic in defining the nature of the revolution, but they overlook both the earlier working-class struggles, which established a popular, anticapitalist political culture, and the later massive entry of rural and urban workers into the political movement.

While the revolutionary process encompasses a variety of social forces—and the timing of entry of these forces varies from situation to situation—it is important not only to count heads but to identify the qualitative position (power) of each social force within the movement. Early or late entry of the working class can be the decisive factor in propelling a revolutionary party or movement toward overthrowing capitalism and collectivizing the means of production. In Russia the working class was the central force initiating and sustaining the revolution; in China it initiated the struggle and the organization of the party; in Vietnam it initiated the struggle and sustained activity on a secondary plane; in Cuba it created a revolutionary culture that was vital for the formation of the Castro leadership and subsequently played a central role in the decisive social struggles after the political regime was transformed. In all cases, the revolution had a socialist character because working-class struggles profoundly influenced the ideas and practices of the revolutionary organization.

The third necessary element in theorizing socialist revolution is a differentiation of the levels at which various social forces participate in the revolutionary process. We can note six levels of organization: leaders, cadres, militants, fighters, sympathizers, and supporters. The ideology and formative experience of participants at each level reflect the particular moment in which they entered the struggle. This qualitative distinction is crucial, insofar as revolutions in the course of their successful trajectory attract a variety of social forces and thus may appear to be polyclass in character, or in some cases they may appear to have no working-class content. This was especially the case in China, where the great mass of militants and fighters were uprooted peasants and largely grounded in rural struggles. That the leaders and many of the cadres were directly or indirectly influenced by the workers' struggle and its ideology has been obscured in many accounts, which have focused on one level of the party organization and its "empirical" rather than its "historical" base. The long-term direction of the revolutionary process was primarily influenced by the historic base in the working class, not in the peasantry: The seizure of power led to the collectivization of production, not to the proliferation of petty-commodity production.

In the case of Cuba the bulk of the leaders and cadres were increasingly committed to building a mass party centered in the working class, even though a substantial number of sympathizers and supporters and even fighters came from bourgeois and petit-bourgeois strata. Because socialist leaders controlled key posts, despite a substantial number of anti-socialist supporters at one (the preinsurrectional) phase, the revolutionary movement could shift gears and expand support among rural and urban workers, creating a mass base of militants and fighters among them. Because the central core of the organization was composed of committed socialist revolutionary forces, the accumulation of petit-bourgeois support did not adversely affect the revolutionary trajectory of the movement. Located primarily in the subcadre levels of the revolutionary movement, the nonrevolutionary forces provided fighters or economic support but were not decisive for the historical content of the revolutionary struggle.

The fourth element in the theorization of socialist revolution concerns the central concepts and ideas that influence and shape the ideology of the revolutionary movement. The ideas are of two types: (1) the core notions that express the motivating forces and historic goals and methods of the revolution; and (2) the tactical/strategic ideas that express the conjunctural struggles and immediate needs of particular strata and organizations and reflect efforts to accumulate forces around the central party cadre. The key notions of twentiety-centry revolutionary socialist movements revolve around class struggle, imperialism, the class nature of the state, and the collectivization of the means of production. The tactical-strategic ideas vary from conjuncture to conjuncture, from one class and stratum to another. Tactical-strategic ideas are essentially directed toward a discrete problem area; for instance, a reform or set of reforms as a means of creating political alliances or fronts. Thus the tactics of a revolutionary socialist party may, at a certain moment, give the appearance of an agrarian-peasant movement, as in China during the 1930s, or of a democratic populism, as in Cuba in the 1950s, or of a nationalist movement, as in Vietnam in the 1950s and 1960s. The shifting terrain of revolutionary struggle requires tactical shifts and an accompanying ideological flexibility. Nevertheless, these changes are informed by core ideas that are largely the product of the historic forces of socialist transformation embodied in the working class and distilled in its organizational expression.

Class Participants in Socialist Revolution

Three social forces have played a decisive role in twentieth-century socialist revolution: the intellectuals, rural labor, and the urban working class. Each has contributed to the organizational, ideological, and military efforts necessary for a successful transformation. Yet the social characteristics that enabled them to take an active and specific part in the revolutionary process, which fundamentally remade their societies, have rarely been adequately identified. These basic characteristics have instead been obscured by an emphasis on sociopsychological and/or vulgar economistic attributes. However, the long-term commitments and large-scale presence of these social forces, through the worst adversities and changing circumstances, cannot be explained in terms of simple individual experience or immediate economic interest. The great personal sacrifices and social suffering that have accompanied the prolonged revolutionary struggles of a country require structural explanations and a broader grasp of the societal crises which engendered the historic alliance that has and continues to transform society.

Most efforts to characterize revolutionary processes have nevertheless relied, in one form or another, on identifying the social characteristics of political participants. One of the most commonplace notions is that these have a class identity that can be readily deduced by noting the family background of individuals. The experiences of class and class struggle, however, are transmitted from one generation to another directly through the family only if parents and offspring continue to inhabit the same situation, affected by the same sets of operative forces. But in the twentieth century, forces of world-historical proportions have intervened in social processes, disrupting the regular reproduction of classes: Imperial wars, colonial conquests, and massive flows of capital have produced severe disjunctions between family and class and the position of individuals within the class structure. The role of imperial force in jarring individuals loose from their class matrix has been a recurrent phenomenon in both European and Third World countries. Visibility in social background may even become a hindrance to understanding the dynamic interplay between political commitment and class position, when class position itself is subject to sudden and massive disruption. The impact of historical forces on the class structure thus has decisive importance in determining whether individuals will conform to the class practices of their forebears.[2]

The Social Identity of the Intellectuals

Intellectual strata are, of course, particularly affected by the tremors that are set off when war, capitalist crisis, or class struggle upsets the equilibrium of exploitative society. Hence, although many revolutionary intellectuals have middle-class backgrounds, this has less significance in determining their social orientation than the worldwide struggles that impinge upon a social formation. No single factor is in fact less useful in understanding the emergence and political action of intellectuals than class background. The experiences, situations, and institutions that intervene between childhood social attachments and adult political practices vitiate any effort to derive behavioral patterns from background. This is especially the case where large-scale, long-term changes in society as a whole undermine the possibilities for children to reproduce themselves in the image of their parents. Equally useless is any attempt to locate intellectuals in the class structure by virtue of their education, income, or lifestyle. The economic and social activities of revolutionary socialist intellectuals are not convertible into the formal roles they occupy in the social structure, emptied of the political content that they carry. The absurd "irony" often discerned in the situation of intellectuals who are in the system yet attack it is at once resolved if one looks not at the routines of everyday work or life, but at the practical political content of the production of that work: The struggles and ideas embodied in the work of, for instance, a teacher or lawyer may themselves function to undermine the reproduction of the social system.

The growth of a revolutionary socialist intelligentsia in Russia and China occurred during a prolonged period of class conflict, in which the economic position of the intellectuals was less important in shaping a political vocation than the class struggles emerging in the society as a whole. The problematic of the revolutionary socialist intellectual cannot be reduced to a determination by declassed forces on the fringes of society.

For lack of anchorage, resulting from large-scale disruptions, is not the main element in determining his or her specific ideological commitments. Rather, for us, the primary force providing a social identity for such intellectuals is their political membership in the working-class movement. Their social identity is a product of the influence, ideas, and activities of an ascending class—which even before it transforms society modifies the conditions in which society produces and reproduces itself. Their incorporation into the mass movement and the process through which this is achieved—class struggle, national wars—provide the basic ingredients for determining the class loyalty of the intellectuals. Insofar as their class situation is in flux, the primary determinants are not to be found in their economic roles, but in the political role they play in the class struggle.

Rural Labor and Socialist Revolution

The relationship of landlord and peasant has been characterized by relatively long periods of stability, punctuated by periods of rebellion and protest. In the classic cases of peasant revolt the land-hungry peasants attack the symbols and substance of landlord domination but are incapable of reordering society in their own image. The twentieth century has witnessed the rise of imperial capital, which appropriates means of production and surplus from the peasantry, but accumulates outside the particular social economy. The separation of the process of exploitation from the locus of accumulation has lead to profound dislocation of the rural labor force. For massive numbers of peasants are stripped of their means of production while being divorced geographically from employment in the locus of accumulation, in centers of industrial production. Rural labor that has been drawn into twentieth-century socialist revolutions is not the same peasantry exploited for centuries by landlords. On the contrary, the features of rural existence and the forces acting upon it, leading to socialist revolution, are unique to the twentieth century and account for the distinct path that "peasant" revolts have taken.

The crucial elements in the internal development of the countryside are found in the uprooting of the peasantry, the proletarianization of the labor force, and the incorporation of part of this displaced and proletarianized rural labor force in forms of disciplined revolutionary organization. The immediate effect of imperial domination has been to accentuate the uprootedness of the rural labor force: The decomposition of the village through force, commercial relations, and/or corporate expansion have been a central feature of prerevolutionary societies. The process of differentiation that capitalism has fomented through the extension of investment from centers of capital to the countryside has been accompanied by large-scale military-political movements, which have dominated and blocked the emergence of indigenous capitalist forces capable of exercising hegemony. The rural labor force, concerned with the occupation of the countryside, is no longer the peasant oppressed by the landlord. The impersonal forces of imperial capital penetration obliterate traces of particularistic domination and establish conditions of generalized exploitation and uprootedness.

Socialist revolution has nowhere been based on an undifferentiated mass peasantry. Rather, it is the dispossessed former peasant, uprooted by the combined politico-military-economic efforts of imperial powers, who has set in motion the movement of peasants toward political action. The dissolution of local ties to the land facilitates participation in revolutionary socialist activity. As the revolution enters into conflict with capitalist or precapitalist relations of production, its reliance on rural labor (which approximates the conditions of the classical proletariat) increases. And although smallholders—or even kulaks—may enter into the revolutionary struggle under conditions of imperial appropriation, despite the cost of dispossession, it nevertheless remains the case that as the revolutionary movement takes on more clearly socialist objectives, landless laborers and uprooted former peasants increasingly become the fulcrum for political action. It is neither middle peasants nor undifferentiated oppressed peasants that are the instruments of a socialist transformation, but the depeasantized rural labor force caught in the maelstrom of urban-led mass struggles.

In addition, as imperialist forces (capital and military) have acted on the countryside, the massive transformations evidenced throughout rural society have provided fertile ground for rural revolutionary movements. The efforts of imperial capital to transform society in accordance with its needs have led to the large-scale intrusion of military technology, without any accompanying alternative form of socioeconomic organization capable of massive integration of the labor force in productive labor. The intervention of imperialist forces on a scale commensurate with the subjugation of whole populations has homogenized or leveled opposition and has provided a common target for quite disparate class forces. The clue to the massive nature of rural participation in twentieth-century revolutions is to be found in common collective experiences resulting from the pervasive impact of imperialism on the countryside. Furthermore, the specific changes wrought in the labor force by the impact of world capitalism—in the form both of colonial and imperial wars and of market investment forces—undermine the notion that "the peasantry" as such has been a revolutionary force. It is rather the case that this peasantry has been transformed and its class situation altered—and that any turn toward socialist solutions is thus a direct response to the new forces impinging upon society, the modern organizational forms of imperial armies and capital. Indeed, this transformation of the peasantry is clearly the reason that rural labor has been so prominent in all successful socialist revolutions to date.

The critical issue, however, is not simply to recognize the immense revolutionary possibilities inherent in rural labor, but to locate precisely the latter's role in the revolutionary process. Specifically, has the mass character of rural labor's participation enabled it to *direct* the process of transformation? Given what has already been said about the vital part played by uprooted former peasants incorporated into the revolutionary organization, is it not possible to view them as the directing force in the confrontation with imperialism, in much the same way as earlier Marxists conceived of the proletariat as the hegemonic class in the revolutionary bloc of forces?[3] The problem with this conception is that it drastically exaggerates the degree to which *socioeconomic changes* and *military experience* are in themselves *sufficient* to shape and create a new socialist consciousness among former peasants.

Close to the recent past, in which petty-commodity relations predominated, ever embedded in a rural matrix containing peasants anchored in productive relations, the rural labor force has never completely severed its ties with the society out of which it emerged. The struggle against the uprootedness generated by imperialism *weakens* these ties; but the ex-peasant never loses sight of the past. There is a continuing tension within the mass consciousness of the revolutionary rural labor force between, on the one hand, a break with the past (incorporation in a socialist movement) and, on the other, a continuity with that past expressed in the tendency, if left to their own devices, to return to petty-commodity production. It is this tension, this ambiguity, and the lack of a formulated collectivist conception that the rural labor force can execute *on its own* that limits the latter's role to that of an *influential base*—and *not a revolutionary vanguard*.

Thus to envision the involvement of rural labor en masse in revolutionary activity as a self-generating process is to overlook the centuries of ties and relationships engendered within the countryside. It was rather the degree to which rural labor was uprooted by imperialism that determined its extent of participation in a collectivist enterprise oriented and organized by the worker-rooted central party cadre. In the U.S.S.R., where peasant revolts were directed essentially against the landlords, the peasants remained wedded to petty-commodity production and showed few inclinations toward collectivist agriculture. Even the millions of uprooted peasants—conscripted for the army or victims of Western military occupation—remained under the hegemony of the core of peasants who remained in petty-commodity production, in the absence of any mass Bolshevik political organization capable of reorganizing production on the land.

In China, by contrast, the revolutionary armies were recruited mainly from the uprooted rural masses and, in turn, provided a discipline and social organization within which peasant agriculture could develop; they thus came to represent an alternative source of hegemony over those displaced and uprooted by wars and class conflict. In Vietnam the process was similar: Collectivism was implanted through the mass integration of uprooted peasants into socialist revolutionary organizations, U.S. bombers, in addition to murdering millions, cleared the fields of centuries of precapitalist or decades of capitalist social relations, providing a carte blanche for the wholesale restructuring of the countryside under the undisputed hegemony of the worker-rooted Communist Party. The case of Cuba reflects a different set of imperialist forces: largely, massive flows of imperial capital into agriculture, which had the equivalent effect of uprooting the peasantry. Moreover, the transformation of the peasantry reached the most advanced state, going beyond uprootedness and actually creating a substantial rural proletariat in factories and in the fields. The more thorough change effected by the impersonal economic forms of imperialism—in contrast with more blatant military-cum-economic depredations—accounts for the more rapid collectivization of agriculture in Cuba than in Russia, China, or Vietnam.

While Cuban rural labor was in a more advanced socioeconomic position to initiate the process of collectivization, the leadership of the revolution did not possess, at least initially, the same direct ties to the rural workers' struggle as the Chinese or Vietnamese Communists. For the degree, extent, and duration of the rural class struggle, independent of the level of the productive forces, can be viewed as a crucial variable in shaping the organization of postrevolutionary social and political institutions in the countryside. In China and Vietnam (unlike in Russia or Cuba), the uprooted rural masses achieved strategic positions at middle-cadre levels as a result of the prolonged and mass rural character of the war; this presence gave them influence over the top leadership and shaped the particular collectivist measures that were instituted. The influence of rural labor in both cases, however, was not a function of its mere numerical strength, but of its position in the party organization.

Rural Labor and Political Organization

The position of rural labor within the revolutionary movement varied from one revolutionary experience to another. In the U.S.S.R. it was always a marginal force, largely an unintegrated mass operating outside the organized movement—although acting on the latter and in turn being acted upon. In Cuba rural labor was incorporated into the mass movement, especially the people's militias and the Committees for the Defense of the Revolution (Comites de defensa de la revolucion). These bodies played a decisive role in carrying out the struggles that culminated in collectivization of the economy. Nevertheless, because they were not essentially and directly political organs that made decisions within productive units, these mass-based organizations did not become organs of political rule. At best, they served as a reminder to the leadership of the specific social and economic interests of rural labor and thus set limits to the types of concession that might be granted to opposing strata.

The effectiveness of rural labor's role in safeguarding its social interests through the mass organizations can be seen in the thoroughness with which their enemies were expropriated, the short shrift given to agro-businessmen, and the care given to legislation benefiting rural labor. Meanwhile, the process of revolutionary struggle in China and Vietnam saw a massive incorporation of rural labor into the politico-military structures, with many former peasants rising to substantial positions of influence, after varying periods of resocialization into the ideas and norms of collectivism. The combined influence of early working-class struggles and ideas on long-term leaders and of confrontation and struggles with imperialist forces on the uprooted rural labor force produced an influential militarized rural cadre. Their presence within the party at upper and middle levels, as well as at the base, was a product of their entry into the party during the middle years of the revolution.

In the Russian case the peasants as a mass never played a major role *within* the organized movement (although they did play a substantial political role informally and provided decisive military support at the base); hence, they were unable to influence and shape rural policy. This is part of the explanation for the savage manner in which collectivization was ultimately imposed on the peasants from above. The case of Cuba is closer to that of China or Vietnam, insofar as rural labor was incorporated into the last but decisive stages of the socialist transformation and, as such, remained to play a role in *indirectly* shaping regime priorities and the allocation of resources. However, the late involvement of the Cuban rural labor force ensured that its position in the strictly organizational structures of the revolutionary movement would remain peripheral. For the earlier rural labor enters the revolutionary struggle, the more influential its role is in political decisionmaking, as well as in military operations. At the same time, it is not sheer numbers alone that determine what say rural labor will have in the revolutionary process. Cuba, for example, had less than 50 percent of its labor force in agriculture—a smaller proportion than in Russia—yet its influence on the revolutionary process was greater. Likewise, in China and Vietnam, rural labor was just as numerous in the 1920s and early 1930s as it was later, yet it became influential only when its numerical strength was embodied in party and military organizations that exercised control over productive units.

The early involvement of rural labor in the revolutionary movement depends above all upon the elaboration by the party of an appropriate program and its application to the concrete struggles emerging in the countryside. In Russia the prior existence of widespread commercial agriculture and a preexisting petty-commodity structure inhibited the

Bolsheviks from developing organic ties to the rural labor force—fearing, as they might, their ideological influence on the party. The different character of the peasantry in Russia and the different development of the class struggle led the Bolsheviks to formulate programs that relegated the peasantry to a supportive role, outside the political organization—thus ensuring that they would continue to follow the view of the petty-commodity producer. Hence, even when the peasants were drafted en masse into the army during World War I, they retained a peasant rather than a proletarian consciousness. In China and Vietnam, by contrast, the prolonged struggles fought and the organic ties forged in rural areas prior to the revolution were accompanied by an early formulation and application of an agrarian program as one of the centerpieces of party policy.

However, that the revolutionary leaderships in China, Cuba, and Vietnam developed a conception of the peasantry as a proto-proletarian mass was itself a reflection of the uprootedness and relative proletarianization that accompanied imperialist penetration in those countries. Thus it was not merely a program that created a political unity between displaced urban cadres and rural labor: It was ultimately the common bonds of uncertainty and uprootedness generated by imperialist penetration that enabled the two to merge in a common organization. While the early presence of a party agrarian program *facilitated* the early entry of rural labor into the party, it was the development of imperialism on a world scale that uprooted and radicalized rural labor en masse and precipitated the conflicts that led to its disciplining and integration into a revolutionary movement.

In this way, the attempt by world capitalism to overcome its historic crisis through external expansion proved, in the specific conditions of its military-economic intervention in Vietnam, China, and Cuba, to carry within it the seeds of capitalism's own destruction: For it catalyzed a rural labor force, uprooted and without the chains of age-old oppression, but with a newly forged revolutionary socialist leadership. Thus the program and ideology of the revolutionary struggle did not express internally generated productive forces, but those resulting from the advanced social formations of the imperial world. A collectivist consciousness developed within rural labor not because of past landlord abuses, but as a direct product of the new forces of destruction and production, operating on a world scale, that originated in the imperialist countries. Thus it is not subjective will or local backwardness that generate revolutionary action among rural labor: there is no inverse relationship between rural radicalization and development of the productive forces. Nor are rural movements for socialist revolution premature, because the productive forces have not been developed within the social formation itself. For from a world-historic perspective, as the most developed forces operated within the backward formations to precipitate revolutionary socialist action, they provided ample testimony to the ripeness of the social situation.

The Role of Urban Workers

Conventional sociology has often downplayed the role of the urban working class in socialist revolutions. A number of attributes imputed to the working class are alleged to have prevented it from making any decisive contribution to the overall success. Not infrequently, the thinly disguised purpose has been to deny the centrality of class struggle in the making of history and to refute Marxism as a science: Revolutions have been explained by conjunctural causes (wars, crises), sociopsychological phenomena (power-drives of intellectuals), and/or the collapse of precapitalist societies.

One fundamental error is the notion that class consciousness is an attribute possessed by an individual, which can be measured outside of the class struggle. The attitude studies, the opinion surveys, the interviews that purport to measure class consciousness—all abstract the individual from the class, the class from the class struggle, the class struggle from the historical process. Yet the essential relationships established prior to the individual's response, the social and political organizations within which he or she acts, the struggles in which he or she is involved, and the global relations between conflicting classes and the state are in fact the crucial determinants of class consciousness. Class consciousness has its basis in the class struggle, and the class struggle is rooted in class consciousness. The study of class consciousness requires the study of classes acting in history: It is a dimension of a historical process, not a static, psychological attribute derived from interpersonal encounters.

When conventional sociology studies consciousness, it tends to isolate the individual and, in the context of immediate circumstances, record responses registering what is most urgent, obvious, and obtainable for him. Hence, most close-up studies of consciousness have discovered over and over again that workers subject to the constraints of local circumstances and pressing needs respond with preferences for immediate economic rewards. From this limited vantage point, the conventional anti-Marxists argue that the working class—conceived of as an aggregate of static individualized responses—is economistic and lacking in revolutionary will. If workers take part in revolutionary movements, it is basically because clever leaders (intellectuals) have manipulated their immediate needs to serve the alien larger ends. This approach denies the reality of larger movements existing in their own right, providing a new reality, existing as a social force capable of increasing the power of individuals insofar as they stand together behind a common set of demands that subsume immediate needs and define new historical projects. It cannot comprehend that the economic interests of isolated individuals are, through the action of the class, converted into collective class demands: The movement of a class that has elaborated on the demands of each member is no longer speaking merely the economistic language of the individual worker.

In reality, that economic issues may initially be felt to be important by isolated individuals does not at all preclude the elaboration of a general class political program. Merely to ascertain the economic stance of the individual worker is to scratch the surface of social reality, leaving unexplored the sociopolitical matrix that constrains or facilitates further elaboration of political and social demands. In the course of the socialist revolutions that have occurred in this century, there have certainly been many instances in which workers have raised economist demands; and these, at a certain point, may have embodied the sentiments of the bulk of the class. Nonetheless, the historic process of working-class struggle soon led to an incorporation of economic with political demands. The greater the scope and intensity of the class struggle, the more closely economic and political, or immediate and historic, demands became merged: wages and redistribution, working conditions and control, repressive laws and state power. And it was in the whole complex of demands and in the struggles, over time, to win them—not in the one-dimensional, immediate wants of individual workers—that the class consciousness of the working class was expressed.

At the same time, history makes clear that class consciousness can continue to exist in a latent form even when repression has enforced an apparent surcease of the class war. For example, in the 1920s the Chinese urban labor movement was clearly spearheading a social and political movement of substantial dimensions. That movement was savagely repressed. Throughout the 1930s and up to the mid-1940s, workers, we are often told, became nonrevolutionary and economistic. Yet with the overthrow of the KMT, the workers became integral elements in the process of social transformation. Similar cycles appear in the cases of Russia, Cuba, or Vietnam. In Russia the revolutionary mobilization of the working class in 1905 was followed by an economistic slide until 1917, when revolutionary struggles and organization reemerged in much the same form (Soviets) as before. In Cuba militancy in the 1930s was followed by repression in the 1940s, then by an urban proletarian resurgence in the anticapitalist, anti-imperialist struggles of the early 1960s. Similarly, Vietnamese workers, active in the mass upsurge of the 1930s and 1940s, were relatively less active in the 1950s; the Tet Offensive, however, gave a fresh indication of worker consciousness, and the postliberation reconstruction of industry has witnessed a massive incorporation of the working class within the revolutionary process. Clearly, therefore, the decline or even disappearance of revolutionary working-class activity in a particular period, whether as the result of repression or, more generally, as a reflection of the possibilities inherent in those specific conditions with that specific state regime, does not mean that the workers have become economistic in any essential historical sense—that they have given up their historic interest in social transformation. It is rather the case that conjunctural circumstances may force revolutionary consciousness to become latent, subject to a change in state relations.

A second (and related) characteristic error of non-Marxist sociology is the mechanistic counterposition of reform to revolution. It is assumed that the presence of reformist demands within the workers' movement ipso facto excludes the possibility that workers will carry the struggle through to a revolutionary outcome. When workers, at a particular moment, put forward a set of discrete demands, the conclusion is drawn that these demands define the nature of the movement. The unspoken assumption is that workers are by nature reformist and incapable of transcending their immediate surroundings. It is ironic indeed that a corollary thesis to this patronizing view of the working class should present the revolutionary party as fundamentally elitist—an outside presence, imposing its values and political beliefs on the class.

In reality, the relation of reform to revolution is by no means so simple. The knowledge the working class obtains of the social system is a function of the scope and depth of the class struggle. Some segments of the class historically arrive at an understanding of the nature of society and its contending forces before others. This uneven process results in differential degrees of political organization and combativity. The class, as a whole, becomes fully involved only at certain key conjunctural moments, thereby signaling a social crisis or even a prerevolutionary situation of dual power. At other times, the process of working-class struggle involves merely segments of the class and partial demands (reforms). But it is the overall trajectory of the movement that determines whether these are mere reforms or the building blocks for the mobilization of the whole class toward a systematic confrontation.

To argue that the working class is inherently reformist because, in a particular historical conjuncture, only part of it is involved in class struggle, or because the class as a whole is demanding only partial changes, is to reduce historical movement to the changing circumstances of the moment. In a word, working-class support for reforms does not make the working class *reformist*. On the contrary, all profound revolutionary changes have had their immediate origins in limited demands for reforms. But what is crucial in the ensuing struggles is the speed and extent to which these immediate issues lead to revolutionary struggles for power, challenging state authority and the dominance of existing ruling classes. In all socialist revolutions the workers' movement has integrated struggles for reform with wider demands for revolutionary change.

The Myth of Working-Class Privilege

A third common misconception (in which Fanonism rubs shoulders with functionalism) sees the working class throughout the Third World as, by and large, incorporated into existing society, its relatively higher wages and greater privileges (by comparison with the rural masses) having been purchased at the price of its subordination to the dominant classes. Once again, this view sees the working class as fundamentally economistic, its consciousness determined in the last resort by its wage levels, whether absolute or relative. However, a consideration, first, of the significance of differential wages within the working class itself and, second, of the relations between workers and peasants will clearly show the spurious nature of this conception.

In the first place, the overwhelming participation of relatively better-paid workers (relative to peasants) in revolutionary mass organizations in Russia both before and after 1917, in China during the 1920s and after 1949, in Cuba during the 1930s and in the late 1950s and early 1960s, and in Vietnam during the 1930s and 1940s and again in 1968 and after Liberation suggests that class consciousness is not reducible to salary payments. The class nature of society is brought home to workers constantly, and in extremely material forms: a repressive state, fluctuations of the economy and of state economic policy, oppressive social relations of production, and so on. Thus the broader sociopolitical context of class society and the exploitative relationships embodied in it have often proved to be more fundamental determinants of class consciousness than wage levels. Moreover, the degree to which certain segments of the working class are paid higher wages may precisely be a function of their greater militancy, and it may reinforce their political allegiance to a revolutionary party. Hence the notion that workers, or even better-paid workers, are in essence privileged strata, incapable of participating in revolutionary struggles, is both historically and logically incorrect. The notion of a privileged working class assumes that higher wages are derived from exploiting others. Yet in reality the workers neither employ labor nor appropriate surplus. Rather, usually located in highly productive imperialist enterprises, they are themselves producers of surplus value and, in fact, are technically subject to greater exploitation (i.e., produce greater surplus value). By not increasing their share of the value that is produced, they would not lessen the exploitation in society or improve the condition of other toilers; rather, they would simply heighten the concentration of wealth in the hands of the capitalist class.

The degree of solidarity in action of the working class, of course, varies with the issue being contested. Structural differentiaton is obvious and extensive. Yet in Russia, China, Cuba, and Vietnam issues arose that made clear the common situation and evoked a class solidarity, despite any historic differences in wage levels. In Russia, the war and the exceptional cost it imposed on the working class blurred over internal differences and hastened the formation of Soviets, incorporating all segments of the class. In China the common demands of all urban labor for improved minimum conditions of payment, hours, and political rights evoked a massive and turbulent mobilization. In Cuba the corrupt and repressive character of the Batista regime, and the generalized insecurity of employment under U.S. dominance, triggered a massive unified working-class movement. In Vietnam the colonial situation combined with state repression of labor struggles forced miners, plantation workers, and municipal employees to unite behind revolutionary socialist forces. Thus internal differentiation of the working class has not historically proved to be an insurmountable obstacle to the unity of high- and low-wage workers in mass revolutionary struggle.

Perhaps more weighty arguments have been adduced in an attempt to establish an incompatibility and even fundamental antagonism between urban and rural labor. These have pointed to disparities in income, standard of living and social relations, and to all the very real inequalities that subsist between countryside and city. The notion has been popularized that the highly organized, better-paid workers are unwilling to support peasant struggles; that the workers' movement is simply another particularistic interest group, intent only on satisfying its immediate demands by negotiating with the State and employers for better terms. For Fanon, the workers are part of colonial society; for others, they form an aristocracy of labor divorced from the revolutionary class struggles waged by the peasants. In addition, it is true that relations between workers' parties and peasant movements have not always been optimal, conducive to the forging of a revolutionary alliance. However, in reality, there is no structural reason why an alliance between workers and peasants cannot be brought about; moreover, the historical experience of the four socialist revolutions we have considered has shown this conclusively. The revolutionary alliance was achieved in each, despite the disparities, and was to prove sufficiently strong to lead to a fundamental transformation of the entire social structure and economic system. In each revolution the role of the working class and its party was to provide moral, political, and material direction for, and support to, the peasant struggles.

The Revolutionary Alliance

In China the Communist Party, which became the leading revolutionary force in the countryside, was formed in and by urban workers' struggles. Throughout the 1920s the workers' movement supported agrarian reform demands and frequently provided material support. Later, after the suppression of the mass workers' movement in 1926–28, thousands of cadres shaped and influenced by those urban struggles turned to the rural masses, organizing and directing revolutionary activity in the countryside. The overthrow of the KMT set the stage subsequently for the full integration of rural and urban labor in the task of collectivizing the economy and transforming social relations. The apparent break in the emerging alliance of urban and rural labor after the 1926–28 urban repression occurred only at the level of *mass* movements. For the Communist Party carried proletarian ideology, embodied in its cadres, to the peasants. Basing itself on past working-class experience, and anticipating the future reassertion of the alliance, the Communist Party during the 1930s and 1940s became the link between working class and the peasantry.[4] The proof lies in the post-1949 overthrow of capitalist relations of production, which was the expression not merely of peasant forces, but of combined elements from both working class and peasantry. Had the working class been completely eclipsed, had only the peasants counted, the subsequent act of alliance in collectivization would be a gratuitous act, an inexplicable occurrence because of fortuitous circumstances. This is hardly convincing.

In Cuba the disintegration of petty-commodity production and the construction of sugar mills in the countryside created a rural proletariat able and willing to politicize and radicalize the remaining peasantry. The differences between urban and rural labor became obliterated: Both were wage workers employed by corporate capital, both were organized in trade unions and engaged in class struggle, and both provided a base for the Communist Party. As the dominant social force in the countryside, rural wage labor thus served as a bridge between urban wage labor and rural petty-commodity production. The struggles of the 1930s and the subsequent revolutionary movement of the 1950s and 1960s saw a convergence in action. And the rural laborers and urban workers, who provided the central core of forces pressing through the elimination of capitalist relations of production, also guaranteed the continued existence of petty producers, making them, in effect, into an auxiliary support group for the revolution.[5]

In Vietnam the semiproletarian rural labor force (part-time petty-commodity and subsistence peasants, part-time migratory laborers), which mingled with wage workers in the mines and plantations, was organized and engaged in class-struggle politics under the leadership of the Communist Party and thereby became linked to the urban working class. The heightened repression in the late 1930s and the subsequent emergence of a Communist-led rural guerrilla movement facilitated the transfer of urban working-class-influenced cadres to the countryside and the communication of ideas and spread of organizations among petty-commodity producers and semiproletarians.

During the 1960s the massive U.S. invasion of Vietnam and the ensuing uprooting of millions of peasants hastened the flow of ex-peasants simultaneously into the guerrilla movement and into the festering slums of Saigon. The forced marches, concentration camps, and terror bombing freed the peasants from their land and from petty-commodity production and facilitated their recruitment by the Communist Party. The synthesis of forcibly uprooted peasants and a revolutionary vanguard party, grounded in past proletarian struggles and ideology, provided the driving force for a mass movement that would be not merely anti-imperialist, but socialist.

In the case of the Russian Revolution, the worker-peasant alliance was less the product of large-scale movements of capital, uprooting and transforming peasants into rural proletarians, than was the case in Cuba; nor were the military incursions of imperialism sufficient to erode the organization of petty-commodity production, as was the case in Vietnam and China. On the contrary, by devastating the cities and the marketing system, imperialist intervention positively encouraged a return to small self-sustaining agriculture. Moreover, huge areas of Russia were without any working-class presence whatsoever, which made the task of extending proletarian hegemony and sustaining the alliance with the peasants more difficult. Thus some of the basic historic forces that facilitated and cemented the worker-peasant alliance in China, Cuba, and Vietnam were absent—or operated in the opposite direction—in Russia. And the alliance, although it was decisive in establishing a workers' state, could not be maintained over time.[6]

The divergences that began in the early 1920s became unbridgeable gaps with the unspeakable measures taken by Stalin during the collectivization drive in the late 1920s and the 1930s. The destruction of industry and a good part of the urban proletariat in the civil war led to a partial peasantization of the working class. Under the conditions that prevailed in the first five years after the revolution, the qualities and attributes associated with rural petty-commodity production were favored, and there was no pressure toward collectivist solutions in the countryside. The introduction of NEP (New Economic Policy) further encouraged these trends, which contrasted with the situation in China, Cuba, and Vietnam, where the momentum of change was toward the expansion (in varying time periods, of varying duration) of large-scale units of agricultural production and toward their progressive collectivization. Thus the Russian experience of a short-lived worker-peasant alliance followed by a profound divergence of interests was the exception, not the rule, in twentieth-century socialist revolutions. The favorite bourgeois myth that socialist revolutions are minority-led transformations in which the majority (peasants) are used temporarily, only to be later abandoned and exploited, is based on the singular experience of Russia under Stalin. The coercive violence used in the name of the working class to convert Russia's peasantry into a rural proletariat has had no equivalent elsewhere. In reality, the historic forces operating in other revolutionary contexts have been seen to work against any similar violent clash of interests, and the worker-peasant alliance has continued to provide the principal basis of support for the postrevolutionary regimes.

We can now summarize the forces that have acted to forge the revolutionary alliance of workers and peasants. Uprooting and proletarianization of the peasantry have reduced some of the crucial structural differences between rural and urban labor. While these processes have not brought about a clean break with the past, they have nevertheless served to sever the primordial ties to local authority, custom, and tradition (what Marx called village idiocy). Stripped of his means of production, the ex-peasant has become more open to proletarian ideology and worker-founded parties. The social and geographic proximity of centers of capitalist production, in the economic enclaves established by imperialism, has helped to spread the organizational skills and ideology of working-class struggle throughout the countryside, incorporating strata only partially linked to the capitalist mode of production. Revolutionary armies and militia have served as mechanisms for the diffusion of socialist ideas and cadres, as transmission belts for the revolutionary party. Paradoxically, the defeat of geographically anchored and concentrated proletarian movements in earlier periods resulted in a greater mobility of revolutionary collectivist ideas and organization throughout the countryside, whereas victorious capital became entrenched and inflexible in limited areas of influence and dominance.

The transmission of revolutionary ideas and organization to the countryside, via productive and politico-military apparatuses, has thus converged with structural changes within the countryside to create a dynamic toward worker-peasant alliance. The crucial subjective force acting upon this objective dynamic to realize the alliance in practice has been the revolutionary party. It is the party that incorporates the experience of class struggle in the cities, forms the cadres in the fields, mines, and armies, and organizes the diffusion of collectivist ideology and practice throughout the countryside, analysing the basic coordinates of the situation and intervening in the crucial political, economic, and military structures to detonate revolutionary struggles. The alliance between the working class and the peasantry is a historic product of the unfolding of capitalist and imperialist development, insofar as this brings the two classes into a common set of exploitative relations. But this objective convergence only becomes a political force and reality if a revolutionary party formulates a program and devises a strategy capable of channeling the energies of both classes toward common goals and against common enemies. Without such a party, the objective situation of common oppression can be dissipated into a thousand secondary struggles involving communal, ethnic, or sectoral interests—struggles that, incidentally, provide the favorite terrain for conventional bourgeois sociologists intent on refuting Marxist class analysis.

The Revolutionary Party and the Working Class

But what is the relationship of the party leading the struggle for socialist revolution to the working class itself?[7] It has often been argued that such parties, made up of professional revolutionaries, mainly intellectuals and other nonworking-class types, are distinct and apart from the class and pursue policies that the workers themselves would not elaborate: The party *of* the working class is in reality the party *over* the working class. Moreover, elitist in composition, it is also elitist in its methods; it acts from "outside," "manipulating" the interests of the workers to serve the power drives and the interests of the intellectual elite that runs the party. In the arena of social struggles, the workers' economic interests are "sacrificed" to the political aims of the party, which stands to gain from its accession to power. The ground is thus prepared for the new exploitative society that will emerge when this proto-class takes power and begins to reorganize society to serve its own as opposed to the workers' interests. Such a view of the party seeks to minimize the extent of working-class participation in the revolutionary struggle; or, if it is clear that masses of workers are active, it seeks to differentiate party involvement from that of workers in general; or, if the two cannot be separated, it argues that the common orientation is merely conjunctural, and that the long-term conflict of interests will become manifest over time. A related line of argument presents the party as basically oriented toward "modernization" and "industrialization," while the workers are allegedly concerned only with immediate problems.

Although this way of presenting the relationship between party and class is misconceived, there does exist a certain material basis for it, in the nature of postrevolutionary developments in a number of countries. "Elites" have emerged and have restratified society; industrial plans have been imposed rather than debated by workers' councils; gaps have appeared between the concrete interests of the workers and the demands of the planners; above all, decisionmaking has been the prerogative of the party, or rather of the party leadership, and the workers have consequently often expressed their interests in narrowly economic terms.[8] Moreover, these real divergences of interest after the revolution have not merely been pointed to by anti-Marxists as evidence of a universal and inherent contradiction between party and class; they have also been endowed with a similarly universal value from the other side, by the postrevolutionary regimes and their apologists. Liberal scholars discover that all subsequent distortions were inscribed in the process, party, and ideology of socialist revolution. Quotations out of context from Lenin, vacuous sociological generalizations about party structures and class/party relations, psychosociological hypotheses about the motives of political and social leaders—all serve as a substitute for concrete analysis of the historical process. Propagandists for the postrevolutionary regimes, for their part, follow an essentially similar procedure, although from a sympathetic rather than a hostile vantage point: once again, out-of-context citations from Lenin, a one-sided emphasis on the role of the party and its leaders, and a claim for absolute continuity between the period of revolutionary change and postrevolutionary policies. The only difference is that the authoritarianism, economic developmentalism, and bureaucratic domination associated with the postrevolutionary period are presented as necessary and positive accompanying features of the revolution, whereas the liberals present them as elements of a new exploitative society.

In fact, however, the problem of relations between the working class and the revolutionary party, and of the role of the working class in the socialist revolutions that have occurred to date and in the societies created by them, is both more complex and dialectical and more historically specific than such simplistic theses suggest. The essential point here is that postrevolutionary undermining of the working classes' power is no reason to omit, distort, or downplay the historic role of the working class in providing the impetus to revolution. And to get at the real relationship between party and class during the revolutionary process itself, it is necessary to clear the field of the two mirror-opposite views described above.

First, the founding of a party does not necessarily reflect the activities of the class it will ultimately represent. Usually, parties are founded by small groups of people from diverse backgrounds, drawn together by a common set of ideas or a common project. Thus the founding meetings of the Communist parties of Russia, China, and Vietnam included substantial numbers of intellectuals, who had as yet little direct connection with the burgeoning social struggles of the period. The small initial organization could hardly be said to "represent" the class. But in a sense, this goes without saying. The crucial test, however, is the capacity of a party to move from a primarily intellectual position outside the working class and to integrate itself into the mass movement, winning new members and transforming itself from a party of the "elite" into a party representing a substantial segment of the working class.

The early history of the Russian, Chinese, or Vietnamese parties shows an evolving relationship with the working class, in the course of which they were progressively transformed into parties increasingly composed of workers. This was achieved by a direct and growing participation in class struggles, and subsequently through the establishment of mass organizations. "Overlap" of membership between party and mass organization, mass organization and working class, is the prime index for the true relationship of party to class. The quantitative growth in working-class membership of the party and the extension of party-affiliated or influenced mass organizations suggest a progressive *integration* of the party in the class, a convergence of political and economic interests. The capacity of the party to sustain its working-class membership and affiliates, to augment the level of struggles, and to extend its influence on the basis of more elaborate programmatic statements (going beyond immediate economic-political interests, in the direction of a full socialist program), suggests that its integration within the class was not conjunctural, but reflects its own historic nature as a working-class party.

A second strand in the argument that the revolutionary party is something alien to the working class concerns the explicit central role of "professional revolutionaries." Since workers work all day, the argument goes, the possibility for them to play any substantial role in the "vanguard party" is necessarily limited. Hence, the party of professional revolutionaries acts *upon* the class, and not vice versa. But this confuses a number of issues. First, the notion of professional revolutionaries should not be taken to mean footloose intellectuals dissociated from the work place. Rather, it refers to workers who are *primarily political activists*, precisely *in work* as well as *after work*. The capacity to act effectively as a serious, committed ("professional") revolutionary presupposes insertion within a network of solidarity and joint activity, at the point of production or within a mass front. The capacity of the Bolshevik Party to enroll tens of thousands of members in the few months after February 1917, or of the Chinese Communist Party to grow by leaps and bounds in the 1924–27 period, was based on the prior recruitment of working-class cadres, who were in a position to insert themselves in the mass upsurge when this erupted. The party could not have created such cadres when the struggle erupted, any more than it could have "imposed" its line or leaders upon the mass movement from outside. After all, there were other organized political forces fighting for hegemony over that movement, some of which could draw on the power of the state (however weakened this may have been).

It is also true, of course, that the revolutionary party has nowhere embodied all of the working class. In the cases we have been considering, not only were there competing political groups with influence in the working class, but many workers were not organizationally committed to any party. The point is that a substantial part of the party was in each case made up of workers, and these in turn acted within the broad working-class movement to provide political direction and leadership, transmitting to the class programmatic demands for transforming society. At the same time, the course of party activity, to the extent it has succeeded, has reflected the capacity of the workers' movement not merely to assimilate but to modify the party's program and orientation. It is not merely the party that has shaped the workers' struggle, but the workers' struggle that has influenced and formed the members of the party: The whole growth of party-class integration is a dialectical process. And, of course, successful policies of the party at moments of class upsurge have resulted in a new influx of members, while severe defeats have resulted in mass exodus.

The Primacy of Politics

The central issue raised by the massive entry of workers into a revolutionary party is that of *representation* of the class and *articulation* of its historic interests. There is no reason to take up the highly politicized and demanding existence of a party militant, unless there is some prior commitment to transforming the *political* role of the working class in society. To enter a revolutionary socialist party presumes a recognition of the inadequacy of existing forms of political representation and, more important, of existing social relations of production—central targets of party program and activity. The positive act of joining the party and the affirmation of its program through party-directed activity reflect a primary concern not for economic issues (whether consumption or production), but rather for political and social ones: political freedom, embodied in direct forms of workers' representation and power; and the replacement of exploitative social relations of production by collective ownership and self-management.

When workers join a revolutionary party and seek to transform society, their aim is evidently not to create a new class society or to become instruments of "modernization." Rather, at the point of transformation, the driving force of the revolution is precisely an attack on class domination and on the instrumental use of workers to capitalize the economy for the benefit of other classes. Moreover, as has already been argued, the fact that postrevolutionary societies have seen new forms of stratification and the imposition of alien and instrumental tasks upon the working class is not in itself a reason to deny the historic role of the working class in providing the impetus to revolution. The restratification process was not "inherent" in the revolution, but the product of specific economic and political conditions at an international and national level, as well as of postrevolutionary social and political conflicts in which the working class suffered a political defeat and the goals of the revolution were redefined (from "representation" to "modernization") and identified with the Inevitable Historical Process.

Stalinists who celebrate this process, and liberal academics (like Barrington Moore) who press it upon us as the fateful way of history, have found no difficulty in suppressing (physically in the one case, intellectually in the other) the essential nature and social content of the revolutionary process.[9] Both see overarching modernization imperatives—transcending class—as subsuming working-class struggles for freedom and an end to exploitation. The struggle to build a socialist society in a world dominated by imperialism becomes a process of the same fundamental nature as imperialist "development." As mere unconscious instruments of such a larger global process, class struggles and the goal of liberation become secondary and utopian, soon to be overtaken by the "real" measures formulated by party bureaucrats and industrial managers. And the absence of an autonomous role for the workers in the postrevolutionary society is writen back into the history of the revolution itself.

In each successful revolutionary experience, the outcome depended upon the fusion of significant segments of the working class with the revolutionary party, and the incorporation of representative demands of the class into the activity of the party. In the Russian Revolution the central slogan of the Bolsheviks was a *political* demand to concentrate power in the hands of the most representative institutions of workers' struggle: "All power to the Soviets." This was the high point of the revolution, the *culmination* of foregoing economic and social struggles; it reflected the intense interaction between the Bolshevik working-class cadre and the class as a whole. In China the massive upsurge of the working class was cut short by the savage repression in 1926–28; nevertheless, the notion of mass representative councils (Soviets), popular militia, and other forms of mass representation in the state remained in the forefront of the rural struggle throughout the prerevolutionary period. That the idea of mass representation, derived from the workers' experiences, should have persisted through the radical-agrarian and antifascist periods—in fact right up to the seizure of state power—suggests that while socioeconomic demands could be downplayed for conjunctural reasons, the issue of representation could not.

In Vietnam the shift from urban class struggle to guerrilla war and national liberation struggle was sustained through the elaboration of a variety of institutions of representation. In liberated villages parallel committees were formed; in factories clandestine councils were established. Everywhere, demands for freedom from bourgeois rule predominated, even while economic and social demands were watered down to accommodate petit-bourgeois and other forces. Political representation and the organizational articulation of worker and peasant interests played a central role in orienting and directing the protracted struggle; this accounts for the relative ease with which the Vietnamese were able to administer the war-devastated country, after the defeat and the departure of the United States and their clients.[10]

In Cuba the revolutionary process emphasized the elimination of class differences to the point where all private businesses, even the most petty, were expropriated during the Great Revolutionary Offensive of 1968. An end to exploitation, and the social relations based on it, was a central priority of the revolution for at least the first decade. The elaboration of representative organs found expression especially in military-security units—the popular militia, the People's Courts, the local Committees for the Defence of the Revolution. This form of representation was confined to acting *against* enemies of the revolution—a key task in the early years, when imperialist intervention was a real and constant threat. Nevertheless, it became increasingly obvious that this was an inadequate form for articulating the workers' demands and interests. The attrition of the trade unions as organs of representation, and the failure to replace them with new institutions, has led to a crisis of consciousness: Confronted with an absence of political channels and with demands for economic performance, workers inevitably tend to revert to economistic demands.

Thus the central importance of the dialectical relationship between the revolutionary party and the working class needs no further emphasis. No twentieth-century socialist revolution occurred without the establishment of such a relationship. The party experience and the class struggles that resulted from the integration of party and class interests were essential in forging the ideology and cadre that made possible the revolution. And that integration was based on political demands—for freedom, representation, and an end to exploitation.

Conclusion

We have seen the many ways in which non-Marxist sociology has misconstrued or distorted working-class activity and consciousness: the counterposition of reforms to revolution; the separation of economic issues from political; the attempt to derive consciousness from a particular set of immediate demands or attitudes, or directly from wage levels, extrapolating from the wider social and political context of class struggle and state; the imputation of fundamental political cleavages between industrial workers and rural labor, on the basis of cultural or conjunctural differences, and so on. We have noted that these conceptions fail to grasp the real historic processes involved in twentieth-century socialist revolutions. Throughout the century, in major social transformations involving Europe, Asia, and Latin America, the workers' movement has played an essential role. In Russia, China, Cuba, and Vietnam, it was the large-scale entry of the working class onto the center stage of political struggle that transformed a process aimed at political reform into one leading to a combined political and social revolution. In Russia it was the workers' parties that moved beyond demands for the overthrow of the autocracy toward a social transformation. In China it was with the large-scale urban and rural movements organized by the working-class-centered Communist Party that the national struggle of the 1920s became also a struggle over land ownership and against class exploitation. In Cuba the extension of the revolutionary process beyond the anti-Batista struggle to the expropriation of land and U.S. enterprises was accompanied by a massive entry of urban and rural labor into the political arena.

Far from being inherently economistic, workers are stimulated by the adoption of broader political and social demands, while their activity in turn radicalizes social and political struggle in general. Thus the development of those working-class movements that have led to social revolutions has been accompanied by an integral interplay between widening working-class participation and an ever-greater combination of political and economic demands. In no sense are immediate demands eliminated; but they become linked to a broader struggle for basic changes in regime and property ownership. Individual demands for land become linked to the expropriation of the landlord class. It thus makes no sense to seek to measure consciousness through observation of individual attitudes; what alone makes sense is to study the political and social organizations that mobilized rural and urban labor and that formulated the goals and found the means to realize them.

Working-class consciousness is not the product of some essential "condition," but rather of all the collective associations and struggles within which an individual worker is correctly located. Hence, in the case of Russia, China, Cuba, and Vietnam, the presence of better-paid as well as lower-paid workers within the same revolutionary organizational matrix was a function of their common exploitation by imperialist capital, warlords, or local businessmen. No matter how great the income disparities, savage encounters with the state and constant efforts by employers to raise the level of exploitation forced "aristocrats" and "coolies" into the same general struggle. What is crucial is not the differential gains that may have accrued to different segments of the working class, but the *method of struggle* adopted to win these. High- and low-paid workers alike engaged in class struggle under the leadership of the Communist Party, which acted to unify the disparate forces and provide a central political focus.

The common methods, political organizations, and programs that embraced high- and low-paid workers thus overrode the internal differentiation of the class. Confronted by a set of overarching problems and adversaries, income differences were subordinated to the common struggle. In Cuba, for example, skilled and semiskilled urban workers and cane cutters united to furnish the backbone of the popular militias that defeated U.S.-backed military incursions, guerrilla attacks, and urban sabotage. A shared experience of class struggle created common bonds between different segments of the working class, and these sustained the revolutionary movement and formed the cadres that eventually succeeded in transforming society. In the absence of revolutionary perspectives and organization, day-to-day economic struggles have reflected the internal differentiation of the working class, taking the form of a whole series of disparate conflicts and demands. But to the degree to which the party has extended its membership and influence in the working class, to the degree to which the entire activity of the class has thus become party-oriented, even the most apparently "economistic" struggles have served as a basis for the large-scale, long-term changes, evidenced in subsequent, societal confrontations. Individual subjectivity has become subsumed within movements-in-struggle, and it is these movements that have defined the level of consciousness of the working class.

The strategic importance of the working class in the development of these revolutions derived, above all, from its qualitatively greater capacity to pose socialist goals. No other class possessed the same degree of cohesiveness and organization, linked to a socialist purpose. For while masses of peasants supported agrarian demands, and dispossessed peasants moved toward collectivist solutions, it was the proletarian forces—clearly separated from the means of production—that initially supported the formulation of a collectivist program. And the disparate strata of intellectuals, petty-commodity producers, shopkeepers, or civil servants were incapable even of themselves uniting as coherent, organized forces, let alone of formulating a program envisioning the socialization of production. That individuals from these strata came over to the working class, and even played a major role within the working-class movement in formulating such a program, does not change the fundamental nature of the strata themselves. Such individuals were *won over* to the revolutionary movement, as a result of the prior existence of an organized revolutionary pole rooted in the working class.

Since the twentieth-century revolutions in which the workers' movement played such an important role occurred in mainly rural societies, it is clear that the numerical size of the working class was less important than its strategic position. Tied to urban industrial centers, largely exploited by imperialist capital, organized in class-based unions, the collective experience of propertylessness and class struggle permeated its political experience and facilitated its mobilization behind socialist objectives. The centers of capitalist production gave birth to the key ideas, organization, and cadres that were to provide leadership and an orientation for the vast, amorphous rural masses. And the strategic role of the proletariat was further made manifest in the outcome of those primarily rural-based revolutions: The means of production, including land, were collectivized, not fragmented into the peasant ideal of small property.

The historic role of the working class as "initiator" and "definer" of the revolutionary process made possible only by the adoption en masse of socialist goals. In Russia, China, Vietnam, and Cuba alike, it was the idea of an end to exploitative relations, to class and class privilege, that detonated the assault on property holders and their instruments of domination. Economic demands became, as it were, only pretexts.

Arguments about inadequate economic performance (important in winning over petit-bourgeois strata) rationalized an attack on the existing regime, whose real motives were far more fundamental. The emotional energy and the political drive behind the mobilization of the masses in the course of these revolutions derived from the thousand indignities they suffered daily at the hands of the authorities—the industrialists, merchants, generals, and police chiefs—with their absolute power concentrated in the state. The appeal of socialism was rooted in this latent class hatred; and the revolutionary movement removed social inhibitions at the same time as it provided a focus for political expression. After the assumption of state power, the working-class character of the postrevolutionary state was in each case consolidated and made manifest in the transformation of property relations (despite programs that, in the Chinese, Cuban, and Vietnamese cases, had before the seizure of power not posed this as an objective). In each case, this was crucial in ensuring the survival of the workers' state, in a world still dominated economically (and, at least until recently, also militarily) by imperialism. Further advance in the direction of socialism, moreover, requires the establishment of forms of *working-class* democracy and power, which alone are capable of transcending the nationally limited, bureaucratic structures of the postrevolutionary regimes.

Notes

1. Mark Selden, *The Yenan Way in Revolutionary China* (Cambridge, Mass., 1974); Chalmers Johnson, *Peasant Nationalism and Communist Power* (Stanford, 1962). See also Benjamin Schwartz, *Chinese Communism and the Rise of Mao* (Cambridge, Mass., 1971), and Edgar Snow, *Red Star over China* (New York, 1941).

2. In a complementary study, the author investigates the highly disruptive effects of imperialism and war on a global scale. James Petras, "Toward a Theory of Twentieth Century Socialist Revolutions," *Journal of Contemporary Asia*, no. 3, 1978. But see also David Horowitz, *Containment and Revolution* (Boston, 1967); Gabriel Kolko, *The Politics of War* (New York, 1968); Gabriel and Joyce Kolko, *The Limits of Power* (New York, 1976); Fernando Claudin, *The Communist Movement: From Comintern to Cominform* (London, 1976); Ernest Mandel, *Late Capitalism* (London, 1975), especially chaps 2 and 11; and Andre Gunder Frank, *Capitalism and Underdevelopment in Latin America* (New York, 1969).

3. See, for example, Eric Wolf, *Peasant Wars of the Twentieth Century* (New York, 1969); Norman Miller and Roderick Aya, *National Liberation Revolution in the Third World* (New York, 1971); Franz Fanon, *The Wretched of the Earth* (New York, 1963).

4. For social forces in the Chinese revolutionary process, see, in particular, Jean Chesneaux, *The Chinese Labor Movement 1919-1927* (Stanford, 1968); Harold Isaacs, *The Tragedy of the Chinese Revolution* (New York, 1966); Lucien Bianco, *The Origins of the Chinese Revolution, 1915-1949* (Stanford, 1971); Jean Chesneaux, *Peasant Revolts in China, 1840-1947* (London, 1973); Nym Wales, *The Chinese Labor Movement* (New York, 1945); and Jack Belden, *China Shakes the World* (London, 1975). The underlying element of political continuity from the 1920s to the 1940s and beyond is discussed in Isaac Deutscher, "Maoism: Its Origins and Outlook," in Robin Blackburn (ed.), *Revolution and Class Struggle* (London, 1977).

5. For social forces in twentieth-century Cuba, see, in particular, *Pensamiento Critico*, no. 39, April 1970 (Havana), special issue on the struggles of the 1920s and 1930s; Lowry Nelson, *Rural Cuba* (Minneapolis, 1950); Luis Aguilar, *Cuba 1933: Prologue to Revolution*

(Ithaca, 1972); Leo Huberman and Paul Sweezy, *Cuba: Anatomy of a Revolution* (New York, 1961); Che Guevara, *Episodes of the Revolutionary War* (Havana, 1966), Maurice Zeitlin, *Revolutionary Politics and the Cuban Working Class* (Princeton, 1967); James Petras (ed.), *Fidel Castro Speaks* (London, 1973); and Vania Bambirra, *La Revolución Cubana* (Mexico, 1974).

6. The popular basis of the Russian Revolution, and the exceptional vitality and initiative displayed by the working class during the period of the conquest of power, is well conveyed in Alexander Rabinowitch, *The Bolsheviks Come to Power* (New York, 1976). But see also Leon Trotsky, *The History of the Russian Revolution*, 3 vols. (London, 1967); E. H. Carr, *The Bolshevik Revolution* (London, 1966), vols. 1 and 2; Isaac Deutscher, *Stalin* (London, 1949); James Bunyan and H. H. Fisher, *The Bolshevik Revolution 1917-1918* (Stanford, 1974); Marcel Liebman, *Leninism under Lenin* (London, 1975); and Moshe Lewin, *Russian Peasants and Soviet Power* (London, 1966).

7. While a great deal of attention has been paid recently by Marxists to the relative autonomy of the state, and correlatively to the extent of its instrumentalization, there has been less discussion of the relative autonomy of political organizations. But see Antonio Gramsci, *Selections from the Prison Notebooks* (London, 1971); Lucio Magri, "Problems of the Marxist Theory of the Revolutionary Party," *NLR* 60, March-April 1970; Ernest Mandel, "The Leninist Theory of Organization," in Blackburn (ed.), *Revolution and Class Struggle*; Louis Althusser, "What Must Change in the Party," *NLR* 109, May-June 1978.

8. On postrevolutionary developments in the Soviet Union and China, with special reference to the relationship between bureaucracy and the working class, see E. H. Carr, *Socialism in One Country*, vols. 1 and 2 (London, 1958 and 1959); Deutscher, *Stalin*, and *The Prophet Unarmed* (London, 1959), Moshe Lewin, *Lenin's Last Struggle* (London, 1969); Roy Medvedev, *Let History Judge* (New York, 1973); Lucio Colletti, "The Question of Stalin," in Blackburn (ed.), *Revolution and Class Struggle*; and Livio Maitan, *Party, Army, Masses in China* (London, 1976).

9. Barrington Moore, Jr., *The Social Origins of Dictatorship and Democracy* (Boston, 1966); and *Terror and Progress* (Cambridge, Mass., 1954).

10. For social forces in the Vietnamese revolutionary struggles, see, in particular, Ho Chi Minh, *Selected Writings* (Hanoi, 1977); Phang Thang Son, "Le mouvement ouvrier vietnamien de 1920 à 1930," in Chesneaux, Boudarel, and Hemery (eds.), *Tradition et Revolution au Vietnam* (Paris, 1971); John T. McAlister, *Vietnam: The Origins of Revolution* (New York, 1965); Joseph Buttinger, *A Dragon Defiant* (New York, 1972); anon., *Brief History of the Vietnam Workers' Party 1930-1975* (Hanoi, 1976); Pierre Rousset, *Le Parti Communiste Vietnamien* (Paris, 1975); William Duiker, *The Rise of Nationalism 1900-1941* (Ithaca, 1976); Van Tien Dung, *Our Great Spring Victory* (New York, 1977); Tiziano Terzani, *Giai Phong: The Fall and Liberation of Saigon* (New York, 1976); Daniel Hemery, *Revolutionnaires Vietnamiens et Pouvoir Colonial en Indochine* (Paris, 1975); I. Milton Sacks, "Communism and Nationalism in Vietnam," (Ph.D. diss., Yale); Ta Thu Yhau, "Indochina: The Construction of the Revolutionary Party," *Fourth International*, November/December 1938; and Hoang Quoc Viet, *Short History of the Vietnamese Workers' and Trade Union Movement* (Hanoi, 1960).

10

Political Opposition and the Rise of Neo-Fascism in Latin America

One of the most striking aspects of the rise of neo-fascism is the relative ease with which it has taken power, despite the growth and extension of mass popular organizations throughout Latin American societies. This was especially the case in Chile and Brazil, where there were virtually no organized protests on a national scale. In Argentina and Uruguay there were prolonged general strikes leading up to the seizure of power, but no civil wars or mass insurrections. Likewise, in the period immediately after the seizure of power, the regime was able to execute, arrest, and purge tens of thousands with very little resistance. While no doubt terror intimidated many, there remained pockets of resistances; nevertheless, the neo-fascist regimes were able to consolidate their power relatively easily. The question of why opposition and dissent were so easily crushed looms as an important issue not only for historical purposes but also because the continuing conditions of neo-fascist rule require a critical examination of the factors that *prevented* opposition in order to determine what might allow for successful opposition to emerge in the future. In this regard, probably the most striking case of the failure of mass opposition to stop fascism is Chile. By briefly examining the Chilean experience before and after 1973, we can perhaps identify some of the general factors that facilitate fascist successes.

The Case of Chile

A simple response to the question of why fascism succeeded would be "unpreparedness" by the antifascist forces. But this simple formula in fact hides a complex set of political organizational and socio-psychological factors that go far and deep in the history of the development of the left and help to explain its relative passivity in the face of the Chilean holocaust. For now, several interrelated areas that combine to shape the political response or lack of response to the events under discussion can be cited. Among the more prominent areas that require investigation are culture, psychology and organization, the political analysis and program, and, finally, the mode of participation in politics—what might be called the "political lifestyle," or the manner in which public and private activities were intertwined.

Leftist politics in Chile embodied the principles of civic culture, in particular, open politics at every level of political life; strategy, tactics, divisions, and debates became public, whether or not by intention. There was a high degree of trust and reciprocity extending to the furthest end of the political spectrum. Personal virtues, such as honor, honesty, and respect for the person, were commonplace and expected. Thus when Augusto Pinochet seized power, prominent cabinet members described to this author with considerable disgust his "dishonorable" behavior and "betrayal"—as if they held common values and pursued common goals. The same was true with regard to the behavior of the U.S. government. After the revelations of congressional committees documenting Henry Kissinger's support for direct intervention, an ex-Cabinet member was indignant because Kissinger had solemnly "promised," after the ITT revelations, not to intervene in Chile's internal politics: Such brazen duplicity and outrageous lying calculated to serve a class interest was seen as a violation of a code of personal ethics, as well as of democratic politics.

These beliefs and practices, which profoundly affected the everyday behavior of most sectors of the left, from government leaders to rank-and-file members, had serious negative consequences in dealing with the quasi-totalitarian internal opposition (the bourgeoisie and military) and the power-driven policymakers in Washington. Each effort by the left at negotiation and bargaining, characteristic features of the political culture, was seen by their internal and external class enemies as a sign of weakness to be exploited in pursuit of a single-minded purpose—to undermine and destroy the mass movement to socialism. The almost totally public nature of political activities and organization meant that all members were easily identified, and their responsibilities and positions were known to their enemies, thus facilitating the zeroing in for the repression. The same ease with which progressive American academics had access to their Chilean counterparts was true also of the CIA, which compiled a lengthy list (more than 50,000 names) that most likely became the hit list for the DINA, the secret political police. Imbued with the traditions of civility and open politics, which their bourgeois opponents publicly articulated while they covertly plotted to destroy the leftist organizations, the left lacked the minimum security precautions and clandestine networks, let alone an organizational tradition of closed, covert operations and simulated behavior so necessary to resist the police state.

The same features of Chilean leftist politics that made it attractive to the North American libertarian, liberal, and Social Democrat were precisely those features that prevented it from acting decisively and ruthlessly to crush the emerging rightist coalition that organized the coup and subsequent massive purge.

Apart from the style of politics, the substance of Chilean leftist politics deeply affected the left's capacity to act. It never seriously attempted to formulate the issues and base its analysis and practice to take account of a rupture in the political system: Less than three weeks before the coup, the leader of the major trade union confederation praised and defended the military high command and its presence in the Cabinet at a raucous and conflictive mass meeting, despite public knowledge that many, if not all, of the commanders were deadly enemies of the regime. A high communist official broke off a long-standing friendship with this author that night for pointing out the putschist tendencies and accused critics of provoking a civil war. The idea of institutional continuity embodied in the notion of the "professional military" was so deeply and widely held among the left leadership that even when the less politically sophisticated members (who were already experiencing the military's repression before the coup) protested these calls for action, they were summarily dismissed.

Lacking an adequate theory to guide the practice of revolutionary transition, the left leadership was incapable of the kind of political mobilization and preparation of mass organizations for combat. Ritual marches on symbolic occasions, affirmations of loyalty to the constitution (which the opposition scorned), and exhortations to sacrifice without consequential efforts to provide the organizational instruments led to a severe decline in morale. Operating with a pluralist conception of the state, especially the military and society, the Left was incapable of bridging the gap between a past in which it was immersed in democratic electoral politics and a present in which armed struggle between polar class interests headed the agenda. Likewise, the significance of imperialism as a political-economic phenomenon in which the imperial state plays a central role, especially in major political confrontations, was overshadowed by an economistic determination, in which the multinationals were identified as the central unit in the anti-imperialist conflict. Thus Salvadore Allende, in his speech before the United Nations denouncing U.S. intervention, differentiated between the ITT and the State—a fatal flaw. For the activities of the multinationals were clumsy and ineffectual efforts compared to the massive resources and complex operations of the imperial state.

The Left's failure to conceptualize adequately the relationship between electoral and armed struggle contributed to the prolonged crises prior to the coup. The profound collapse after the coup, evidenced in the absence of any national mobilization and resistance, was striking evidence of the total disorientation of the leadership, a product of their political assumptions, analyses, and strategy. Indeed, at the very time of the coup, Communist leader Godoy, speaking on television, asked the Party followers to hold tight and not act prematurely, because it was not clear what direction the military would go. With the Moneda (the executive house) in flames, and his followers being hunted and shot down in the streets, Godoy still clung to his Party's pluralist dogma. The same position probably explains in part the total immobility of the trade union leadership. Unlike Uruguay, where the trade unions engaged in a massive fifteen-day strike before succumbing to the military, in Chile the national leftists in the trade unions provided no leadership and direction. Since the coup, a large part of their activity has been directed at pressuring the current Christian Democratic collaborators and self-appointed leaders into making wage demands and rhetorical criticisms.

The key to the political behavior of the Chilean Left is found in its immersion in the routines of everyday bourgeois democratic political life. The rituals of parliamentary life, the duties, obligations, courtesies, and favors erased the single-minded, purposeful exercise of revolutionary power. The detailed parliamentary report, rather than audacious revolutionary action, was the norm. The tradition of peaceful bargaining and civility predisposed the Left to avoid civil war at all costs—in a prerevolutionary class context that made it inevitable. This changing political context and the terms in which it was to be waged made these values extremely dysfunctional. There was, among the leftist opposition to Allende and the Communists, a recognition of the total absence of a sense of power and its real locus in the state apparatus. But many of these critics played at class war, a verbal militancy, while rightist preparations went on apace. In fact, this verbal militancy served as a pretext for the Right to accelerate and camouflage its ongoing activities while attacking the "undemocratic" rhetoric of the Left as if it were a real threat, which unfortunately it was not. In contrast to the Left, the Right moved ahead with military preparedness: organizing support in the military and purging dissidents—from generals to privates in the navy and army—who were not taken in by the democratic mythology that their civilian supporters were mouthing. It is in this context that the statements by some American academics that the ultra-Left provoked the coup should be evaluated. It serves to further disguise the class basis of rightist politics, the antidemocratic aims of the self-styled moderate collaborators with totalitarians, and the severe political weaknesses of a democratic transition to socialism. The right (which included the ultraright Fatherland and Liberty, the conservative National Party, most of the leadership of the Christian Democratic Party led by Eduardo Frei, and the U.S. Embassy and its cohorts in the C.I.A.) from beginning to end moved with a single purpose—to destroy the experiment at democratic socialism. The tragedy is that the politics, background, traditions, and political style of the traditional left leadership could do little to prevent it.

Contradictions and Opposition to Neo-Fascism

The rise and consolidation of neo-fascist regimes in Latin America has set off contradictions and conflicts throughout society. In the ideological-organizational sphere, the state monopoly of power has led to conflicts with church people, most specifically but not exclusively among those oriented by a "social action" orientation. The Church in Brazil has attacked the doctrine of national security as an instrument for denying political rights and the doctrine of elite-directed economic modernization as a means of oppressing the poor. While the Church has been and continues to be deeply divided over social questions, the neo-fascists' disregard of the organizational autonomy of the Church, its arrest and assassination of Church officials, and its violation of religious sanctuaries have forced even conservative church people to rally around the repressed in the name of organizational solidarity. In a number of countries the highest officials of the Church have attacked the "totalitarian" tendencies of the regimes, giving legitimacy and support to grassroots Church workers and weakening the still substantial position of certain reactionary sectors of the Church. Thus one of the significant sectors of opposition to neo-fascism is located among the clergy. The political basis of opposition varies and the range includes those who oppose:

1. The arbitrary use of force and torture—the "human rights" critics.
2. The lack of democracy and political rights and the absence of political parties and elections.
3. The lack of equity, the socioeconomic policies that produce unemployment, low living standards, and widening inequalities.
4. The socioeconomic system, which underlies the repression, oppression, and exploitation.

While the opposition to neo-fascism has been growing among church people, the basis of opposition still reflects the conservative/liberal/radical divisions. Only the current extremism of the regimes creates the appearance of unity. Nevertheless, the attacks of church people by the regime, its attempt to monopolize the media and information, and the failure to observe the areas of autonomy and power of ecclesiastical authority have led to conflict with the hierarchy as a whole—conflict, however, that has led to negotiations and sharp exchanges more often than confrontation.

The second group in opposition to the neo-fascist regime is the national bourgeoisie. The development model undermines the operations of this strata by reducing protective tariffs, subsidies, credits, and the size of the internal market, through reductions in wages and public spending. In addition, the promotion of multinational corporations and the expansion of the state further displace the local bourgeoisie to a secondary role. Bankruptcy and economic losses have propelled sectors of the bourgeoisie in Brazil, Argentina, and Chile to adopt two forms of opposition: (1) demands for shifts by the regime in economic policy, toward "national development," and (2) demands for a return to democracy "without the Marxists." In both cases, there is a direct link between economic losses and political opposition. However, given the constraints of the political regime and the fear of mass upheaval, the national bourgeoisie has confined its appeals to the political and economic elite and has not engaged in any far-reaching public mobilization.

The third source of opposition has been among professionals, lawyers, and jurists, who have attempted to use their professional associations to call for the ending of arbitrary arrests and the return of juridical norms. The occupations of these professionals in direct ways have been adversely affected by the regime. This group combines appeals for human rights (end to torture) and legalistic appeals. During the periods in which repression lessens, there are also appeals for a return to democracy, essentially tying sectors of the liberal professionals to the return of liberal politics.

There has also appeared among the military three types of opposition:

1. Those who call for a return of a form of civilian "democratic" government with military veto and restrictions on the Left. This includes groups in Brazil, Argentina, and Chile.
2. A nationalist sector that supports the repressive political structure and opposes the liberal "open-door" economic policies favoring the multinational corporations. This group can be referred to as the nationalist-fascist wing, occasionally citing the fascist experience in Europe, as is the case in Argentina.
3. An ultra-fascist faction that supports sustained massive repression independently of economic cost and international isolation. The existence of this group is the usual pretext for American journalists to refer to the existing regime spokesmen as "moderates."

Thus far, however, there has not emerged any broad alliance of national bourgeoisie, liberal professionals, church people, and enlightened military capable of coordinating joint action and appealing for mass support. Each group tends to concentrate its activities to its own institutional setting. Attempts to move from one arena to another—liberal professionals and military—have been suppressed, and most public activity outside of the Church is combined with professions of loyalty to the regime. Thus, while recognizing the existence and even potential of these opposition groups, their lack of consequential ties and their willingness to work through institutional channels seems to limit their ultimate effectiveness in overthrowing the neo-fascist regimes. At best, they may substitute a new form of authoritarianism—one that provides limited rights to restricted groups and political parties.

Outside of these political elites and operating within a more shadowy existence—between legality and illegality, although more the latter than the former—are the popular organizations of workers, students, and slum dwellers. In all of the neo-fascist regimes, all basic democratic rights have been denied to mass organizations and their members: Their internal activities are regulated by the state and their rights of protest denied. Massive purges generally have left in place leaders who have no political past or who are acceptable to the regime. In any case, the right to mobilize the membership or to engage in demonstrations and strikes is illegal. In these circumstances, dissent has taken several forms:

(1) Existing leaders, even those trusted by the regime, have been pressured by the masses, in the face of gross declines of standard of living, into making public protests and demands for economic improvements.

(2) Clandestine grassroots groups operating in parallel organizations have been able to organize wildcat or unauthorized strikes. Brazil's auto workers, Argentina's railroad and subway workers, and Chile's copper miners have resorted to this form of protest. While the prime emphasis is on wage and salary issues, implicit is an attack on the whole apparatus of state control. There have been protests also concerning leaders kidnapped and assassinated by the regime. Not infrequently, the neo-fascist regime will concede the economic demands of the mass of workers and selectively arrest the dissident leaders, if it can identify them.

Student opposition has been sporadic and generally ineffectual. The universities have been massively purged, and widespread arrests and assassinations have been combined with perpetual military-secret police infiltration and intervention to limit student effectiveness. Nevertheless, in Brazil students have raised demands that range from university freedom to a general call for the restoration of democracy. The bulk of the critical intelligentsia has been forced into exile or has engaged in prudent critiques of policies and indirect or Aesopian criticism of the regime. While the neo-fascist regime and the main supporting forces have remained relatively cohesive, mass movements from below have not been able to secure the political space and freedom to communicate and organize sustained and massive protests. The distrust of the elite opposition, the latter's unwillingness to include mass socioeconomic interests into their political program (confining themselves to democratic/national appeals), and the elite's fear of a larger mass revolution have prevented the linking up of mass/elite opposition. Limited common struggles have emerged over human rights issues, such as demands that the regime account for "disappeared prisoners," torture in interrogation, the existence of death squads staffed by the police, and so on. Beyond that, the differences between the dissidents increase.

The major factor that has favored cooperation between elite opposition for limited political changes and mass-based groups has been the Communist Party and, to a lesser extent, "nationalist populist" groups. Communist parties have fostered a concept of an all-inclusive alliance that is based on the minimal demands of the elite opposition and depends on their negotiations and the tactical backing of the latter. Hence, Church hierarchs and bourgeois nationalists are supported, and mass demands are contained within the constraints imposed by these groups. These conditions have led to the slowing down of mass pressure in order not to frighten or alienate what are described as the "democratic forces." The arena of struggle is likewise sharply limited to pressuring existing organizations and leaders allowed by the junta—whose behavior throughout has been one of negotiated and limited conflict and ineffectual appeals to the regime.

Outside of these official oppositions there exists a great mass of discontent linked to local groups and leaders and with little respect and great fear of the regime. The great strikes in Brazil in May 1978, in Argentina in November 1977, and the Chilean May Day protest led by syndicalist leader, Clotario Blest, testify to the vitality of the popular classes, rather than to their mere passivity. The emergence of clandestine workers' commissions in the factories leaves the would-be "corporatist" projects empty bureaucratic husks devoid of any mass participation and significance. The massive opposition vote against the Brazilian regime and for the Democratic Movement in the great industrial centers testifies more to the mass dislike of the regime than it does to the appeal of the bourgeois politicians who run the party. This mass opposition, which exists in all neo-fascist countries, however, remains fragmented, tied to industries, regions, and particular sets of grievances at the moment. Lacking any national leadership, it can be captured by ambitious political leaders among the professional and bourgeois classes, or even perhaps by populist demagogues among the dissident military. The lack of any viable vertical movement of national and democratic changes, however, could lead in the long run to the emergence of socialist-led dissidence from below.

Conclusion

We have seen how neo-fascism generates contradictions within its own bloc of forces, forcing divisions among its own potential followers: choosing the multinational corporations over the national bourgeoisie, seeking absolute control at the expense of the Church, and undermining the conditions of employment of professionals in reorganizing the state and the juridical and law enforcement structure. The consolidation of neo-fascism, then, is at the same time the unmaking of the class basis of its rule. The concomitant appearance of solidity based on the use of force and the crushing of critics is matched by the multiplicity of groups and classes that, in one form or another, oppose it. The capacity of the regime to thus far prevent consequential alliances among the opposition nevertheless should not mask the spread of opposition. Neo-fascism, while maintaining power in Brazil since 1964, in Chile since 1973, in Uruguay since 1974, and in Argentina since 1976, has created a series of points of opposition that open up the possible demise of the regimes.

11

The Working Class and
the Cuban Revolution

Introduction

The Cuban revolution must be studied and understood as a *process*, not as an event, although particular configurations of activities and personalities at given moments certainly define important benchmarks or turning points in history. In particular, to establish the boundaries of the Cuban revolution, we must identify the essential features of the revolutionary process. It is clear that the Cuban revolution was a *socialist* revolution in the sense that its overall thrust was to expropriate the major privately owned productive forces and collectivize them. This is not to deny the importance of other elements of the revolutionary process—the nationalist, antidictatorial, anticorruption aspects, which were certainly present. However, all these components were ultimately subsumed within the social process that transformed all of Cuba's property relations.

Thus to periodize the Cuban revolution, the point must be identified in Cuban history when socialism ceased being an idea discussed in limited circles and became the driving force of a social movement and immediately threatened the capitalist relations of production. The starting point is the popular upheaval of 1933.

The 1933 revolution contained within it the first massive socialist movement of the Cuban working class. Under socialist leadership (and sometimes without), major sections of the Cuban working class directly attacked the owners of property, took control over a number of the productive units in several regions of the country, and established class hegemony over important sectors of the non-working-class regions of the country and sectors of the state apparatus (municipal government, police, and army).

While this uprising was eventually defeated, this movement had long-term influence on the consciousness of the working class and on all subsequent governments, parties and trade union activities. The uprising and the threat it represented was always present in the minds of most decisionmakers. Policies formulated henceforth, even by non-working-class (and even anti-working-class) governments had to take account of the presence of the working class. Moreover, all revolutionary and pseudorevolutionary parties and groups, each in its own way, attempted to derive their legitimacy, inspiration, and lessons from the experience of 1933. The legacy of the popular uprising was not directly expressed in new revolutionary upheavals, but permeated society at all levels and found multiple expression institutionally and legally, as well as in the memories of the participants.

If 1933 defines the beginning period in the struggle for a socialist revolution, it must be kept in mind that its trajectory did not follow a straight line but was refracted through a variety of nonrevolutionary working-class experiences that nonetheless generated a crisis of regime. Capitalism was secured at the level of the state, but labor's presence was codified and institutionalized to the point of seriously impairing capitalism's capacity to reproduce itself with any dynamism. The development of the anticapitalist struggle was a contradictory one, combining socialist and reformist elements. The result was a deadlock in which *both* capitalist development and working-class struggle was contained. This contradictory development found reflection in myriad economistic strikes, flights of capital abroad, investment in nonproductive areas, pillage of the state treasury, and, in general, an emphasis on short-term gains. Class consciousness among all social strata created a perspective based on uncertainty, in which systemic crisis was always present although mostly latent.

The armed struggle initiated in the 1950s by the July 26th Movement broke with and continued this contradictory development in a new form: State power was challenged, but seemingly for narrow ends. The previous pattern espoused by the Cuban Communist Party of advocating socialist ideology and practicing state subordination was reversed. The pattern followed by the July 26th Movement in the 1950s involved a conventional national-popular program and sustained efforts at breaking the state apparatus. The July 26th Movement accumulated social forces, many politicized and radicalized in previous decades. It gained massive support in provincial productive regions, and it drew support from a variety of fractions of classes and races open to its appeal. Traditional, regionalist, and antiimperialist forces were recruited and combined with new social revolutionary forces seeking state power. The social revolutionary process was accelerated with the overthrow of Batista in 1959 and culminated four years later with the expropriation of the major productive forces, the destruction of the old repressive apparatus, and the creation of the revolutionary state.

In summary this argument can be summed up in propositional form. (1) The socialist revolution in Cuba was the product of an accumulation of social and political forces and experiences resulting from the social upheaval of the early 1930s. (2) The content and legacy of that defeated revolution and the threat that it represented for all propertied groups shaped the content and style of Cuban politics in the direction of labor-influenced policies and institutions. (3) The central contradiction of Cuban society was rooted in the fact that while capitalistic forces controlled the state, the labor movement's presence blocked the accumulation of capital, thus both capitalist development and the working-class struggle for socialism were contained. (4) The consequences of this stalemate were an emphasis by both labor and capital on short-term gains, reflecting the general perception by all social strata that a systemic crisis was always imminent. (5) The coup by Batista in 1952 was aimed at breaking this deadlock at the expense of labor and unleashing a new phase of capitalist development from above, promoting large-scale foreign investment. (6) The revolutionary struggle led by the July 26th Movement represented an effort to break the deadlock by mobilizing forces from below, extending the social gains and in the postrevolutionary period moving toward an effort to reorganize the pattern of collective ownership and control to create a new base for economic expansion.

Four distinct periods can be identified within the overall time frame of the social revolutionary process encompassed in the 1932-63 period, which reflect changes in the scope, size, and orientation of the mass movement and working class. Within each period, activities and organizations emerged that conditioned the context and struggles in the ensuing period and the overall character of the political-economic system. Thus the revolution in Cuba must be seen as a complex mosaic involving overlapping events and activities whose cumulative effects created the context and movement for a socialist transformation.

In this interpretation the Cuban revolution is not seen as a willfull act of a handful of dedicated idealistic guerrillas. In contrast to this voluntaristic approach, historical processes—structure and action—that created the "will" should be emphasized, as well as the political and social conditions for its realization.

Mass Socialist Revolutionary Mobilization, 1932-35

The struggle against the Machado dictatorship took place in the context of a society that had been profoundly transformed by advanced capitalist expansion and the subsequent world capitalist depression. The former created a large class of wage workers linked to the productive process through the cash nexus; the latter led to the massive displacement of labor and depression of wages.

As James O'Connor notes "By 1907 the island's social economy already featured a typically capitalist class structure. The rural proletariat was (statistically) well developed; according to the census of that year, of roughly 770,000 Cuban wage workers about 40% or 310,000 laborers were farm workers. Also included in the agricultural labor force were 40,000 tenant farmers and 17,000 farm owners."[1] The process of proletarianization was evidenced in the declining number of small farmers. Before 1894 there were 90,960 small and lease farms; in 1899 this was reduced to 60,711, and by 1935 this was reduced to 38,105 small farm plots.[2]

Real per-capita income in Cuba fell from 239 pesos per year in 1924 to 109 in 1933. The combined process of massive proletarianization and precipitous socioeconomic dislocation created propitious conditions for class organization. The revolutionary political and social forms within which class organization developed reflected the absence of any substantial reformist-mediating structures capable of channeling the discontent. Machado's repression of the anarchist and socialist trade unions, newspapers, and offices undermined their organizational position in the labor movement and laid the groundwork for the emergence of the Communist Party.[3]

The rapid and massive incorporation of employed/unemployed wage workers into social revolutionary activity was largely the result of the autocratic/centralized structure of the Cuban political system, which undermined independent forms of representation and articulation. Autocratic centralism, however, was one of the basic ingredients, conditioning the massive and sustained flow of capital, guaranteeing its reproduction and accumulation. Massive proletarianization of labor, the product of large-scale and precipitous expansion of capital, emerged in the context of an autocratic-centralized state: The cohesion of the whole ensemble was sustained by the expanding world economy during the 1920s. Cuba's thorough transformation into a capitalist society was rooted in its incorporation into the productive and exchange relations of the world capitalist system. The crises of that system, beginning with the crash of 1929, directly and massively affected the Cuban class structure in much the same way that it affected the economies and societies of the United States and Europe: There were few precapitalist subsistence units to cushion this collapse of capitalist relations of production. Moreover, unlike Europe, Cuba's capitalist transformation was telescoped into a few decades, under the aegis of autocratic regimes, and thus lacked the accumulation of bureaucratic working-class reformist organization capable of deflecting the working-class struggle into purely economistic channels or into demands for change of regime.[4]

The objective transformations wrought in the organization of productive units (concentrating masses of propertyless workers in large-scale integrated production and processing networks) and social relations (cash payments tied to the creation of surplus value and privately accumulated capital) found social expression in the massive organization of class-oriented unions. The generalized depression served to homogenize wage-labor demands, because all workers, independent of wage difference, suffered sharp declines in salary and were threatened by unemployment. The autocratic-centralized regime of Machado, which penetrated relations down to the local enterprise level—intervening to repress struggles at the point of production—politicized the working class. One partici-pant observer early on noted Machado's tendency to either subordinate and emasculate representative organization or to repress it: "In 1926 Machado crushed the railroad strike and the strike of the Camaguay sugar workers, thereby fulfilling his promise that under his government 'no strike in Cuba would last more than 24 hours.' The dictatorship laun-ched an uncontrolled terror. It dissolved unions, arrested or deported hundreds of militant workers, and assassinated such outstanding leaders as Enrique Varona and Alfredo Lopez."[5]

The extensive control exercised by absentee U.S. corporate owners and the impersonal relations within production eroded the exercise of "cultural hegemony"—highlighting the specific socioeconomic forms of exploitation, the unequal relations within the enterprise, and the polariz-ed nature of the productive process (between owners and producers). Thus to the objective effects of capital accumulation at the global level were added the class *homogenizing* effects of economic crisis, the *politicization* effects of a centralized state and the *polarizing* effects re-sultant from the absence of a culturally hegemonic ruling class. These in-gredients set the stage for the political confrontation between capital and labor, culminating in the insurrectionary efforts embodied in the short-lived "Soviets" encountered in many parts of Cuba. "Direct-action" syndicalist activity had been prominent within the working-class move-ment preceding the insurrectionary phase. This tradition was embodied in the anarcho-sindicalist leadership that led the Cuban trade unions in the 1920s. The impact of anarcho-sindicalist tradition and rank and file on the increasingly Communist-led labor struggle was clear in the strike wave of 1932. As one writer notes: "The strike movement of these years (1930-1932) was strongly influenced by the traditions and tendencies of anarcho-syndicalism . . . the application of the united front, the im-placable struggle against reformist leaders and the systematic and daily propaganda on the necessity of applying revolutionary union methods involving mass participation, strike committees elected by the workers, pickets."[6]

The destruction and demise of this leadership during the Machado dic-tatorship led to the disarticulation of the organization, but not the methods of struggle, which remained ingrained in the consciousness of working-class militants. In the preinsurrectionary period, the Com-munist Party laid claim to the tradition of direct action, class struggle, and class solidarity that preceded, although not always acknowledging it. The Communist innovation was the diffusion of these ideas and their translation into mass organizational forms among the sugar workers, located in the new, modern industrial areas. The responsiveness of the rural working class to revolutionary Communist organizing efforts and the dedication and commitment of the latter are attested to in a citation in the 1935 Foreign Policy Association study of Cuba: "As one young Communist leader stated: 'The Confederation did not need much money. We traveled free of charge thanks to the drivers, who were comrades, and when we arrived in any town or central the comrades gave us lodging and food and even offered us shirts and pants. A member of the Student Left Wing stated that: 'I was in a central three days during the November strike. In the daytime they hid me in a decaying peasant hut (bohio) and fed me and only during the evening did I walk several kilometers between sugar fields distributing progaganda.' "[7] The creation of mass industrial unions in the sugar fields and factories linked to a revolutionary Communist party conditioned the further development of the class struggle in Cuba. The centrality of this sector of the working class to Cuban capitalism and its organization laid the basis for the challenge to state power. Having moved to the center of capitalist development, the Communist Party confronted the main task of organizing its overthrow. This strategically correct move, however, was dissipated by a series of tactical political errors compounded by a leadership that failed to evaluate the pulse and rhythm of the class struggle and the particularities of the Cuban social formation. For example, in the midst of a revolutionary situation in August 1933, the Communists came to an agreement with Machado to call off the general strike in exchange for wages and legality, a move they later repudiated.

During this insurrectionary period, political and economic demands were combined: Wage demands were linked to general strikes to overthrow the regime; struggles for trade union rights were joined with the organization of organs of dual-power workers' councils. The revolution against the Machado dictatorship and its supporters was quickly transformed into a struggle against the major corporate property holdings on the island—many of the same owners who were nourished and sustained by the Machado regime.

The observations by the researchers of the Foreign Policy Association present us with a detailed and vivid account of the worker-led social revolution.

The discontent was generalized throughout the interior. Students, communists and some members of the ABC were reported active in the task of labor organization. Strikes were spreading on the sugar plantations, the workers demanding higher wages, recognition of their unions and better living conditions. On August 21, the workers seized the first sugar mill—at Punta Alegre in Camaguey Province. Within less than a month the number of mills under labor control was estimated at thirty-six. Soviets were reported to have been organized at Mabay,

Jaronu, Senado, Santa Lucia and other *centrales*. At various points mill managers were held prisoners by the workers. Labor guards were formed, armed with clubs, sticks and a few revolvers, a red armband serving as uniform. Workers fraternized with soldiers and police. During the first stage of the movement, demonstrations in Camaguey and Oriente were often headed by a worker, a peasant and a soldier. At some of the centrales in Santa Clara, Camaguey and Oriente provinces the workers occupied not only the mills but also the company railroad systems and extended their control to the subports and the neighboring small towns and agricultural areas. Relief committees supplied food to the strikes and their families, and in some cases became subsistence commission for the whole population of the strike area. At various points these committees allocated parcels of land to be cultivated by the field workers. This wave of agitation and discontent extended to almost all the sugar mills and zones, reaching even the most remote areas. In the far west of the island, in the province of Pinar del Rio the tobacco workers declared themselves on strike; the coffee workers of Oriente did likewise. In the same region the Bethlehem Steel mines in Daiqiuri were closed and in the hands of the working class . . . . In Antilla the red flag waved from the city hall and in Santiago a communist demonstration obliged the mayor to abandon the province.[8]

The transparent linkages between the Machado state and U.S. capitalist expansion and exploitation facilitated mass mobilization against both: The antidictatorial and the anti-imperialist struggle were fused and, among workers, anticapitalist consciousness flourished. As the movement grew in size, this animus to corporate capitalism was extended to new strata of the population.

At the height of the insurrectionary movement, observers noted that

The strikers included young and old, whites and blacks, natives and foreign [workers]. In many places the whole working class was drawn into the movement; joining the sugar-mill workers were field workers, office and shop employees, and even inspectors and guards. The tenant farmers formulated their own demands. In some sugar mills the cooks, laundry workers, and domestic servants went on strike asking for higher pay. The small farmers and businessmen of the neighboring towns lent their solidarity.[9]

This opposition movement was instrumental in engraving a profound antagonism to labor's relation to capital. The expression of hostility to capital provided one impetus to the social revolution. More important, however, was the organization of class-anchored revolutionary organs—workers' councils that threatened to disintegrate capital's state and property relations.

The original nationalist and antidictatorial movement based on petit-bourgeois and working-class forces found expression in the populist Grau San Martin regime (1933-34). The latter, while purging the old bourgeois officers, retained the lower echelon of the capitalist state as its own guardian against the *social* threat embodied in a working-class movement, which was not to be contained within the bourgeois-nationalist program espoused by the Grau regime. The military sectors of the reconstructed capitalist state retained by Grau and led by Batista were not content with repressing workers. Sergeant Batista turned against his petit-bourgeois political mentors, including Grau, in the course of reconstructing an alliance with U.S. imperialism.

Above everything else, the 1933 revolution demonstrated the capability of the Cuban working class to organize and actively support a revolutionary socialist insurrection. This fact was deeply etched in the minds of U.S. investors and officials, as well as among Cuban politicians and bourgeois leaders. Henceforth, the Cuban working class was seen as an important factor to be taken into account in any political calculation—whether the regime pursued policies of repression, concession, or a combination of both. The threat of another "1933" was an ever-present reality that hung over Cuban politics for the next twenty-five years and was evident in much of the debate and discussion that surrounded government policy to labor organizations and legislation, as well as its attitude toward strikes and labor/management conflicts.

In terms of its long-term diffuse impact on the political system, the insurrectionary period of 1933 had a profound effect in shaping the boundaries and content of all subsequent developments in Cuba. U.S. investments, the development of a Cuban bourgeoisie, the position of the colonos, the overall process of capital accumulation (and lack of it—the problem of stagnation), and the orientation of investors toward short-term speculative gain and politicians to immediate pay-off (graft) must be seen in the context of the constraints imposed by the organizational strength of labor against capital, one of the long-term results of the 1933-35 period.

The Working-Class Presence, 1936-52

In the period following the insurrection (1933-34) and its repression (1935-36), the Cuban working-class movement reemerged as a major actor in the Cuban political and social system. Throughout this period, a whole series of legislation and policy decisions were instituted that reflected the real power and potential threat of a reenactment of 1933. This period was marked by the growth and institutionalization of workers' power, providing incremental gains to the working class and confining it within the framework of the capitalist state. The policies of the Communist and later Auténtico parties and their representatives in the labor movement followed a similar policy of actively collaborating with the state as a means of enlarging the institutional influence and economic share of the labor movement. The net result was a vast labor presence focused on a narrow set of interests. The consequences of this set of circumstances, however, were adversely to affect the capacity and willingness of capital, especially U.S. capital, to expand where labor was organized.

From the 1930s U.S. capital begins to divest itself of holdings in Cuban sugar, and, even after the crisis, Cuban sugar production remains at levels commensurate with the 1920s. U.S. mills produced 62 percent of sugar prior to 1933; this dropped to 55 percent in 1939, 43 percent in 1951, and by 1958 only 37 percent. Likewise the number of U.S. mills declined from 66 to 1939 to 36 in 1958. Foreign-owned land declined from 1.7 million hectares in 1946 to 1.2 million hectares in 1958.[10] The crucial problem cited repeatedly by foreign and domestic capitalists for Cuba's accumulation crisis was "the labor problem."

One of the most thorough and searching reports of Cuban economic development, prepared by the International Bank for Reconstruction and Development, concludes that "Conflicts in labor management relations in Cuba today [1951] are undoubtedly among the chief obstacles to economic progress."[11] The report went on to provide the historical and sociopolitical reasons underlying capitalist stagnation.

In view of the important role by the government in these matters [collective bargaining] the political strength of organized labor, which has become very great since the political and social revolution of 1933 is in many respects a more important factor than its economic bargaining power. Before the 1933 revolution, the government was usually on the side of the employers in disputes with workers. Since then the pendulum has swung so far towards the other extreme that it is now employers and investors who complain that every issue seems to be settled against them.[12]

The crisis expressed in Cuba's economic stagnation was thus a result of the class struggle and the institutional strength of labor. The electoral regimes that sought to promote capitalist development by necessity of survival gave way to labor pressure. Batista's second regime, following the coup of 1952, sought to resolve this crisis by weakening the institutional constraints that labor imposed on efforts at capitalist rationality. Even in this case, however, Batista's efforts were constantly stymied by his efforts to secure the support of the labor bureaucracy to enable him to sustain political power. Thus his regime vacillated between overtures to capitalist investors and promises of labor discipline, on the one hand, and the need to recognize and concede concessions to trade unions, on the other. The crisis of accumulation was exacerbated in both directions; insufficient capital responded, labor discontent multiplied, repression increased, the labor bureaucracy became more isolated, the political legitimacy of the regime declined, and the July 26th and other revolutionary movements consolidated their support.

The convergence of guerrilla and insurrectionary forces in the general strike that toppled Batista at the end of 1958 symbolized the merger of the forces of revolution of the 1930s with those of the 1950s. The stalemate between capital-labor, which paralyzed Cuban society, was once again challenged, only this time from the Left: The pattern of the 1930s, the reemergence of workers' militias, the intervention of *centrales*, and the takeover of land was repeated, only this time with the backing of the national government and the rebel army. Cuba had come full circle: The aborted social revolution of 1933 was consummated in 1963. The role of the mass labor movement was decisive in initiating the process, sustaining the anticapitalist animus, constraining the development of capital, and providing the organized mass forces to sustain the reorganization of the state and the collectivization of property. The period between 1936 and 1952 can be subdivided into several phases, each corresponding to different moments in the working-class struggle.

The Repression of Insurrection, 1935-36

The defeat of the revolutionary wave of 1932-34 was organized and directed by Batista in consort with U.S. imperialism. Essentially, the defeat was the result of the "regional" nature of the revolutionary movement, the sectarian policies of the Communist Party, the fragmentation of the Left forces (revolutionary petit-bourgeois nationalists and the Communist working class), and, most important, the fact that the workers were not armed or able to politicize the army sufficiently and win decisive sectors over to its side. The result was a confrontation between the reconstructed capitalist state appartus, armed and disciplined, versus a mobilized but unarmed working-class movement. The outcome was predetermined: The general strikes were broken, land and factory occupiers were dislodged, and local councils and elected officials responsible to the working class were purged and replaced by functionaries loyal to the regime.

The immediate and direct targets of the repression were the revolutionary organs of the working class: the areas of greatest concentration of working-class militancy; the leaders and political parties most directly linked to the anti-imperialist, anticapitalist movement. Although the counterrevolutionary repression soon spread to encompass nationalists, middle-class political leaders, and the less radical trade unionists, its prime goal was to destroy the basis of revolutionary working-class action. The Soviets (workers' councils) were the earliest targets, followed by the Communist Party, the left-wing nationalists around Antonio Guiteres, (a member of the cabinet of Grau San Martin), the trade unionists affiliated with them, and the industrial workers who were militants in one or another of the direct-action groups.

A confidential memorandum written by the U.S. Consul in Havana sums up the repressive policies of Batista-backed President Mendieta's regime and its political isolation:

The Mendieta Government has unquestionably met the issue of labor, red as it has seemed, squarely if not fairly. Its defense of the Republic Decree virtually suspending constitutional guarantees—the word "constitutional" seems out of place in these days of government by executive decree—and resorting again to military law to forestall the general strike was undoubtedly most opportune and necessary for the preservation of civil peace. It had reached its limits in negotiating with the strike organization. Only the use of troops with threats of violence and actual jailing of the communistic agitators could have saved it from downfall . . . . Its hold on power in the final analysis still rests upon the backing it receives from the military branch of the Government. Without this support last week the general strike would have been consummated . . . .

However, if his government does not proceed with the dissolution of the syndicates declared by decree illegal, and continues to take drastic measures against the communistic labor agitators, arresting the natives and deporting aliens, danger of another revolution threatens.''[13]

The dismantling of revolutionary organizations was accompanied by physical assaults on trade union and party facilities and assassination of revolutionary leaders and militants. The purges in the trade unions and working-class centers were destined to prevent any counterattack by the revolutionary Left. More fundamentally, the repression was not only designed to *prevent* revolutionary action, but to put the workers back in their place within the organization of capitalist production—to re-create capitalist work discipline among the labor force and restore managerial prerogatives at the plant level and government authority at the state level. The rupture in the system evidenced during the 1932-34 period raised grave problems for the functioning of the capitalist state and enterprise: The incapacity to rule and enforce capitalist laws and the threat of massive flight of capital and/or U.S. military intervention were uppermost concerns in the minds of the leaders of the counterrevolution. The growth of a "dual-power" situation, in which two sets of competing authorities governed within the same national boundaries, was incompatible with the development of capital: The counterrevolution was designed to resolve this anomaly.

The targeting of the revolutionary vanguard and its immediate periphery was designed to try to divide the working class—to separate the socialist revolutionaries from the less politicized workers. The purges were extensive and affected almost all areas of public life, reaching beyond working-class organs and affecting the press, the rights of free speech, assembly, and so on. The relentless pursuit of all protesters and the breakup of all opposition activity was designed to fragment the working class and its organization and dissolve the material basis for class consciousness rooted in collective mobility through collective activity. By destroying the *political* basis of class organization, the regime sought to restructure the working class in corporate bodies that were dependent on the state and cooperated with capital. To this end, the regime sought to retain most of the social legislation approved during the insurrectionary period, while destroying the organizations that had brought it about.

Clearly, repression was a short-term measure that could be applied to limited sectors of the working class: Its continual application to broad sectors of the class would destablize and dislocate production, in addition to homogenizing the class experience of all sectors of labor and creating a common basis and bond for future action. The policy of the counterrevolution—to combine repression against the revolutionary sectors of the working class and attempt to gain the loyalty of the rest through nationalist rhetoric and the retention of the progressive social legislation—did not succeed because the working class was denied the instruments by which to enforce the legislation and to raise its most elementary demands. The employers and their supporters within the regime took advantage of the counterrevolution to attack all the gains of the labor movement, thus undermining the regime's attempt to impose a new order in which deradicalized labor participated in the system through its ties to social welfare programs.

The immediate outcome of the counterrevolutionary offensive was quite successful. There was a sharp decrease in strikes, political or economic, and other forms of mass activity. The working-class movement suffered a historical defeat that set the movement back in terms of organizational capabilities. The democratic gains that had created the space for further mobilization were destroyed. The terror unleashed by the regime, compounded by disintegration of mass organization, led to widespread political intimidation: Political demobilization and disarticulation of organizations isolated the revolutionary forces, who fell back on their organizational nuclei and seasoned cadres.

However, these political victories of the counterrevolutionary regime over the working-class movement at the same time destroyed any capacity to secure substantial support. Cuba's labor force, composed of wage workers, and petty-commodity producers and employees, who suffered the brunt of the repressive measures, were in no mood to concede any legitimacy to the regime. Cuba's capitalist class was weak and ineffective (where they were not on the verge of bankruptcy). Only the U.S. corporations and state stood as staunch allies of the regime, and, in a sense, this support undermined the only nonclass appeal, "nationalism," that the regime could float in an effort to capture some semblance of popular support. Hence the very terms (its social base and political program) of the counterrevolutionary success created the conditions for its *political isolation*, a condition which, by its pervasiveness, threatened the middle-range stability of the regime and the operation of the social system.

Equally important, the regime recognized that the repression was not destroying the social commitments of the working class but driving it underground: Whatever the lack of public expression, there existed widespread and substantial loyalty to the revolutionary Left and more fundamentally to the working-class organizations that had gained the social benefits and had provided a certain degree of job freedom and protection from the employers. The experience of 1932-34 could not be obliterated from the consciousness of the working class, which could directly contrast its present adversities and its recent liberties. Beneath the satisfaction that the holders of power expressed was fear that a generalized decline in workers' standard of living could once again coalesce with the residual revolutionary forces in a new insurrectionary wave. The continued economic crisis, the pervasive presence of U.S. corporate power, and the lack of any popular loyalties to the state dictated that Batista adopt a new approach to securing the stability of the capitalist system that went beyond repression.

The Reemergence of Working-Class Institutions, 1937–44

Beginning in early 1936, the Communist Party in Cuba, as elsewhere, shifted its political orientation toward what is described as "popular fronts," essentially political alliances in which the Communist Party allied itself with capitalist parties and subordinated the struggle for socialism to a variety of reform goals, including welfare legislation, democratic rights, modified colonial rule (in the colonies), and, above all, antifascist declarations. In Cuba the shift from a revolutionary to a reformist perspective was aided by the defeat of the revolutionary upsurge and the demise of revolutionary democratic institutions. Hence, the counterrevolutionary ascendancy, the disarticulation of popular organizations, argued for a *reconstruction* of the movement, which in turn depended on reattaining democratic rights. However, while the conditions in Cuba facilitated the shift in political orientation, as the circumstances changed and the Left regained its organizational position, it became clear that the reformist orientation was not contingent on the adversities resulting from the repressive phase of the counterrevolution (nor on the "mistakes" during the insurrectionary period). Rather, it reflected a fundamentally different conception of Cuban sociopolitical reality and thus a different strategy, one in which socialist transformation was put on the back burner.

Between 1937 and 1944 the Communist Party developed a close and cooperative relationship with the Batista regime, exchanging political support of the capitalist state for legality, organizational freedom to organize the working class, and access to cabinet ministers, especially the labor ministry. In affirming Communist support for Batista in 1942, Blas Roca, the Party's general secretary, cited his "democratic positions . . . his categorical declaration in favor of popular demands, opposition to fascism and finance capital, his support of democracy and the complete independence of our country."[14] Batista reciprocated by stating that "the Communist Party has my respect and my greatest consideration".[15]

Thus the move toward "popular-front" politics translated itself into a policy of state collaboration, organizational expansion, and incrementalist social gains, especially prior to World War II. With the coming of the war, the social gains diminished, and what remained was essentially the consolidation of state/party ties and organizational expansion, as the Communist Party, in line with its "antifascist" program, opposed even the limited economic struggles for incremental gains that it promoted until 1941.

The shift in Communist orientation during the late 1930s and the emerging political crises facing the regime (isolation, illegitimacy) converged and allowed Batista to forge a new political orientation. The Batista of the counterrevolutionary terror was set aside and the image of Batista the Social Democrat was fashioned. For Batista, there were two basic concerns within which his "popular turn" operated: (1) to prevent any overturn of capitalist property-relations, including U.S. corporate holdings, and (2) to secure governmental power for his particular political entourage to facilitate personal enrichment and the expansion of economic holdings. Within those boundaries, Batista was willing to pursue a very flexible program of reforms and concessions to a variety of groups and classes, including the working class. The Communist Party accepted those boundaries and fashioned its party and trade union activities to maximize its gains and those of its followers within that framework. The problem was no longer one of state power but of elaborating a reform program that was sufficiently "advanced" or "progressive" to secure immediate gains for the working class and institutional stability for the party and the unions. The new nonclass vocabulary introduced was symptomatic of the larger shift from socialist revolution to capitalist reform.

The relationship between Batista and the CCP, however, was reciprocal: The Communists did not surrender the social revolution gratis but realized a series of substantial gains that had far-reaching, if indirect, effects on the operations of the capitalist system. While Batista received mass support, mobilized by the Communist Party, he had to recompense those supporters with more than symbolic payoffs. Batista granted the sugar workers 15- to 25-percent wage raises prior to the 1942 harvest, 50 percent prior to the 1943 harvest, and 10 percent prior to the 1944 harvest.

Per-capita income increased from 109 pesos in 1933 to 240 pesos in 1944. Laws dealing with minimum wages, maternity insurance (women workers received full pay six weeks before and after giving birth), and labor immobility (guaranteeing workers against dismissal) were instituted. Laws passed during the Grau period creating a Ministry of Labor, providing an eight-hour day and guaranteeing 50 percent of all employees in a given category were Cuban were maintained.[16]

As early as 1936 and continuing throughout the 1930s, businessmen complained about the prolabor policies of the regime, and the U.S. Embassy frequently intervened with the Cuban government on their behalf. One among many memos from the U.S. Embassy to the State

Department reported that the president of the American Chamber of Commerce complained that "the present administration of Cuba's labor laws is causing great hardship to American companies established in Cuba." The memo accused the Secretary of Labor of "seeking to secure the support of labor" and thus going "much further in instituting measures favoring labor than previous administrations."[17]

The cost of popular legitimacy and Communist support, at least up to 1941, was not at all cheap. New legislation was passed, and previous legislation approved during the insurrectionary period was enforced. Trade unions were recognized and union organizing drives, collective bargaining, and strikes were legalized. Moreover, the regime frequently intervened to support the economic demands of labor or, more likely, refrained from the use of force. The Communist Party was legalized, and while it promoted Batista's candidacy and gave support to his regime, it also, until 1941, disseminated socialist and anti-imperialist ideas, recruited and organized working-class militants and developed a "subculture" of working-class solidarity. While the Communist Party and its trade union leaders eschewed the general strike as a political weapon against Batista, they were not averse to organizing strikes at the industrial level on the basis of economic and social issues. Moreover, the Communist Party used its political influence to secure a series of laws that virtually made it impossible to fire workers, thus overcoming one of the great fears that had always plagued the Cuban working class in a high-unemployment economy. The combined impact of organizational legality, political access, limited class struggle, social legislation, and prolabor state intervention in wage disputes contributed to incremental gains in income for the working class and substantial expansion in labor organization.

Using dues collected as an indicator of the growth of the organizational strength of the Cuban Labor Confederation (CTC) demonstrates the extraordinary growth of the labor movement. In 1939, 4.7 million pesos were collected, while in 1944, 41.5 million pesos filled the treasury. In 1939, 282 unions were dues-paying members; in 1944, there were 913.[18] By 1945 approximately one-third or 406,776 workers were organized out of a labor force of 1.2 million.[19]

The spread of reforms and the resurgence of Communist influence in the labor movement were, however, premised on the institutionalization of that power: It was confined and defined by its class collaboration at the political level. While class struggle at the point of production reemerged, it was dissociated from political radicalism. The cooperation between labor and the regime was translated into the election of Batista and the demise of mass revolutionary political action. Nevertheless, an unforeseen consequence that resulted from the institutionalization of the labor movement was that its increasing capacity to impose wage solutions, and its ability to curtail some of the prerogatives of capital regarding control over labor in production, limited the process of capital accumulation. The continual needs of capital to modernize and rationalize production, to hire and fire labor, were in constant conflict with the institutional power of labor. Hence, while Batista sought and effectively did co-opt labor to preserve capital, he did so in such a fashion as to hinder the mechanism that facilitated its dynamic development.

This was not altogether evident during the war years (1941-45), for both the Communists and Auténticos outdid each other in collaborating with the "allies," their corporate subsidiaries, and the local capitalist class: Incrementalism, wage gains, and social legislation were put on the shelf in the interests of supporting the antifascist effort, democracy, and the Soviet Union. A resolution passed at the 1942 CTC Congress succinctly summed up the position of the Communist leadership:

While war conditions last, the Cuban workers wish to avoid all strikes and conflicts capable of paralyzing production but at the same time they insist that their suggestions for the creation of machinery for conciliation and arbitration shall be given due consideration as well as the suggestion for direct negotiations between the unions and management.[20]

One U.S. Embassy intelligence study provides the figures in Table 11.1 on Communist Party growth between its founding the immediate post-World War II period.[21] The first big gain (six-fold) occurred during the 1933 insurrection. The subsequent expansion occurred during the alliance with Batista, beginning in 1937. The war period thus witnessed the deepening ties with the state apparatus: organizational growth and the further weakening of the class-struggle ideology. The trade unions were more concerned with maintaining production than with defending workers' interests. The extension of working-class membership was more the result of cooperation with the employers than the result of organization from below.

Institutionalization, and Class Collaboration, 1945-52

The degree to which the Communist Party contributed to the growth

Table 11.1   Growth of the Cuban Communist Party, 1925–46

Year	Number of Members
1925	80
1930	500
1933	3,000
1937	5,000
1938	10,000
1940	40,000
1946	151,000

and conservatism of the labor movement cannot be overemphasized, especially during the war years. The basic relations of state collaboration in exchange for labor legislation between regime and labor confederation were established, extended, and sustained during the years of Communist leadership. The process, however, was contradictory: For as the Communists extended organizational networks, they limited class conflict; as they cooperated with capitalist regimes, they diffused socialist ideas; as they promoted the Marxist doctrine of class struggle, they practiced the politics of class collaboration; as they purported to represent the historic interest of the working class, they became integrated into the capitalist state apparatus.

The contradictory class position of the Communist Party and its working-class organizations reflected the dual realities of Cuban political economy: Its flexibility and capacity for absorption of labor demands filtered through a bureaucratized labor movement and the perennial struggles generated by stagnant capitalist development with chronic high rates of unemployment. The change of government in 1944—the victory of the Auténtico Grau San Martin—did not lead to any qualitative changes in working-class politics. Grau was amenable to the same relationship with the CCP that Batista cultivated: exchange of incremental reforms and salary increases for political support of his essentially capitalist regime. Shortly after taking office, Grau raised the wages of the sugar workers 32 percent prior to the 1945 harvest.[22]

With the end of World War II, limited class conflict again reemerged, fanned in part by the competition between the Auténticos and Communists for leadership of the CTC. While the labor unions were firmly entrenched, Communist leadership within them was less so. Years of dependence on regime support, years without any serious effort at revolutionary mobilization, and constant emphasis on immediate gains over and against the historic goals of socialism obscured the differences between the socialist and nonsocialist working-class struggle. The blurring of political differences, the decline in socialist consciousness among the trade unionists, and the dependence on agreements at the top contributed to the displacement of the Communist leadership from the labor movement once the regime changed hands. Despite its apparent massive growth, the *quality* of membership and leadership had changed. As Charles Page noted: "During the Batista-Communist Party pact many young would be proletarians without legal education saw the way open to political power through the Communist organized labor movement . . . . The aspirants to these positions . . . with scant Communist ideology, easily recanted."[23]

The organizational challenge mounted by the Auténticos could not be answered in the streets, but in the offices of the government: Offers to share power, to divide leadership posts, and to proffer support to the regime were of no avail. When the Grau regime finally endorsed the

Auténtico seizure of the CTC offices and buildings in 1948, the Communist Party was no longer politically or psychologically in a position to offer any resistance. The years of practice involving the extension and enforcement of legislation, the limited struggles for economic demands, and the bureaucratic nature of the organization vitiated the capacity for political warfare. The Communist labor movement was a giant with clay feet. Many members transferred their loyalties to the new bureaucracy, which sustained the old policies of the Communist Party, engaging in struggles and demands for wages increases, new legislation, and so forth, without the accompanying socialist educational campaigns.

As Page observes: "The Popular Front in union affairs proved to be a weakness for the Communists. One after another, formerly subservient syndicate officials joined the Auténtico rebellion. Only those syndicates with large rank and file Communist membership remained loyal."[24] Union membership grew along with the economic demands, continuing the pressures on the accumulation process. The labor movement, and its organization and demands, was so institutionalized that it easily withstood the shift in leadership and continued on its bureaucratic way. The purge of the Communist Party during 1948-52 did not have any noticeable effects at the level of labor-state relations. The Auténtico-President Prío relationship was not very different from the Communist Party/Batista/Grau relationship: Wages and salaries were increased, protective legislation was pursued, and so on. The only difference was an increase in class conflict at the plant level, as both factions competed for worker loyalty, thus fanning greater labor strife.

The conspicuous loser in this situation was the Cuban economy: Economic stagnation, speculative investments, overseas bank accounts, and political corruption highlighted a society in which local and foreign capital refused to invest in an economy that had powerful labor influence. With Communist leadership and without, the labor movement was a major force *within* capitalist society, but it was impotent to change it. Likewise, capitalism controlled the means of production but was unable to develop them. This stalemate defined the prolonged crisis in Cuban society, which the Batista coup of 1952 sought to resolve.

Military Dictatorship and Revolution, 1952-58

Many episodes and idiosyncratic factors can be analyzed to account for the coup of 1952. But the long-term structural factors that underlay the coup must be taken into account. Cuba's economy was stagnating: Sugar production, the mainstay of the economy, remained at levels comparable to earlier decades. Cuba was still overwhelmingly dependent on sugar, productivity was low, the local bourgeoisie was not investing on a significant scale or in areas to promote structural changes.

As James O'Connor noted:

. . . productivity of investments in Cuba was unusually low, reaching barely one-third of the level of capital productivity in most advanced capitalist countries. One of the reasons was that commercial and public construction took a relatively large share of total capital outlays; also an inordinate amount of investment funds were expended in trade and commerce and in consumer goods industry.[25]

Moreover, foreign capital regarded Cuba as unattractive because of its strong labor movement and the constraints that it imposed on the development of capitalism. In 1950 a thorough survey of the Cuban economy by the International Bank for Reconstruction and Development (IBRD) documented the constraints that existed and were felt by the capitalist class: The power of labor and social legislation were cited as fundamental concerns for the lack of capitalist involvement. The IBRD report complained that "few of them [Cuban workers] have had good educational opportunities, and any economic education has probably been at the hands of class struggle doctrinaries."[26]

Batista's "historic mission" was to break this paralysis, to restructure Cuban society to facilitate capital accumulation. In the 1930s his mission had been to prevent a socialist revolution and to stabilize a capitalist regime, which he did, first through repression and then through co-optation. The very terms of his success in stabilizing and legitimatizing his regime, however, created the conditions for the paralysis of capitalist expansion. In 1952 capitalism appeared to be secure from any insurrectionary threat, and Batista's efforts were turned toward creating conditions for rapid and substantial capital expansion—at the cost of the very labor programs that he had initiated earlier. In launching his offensive against labor, Batista not only failed to restructure society to facilitate capitalist advance, but he also succeeded in re-creating the conditions that undermined the security of the system of labor/regime collaboration, which he had so laboriously contributed to creating in an earlier period.

During the period immediately preceding Batista's coup, the labor movement, largely purged of Communist Party leaders and militants, extended and deepened its collaboration and subordination to the state. As Page observed:

The rank and file of the left-wing labor were intimidated by the arrests of its leadership—assemblies removed their former officers and elected pro Cofiño [*Autentico*, anti-communists]. Where assemblies did not act the Ministry of Labor intervened . . . Management proceeded to fire thousands of Communist supporters for participating in the strike.[27]

Militancy at the local level was attacked, and national union leaders kept a heavy hand on radicalized locals and an open hand toward the employers and state. Corruption within the labor movement eroded the loyalty of many members and went far beyond any previously experienced during Communist Party leadership. Bureaucratization and purges forced the labor movement to depend more and more on top-level agreements with the regime to secure minimal gains—which were necessary to maintain organizational control. Differentiation between national union leaders and their apparatus supporters and the rank and file became very marked. Page noted that "in the federation we find scant contact between the leadership and the rank and file."[28]

The virtual integration of the labor bureaucracy into the state allowed for specific union protection, legislation, and trade union cooperation with the state, but it led to the neglect of the broader social problems of unemployment (20 percent), underemployment (seasonal work in the sugar fields), vast regional and class disparities, and racism. Page summarizes the situation:

The present CTC(A) leaders drew their strength from the government. They are the government's lobby with the labor movement. Since 1947 . . . the workers pressure has been directed against their leaders and the government, rather than with their leaders against the government. . . . The most advanced social legislation . . . are circumvented by all parties concerned. Economic and political strength still dictates the solution of an issue outside of an artificial legal framework.[29]

Nevertheless, the class struggle existed within industries and especially because of rank-and-file pressure. The Communist Party, now in opposition and lacking ties to the regime, was more responsive to local rank-and-file demands for direct action. The Auténtico militants at the local level, fearful of losing their following, competed with the Communist Party in militancy. Thus clear and profound breaches began to appear within the labor movement: between a militant rank and file organized in local unions and an increasingly privileged and corrupt bureaucracy tied more to the state than to the membership; between the regional unions located in the provinces and the Havana headquarters; between certain national federations and the central federation. There were several crosscurrents operating to realign working-class forces within the national pattern of class collaboration, immobilization, and corruption.

The ease with which Batista took power—the lack of any sustained opposition—appeared to vindicate his assessment of the weakness of his political opponents and his shrewd understanding of the dependence and immobilism of the so-called mass organizations. As the leader of the CTC, Eusebio Mujal, described it, "only one out of seventy CTC leaders voted for a general strike to protest the coup—the remaining sixty nine said that 'Batista was useful.' "[30] The bureaucratized nature of Cuban political and social life and the lack of any consequential mobilization and sustained participation from below prevented any effective response. President Prio ran for an Embassy: Mujal and the trade union bureaucracy almost immediately and unanimously sought to come to terms with Batista. According to Mujal, Batista offered the CTC bureaucracy "legality and social legislation"[31] in exchange for support of the dictatorship. The ease of the transfer of political loyalties captures well the fundamental concern with maintaining organizational control and political sinecures over and against membership concerns and political programs.

Batista's inheritance included a strong labor presence and a crisis in capital accumulation. The needs of capital dictated a break with the constraints that labor represented. However, Batista, an experienced politician, recognized that he needed some form of labor cooperation. He resolved the apparent dilemma by relying on the labor bureaucracy, signing a pact with its leaders and attacking regional, sectional, and rank-and-file members who created obstacles to the expansion of capital. The Batista-CTC bureaucracy pact was successful: Each respected the other. According to Mujal, "Batista offered a pact that he honorably and loyally fulfilled."[32] Batista allowed the CTC bureaucrats to draw their salaries, secure favors, and even to make selective gains, while the bureaucracy attempted to block each and every effort by rank-and-file groups to oppose Batista's economic policies and political regime.

As the policies of the Batista regime began to affect the labor movement adversely, and as the bureaucracy continued to support Batista against the rank and file, a crisis within the labor movement and outside among nonaffiliated wage workers began to develop: Divisions reflecting class, regional, and generational differences began to appear. Among bank, telephone, and transport workers, dissidents gained strength. An editorial in *El Rodante* of the Transport Workers Union, captures the emerging opposition to Batista regime.

What attitude should we adopt before these measures . . . ? Should we allow our miserable salaries to be lowered and that they throw us out in the streets, so many family heads . . . ? If these functionaries do not resolve our problems we will go directly to General Batista . . . and explain our rights. . . . [33]

The failure to secure a response through petitions to the Labor Ministry in the traditional fashion, "radicalized" workers around "standard of living" arguments.

Within the CTC, Mujal attempted to disguise his subordination of the trade unions to the Batista regime by defining his program as "Third Force." Nonetheless, his "Third Force" rhetoric was fundamentally directed toward destroying any dissident reformist or revolutionary trade unionist group. Mujal editorialized:

We close ranks in the great struggle for the liberation against all totalitarianisms and repressive regimes, but we know who we have to defeat first, in order to pursue the struggle. The CTC supports free thought among its members but we have a statute and program to defend and that is anti-communist and absolutely democratic. . . . The Communists are not workers, they do not have a race, nor sex, they are simply communists.[34]

Within the official publications of the union bureaucracy and the hierarchically controlled conventions, there were few signs of the increasing discontent evidenced among rank-and-file workers, who were increasingly turning to other forms of pressure and protest and closer to the direct-action tactics proposed by new groups outside of the official labor movement.

Batista's main preoccupation after the coup, in addition to self-enrichment, was to seek ways and means of implementing the IBRD recommendations. The strongly entrenched position of labor, however, dictated a cautious piecemeal approach in close cooperation with the labor bureaucracy, lest a broadside unite labor and provoke a massive response. Thus while Batista appears to follow the same co-optive strategy of the earlier period, in reality his position rested, of necessity, on a much narrower base. Rather than attack the bureaucratic institutions per se, his policies were designed to weaken labor's positions in the factories and at the point of production. Although cordial relations were maintained with the labor bureaucracy at the top, there was no concomitant payoff at the bottom. Thus, in place of the sustained and effective trickle-down approach promoted between 1936 and 1944 through the trade unions, there developed a policy of horizontal payoffs to the leaders and tightening of political and social controls at the bottom.

In pursuring this different policy, Batista no longer faced the immediate threat of 1933, and he discounted the new challenge embodied in the armed movements of the 1950s. Operating within the framework of the old parties of the 1930s and 1940s, he was unimpressed by a weak and isolated Communist Party and ineffectual, corrupt Auténticos, a divided bureaucratized trade union movement, and a less politicized working class. The fading out of the past threat of 1933 blinded Batista to the reemergence of a new opposition; the July 26th movement based on a new tactical and strategic approach, although rooted, in some cases, in social forces similar to those that exploded earlier. While Batista guarded against and looked for ways to crush an urban insurrection, he overlooked the possible success emanating from combined urban mass struggle and rural guerrilla activity.

Batista set the stage for the outbreak in the new revolutionary struggles by his increasing attacks on the cumulative economic, social, and political gains achieved by the working class over the previous twenty years. His forceful intervention against labor strikes, unions, and the steady increase in pressure on behalf of the employers reactivated working-class opposition and alienated an increasing number of local trade union leaders. State repression penetrating to the local level politicized union and nonunion members, independently of the trade union bureaucracy. Herbert Mathews's reports in Santiago de Cuba best captured the emerging working-class revolt:

A group of nine trade union leaders representing a cross section of the workers of the province came to see me at the hotel. . . . "None of us is political or partisan. We speak to you as Cubans. We represent and we are the people of Cuba and we are against Batista and his clique. You may be sure that all workers are good Cubans and feel the way we do, all except our top national leaders who are chosen by Batista and are in his pay." . . . Anti-U.S. feeling runs high in this city because of what is considered United States support for General Batista. There is a constant exodus from the city of youths who try to join Fidel Castro . . . the center and symbol of Santiago de Cuba's resistence. . . . The tension is almost palpable and is certainly very dangerous to the regime. Santiago de Cuba is a city living in a state of fear and exaltation and it is the exaltation that dominates.[35]

The unwillingness of the bureaucrats to channel this discontent or to provide any leadership opened the field to the direct-action groups organized against Batista. The principal conflict within Cuban society was between the capitalist state embodied in the Batista dictatorship, which sought to restructure Cuban society for the capitalist class as a whole, and the Cuban working class, increasingly disposed to act outside the official party and trade union organizations. Thus, because the capital labor struggle did not take place primarily between private owners and labor unions, the fact that a highly politicized class struggle was taking place—and not merely an amorphous political struggle against a dictatorial regime—should not be obscured.

Moreover, while Batista was pushing to reverse previous gains, the working class in Cuba was looking beyond its previous achievements toward a new set of demands that went beyond the capacity of Cuba's dependent capitalist society: The demands for full employment and improved and increasing social services came into conflict with the imperatives of capitalist rationality, which demanded an end to work definitions that multiplied employment. The reinsertion of U.S. capital to promote a diversified economy necessitated a lowering of social overhead costs and a reallocation of state expenditures from social services to capital expenditures and infrastructure investments. The pursuit of this new development strategy forced Batista to cut off labor's access to the state and to increase his ties with U.S. and domestic capital. The result was to re-create the basis for mass confrontation politics—similar to the early 1930s. Following a similar development model—"from above and outside"—Batista ended up creating the same revolutionary situation in which a military-centralist autocrat state linked to U.S. business provoked a massive popular movement that fused democratic, anti-imperialist, and anticapitalist forces into one broad movement outside of the official parties and trade unions.

From General Strike to Collectivization, 1959–63

A number of striking aspects of the social revolutionary process that occurred between 1959 and 1963 have been inadequately dealt with both by friends and foes of the Cuban revolutionary process. The first is the

massive activity and active support of the working class in the collectivization of capitalist property and the construction of revolutionary
organs of state power. The second is the *speed* and *scope* of the action
directed toward realizing these revolutionary ends. Third is the unques-
tioned and unambiguous *success* of these efforts. The explanation usually
set forth is that Castro and his inner circle were able, because of their
personal influence and because of the deficiencies in political organization of the local bourgeoisie, to engineer this revolution with the support
of the masses who were brought into this process. The conflict with the
United States facilitated this change, for the leadership was able to
mobilize on a nationalist basis forces that otherwise might not have
responded to a purely anticapitalist or socialist appeal. The long and
short of these "explanations" is that they do not go far enough—
whatever their simplicity and appeal to "obvious" facts. Why was there
such a massive response in such a short period for such monumental
changes if there was not a whole history of struggles and activities that
preceded it? What elements in Cuban society weakened the bourgeoisie's
social and political position, vis-à-vis labor, even as the former's position
with relationshp to U.S. capital was improving?

It is clear that Cuban national capital was growing in importance in
sugar, relative to the United States, yet its capacity to exercise hegemony
was severely constrained. Hence, the thesis of U.S. corporate capital
"undermining" the basis of social domination by the bourgeoisie was
less tenable in the late 1950s than it was earlier. Castro's actions and
revolutionary measures—intervening enterprises, nationalizing large-
scale foreign enterprises—followed a pattern that had been initiated by
the workers' movement in the early 1930s and followed the labor/capital
strife that was endemic to Cuban labor relations throughout the
preceding period. The post-1959 struggles in Cuba, culminating in nationalization and collectivization, deepened and extended the class struggle,
frequently a direct response to the labor/capital conflicts emerging in the
post-1959 period. The leadership drew sustenance and, in turn, was influenced by the generalized anticapitalist animus that pervaded rank-
and-file labor and animated its activities for a quarter of a century. The
revolutionary regime was able initially to build on the juridical structure
and social legislation, which reflected past working-class struggles, in implementing and extending laws to secure and provide employment, increase the standard of living, and lower costs of essentials. The "continuities" with the past, however, were in some ways superficial: The
depth, scope, consistency, and coherence of application were *qualitatively*
different after 1959 because the state was not trying to deflect working-
class action from a revolutionary overturn, but to provide space for its
consummation.

But it is a mistake to speak of the "state" at least in the immediate
period following Batista's overturn, for the situation was much more

fluid: The dismantling of the military/police apparatus was in full force (the civil bureaucracy was still in place, although quite passive), cautiously waiting to see whether they could be individually or collectively assimilated to the new order. The expansion and growth of the rebel guerrilla army and the proliferation of local armed committees served as transitional forms of state power in the immediate circumstances. The armed struggle launched by the counterrevolutionaries against the regime precipitated a massive movement demanding the arming of the people—a movement that paralleled the insurrectionary experiences of the 1930s *and* grew out of the armed struggle of the 1950s.

The extension and deepening of the revolutionary process was as much through mass pressure as it was through leadership initiative. In the sugar fields mass action occurred: "The revolutionary militia have converted the 161 sugar centrales of the island into 161 bulwarks of the revolution. These militias guard their own work centers against criminal sabotage."[36] In the petroleum refineries similar mass action occurred: "It was the militias of these work centers, those who were alert and vigilant before the interventions and who proceeded to make them function, with the decided support of the Cuban technicians and engineers."[37]

In all the major unions—railroad, metallurgical, and sugar workers—new revolutionary slates were elected. In addition, the Castro Government was pressured from below for a militia form of army. "But in the same measure that these [U.S.] aggressions were consumated the Cuban people with a profound revolutionary spirit . . . clamored for military instruction and necessary preparation in order to defend the country. . . . Thus emerged the National Revolutionary Militia."[38] This popular working-class army was instrumental in defeating the U.S.-backed invading force at the Bay of Pigs in April 1961. The movement from below for a working-class militia as an alternative form of state power culminated in the transfer of state power from the capitalist to the working class, deepening U.S. and Cuban bourgeois opposition. If this mass movement for militias *originated* in a struggle to defend the limited gains attained in early 1959, it resulted in further polarizing class forces, internally and internationally, and ultimately extending the collectivization process throughout the productive units within which the armed workers were employed.

The genius of the Castro leadership was not to "create" consciousness among Cuban workers, but rather to respond to the historic legacy of Cuban class politics, to facilitate its organizational expression, and to synthesize and articulate the sometimes inchoate strivings and tumultuous activities. In many ways, Castro's success was based on the fact that his revolutionary trajectory was similar to the "average" class-conscious militant: a historic sense of capitalist and imperialist exploitation that had built upon an organizational movement defending Cuban national and working-class interests, a commitment to new forms of struggle, including arms, and a profound rejection of the compromised parties of the past. In other words, it was a clear understanding of the adversaries and a commitment to defeat them, a willingness to use all necessary political and military means, and a vague general idea of what postcapitalist society and state should emerge. The strong point of both Castro and the militants in the Cuban working class was a concrete sense of the past and present and a consequential commitment to rectify or abolish exploitative relations. Where they both were weak was in their sense of the social system that should emerge. The movement of militants and leadership were more anti-imperialist and anticapitalist than socialist—the product of twenty-five years in which immediate militant struggles were not illuminated by a socialist perspective.

The resurgence of revolutionary class struggle began in the mid-1950s. Among the myriad forces that began to percolate in the campaign against the Batista dictatorship were sectors of the working class. Beginning in mid-1955 strikes and demonstrations by employees in diverse industries, including the sugar industry, began to be manifested. The original impetuses in many cases were "economic"—wages, bonus payments, job security. The limitations that Batista tried to impose on labor's power in relation to capital and the collaboration of the CTC leadership with his "development" scheme *alienated* rank-and-file labor and politicized the stuggle. As worker discontent was not deflected by regime policy and as the CTC leadership was incapable of mediating the disputes, new local leadership emerged to articulate grievances.

The expression of labor discontent outside of official channels was repressed by the regime, transforming the economic discontent into political opposition to the regime. The first major indication of mass working-class opposition was the successful general strike organized by Frank Pais and others in Santiago de Cuba in Oriente Province in 1956. This mass working-class action was not an isolated event but reflected the constant tension and hostility that existed there between the regime and the laboring masses and included a substantial number of local and provincial working-class leaders. The revolutionary mobilization reflected the dialectical interplay between the mass struggle of the cities and the armed guerrilla movement in the countryside. Beyond the tactical differences, the success of the struggle depended upon the interdependence and articulation of both struggles.

Castro's rupture with the conventional collaborationist politics of the 1940s, and his mass appeal to join the revolutionary movement, was based on an accurate perception of two basic facts: that the insurrectionary tradition of the 1930s was still alive; and that a significant mass of Cubans, in and out of the official labor organizations, who were not represented in the class struggle, were capable of engaging in a confrontation with the regime. The guerrilla movement was seen by its organizers as an instrument to weaken the regime and organize the general strike leading to the mass insurrection. The "foco" concept, of guerrilla action being a substitute for mass action, was foreign to Cuban history and thus to the thinking of the revolutionary vanguard of the July 26th Movement. The Movement was a national political formation, anchored in the mass struggle of provincial towns, drawing support from wage and salaried workers of the cities and peasants in the countryside, and finding active collaboration among the younger generation of local trade union leaders. As the struggles developed, the movement expanded and drew to itself and reactivated many of the militants from the earlier insurrectionary period. These physical links between the revolutionary past and the younger militants of the 1950s laid the groundwork for the radicalization of the post-Batista period.

The working-class presence in the anti-Batista struggle and its specific class interests were subsumed within the general democratic, antidictatorial framework. It shared, along with other petit-bourgeois and bourgeois forces, an opposition to the political repression of the regime—but from a different class perspective. This temporary convergence would immediately dissolve after the overthrow of Batista in the competing and conflictive efforts to restructure and define the nature of the state apparatus. The working-class struggle against Batista was directed toward maximizing its weight and interests within the state and society and ensuring that its gains would not be endangered. Hence, the historic importance of the working-class demand for "arming the people"—thus blocking the attempt by the bourgeois coalition to demobilize the populace and to restructure an armed apparatus sympathetic to its class interests. The precipitous reaction of the more extreme sectors of the bourgeoisie in launching armed actions against the initial structural changes of the coalition regime served as a catalytic force, alerting the working class to the inherent dangers in the politically fluid post-Batista period. The armed mobilization of the masses, accompanied by sociopolitical pressures within each productive sector and firm in which they were employed, accelerated the radicalization process. Nationalization and state interventions multiplied, breaking up the coalition regime and forcing the bougeois cabinet minister to abandon responsibility for the expropriation of their closest capitalist associates.

The emerging power bloc of guerrilla leaders and armed mass working-class organizations overwhelmed both the political and economic organizations of the bourgeoisie. The latter lacked comparable instruments to "confront" the revolutionary forces with the disintegration of the old (Batista) state apparatus; they lacked any comparable organization within the trade union apparatus and any "special formations" derived from the anti-Batista struggle. Their only recourse was the U.S. imperial state apparatus, to which they had recourse. The surprisingly rapid and drastic shift from "reformist" ministers of a "democratic," "nationalist' regime to open collaborators with imperialist and dictatorial forces (as one encounters during the Bay of Pigs invasion) is explained by the absence of any alternatives between the organized armed power of the Cuban working-class and the organizational apparatus of U.S. imperialism. Having broken with the first, the second remained the only choice; having to choose to live under working-class power or dependent dictatorial capitalism, the bourgeoisie belatedly chose the latter—symptomatic of the behavior of the bourgeoisie throughout the continent for the next two decades.

For the working class, the anti-Batista mobilization was a form of class struggle, directly political and with an immediate set of grievances directed at the capitalist system. The original limitations of that struggle —that it was confined at the political level and was informed by a series of social reforms—did not prevent it from deepening and extending in the postdictatorial period. The multiple conflicts between labor and capital after the overthrow and the enormous number of demands that the populace placed on the new leadership can be seen as attempts by the working class to put its social class content into the emerging democratic forms. The class struggle in the post-Batista period became clearer, and the social dimension of the revolution became predominant—essentially through the penetration by the working class of the critical new institutions, the embryonic revolutionary state, the Rebel Army, and the popular militias. The transition from the democratic to the socialist phase of the revolution, punctured as it was by conflicts and some violence, was relatively peaceful, because the working-class role in the armed struggle for democracy had secured it a strategic position, allowing it to undermine all bourgeois opposition.

Notes

1. James O'Connor, *The Origins of Socialism in Cuba* (Ithaca: Cornell University Press, 1970), p. 22.

2. *Problems of the New Cuba* (New York: Foreign Policy Association: New York, 1935), p. 54.

3. Charles Page, "The Development of Organized Labor in Cuba" (Ph.D diss., University of California, Berkeley, 1952), p. 62. Evelio Telleria Toca, *Los Congresos obreros en Cuba* (Havana, 1974), p. 230 passim. Telleria cites Machado's destruction of the anarchist-controlled Sindicato Fabril as a crucial element in its decline.

4. Paradoxically, one of the outcomes of the defeat of the social revolutionary movement was the deliberate effort by Batista after 1935 to cultivate working-class organizations that would mediate the struggles in a fashion to contain them within capitalist state structures.

5. Fabio Grobart, "The Cuban Working Class Movement from 1925 to 1933," *Science and Society* 34, no. 1, Spring 1975, p. 86. See also Mirtz Rosell, *Luchas obreras contra Machado* (Havana, 1973). José Tabares del Real, *La revolucion del 30: Sus dos últimos años* (Havana: 1971). Lionel Soto, *La revolucion del 33*, 3 vols. (Editorial ciencias Sociales: Havana, 1977).

6. Evelio Telleria Toca, *Los Congresos*, p. 235.

7. *Problems of the New Cuba*, p. 204.

8. Ibid., pp. 201–2.

9. Ibid., p. 202.

10. O'Connor, *The Origins of Socialism in Cuba*, p. 27.

11. *Report on Cuba*, International Bank for Reconstruction and Development, Economic and Technical Mission (Washington, D.C., 1951), p. 357. See also, *Summary of the Labor Situation in Cuba*, International Co-operation Administration, Office of Labor Affairs, U.S. Department of Labor, 1956, pp. 1–3.

12. *Report on Cuba*, p. 361.

13. U.S. Consul Lee R. Blohm to Department of State, March 15, 1934. *Cuba Labor Notes*, U.S. Archives.

14. *El recibimiento al Coronel Batista* (Partido Communista: Cuba, 1938).

15. *Carta del Coronel Batista a Pepin Rivero* (Havana: May 25, 1940).

16. Page, "The Development of Organized Labor in Cuba," p. 89 passim.

17. Memo from Laurence Duggan, U.S. Embassy in Havana, to Department of State, Division of Latin American Affairs, August 19, 1936.

18. *Balance General 1943* C.T.C. Secretaria Financias (Editorial CENIT Havana, 1944).

19. *Informe rendido al día 2 de diciembre 1944*, IV Congreso Nacional de la CTC.

20. Lazaro Pena, *El proletariado, las huelgas y la lucha contra el nazismo* (Havana, 1943). The clearest expression of the collaborationists' perspective is found in "La colaboración nacional entre obreros y patronas" *CTC* Marzo 1945, no. 61, pp. 14–15.

21. U.S. Embassy Report, *The Communist Party in Cuba*, March 1947.

22. Page, *The Development of Organized Labor in Cuba*, p. 96.

23. Ibid., p. 217.

24. Ibid, p. 121.

25. O'Connor, *The Origins of Socialism in Cuba*, p. 18–19.

26. IBRD, *Report on Cuba*, p. 358.

27. Page, *The Development of Organized Labor in Cuba*, p. 128.

28. Ibid., p. 218.

29. Ibid., p. 223.

30. Interview with Eusebio Mujal, April 11, 1979.

31. Ibid.

32. Ibid.

33. *El Rodante*, September 1952, pp. 1–2.

34. Ibid., August 1954, pp. 7–8.

35. *New York Times*, June 10, 1957, p. 10. According to one account among the known participants in the Moncado attack, the bulk were wage and salaried workers.

Factory and shop workers (including truck drivers, stevedores, construction workers, and one taxi driver	44
Office Workers and store clerks (including restaurant workers)	33
Students	13
Agricultural laborers	11
Professionals	4
Small businessmen	6
Self-employed workers and traveling salesmen	10
Teachers	1
Housewives	1
Soldiers	1
Employed in father's business	3
Occupations unknown to author	20

See Lionel Martin, *The Early Fidel* (Lyle Stuart: Secaucus, N.J., 1978).

36. *Verde Olivo*, no. 17, July 10, 1960, pp. 28–29.

37. Ibid., July 17, 1960, p. 15.

38. Ibid., November 12, 1960, p. 8.

12

Peasant Movements and Social Change: Cooperatives in Peru

by JAMES F. PETRAS and A. EUGENE HAVENS

Introduction

Over the past several years the notion has been popularized that cooperative farming is the most rational, efficient, and equitable approach to developing agriculture in societies experiencing agrarian reforms or other forms of structural change. The demise of traditional landlord systems under the pressure of peasant movements has proceeded apace in a number of societies. In the face of centuries of exploitation and deprivation, peasant-based movements have either directly taken control of large landed estates or forced governments, through specialized agencies, to expropriate landed property. The disintegration of traditional landholding patterns immediately raises a basic policy question: What system of land tenure should take its place?

Cooperative farming has been frequently proposed as the most viable alternative. By combining resources it cuts back on the duplication of costs, allows the enterprise to take advantage of economies of scale, facilitates large-scale purchases, and lessens the possibility of social inequalities, thus promoting collective in place of individual mobility and sustaining "communitarian" values. Economic rationality (scale of production and distribution) is supposedly combined with equity (greater social good for the greater number).

Moreover, a number of writers, anthropologists included, stress the continuity between the past precapitalist collectivity and the post-reform cooperative, with the latter seen as fitting in better with the cultural-historical traditions, thereby ensuring the integrity of the community as against the divisive effects of unmitigated market activities (Cf. Erasmus 1961 and Wolf 1978). The cooperative thus serves to sustain cultural continuity and promotes social integration while augmenting the levels of production and income.

What has been lacking in much of this literature is a discussion of the larger political and social context, which influences the internal structure, social relations of production, and economic exchange—all in turn determining the viability of the cooperatives and thus the attitudes of their members. The policies and social nature of the state, under whose auspices the cooperatives are initiated, are crucial to understanding peasant behavior.

The thesis here is that peasants are neither inherently in favor of nor against cooperative or individual holdings but will respond to either according to their own practical experiences and how these experiences affect their everyday calculations of their private interests. If peasants experience cooperatives as agencies through which they can maximize their interests, they will support and participate in them. If they experience them as exploitative or adversely affecting their private interests, they will reject them or act to undermine their operation.

Peru: From Hacienda to Cooperative

The focus here will be on the recent experience of extensive and widely publicized land reform and cooperativization initiated in Peru over the past ten years. The "model" of agriculture promoted by the "reformist" military regime was essentially rooted in the notion that the highland traditional *latifundio* and coastal plantation systems were serious obstacles to economic development, social and regional integration, and political participation. The Peruvian agricultural system had been characterized by great concentrations of land in the hands of a few domestic and foreign landowners, while the bulk of the rural labor force was located in tiny plots of land (*minifundistas*) and Indian communities, frequently employed as wage laborers or even held in semifeudal obligations to the landowners. (See Table 12.1).

The military coup of 1968 brought a reformist military regime led by General Velasco with a different vision of rural society—one that emphasized the centrality of cooperatives in transforming the rural sector. Three ideas informed Velasco's vision: First was the notion that the cooperatives were part and parcel of Peru's communal past. This fit in nicely with the search for a nationalist developmental conception that claimed the necessity to adapt processes of social change to "national realities." The second idea (and closely related to the first) was that the "Peruvian Revolution" (as its leaders described it) would follow a "third way," between the capitalist market of the West and the centralized collectivism of the East. The cooperative idea was seen as a means of combining features of both worlds in a way that optimized collective work and individual enterprise. The third idea was rooted in Catholic-humanist ideology, which stressed the notion of an organic community over and against individual gain, in which leaders and followers (government and cooperative members) were bound together by a set of mutual obligations and duties. What was never set clear in the ideology was who would decide the distribution of obligations and duties. And in case of conflicts between government and cooperative, it was not clear who would serve as arbiter, since the divine spirit could be seen to talk in many tongues, ranging from (1) state technocrats interested in harnessing peasant production to industrial growth to (2) Marxist peasant organizers encouraging peasants to keep the whole of the social product that they produced.

As the government moved beyond the expropriation of landed estates to the establishment of cooperatives, the crucial question arose as to the organization of the cooperatives. The meaning of the co-ops to the peasants, their role and experiences, was substantially determined by the structure and organization of the co-ops. The philosophical and vi-sionary cooperatives of humanistic thought and communitary ideology were operationalized by military generals and colonels. Thus the ideology of cooperatives was presented as an abstract plan that would stand above class structure and class struggle; but the official who presided over its implementation maintained concrete and tenacious ties to the class structure and the state apparatus.

Table 12.1   Distribution of Total Land Area, Arable Land, Permanent Crop-Land Natural Pastures by Size of Production Unit, 1961

Size of production unit	Percent of number of production units	Percent of total land in farms	Average size of holdings (Has.)
Hectares			
0–5 Has.	82.9	5.8	1.5
5–100 Has.	15.7	10.4	15.8
100–500 Has.	0.9	8.8	133.5
More than 500 Has.	0.5	75.0	1,212.5
Total	100.0	100.0	

Source: Peru. Dirección Nacional de Estadísticos y Censos. Primer Censo Nacional Agropecuario. Lima, 1965.

The Structure and Organization of the Cooperatives

The formative period in the establishment of the cooperatives played a decisive role in determining their long-term operation and ultimate demise. The relation between mass peasant movements and the military was crucial in this period. From the mid-1950s to the mid-1960s large-scale peasant movements developed in many parts of Peru. One indication of this mobilization was the rising number of strikes in agriculture. (See Table 12.2) These movements, sometimes organized by Marxists, frequently took over estates and confronted military and police detachments dispatched to restore landlord possession. The high point of these movements occured in Convención-Lares. Many officers who had

Table 12.2   **Strikes in the Agricultural Sector, 1957–68, Officially Recognized by the Ministry of Labor**

	Total number of strikes in all sectors	*Strikes in agriculture*	
		Number	*Percent*
1957	161	19	11.8
1958	213	21	12.6
1959	233	31	13.3
1960	285	40	14.0
1961	341	32	9.3
1962	380	55	14.4
1963	442	58	13.7
1964	398	71	17.8
1965	397	36	9.0
1966	394	51	12.9
1967	414	77	18.5
1968	364	69	18.9

Source: Mejia and Diaz, 1975 : 23.

witnessed the radicalization and mobilization of the peasants—and not infrequently had participated in the repression—helped form the post-1968 reformist military regime. Notwithstanding their coercive role, they were cognizant of the underlying social realities, or so they thought.

A classic example of the intervention of the military in peasant uprisings was that of La Convención-Lares. When this movement began in the late 1950s, the police were sent in to control it. However, they were incapable of putting down a movement that was spreading so rapidly and was becoming more and more organized. So, the army was called on to "restore order." This was the first time that the military became involved in a popular movement in the interior of the country. They were able to confirm for themselves the precapitalist conditions under which the peasant had to work and that the demands made by the peasantry were not only justified but were directed against illegal labor conditions practiced by the landowners. This experience convinced the more progressive elements of the military that an agrarian reform was necessary not only to destroy the backwardness of a great portion of the Peruvian socioeconomic structures, but to avoid future popular uprisings

(Villaneuva, 1973). The success of the Convención-Lares movement demonstrated to the military the danger of ignoring the conditions that make a popular movement possible.

Once in power, the military thought that by expropriating the landlords and organizing the landless in cooperatives they would dampen the revolutionary fires, improve the lot of the peasants, secure their loyalty, and link the agriculture sector to the development process. Table 12.3 shows how land was distributed in Peru from 1969 to 1979.

Table 12.3   Land Redistribution in Peru, 1969–79

	Units	Area distributed (Has.)	Beneficiaries
CAP[a] (excluding sugar)	566	2,096,069	79,354
Sugar CAP	12	128,566	27,783
Peasant groups	798	1,585,561	43,945
Peasant communities	408	715,850	110,971
SAIS[b]	60	2,802,435	60,930
Social property	11	232,653	1,375
Individuals		542,794	31,918
Total	1,855	8,103,948	356,276

Source: Dirección General de Reforma Agraria, Lima, Peru.

[a]Cooperativas Agrarias de Producción (Agrarian Production Cooperatives).

[b]Social Interest Agrarian Societies (including several haciendas and adjoining small producers, and day laborers in an organized community).

While there were some 356,000 beneficiaries—and more than half of the total cultivatable land was affected—the reform did not affect the one-million-plus, small (less than two hectares) landholder. The cooperatives were essentially in the hands of the military, who chose the targets, the timetable, the ideas. Clearly, this was a case of "reform from above." To "popularize" the idea of "cooperativization" among peasants, SINAMOS, or The National System of Mobilization and Support, was later established to provide political leadership and to encourage peasant participation (Caballero 1978; Havens, et al., 1979).

The organization of the co-ops was essentially centralized in the military or in civilian officials under their orders (Caballero 1978; Havens, et al., 1979). Both locally and nationally, hierarchical patterns of authority—not dissimilar to those of the previous landowners—were pervasive, even to the point where the "cooperative colonel" who ran the farm occupied the house of the former landowner. (An apocryphal story circulating in Peru tells of the colonel who took over the Guildermeister estates and after two days spoke with a German accent.) Centralized control of the management and operation of the cooperative reflected the concern of the military that change be "ordered" and "controlled," i.e., that it would not spill over and challenge its authority by creating independent bases of social and political activity. While the military expropriated the landowners, they did not do so to allow "the Marxists" to take advantage of the changes to gain new adherents. Lacking a capacity to compete politically with their Marxist rivals, the military substituted bureaucratic-administrative measures to try to exclude critics and to "integrate" peasants into their national development plans through centralized power.

Within the larger scheme of development, the cooperatives were essentially subordinated to economic projects elaborated by a regime primarily concerned with rapid industrial and mineral growth. The agro-cooperative setup, apart from eliciting political support from the peasants to the regime, was seen as providing export earnings to help finance industrial growth and as growing inexpensive food to lower the costs of reproducing industrial wage labor in the cities (Caballero and Alvarez, 1978). According to Legal Decree 20610 of 1972, all cooperatives located in the departments of Ancash, Lima, and Ica were obligated to dedicate 40 percent of their cultivable lands to basic foodstuff production. These foodstuffs were subject to price controls that favored the urban consumer. By 1976 more than 50 percent of the co-ops were conforming to this decree (see Peru, 1977 : 32–35). Thus the formation, organization, and operation of the cooperatives were largely directed "from above and outside" the control of the peasants, who were instrumentalized to serve ends that, over time, they began to see as alien to their interests.

Consequences of Cooperativization

The centralized redistributive politics of the regime had far-reaching effects on many levels within the reformed sector. The centralized policy-making structures of the cooperatives came into conflict with the participatory ideology promoted by the regime's mobilization agencies. The new structures were viewed by the peasants as replays of the old—merely a change of *patrones*. Decisions were taken at the top, and the peasants were "mobilized" to carry out the policies commanded by the new bureaucratic-technocratic elite. For example, in the case of the CAPs, the law established four groups of workers: (1) manual workers on the land, (2) manual workers in agro-industrial plants, (3) service workers, and (4) high-level managerial officials. Although these groups vary greatly as to the number of persons in each, the law provided that each group be given 25 percent of the membership of the governing and managing bodies (Pasara, 1971b : 49).

Thus the workers were co-opted into participating in a system of entrepreneurial organizations dominated by technocratic leaders oriented toward productionist goals. Politically, military reformism wanted their support in its struggle against emerging urban-worker struggles. Criticism and debate from below was dubbed "politicization," "counter-revolutionary," or "subversive." Little initiative and direction was vested in the hands of the supposed beneficiaries of the land reform. In most instances, only one worker was included in the Production Committee, with the rest of the twelve-member directive committee composed of technocrats (see Caballero, 1978b). Conflicts were largely resolved through the traditional means of government (police) intervention or threats of work stoppages.

Increasingly, "mobilized participation" came to be experienced by the peasants as manipulation. The persistence of suspicion and its pervasiveness among peasants eroded the trust between government technicians and peasants, which was essential for the successful operation of the cooperative. Centralized policy making undercut the positive responses initially elicited through the redistributive measures and re-created an alienated peasantry. Given the role of the peasant as "object" of cooperativization rather than as the subject actively restructuring his social role in production, it is not surprising that the peasants came to view cooperative organization as a new form of manipulation and subjection.

The authority of the centralized policy-making structure was further eroded by its very inadequate administrative performance and by the substantive policies that it pursued. One could imagine circumstances in which the co-ops were efficiently managed and in which substantive policies that provided tangible benefits to the peasants could have elicited at least the passive approval or acquiescence of the peasants. In fact (as was suggested above), the bureaucratic-centralist administration was linked to a development strategy that subordinated agricultural development to capital accumulation in the industrial and mining sector (Havens, et al., 1979). Rather than being a recipient of massive government investments, the rural sector was viewed as a means of pumping out surplus to finance development in the urban-industrial areas. Inadequate financing of infrastructure, resource-development research, and agricultural machinery led to a pattern of "redistribution without development." Insufficient credits and poor administration and investment decisions by co-op managers led to debts without expanding the productive base to repay them. Data for the IV Agricultural Zone (Huacho, Lima, Canete) indicate that credit for the CAPs declined 52 percent in real terms from 1970 to 1975 (Peru, 1977).

Increases in the cost of agro-inputs and high profittaking in processing defined the unequal exchanges that reduced peasant incomes. To defend threatened incomes, cooperative members increasingly engaged in political and social protest against the local representative of the central government in the leadership of the co-ops. While the costs of agricultural implements and food at retail prices shot up, the government attempted to hold back agricultural prices paid to the co-ops, putting them in a cost/price scissors. This situation was further exacerbated by austerity programs dictated by the International Monetary Fund, which led to further cutbacks in public spending (especially in the financing of debtridden public enterprises) at a time when agricultural debts had increased, thus limiting possibilities of new lines of government credit (see Petras and Havens, 1977; and Stallings, 1978). The centralized policy-making structure sought to extract the surplus from the co-ops, thus creating multiple points of conflict and opposition—at the level of specific policies (prices, income, credits, marketing) and at the level of structure (the overall organization of the firm). (For details see *Latin American Economic Report*, 1979; Cabellero, 1979; and Montoya, 1979).

Peasant Responses: Stages in the Anticooperative Movement

The peasant co-op members' response to the government's efforts at agrarian reform and cooperativization went through three phases, each more radical than the first: (1) policy criticism and a "reformist approach," (2) institutional attack, and (3) dismantling of co-ops and demands for individual subdivision of land. This sequence suggests that the ongoing day-to-day experience and rational calculations of the peasantry, rather than any preconceived notions of "communalism" or "individualism," shaped peasant response. In fact, peasants made various efforts to correct perceived wrongs and inadequacies within the cooperative experience before turning away from it (Guillet, 1978). Thus in each phase peasants sought to utilize the existing institutional arrangements to maximize gains, and it was only the continued losses that deepened their alienation to the point of institutional break.

Tables 12.4 and 12.5 indicate the productivity decline in the face of declining farm prices and the decline in income levels and real wages.

The choice of the peasants to work out of the existing institutional arrangements initially was based largely on their positive assessment of the government's action in expropriating the traditional estates and plantations. Thus the initial "good will" of the peasants expressed in taking the "insider" approach was conditioned by the common cause that united peasants and government against big property owners. The opportunity for collaborative efforts and successful organization thus were present. The cooperative idea did not fail because of any notions of *inherent* distrust or individualism; they failed as a result of regime policies, which in turn reflected the overall orientation toward the class structure and the organization of political power. A classic example of this process is found in the eventual dissolution by decree of the National Agricultural Confederation, or CNA (see Havens, et al., 1979).

Table 12.4   Agricultural Output Per Capita for Selected Crops, 1961-77

	Output/year in kg/person		
Selected crop	1961–65	1966–70	1971–77
Wheat	13.5	10.2	9.6
Rice	28.5	33.3	32.6
Potatoes	122.9	131.8	109.8
Corn	45.2	45.9	38.1
Cassava	52.9	47.4	40.8
Barley	16.4	12.5	9.7
Cotton	34.5	21.1	13.7
Sugar	73.5	60.8	60.8
Beef	6.5	5.9	5.0

Source: Caballero and Alvarez, 1978 : 12.

Stage I: During the initial period, peasant opposition essentially focused on criticizing particular aspects of the cooperatives. Attacks were directed at particular government directors, advisers, and policies. Conflicts emerged over the way the administrators functioned, the way the profits were divided, and the way in which advisers intervened in decisions on crop selection, planting, and so forth. This criticism was directed basically at reforming the cooperative—to make it more responsive to its members' needs (Horton, 1974). Pressure was exercised through government-sponsored mobilization organizations (such as the CNA), which mediated the disputes, reviewed the sources of criticism (to isolate the radicals), and kept them within the overall confines of government-sponsored programs. As the criticism mounted, and as the

Table 12.5   Index of Declining Real Wage on Coastal Agro-Industrial CAPs Compared with Metropolitan Lima, 1970-78

	Salaries in coastal CAPs	Salaries in Lima
1970	100	100
1971	102	110
1972	104	117
1973	106	124
1974	113	120
1975	128	119
1976	138	123
1977	111	104
1978	84	95

Source: *Actualidad Económica*, 1979.

central government responses were found wanting, there was a tendency to withdraw from the officially sponsored activities: Disillusionment preceded mass defection and active opposition.

Long-term passivity was precluded by the sharp and precipitous deterioration of the standard of living, which reactivated peasant cooperative members, but now in nonofficial roles. The channels for this reactivation were largely found in the persistence of rural union organizations, which succeeded in sustaining their existence parallel to, and in many cases within, the cooperatives. Nourished by the government's heavy-handedness in managing peasant affairs within the co-op, the peasant unions began to reemerge as the defenders of peasant rights within the co-op, adapting the class-struggle perspective to the change from private owners to state managers. Thus the class-oriented peasant organization—Confederación de Campesinos Peruanos (CCP)—began to grow in size and, in some areas, recruited members from the government-controlled CNA. The CCP defended peasants' work rights, resisted payments of the agrarian debt, and demanded higher farm prices (Rainbird and Taylor, 1977).

Stage II: The conflicts within the co-ops between the bureaucratic leadership and the peasants deepened and extended. Debts accumulated, prices declined, strikes and protests were repressed, and substantial income differences between managers and producers persisted and became transparent to all. Increasingly, the cooperatives as an institution began to be attacked. Rather than deepening its roots among the producers, there began to be a fundamental questioning among peasants of whether the cooperative was the most rational choice for channeling their energies. While permanent workers initially realized income gains until 1975, their wages have steadily declined since then (*Actualidad Económica*, 1979). (See Table 12.6) Moreover, most CAPs employed pastoral workers who did not participate in salary gains and improved work conditions. In the critical stage they would frequently protest their

Table 12.6 Wage Differentials on 73 Production Cooperatives in Peru between Permanent and Seasonal Workers, 1975

Wage rates in soles/day	Permanent workers		Seasonal workers	
	Number	Percent	Number	Percent
Less than 100	2,194	19	2,159	49
105–150	6,711	57	2,080	47
More than 150	2,802	24	180	4
Total	11,707	100	4,419	100

Source: Ministerio de Alimentación, Boletín Analítico, no. 1, April 1977.

own wages by cultivating private plots and abandoning the co-op, assigning stoop work and hand labor to seasonal workers. However, as economic conditions continued to deteriorate, seasonal and permanent workers began to define common interests and struggle together against the co-op managers.

Increasingly, peasant activities shifted from requests that officials be replaced to the physical ousting of unresponsive managers. Price and income policy disputes were carried over into the capital city and became politicized and subject to national political controversy. Parties of the left and center began to respond with new and more vehement attacks on government policy. Their organizing efforts began to be well received within the co-ops. This was clearly the transitional period for the co-ops, meaning either a profound rectification would have to be launched or the whole enterprise would be called into question. For just as the peasants were turning to political and social opposition of the Left, to serve their interests within the co-ops, they also began parallel activity, cultivating private land and engaging in private exchanges. The choice to move toward "privatization" and "radicalization" was conditioned by the adverse experience with the cooperatives. The predominance of one or the other would depend on which set of forces—leftist unions or the market—seemed to be able to structure the peasant's postcooperative response.

Stage III: The institutional crises found in the cooperatives were merely a reflection of the larger institutional crises of the military regime. After eight years, the nationalist-reformist Velasco regime was overthrown and replaced by a leadership oriented toward greater freedom for private enterprise and less interested in cooperative or public ownership. Further cutbacks in public spending and government efforts to destatify the economy heightened conflicts between the regime and its mobilization agencies, leading to a break. The regime-sponsored peasant unions (CNA) moved closer to the Left-sponsored peasant organization, the Peruvian Peasant Confederation. More fundamental changes, however, were in store, because peasant discontent could no longer be contained within the cooperative framework: Widespread peasant takeovers of cooperatives were accompanied by demands for subdivision and individual holdings. Paradoxically, the Left was drawn into this movement against cooperatives and for private holdings. The Left could not resist the peasant choice of privatization against forced and unprofitable cooperativization. The dismantling of the co-ops was thus the culmination of a series of choices that preceded from everyday experiences in which peasants found the costs and benefits of membership wanting. The left opposition was strong enough to sustain a presence in the coop, but not strong enough to create an alternative that could resist market pressures. While the subdivision is perceived by the peasants as a way of escaping from the confines of the co-op, it is hardly likely to provide any durable or substantial rewards.

Individual small landholders face many of the same problems that confronted the cooperative: lack of credit, inflationary prices for inputs, price controls on some marketable food items, lack of access to technical assistance and farm machinery, and the extraction of surplus by commercial middlemen, transport haulers, and money lenders. In the short run individual small landholders may be able to market their produce and secure a better price, avoiding the overhead cost of sustaining an inefficient administration. If prices are too low, they may decide to increase their personal consumption. Moreover, by subdividing the farm they may in effect repudiate the collective debt accumulated during the co-op's operation. In the absence of formal lines of credit, they may secure loans on crops from the informal money market. Finally, having control over the land, they may have at their discretion the decisions as to what and when to plant and harvest—thus perhaps maximizing gains according to market fluctuations.

In the middle and long run, however, the process of subdivision will lead to excessive fragmentation beyond the yield possibilities that could support an extended household. Competition among the small landholders, the natural and political advantages that accrue to some peasants will lead to the displacement and dispossession of others. The wide dispersion of small landholders will undermine most efforts to provide credit and technical assistance. The predominance of urban industrial, commercial, and financial elites will ensure that agriculture will continue to "subsidize" industrial imports and to sustain a higher standard of living. The market exchanges will not favor the small landholders—given the asymmetrical relations between an oligopolistic industrial commercial and a competitive agrarian sector. The end result will be the general deterioration of living standards, accompanied by the reemergence and accentuation of rural stratification: A few peasants may become commercial farmers, but most will enter the large labor pool and probably increase the indebtedness of the small landholders, leading to loss of property and/or a return to some form of debt peonage. In the end the possible short-term advantages accruing to the peasants from the shift from co-ops to individual holdings will evaporate.

Peasants Against Co-ops

The peasant's negative responses to the co-ops were not a reflection of a "traditional way of life," the blind responses to custom and prejudice. On the contrary, the Peruvian experience suggests that no such "irrationality" guided peasant behavior. Rather, the experiential base of a series of decisions, ranging from positive to critical but supportive, preceded the outright rejection of cooperatives. At each point, collective choices were made that reflected the collective interests of the peasantry, and by and large each was based on very real concrete interests—namely, organizational autonomy, local initiative, and income. The regime's vision of a community of shared obligations and rights was not shared by the peasants. Their view of the co-op division of labor was one in which they shared all the obligations and the officials commanded all the rights. This asymmetrical relationship reproduced within peasant consciousness the them/us dichotomy, the idea of the exchange of *patrones* (see Guillet, 1978). This adversary relation was heightened by the gap between the rhetoric of "local autonomy" and the reality of state tutelage. Peasants "tested" government policy commitments to the co-ops in any number of areas: the promise of credits and the lack of them; the accumulation of debts and the lack of growth; the exhortation to produce more and the declining terms of exchange; and the vision of cooperative prosperity and the reality of deteriorating living standards.

Indeed, the terms of trade became progressively more unfavorable in three ways. First, the State set the internal price of sugar and cotton based on costs of production rather than on international market prices. This in effect reduced the end-of-year surplus, which was theoretically available for distribution to the cooperative members to supplement their wages. Since 1972 end-of-year profits were almost totally exhausted after paying the interest on the agrarian debt and management costs. Thus cooperative members were essentially dependent on wages for their sole source of income (Vega Centeno, 1978). The other manner of affecting the terms of trade was to force the CAPs to produce basic foodstuffs on 40 percent of their lands. These were the same foodstuffs that were subject to internal price controls aimed at "protecting urban consumers" (Caballero and Alvarez, 1978 : 13).

Finally, the cost of inputs for agricultural production increased dramatically. For example, from 1974 to 1979 the price of a tractor increased 590 percent, insecticides 530 percent, and fertilizer 180 percent. But the farm gate prices to agricultural producers held constant in real terms. Under these circumstances the collective enterprise was rejected, and the peasants turned to private subdivision as the only means of grasping a piece of immediate security. During 1978 twenty-eight highland cooperatives were taken over and parceled by peasants (Havens, et al., 1979). In addition, military occupation was necessary to prevent seven coastal cooperatives from ousting government administrators and replacing them with peasant-controlled administrators (*Latin America Economic Report*, 1979).

Conclusion

The notions of the abstract rationality of cooperatives are wanting: The primary assumption underlying these notions was that the state and the rest of the economy were geared to the logic of the operations of the agricultural cooperatives. Furthermore, the "abstract rationality" view of the cooperatives assumes rather than demonstrates the basic harmony of interests between cooperative decisionmakers and members, an assumption that was not warranted. Clearly, the success or failure of cooperative production is dependent on how well its operations fit with the larger social system. The congruity between the socioeconomic nature and policy of the state and the cooperatives is one fundamental determinant of the success and failure of cooperative activities. Likewise, the social relations of production between producers and decisionmakers defines the level of conflict and compatability within the co-op. These two levels, one located at the social formation, the other at the level of the enterprise, and the links between them shaped the commitments and choices of the rank and file. The peasants linked central bureaucratic control with local exploitation and perceived both as irrational mechanisms for maximizing production and minimizing local collective and individual benefits.

The evaluation of the Peruvian agrarian reform by the Institute of Peruvian Studies indicates that more than 70 percent of cooperative members felt that lack of participation in decisions about production and distribution of surplus was the biggest single failing of the cooperative reform efforts. Indeed, this failure was given greater importance by the members interviewed than low wages (Mejia and Matos, 1979). Initial and subsequent peasant response to cooperative organization was rooted in an instrumental view of social reality; it was not a reflection of residual precapitalist allegiances. The changes in choice and attempts to modify the institutional setting reflected the accumulation of experiences in the contemporary setting and a recognition of the constraints imposed by market exchanges, state policies, and local structures of power.

The shift from cooperatives to private parcels does not reflect any primordial attachment to markets or a private-property mystique. Rather, it reflects the rational response of peasants seeking to discontinue the immediate constraints of an unresponsive, exploitative state whose policies fail to meet their most essential needs (i.e., increased family income in the face of rampant inflation, improved schools for children, potable water, rural electrification). The new constraints and exploitative relations confronting the individual entrepreneur may generate a new set of responses toward a system that combines decentralized collective production and the flow of substantive payoffs to co-op members.

What are the alternatives to atomized individual holdings and centralized cooperatives? The immediate answer is decentralized cooperatives. But the general problem remains of locating the co-op within the overall economic strategy of the government. No matter how democratic and decentralized a co-op, if state policy allocates resources, credits, and investment and sets prices to the disadvantage of the co-ops, they will be in trouble. Given the interdependent nature of the economy—between sectors—the success of a co-op responsive to its members depends on its centrality in the overall development plans of the state. Agricultural expansion as a major component of a growth strategy presupposes direct representatives of the democratically controlled co-ops in the seats of power.

The formulation of a successful co-op policy is premised on the restructuring of the centers of decisionmaking and a shift in development priorities—from heavy industry to industrial expansion linked to the production of inputs in agriculture and the processing of agrarian products. The economic linkage between industry and agriculture may also facilitate social alliances between wage workers and co-op members, reinforcing the reorientation of policy. The organization of industrial production linked to agriculture could allow for the physical decentralization of production: Agro-industrial complexes regionally anchored would make good sense economically, as well as socially and politically. Lower transport costs is one advantage; increased interaction and communication could lead to organization of agrarian and industrial producers. The increased availability of goods generated by a shift in development priorities and the autonomy of organization resulting from decentralization could begin to meet some of the criteria upon which peasants base their choices, and they could facilitate the acceptance of collective forms of production.

References

Actualidad Económica. 1979. "La Industria Azucarera al Ritmo de la Crises." *Actualidad Económica*, March 13–15.

Amat y Leon, Carlos. 1979. *Estructura y Niveles de Ingresos Familiares en el Peru.* (Gobierno del Peru, Ministerio de Economia y Finananzas.

Caballero, José Maria. 1978a. "Los eventuales en las cooperatives costenas peruanas un modelo analitico." *Economia* (Lima), no. 2, Agosto.

———. 1978b. "La Reforma Agraria y Mas Alla: Del fracaso del modelo agrarlo y del regimen militar." *Critica Andina* (Cuzco), no. 2, pp. 23–53.

Caballero, José Maria, and Elena Alvarez. 1978. "Agriculture Under Import-Substitution Industrialization: The Peruvian Case." Conference on Agriculture and Industrialization in Africa and Latin America, Dakar, December.

Erasmus, Charles. 1961. *Man Takes Control.* Detroit: Bobbs-Merrill.

Guillet, D. 1978. "Peasant Participation in a Peruvian Agrarian Reform Cooperative." *Journal of Rural Cooperation*, vol. 6, no. 1, pp. 21–35.

Havens, A. Eugene, et al. 1979. *Class Relations and Peru's Agrarian Reform.* Madison: Center for Research on Politics and Society, mimeographed.

Horton, Douglas. 1974. "Land Reform and Reform Enterprises in Peru." Madison: Land Tenure Center, University of Wisconsin.

Latin America Economic Report. 1979. July 29, p. 196.

Mejia, José, and Rosa Díaz. 1975. *Sindicalismo y Reforma Agraria.* Lima: Instituto de Estudios Peruanos.

Mejia, José, and José Matos Mar. 1979. *El Fracaso de la Reforma Agraria.* Lima: Caretas. June.

Montoya, Rodrigo. 1979. "Changes in Rural Class Structure Under the Peruvian Agrarian Reform," *Latin American Perspectives*, vol. 5, no. 4, pp. 113-27.

Pasara, Luis, 1971a. "Un año de vigencia de la ley de Reforma Agraria," *Derecho* (Poutificia Universidad Católica del Peru), no. 29, pp. 104-31.

———. 1971b. "The Vicissitudes of a Labor Reform," *CERES: FAO Review*, vol. 4, no. 5, September-October, pp. 47-51.

Peru. 1977. Ministerio de Alimentación, Boletín Analitico, no. 1.

Petras, James, and A. Eugene Havens. 1979. "Peru: Economic Crises and Class Confrontation," *Monthly Review*, vol. 30, no. 9, February, pp. 25-42.

Rainbird, Helen, and Lewis Taylor. 1977. "Relations of Production or Relations of Exploitation: A Re-Analysis of Andean Haciendas," *Bulletin of the Society for Latin American Studies* (U.K.), no. 27, November, pp. 50-67.

Stallings, Barbara. 1978. "Peru and the Banks," NACLA Report on Public Debt (August).

Wolf, Eric. 1978. "Aspects of Group Relations in a Complex Society: Mexico," *American Anthropologist*, no. 58, pp. 1065-78.

Vega-Centeno, Cecilia. 1978. "Comparación de los Precios Agropecuarios del Peru con los del Area Andina 1970-1976." Pontificia Universidad Católica del Peru: Departamento de Economica.

Villaneuva, Victor. 1973. *Ejercita Peruano*. Lima: Editorial Juan Mejia Baca.

13

Urban Radicalism in Peru

by JAMES F. PETRAS and A. EUGENE HAVENS

Introduction

There have been two rather mutually reinforcing views concerning the relationship between urbanization and political behavior that have emanated from the desks and pens of American liberal academics. These interrelated views are simultaneously simplistic and obfuscating rather than revealing the historical dynamics of urban radicalism. This chapter will analyze the historical conjuncture in Peru in 1978, wherein urban radicalism reached a peak (indeed, it has since declined). For the purposes here, radicalism refers to attitudes and behaviors that are anticapitalist and take on a class character.

The most general assumption of U.S. modernization literature turns around the notion that urbanized nations are more mobilized and thus are defined by high political demands (e.g., Thompson, 1975 : 477). When this generalization has been extended to social formations experiencing a breakdown of precapitalist relations in the countryside, with a corresponding high rate of migration to the cities, the argument has been advanced that these nations will become more violent and politically unstable unless these new demands generated by urbanism are satisfied or managed by capable political institutions (Huntington, 1968 : 50–58; and Tiryakian, 1967 : 92). These precapitalist breakdown studies have generated a series of simplistic ideas about urban radicalism. Apparently, there is something magical about the single datum of percent urban population and increased political demands (Morrison and Stevenson, 1974; Smith, 1969; Ruhl, 1975; and Dix, 1967). A more sophisticated version of this simplistic relationship has argued for a generational lag between urbanism and radicalism. That is, first-generation rural-urban migrants tend to remain politically passive, while second-generation migrants become more politically active (Peattie, 1968; and Mangin, 1967).

However, none of these views captures the dynamics of urban radicalism. By focusing on a *breakdown* of precapitalist relations, they ignore the nature of the new social relationships that are emerging. Our central hypothesis is that it is the emergence of capitalist forms of social relationships that are central to urban radicalism, rather than a simple breakdown of precapitalist forms. Specifically, we suggest that (1) the level of capitalist development and its impact on workers, and (2) the visibility of relationships of economic exploitation and political repression *produce* urban radicalism, while (3) the promulgation of a radical working-class view, coupled with a political organization organically linked to mobilized urban residents, *reproduces* urban radicalism.

The second major dominant viewpoint concerning urban squatter settlements is that a self-help ideological campaign coupled with a minimum of support facilities (lights, sewers, schools) will defuse urban mobilization (See Handelman, 1975; Cornelius, 1974; and Fagan and Tuohy, 1972). For years squatter settlements have been under the political control and manipulation of a broad array of state and private organizations linked to foreign and national corporate interests (Gianella, 1970). Within the political confines imposed by authoritarian and repressive governments and the limited economic resources resulting from exploitive social relations of production, the heterogeneous social strata making up the settlements have been pressed into extending the working day to construct housing, toward what apologists describe as "self-help." The housing policy of the state is largely directed toward the big construction companies and middle- and upper-income groups. The class-based policy in state expenditures, and the necessity of settlers to create liveable quarters, requires them to extend the work day—since the surplus extracted by their employers does not allow them any other mechanism by which to create homes and reproduce labor. "Self-help" thus became the mechanism through which the state and private enterprises maintained a subsistence sector that partially subsidizes the labor force at its own expense. Such programs have been underway in Peru since 1922, when Alexander (1922) published his classic study on Lima. It reached its zenith in the late 1950s and early 1960s under President Beirtran's infamous program based on *"la casa barata que crece"* (See Peru, 1959; Dorich, 1961; and Dietz, 1969).

The formidable reduction in costs to the capitalist state of this self-sustaining aspect was not its only benefit. The political and social advantages that accrued from the ideological-organizational derivatives of "self-help" movements were preponderant. Emphasis on individual efforts and ownership coupled with differential levels of achievement served to fragment and isolate the "settlers" from each other. Self-help was counterposed to collective struggle, and the promotion of its achievements by its academic publicists served to accelerate greater external intervention, especially by international funding agencies and AID. The organizational basis of group action was largely tied to local and immediate goals and the making of marginal claims on state resources: title to the land, laying of lights, and so on. Subsidies, political controls, and the organizational link between the local associations' leaders and the state ensured a screening out of militant organizers and challenges to the dominant structure of power. The only "legitimate" claims were those that the organizational "leader," "bargaining" with the state, would consider feasible, meaning those compatible with the existing configuration of society and state expenditures. The *barriadas*, or squatter settlements, were under the complete hegemony of the ruling class's ideas of "self-help" based on incrementalism: gradual improvements based on greater individual efforts. These basic notions were codified in Peru's squatter-settlement legislation, Law 13517 of 1961. One of the major provisions of the law was to give free title to urban lots if major housing improvements had been made on the lot (Peru, 1965).

During the mid-1960s under President Belaunde, little attention was given to the urban sector as a result of mass mobilization of the Peruvian peasantry. However, the need to reduce urban tension reappeared in 1968 and was formalized and institutionalized during the Velasco period, with the added dimensons of greater allocation of state resources. The Velasco regime dubbed the squatter settlements "pueblos jovenes" (young towns) instead of barriadas and attempted to create formal state linkages through the agencies of ONDEPJOV and SINAMOS, as a means of creating a popular social base of support. ONDEPJOV, created in December 1968, stood for the National Organization for the Development of Young Towns, which first introduced into the Limeño lexicon the term "pueblos jovenes." SINAMOS, the National System of Mobilization and Support, was created in 1971 and was charged with co-opting mobilizations throughout the country.

The regime took over and extended the whole notion of "popular participation" and attempted to instrumentalize, centralize, and coordinate the preexisting forms of domination exercised by "voluntary associations." Despite the construction of a whole new popular settlement ("Villa Salvador") and enormous expenditures in promotion and publicity, the changes remained marginal, well within the framework of incrementalism previously supported by private real estate, banking, and construction interests.

The advancing of capitalist development under the military, the accompanying and deepening economic crises, which made exploitation and repression totally visable, and the international and local capital offensive undermined the patterns of limited change, laying the groundwork for independent political action, the emergence of new leaders, and the combining of barriada and working-class struggle under Marxist leadership.

Capitalist Growth and Political Change

While the formal political institutions of military rule have changed little over the past few years, significant political changes are taking place among substantial sectors of the population, especially within the urban working class and "poor." Radical opposition to the existing military regime and total rejection of "corporatist" structures of domination have spread from students, intellectuals, and militant fractions of the trade union movement to substantial majorities of the urban working class and poor. The incorporation of these new sectors of the population into the political struggle is one of the most significant aspects of the political process in the present period, and one that evokes the possibilities of a radical transformation of the social order.

Within the process of political change in contemporary Peruvian society, one of the most striking and significant changes is the radicalization in the behavior of the inhabitants of the barriadas. The process of political radicalization in the barriadas has yet to be analyzed. Because of their numerical importance and strategic location, the barriadas have decisive political consequences for the overall structure and development of Peruvian society. Two interrelated factors have been central to the political changes: Structural developments and changes in the social and political process have been instrumental in redefining the political orientations of barriada residents.

In the past, both in terms of electoral behavior and collective activity, the barriadas were not prominent supporters of the Left. Electorally, most of their support was distributed among one or the other of the bourgeois parties, either the Center-Right APRA or the "paternalistic "Right" of General Odria (Collier, 1975). Insofar as organizations within the barriadas promoted social action, it was around local and immediate issues and located within a bargaining and pressure-group style of politics. In contrast, in the recent period the barriadas have turned out in great numbers as active supporters of the leftist general strikes and into a massive electoral base for the leftist parties. The barriadas, as many studies have shown, are heterogeneous communities containing several strata, from unemployed and self-employed to factory workers and a sprinkling of public employees.

In the past, working-class struggles in production were always separated and dissociated from the struggles in the barriadas: Production and habitation reflected different sets of leaders, strategies, and demands. The class content of the working-class core within the barriadas was muffled by the vast numbers of immediate issues confronting the settlements and the overwhelmingly non-working-class nature of the organization. In the present period working-class consciousness has permeated the barriadas and is expressed in the increasing participation of working-class militants in the organizations, permitting increasing union between barriada and factory struggles. Although the size of the working class probably has not increased, some evidence of increasing industrial proletarist residency in the barriadas is becoming available, and working-class leadership of the political life of the barriadas is becoming significant.

All evidence points to the fact that the pueblos jovenes are the key residential location for migrants to Lima. Few Lima-born residents over twenty years of age reside in the barriadas (Robin and Terzo, 1973; and ENCA, 1976). Havens (1977) merged a random sample of 1,267 Lima residents with census-trait information to determine certain characteristics of migrants of five years or more residence in Lima. Tables 13.1, 13.2, and 13.3 show that rural and urban migrants to Lima tend to be unskilled workers, working more than forty hours a week for twelve months out of the year. Lima-born adults tend to be bureaucrats. Thus the barriada residents in 1972 were workers generally employed full-time. With the economic crisis in 1975, many of these workers were the first to be laid off or fired or jailed for being strike leaders. Radicalism in a proletarian work place was directly entering the homes of many barriada residents.

What is also significant in weighing the relative importance of this newly aroused radicalism is the fact that it is occurring through a massive and conscious rejection of corporatist forms of organization. In the competition between political forms, the growth of urban radicalism and the increasing attraction of masses to socialist ideas take place *against* regime-sponsored corporatist institutions and in favor of forms of democratic representation and self-determination with a substantive socioeconomic content. The second major feature, accompanying the ascent of the class struggle and democratic-socialist politics is the demise of corporatism under the onslaught of mass uprisings from below. The new wave of mass participation has not only laid to rest the corporatist specter, but hopefully has written an epitaph for the corporatist writing emanating from the desk of American academics (cf. Chaplin, 1975; and Stepan, 1978).

Parenthetically, Peru never experienced a corporate system; rather, it experienced elements of a corporate structure that were tempered by populist reforms and penetrated by forces promoted by class struggle. Over time, there was massive and unequivocal rejection of corporate structures and prescriptions by those for whom they were intended. Their precipitous demise attests to their fragile status, their weak roots in Peruvian society and history, and especially their unpopularity among the mass of the working class. The notion popularized by some academics that "corporatism" faithfully reflected Latin cultures or traditions, and thus was an appropriate political form for the region, was not acceptable to the great majority of the Peruvian working class (cf. Wiarda, 1973; Dealy, 1974; and Morse, 1974). Rather, the corporatist notions must be seen for what they were, the products of factions of the governing military class intent on containing class conflict and promoting capitalist industrialization. In fact, the marginal changes achieved within the elaborate "corporatist" organizational schemes were in no way superior to the incremental changes achieved in the previous period, and thus added little to the process of social change.

Capitalist Relations of Exploitation and Repression

The industrial and general economic expansion from the 1950s to the early 1970s was accompanied by incremental gains at the level of wages and home improvements for broad sectors of the urban labor force (Petras and Havens, 1979). Although absolute levels continued to be very low, especially relative to the better-off classes in urban-industrial society, there was a sense among the barriada residents that through extra work and long hours they could compensate for low wages and accumulate savings, gradually providing themselves with the socially necessary goods and services.

In fact, with time, large numbers of barriada residents were able to achieve limited success; they did obtain electricity, water, paved streets, and transportation—no matter how inadequate they actually functioned (Andrews and Phillips, 1970). Increasingly, for those with longer urban residence, their incorporation into factory employment allowed the bar- riada resident to press for increasing social demands that transcended im- mediate subsistence requirements. Wage levels, employment, health and school services, and food prices were among the central issues raised by the barriada residents in their confrontations with the state. Certainly, the *habitacional* conditions in Comas (one of the better-known barriadas located close to the center of Lima and the cite of radical mobilization in 1978) were far "better off" at the time of the general strikes of 1977–78 than they were ten or fifteen years before, and yet the residents were far more radical in the later period.

Apparently, the limited successes in overcoming "marginality" and achieving integration into the urban-industrial networks have led to greater demands. One effect seems to be to reduce the political distance between the barriada and the factory struggles. Yet the physical changes in themselves did not precipitate the changes in demands; rather, the eruption of the economic crises of the mid-1970s aborted the incremental pattern and set in motion the forces leading to radicalization.

The Velasco regime made a concerted effort to organize and contain, politicize and control, the barriadas to create a base of mass support to counterweigh the influence of the organized labor movement. On the practices and policies of previously nonradical barriada organizations, he hoped to create a social base through the introduction of *state* monopolized and promoted self-help programs linked to state mobiliza- tion agencies. The regime-sponsored burst of activity, followed abruptly by massive retrenchment and cutbacks, made available for the Left an in-

Table 13.1 Occupational Category of Lima Residents in 1972 by Migration Status

| | Occupational category | | | | | | | | | | | | |
| Migration status | Employer | | Independent worker | | Empleado | | Worker (obrero) | | Domestic | | Unknown | | Total |
	Number	Percent	Number	Percent	Number	Percent	Number	Percent	Number	Percent	Number	Percent	
Direct from rural area	10	3.4	62	21.2	75	25.7	140	47.9	5	1.7	0	0.0	292
From other urban area	29	4.3	125	18.7	241	36.0	258	38.6	5	0.7	10	1.5	669
Born in Lima	19	6.2	42	13.7	158	51.6	83	27.1	1	.03	3	1.0	306
Total	58	4.6	229	18.1	474	37.4	481	38.0	11	0.9	13	1.0	1267

Table 13.2 Hours Worked per Week by Migration Status in Lima in 1972

| | Hours worked per week | | | | | | | | | | | | |
| Migration status | 0–7 | | 8–16 | | 17–24 | | 25–32 | | 33–40 | | 41 or more | | Totals |
	Number	Percent	Number	Percent	Number	Percent	Number	Percent	Number	Percent	Number	Percent	
Direct from rural area	2	0.7	4	1.4	7	2.4	9	3.1	57	19.5	213	72.9	292
Migrated from other urban	1	0.1	11	1.6	9	1.3	31	4.6	117	17.5	500	74.7	669
Born in Lima	0	0.0	4	1.3	4	1.3	7	2.3	71	23.2	220	71.9	306
Total	3	0.2	19	1.5	20	1.6	47	3.7	245	19.3	933	73.6	1267

Table 13.3 Number of Months Worked during 1972 in Lima by Migration Status

| | | | | | Months worked during year | | | | | |
| | 1-3 | | 4-6 | | 7-9 | | 10-12 | | |
Migration Status	Number	Percent	Number	Percent	Number	Percent	Number	Percent	Total
Direct from rural area	3	1.0	3	0.9	9	3.1	277	95.0	292
Migrated from other urban	7	1.0	8	1.2	26	3.8	628	94.0	669
Born in Lima	2	0.6	2	0.6	5	1.6	297	97.2	306
Total	12	1.0	13	1.0	40	3.1	1202	94.9	1267

creasingly organized and politicized population without any further basis for loyalty to the regime. (For a review of the Velasco program for pueblos jovenes, see Collier, 1975.)

The very programs of "self-help" that were formulated and promoted by the government remained frozen. The general crises had as an immediate effect massive cutbacks in construction, leading to increased unemployment, while devaluation and price policies increased building costs beyond the reach of most barriada residents (See *Actualidad Económica*, 1978). The combined effects of the crisis on income and cost—affecting both employment and habitation—facilitated the growth of solidarity movements between factories and slum settlements. The collapse of incrementalism and the accompanying demise of expectations of relative improvement fastened the barriada dwellers within a static social universe: Social mobility, never great to begin with, gave way to immobility and, along with it, a growing attraction to class politics. Collective mobility through class action increasingly appeared as a more realistic strategy in the face of the deteriorating prospects of individual ascent.

The increasing radicalization of the inhabitants of the barriada— whom we will refer to as the *pobladores*—was manifest in at least two major events: the three general strikes and the electoral results of the Constitutional Assembly. Both types of action represented a clear definition of social and political orientation regarding fundamental issues concerning the economy and society, as well as the political system.

The general strike, especially the third one, emphasized both economic and political demands—a protest against price increase, an affirmation of the standard of living of the working class, as well as a call for the establishment of a popularly elected democratic government. Some more specific demands attacked the International Monetary Fund's influence over the regime, as well as the austerity measures they were advocating. Government proposals to denationalize public enterprise and increase opportunities for foreign capital were likewise attacked. The general strike thus embraced "defensive" measures designed to protect previous gains, as well as "offensive" demands designed to transform the structure of political power; while the detonating issues were clearly economistic in character, the scope and reach of the movement had larger historical implications.

Through leaflets, public meetings, and murals, these ideas informed the mass of the pobladores about the nature of the general strike. The regime-controlled mass media missed no chance to emphasize the radical, extremist, or Marxist nature of the leadership. Thus the choice of the masses to support the general strikes was not a fortuitous act, but was one based on at least a rudimentary understanding of the political orientation and demands of the strike leaders. Despite government threats evidenced in a massive display of firepower and intense propaganda efforts, the great majority of the pobladores supported the general strikes—thus identifying with the radical Left's leadership and programmatic struggle against the regime and those bourgeois civilian parties (APRA, PPC) that openly condemned the call for mass action.

There were generally two types of participation in the general strike—passive and active. Passive participation involved the withdrawal of labor power from productive activity but without an active role in the mass public activity: It usually involved staying indoors, at home, or visiting friends during a scheduled workday. Political discussion usually occurred between friends, relatives, and neighbors. Active opposition, on the other hand, involved participation in street demonstrations, blocking of traffic, public meetings, and, in some cases, confrontations with the police. The active supporters were drawn largely from the younger members of the barriadas, including workers, unemployed, and students. The extremely high rates of teenage unemployment, the lack of attachments to any of the older parties, and the fact that many of the adolescents have experienced the deepening of the economic crises without any previous "cushion" created a volatile social stratum capable of responding to radical appeals for direct action.

Among the barriadas, those that adjoined industrial belts were among the most active and supportive of the general strike. In these areas, the overlap between barriada membership and factory work is substantial—thus the leadership and organization within the factories served as a detonator for the organization of mass protest within the barriada. In some cases, workers previously fired for leading militant struggles in the factory transferred their organizational abilities into barriada organizations, infusing them with a new combative spirit, which overcame the bureaucratic inertia of the established groups. The barriadas that were industrial satellites expressed the dual aspects of the protest: both against price increases and against decline in real wage earnings. The greater the predominance of worker influence in the barriada, the more active the role of its members in the public action. The newer barriadas, experiencing greater unemployment and instability, tended also to exhibit a greater proclivity for direct action. Passive support was more manifest among established venders, small businessmen, and, in general, among the more individualistic older employees. However, the younger, better-educated students within the older barriadas were an active element in public demonstration. The crisscrossing of relative deprivation, factory experience, and generational cohesion combined with socioeconomic rootlessness within a deteriorating urban-industrial context, created a basic set of reinforcing experiences that forged, at least temporarily, social bonds that propelled the barriada movement against the military regime. The massacre of barriada street demonstrators served further to solidify the residents *against* the regime, overcoming their rather disparate individual interests. Both the economic crisis and the repression provided homogenizing experiences overcoming internal particularistic differences that had earlier prevented the development of broad solidarity, antiregime movements within the barriadas.

The increasing flow of radical ideas promulgated by activists and politicians from the factory belts into adjoining barriadas must be added to the radicalization of older barriada residents, who were previously caught up in the incrementalist bargaining organizations. The decline of government services and the increasing cost of living, and especially of items related to home improvements (construction materials, for example), have undermined the authority of the established barriada organizations. The working relations between formal barriada associations and the state to secure small gains no longer operates in favor of the association in the context of the massive cuts in standard of living. The scope of activities and solutions proposed by traditional barriada organizations are dwarfed by the economic crisis, which presents itself to barriada residents as rocketing prices and unemployment. The impotence of the old barriada organizations and strategies, and the discrediting of local leaders for their collaboration with an unresponsive government bureaucracy, has led to the growth of new autonomous structures, as well as the transformation of old organizations. Committees of struggle, many of them on an ad hoc basis, have sprung up before or during the strikes, involving participants in the day-to-day activities organized by the burgeoning movement. These committees, however, have a tendency to be transitory—rising and falling in the face of emergency situations.

The Reproduction of Urban Radicalism

With the end of a strike and back-to-work movement, some organizations lost their reason for being. In a few cases, where experienced political cadres were present, the committees continued functioning, attempting to sustain activity through local meetings and demands. The growth of these autonomous structures based on the barriada, and their capacity to engage in political confrontation with the state, opens up the possibility of creating interbarriada organizations that could lead to citywide groupings capable of mobilization and further politicization. The problems are numerous, however. In addition to the transitory nature of some of the committees, there is the problem that many of the nuclei that organize are affiliated to competing leftist parties, and it appears to be difficult for them to overcome their differences, since no group has overwhelming organizational hegemony. Perhaps unity at the party or front level will permit the coalescence of grassroots organization at the barriada level. In the meantime, in some areas, older associations have been influenced or taken over by more radical members, thus deepening and broadening the scope of politicization. Under the domination of the older "self-help" bureaucrats and ideologues, the members were discouraged from engaging in discussions—let alone action—against the state and the capitalist class. Discussions about imperialism were ruled out as "politics," while the local officials practiced their own brand of incremental politics. Under the impact of the economic crises and with the transparent role of the International Monetary Fund and the U.S. banks, militant activists have no problem linking private needs with global issues.

The spread of radical political ideas and the activation of substantial sectors of the barriadas does not mean, however, that local concerns no longer have relevance to the inhabitants. The pressing needs for better transportation, local services, and drainage systems have not been replaced but have been joined with the larger struggles against the military regime and its economic policies. To the extent that new radical leaders or groups have emerged within the barriadas, it has been on the basis of their ability to handle *both* levels of demands. The local militants are the pivotal agents who link the local barriada residents to the national political struggle, because they are known through the struggles on local issues. This does not mean that there are no differences between militants and residents. After the high moments of general strikes and mass action, during the ebbtide, the "localist" orientation reappears to dominate barriada discussions; and it is a constant struggle for the militants continually to raise the broader perspectives within which local problems are viewed.

One of the seeming paradoxes that seems to emerge from barriada politics is the manner in which old and new political orientations are combined. In one barriada, a previous bulwark of the paternalistic, rightist Odria, the support for FOCEP, or the Peruvian Front of Workers, Peasants, and Students (a largely Trotskyist coalition) and the Left was very high. The shift from extreme right to left, from clientele politics to revolutionary politics, suggests that at least in the eyes of some sectors of the barriadas the incapacity of the establishment to deliver the goods has pushed them toward new political figures on the Left capable of providing solutions. The ability to substitute a Hugo Blanco for a General Odria suggests a substantial floating vote, available to a political movement that projects "strong" leadership, intransigent opposition to the regime (the source of the ongoing deteriorating situation), and has the capacity to translate complex problems into meaningful popular terms. Thus clientelistic orientations are not incompatible with charismatic followers or revolutionary leadership: The possibility of large-scale change does not exclude the opportunity for immediate pickings. One indication of radicalism that also reflects both immediate and fundamental interests is the vote for the Constitutional Assembly.

The elections to the Constitutional Assembly called by the military junta were the first in more than a decade and occurred under very

Table 13.4 Voting Patterns in the 1978 Election for the Constituent Assembly in Five Pueblos Jovenes In Lima

Parties or Coalitions	Pueblo Joven			
	San Juan and Lurigancho	San Juan de Miraflores	El Augustino	Comas Carabayllo
1. Left groups				
FOCEP	7,728	6,477	6,758	24,131
UDP	1,443	1,281	1,646	2,800
PCP	2,276	2,488	3,076	5,108
PSR	2,146	2,946	2,729	4,878
PDC	341	1,903	390	783
Subtotal	13,934 (40.9%)	15,095 (40.5%)	14,599 (35.6%)	37,700 (47.8%)
2. APRA	7,104 (20.9%)	8,379 (22.5%)	8,145 (19.8%)	16,171 (20.5%)
3. PPC[a]	4,828 (14.2%)	7,172 (19.3%)	6,022 (14.9%)	7,542 (9.5%)
4. All others	1,913	2,990	3,380	4,483
5. Blank votes	3,161	2,049	433	1,316
Declared void	399	1,500	5,329	6,351
7. Nonvoters	2,711	73	3,119	5,380
Total	34,050	37,250	41,027	78,943

[a]The PPC (Popular Christian Party) is a right-wing group led by a past mayor of Lima.

inauspicious circumstances for the Left. Widespread arrest and exile of most of the prominent candidates and leaders certainly hampered their campaigning. The mass media were, with a few notable exceptions, dominated by right-wing parties. The literacy requirements disqualified almost exclusively potential lower-class voters for the Left. In brief, the circumstances surrounding the election were decidedly structured by the military to favor the Right and to isolate the Left. As a result, the combined Left vote of approximately 30 percent should be considered the minimum electoral support. Given a free atmosphere, greater access to the media, and an unrestrictive adult suffrage, there is little doubt that the vote would have been much higher, possibly up to half of the voting population. Table 13.4 presents data on voting patterns in five pueblos jovenes.

The change in electoral behavior parallels and reflects the general political transformation taking place in Peru. Fifteen years earlier the Left received less than 5 percent of the vote, mainly in limited working class areas (Collier, 1975). The barriadas were overwhelmingly behind APRA, Odria, or one of the other bourgeois candidates. In the 1978 elections the combined vote of the Left increased six to eightfold. In some barriadas absolute majorities were attained, while in others from one-third to near majorities were the order of the day. The radicalization of the electorate within the barriadas was further evidenced by the fact that within the Left, the most radical coalitions gained the majority of support. Without precedent in Peruvian political history, 30 percent of the seats in the Assembly were won by leftist parties. More surprising for the Right was the support for the FOCEP, led by Hugo Blanco and with support from some Maoist splinter groups, which won seventeen seats out of the 100-person Assembly. Another coalition, UDP, essentially a Maoist-oriented grouping, won four seats. The pro-Moscow Communist Party (PCP) won a mere six seats, reflecting the mass rejection of the military regime and the PCP's support for both the Velasco and Morales Bermudez regimes until 1978. Popular antimilitarism was evidenced in the small vote for the ex-Velasquistas in the Socialist Revolutionary Party (PSR), which won only six seats.

Thus within a general move to the left, there was further radicalization toward the revolutionary Left. Those leftist parties identified with the Velasco period were eclipsed by those that were most vehemently opposed to both military regimes and most consistently in favor of replacing military regimes with popular power. Clearly, the revolutionary Left was tapping sentiments and beliefs that went beyond a "protest" vote—since a vote for the moderate Left would have served the same purpose. The fact that the majority of leftist voters went beyond to register a vote for the revolutionary Left suggests that more fundamental issues were perceived to be at stake.

Many of the leaders of the Left—the very recipients of this vote—expressed surprise at the outcome, but this is completely comprehensible given the high level of class conflict that preceded and followed the elections. Indeed, the underlying causes for both the high levels of participation in the general strike and the massive increase in leftist voting are the deteriorating economic conditions for vast sectors of the population. Nevertheless, strikes and economic crises in themselves do not account for the particular radical expression: Rather, the nature of the crises in which the international and local financial and business groups, through the active intervention of the state, attempt to recover from the crises by adopting measures directed against wage and salaried strata as a whole created sharp class cleavages. The cumulative effect of the general strikes against the regime served to highlight class solidarity, involving communities and factories in joint action. The political nature and the classwide basis of the general strike contributed directly to the radicalization of the barriada electorate: It began to envision the world in class terms. Hence, the class appeals by the Marxist Left found a receptive audience in groups that had already been prepared by two years of direct tumultuous experience of class struggle. Neither the language nor the forceful attacks on the regime appeared as alien as in the past.

Hugo Blanco became a charismatic figure because he was most effective in projecting the profound rejection and intransigent opposition that was surfacing in the barriadas. The whole complex of institutions of control and manipulation, which the corporatist dictators and their ideologues had imposed on the masses, has been one of the first targets of attack. In the preelectoral as well as postelectoral period, the common theme among the populace is a deep rejection of the authoritarians. In this sense, Blanco's appeals for democratic control from below, his personal disdain for the pomp and pretense of the establishment, struck a powerful chord in the plebeian masses—and the violent hostility of the upper classes.

Those interpretations that emphasize Blanco's "charisma" as the basis for leftist voting do not take into account the political context and appeals that evoked the massive vote (almost a half-million). Blanco has been in Peru (in jail and out) for some time and has never built a mass following in the cities. His charisma, the building of a personal following, could not occur outside of the massive strikes and struggles that preceded his campaign. His "persona" symbolized a whole set of experiences and the first gropings toward a redefinition of the social system. Blanco was the lightening rod for those forces looking for a rupture in the system but lacking the organizational form. The rise of FOCEP and the decline of APRA in the barriadas reflects the increasing integration of the latter into the system of domination and its clear incapacity to respond to the most elementary needs of its former constituents.

On the other hand, the FOCEP electorate is not an organized force, but rather an unstructured movement of opinion. In all of Comas and Carabayllo, where FOCEP obtained more than twenty thousand votes, there were fewer than a dozen party members. The disjuncture between the radicalized mass movement and the small party nucleus appears to present a series of problems that center around the need to transform the methods of work and practice of small organizations in order to deal with the new mass constituency. On the other hand, rising tensions within the unstructured masses could lead not only to a sudden and explosive uprising without any organizational direction, but severe repression. The disjuncture between the electoral radicalism of the barriadas, and the organizational strength of the Left, is one indication of the precipitous and rapid nature of political change. However, unless the Left can begin to organize and consolidate its influence—i.e., develop organic ties—the stability of electoral behavior could be jeopardized. Premature rebellions, demoralization, fragmentation, and political controls could all lead to a decline in leftist voting.

Conclusion

Urban radicalism is a consequence of a complex set of social relations that relate directly to capitalist development. It cannot be understood by a descriptive statement concerning the breakdown of precapitalist relations in agriculture that produce high rates of urban migration. Not all urban migrants automatically become radical. Those who have experienced a direct contact with capitalist relations of exploitation and the accompanying repression necessaary to reproduce capitalist relations of production become radical. However, the *reproduction* of radicalism requires the availability of a radical working-class world view and political organization.

The growth of socialist consciousness in Peru is far from finished: The very constraints of the Left prevent any broad historical generalizations. Yet the scope and strength of the action warrant consideration. Certainly, the concerns of local and international business, to say nothing of the military, are evidence of the potential threat that it represents to their interests. The conversion of union militance and electoral behavior into socialist consciousness would be a major step toward the transformation of Peruvian society. Certainly, the old formulas about the conservatism and localism of barriada residents are no longer applicable. It remains to be seen whether the Left is capable or transcending its own sectarian struggles and providing organizational forms to channel the new radical currents.

References

Actualidad Economica. 1978. "Costo de Vida y Desempleo en Lima: Consecuencias de la Crisis." *Actualidad Económica*, August 16–19.

Andrews, Frank, and George Phillips. 1970. The Squatters of Lima: Who They Are and What They Want." *Journal of Developing Areas*, vol. 4, January.

Chaplin, David (ed.). 1975. *Peruvian Nationalism: A Corporatist Revolution*. New Brunswick: Transaction Books.

Collier, David. 1975. "Squatter Settlements and Policy Innovations in Peru," in Abraham Lowenthal (ed.), *The Peruvian Experiment*. Princeton: Princeton University Press.

Cornelius, W. A. 1974. "Urbanization and Political Demand Making: Political Participation Among the Migrant Poor in Latin American Cities." *American Political Science Review* 68, September.

Dealy, Glen Caudill. 1974. "The Tradition of Monistic Democracy in Latin America." *Journal of the History of Ideas*, October-December.

Dietz, Henry A. 1969. "Urban Squatter Settlements in Peru: A Case History and Analysis," *Journal of Inter-American Studies* 11, no. 3, July, pp. 353–70.

Dix, R. H. 1967. *The Political Dimension of Change*. New Haven: Yale University Press.

Dorich T., Luis. 1961. "Urbanization and Physical Planning in Peru," in Philip M. Hauser (ed.), *Urbanization in Latin America*. New York: Columbia University Press.

ENCA. 1976. *Características de la muestra de Lima Metropolitana*. Lima: Ministerio de Alimentación.

Fagen, R. R., and W. S. Tuohy. 1972. *Politics and Privilege in a Mexican City*. Stanford: Stanford University Press.

Gianella, Jaime. 1970. *Marginalidad en Lima Metropolitana*. Lima: DESCO.

Handelman, Howard. 1975. "The Political Mobilization of Urban Squatter Settlements: Santiago's Recent Experience and Its Implications for Urban Research." *Latin American Research Review* 10, no. 2, Summer.

Havens, A. Eugene. 1977. *Manual Sobre las Técnicas Cuantitativas dentro del Materialismo Histórico*. Lima: PUCP.

Huntington, S. P. 1968. *Political Order in Changing Societies*. New Haven: Yale University Press.

Mangin, W. 1967. "Latin American Squatter Settlements." *Latin American Research Review* 2, no. 3, Summer.

Morrison, D. G., and H. M. Stevenson. 1974. "Measuring Social and Political Instability in Latin America: A Test of Huntington's Theory." *Inter-American Economic Affairs* 29, Fall.

Morse, Richard, M. 1964. "The Heritage of Latin America," in Louis Hartz (ed.), *The Founding of New Nations*. New York: Harcourt, Brace, and World.

Peattie, L. R. 1968. *The View from the Barrio*. Ann Arbor: University of Michigan Press.

Peru, Comisión para La Reforma Agraria y Vivienda. 1959. *Report on Housing in Peru*. Mexico: International Cooperation Administration.

Peru, Oficina de la Presidencia. 1965. *Ley de Barriadas*. Lima: Distribuidora Benedzu.

Petras, James, and A. Eugene Havens. 1979. "Peru: Economic Crises and Class Confrontation." *Monthly Review* 30, no. 9, February.

Robin, John P., and Frederick C. Tezo. 1973. *Urbanization in Peru*. New York: Ford Foundation.

Ruhl, J. M. 1975. "Social Mobilization and Political Instability in Latin America: A Test of Huntington's Theory." *Inter-American Economic Affairs* 29, Fall.

Smith, P. H. 1969. "Social Mobilization, Political Participation and the Rise of Juan Perón." *Political Science Quarterly* 87, March.

Stepan, Alfred. 1978. *The State and Society: Peru in Comparative Perspective*. Princeton: Princeton University Press.

Thompson, W. R. 1975. "Regime Vulnerability and the Military Coup." *Compactive Politics* 7, July.

Tiryakin, Edward A. 1967. "A Model of Societal Change and its Lead Indicators," in S. Z. Klausner (ed.), *The Study of Total Societies*. Garden City, N.Y.: Doubleday.

Wiarda, Howard. 1973. "Toward a Framework for the Study of Political Change in the Iberie-Latin Tradition." *World Politics*, January.

14

Terror and the Hydra:
The Resurgence of the
Argentine Working Class

Introduction

In 1971, in the offices of the Argentine Industrialists Union (UIA), the organization of the largest industrial firms, this author interviewed the head of the organization. We discussed the political options most attractive to Argentine capitalists. When I asked what he thought of the Brazilian model, he looked ecstatic: "It's an industrialist's paradise." I then asked, "Why not in Argentina?" His brow furrowed, and he replied in a measured tone: "The Argentine trade unions are too strong; they would resist. There might be a civil war and we don't know who would win, how it would come out." Faced with this uncertainty, he thought under the circumstances that it would be best for the military to return power to the civilian politicians, to defuse the polarization and tension racking Argentina at the time, which the military was not in a position to control. What was striking at the time (but became more apparent in retrospect) was the fact that the business leaders' hesitation in accepting a terrorist regime and bloody repression was all contingent on the issue of the probability of success. There was not a moment's consideration of lives lost or democratic values; rather there was a fear that if the battle was engaged in and lost, there would be an even greater degree of working-class power.

The implication was clear: If a Brazilian solution could be imposed through a successful civil war against the working class, then by all means the big business community was all for it. Unquestionably, what was a central concern to the most prominent and leading industrialists was the industrial paradise of Brazil of the late 1960s: no strikes, labor unions controlled by a police state, social security, and wage cuts imposed by the capitalist class, dismantling of the state sector, freeing of prices. The phrase "industrial paradise" signified the capacity of the industrialists to do whatever they wished without hindrance from workers' organizations and a nationalist-populist state.

But as the industrialists knew too well, there were formidable obstacles to realizing their Molochian-erotic fantasies: the insurrectionary movements in Córdoba and Rosario, the incendiary uprising in Tucuman, the total shutdown of the economy resulting from the general strikes decreed by the CGT. Only a regime willing to take the most extreme measures in the most determined fashion was capable of paving the road to that "paradise." The industrialists were willing to support such a regime if and when it emerged. The regime of March 1976 was up to its "historic task" set forth by the capitalist class: It proceeded to the most radical transformation of society in modern Argentine history as a means of realizing the industrialists' paradise.

This discussion will focus on the uniqueness of this terrorist regime and its impact on Argentine society. The scope and depth of terror practiced by this government is inadequately described by terms such as "bureaucratic authoritarian." Rather, it suggests something akin to fascist terrorist regimes. The purpose, however, is to examine the impact of this terror and repression on the Argentine Left and to examine the differential impact on formal and informal organization. While the repression has been successful in decimating the formal organizational apparatus of the "left," it has failed to destroy the informal popular movement.

The other unique aspect of the Argentine situation is the massive resurgence of working-class struggle—despite the fascist terror—on a scale and scope unheard of in any other country with a similar type of regime. Moreover, this working-class resurgence occurs despite the inactivity of formal democratic political institutions, the illegalization of the trade unions, and the murder, jailing, and exile of practically all the known official leaders, especially those known at the national or regional level. Finally, the resurgence occurs despite the massive and continuing purges of grassroots leaders. The central issue of concern, then, is where does this "undirected" rank-and-file resurgence come from, and what sustains it in the absence of official organization and in the face of an all pervasive terroristic police apparatus?

The Transformation of Argentina

Although Argentina has been ruled off and on by military dictators since the 1930s, the military regime of March 1976 represents an entirely new form of domination, both in terms of the scale, scope, and duration of repression. Never has the Argentine working class been subject to the level of terror and sustained attack that it has experienced during the regime of General Videla, who seized power in a coup in 1976. The singular effort by the military, paramilitary, and police forces to abolish all forms of political opposition has produced an unprecedented level of political assassinations, jailings, and exiles: more than 30,000 deaths and disappearances, thousands of jailings, hundreds of thousands of exiles, tens of thousands tortured, mutilated, and disfigured. Practically everyone in Argentina has direct personal ties with at least someone affected by the repression. Moreover, millions of Argentine workers and salaried employees have seen their political parties, trade unions, and community and social service organizations intervened and/or closed down—thus eliminating all the organization that had been created over the past fifty years. The regime of 1976 has set in motion forces and policies that are uprooting institutions and relationships established through the greater part of the twentieth century. In that precise historic context we cannot consider this a "conservative" or "traditional" dictatorship.

Previous dictatorships from the 1950s through the early 1970s (Aramburo, Ongania, Lanusse) were either "caretaker" regimes—seizing power to displace a populist government and prepare conditions for the return of a civilian regime—or engaged in haphazard, limited assaults, selective assassinations, and official imprisonment. In contrast, the neo-fascist regime engages in massive assassination, "disappearances" of political prisoners by paramilitary death squads in a systematic and sustained fashion. The institutionalization of terror and the permanent purge mark a qualitatively different form of dictatorship. The needs of large-scale capital for long-term security and sweeping access to all sectors of the economy confronted the obstacle of a highly organized working class: The end result was the long-term all-pervasive police state.

The central object of the state was the transformation of the major obstacle to capital expansion: the organized class-conscious working class. The major goal of the terror was to transform the working class from an obstacle to capital accumulation to an instrument of it. The purpose of the terror was a sustained effort to abolish systematically the memory of solidarity and the social bonds within the working class and to atomize the class and inculcate the feelings of subordination, inferiority, and servility characteristic of the pre-Perónist period: The ideal is to reproduce the docile *cabecitas negras* (a derogatory term used to refer to migrants from the interior) found in the past on the rural estates within the urban working class.

Much of the world's media has focused on the plight of the refugees, the regime's persecution of the intellectuals and professionals, and the killing and torture of well-known personalities and guerrilla leaders. But as Juan Carlos Marin has demonstrated (in *Argentina, 1973–1976*), the great bulk of those murdered by the regime were rank-and-file workers. The regime has launched wholesale attacks on militants in the factories—entire executive councils of locals have "disappeared"—and local officials: Grassroots leaders, shop stewards, class-oriented unionists, and rank-and-file-oriented Perónists all have been subject to one form of repression or another. Every major enterprise that has had "labor conflict" has been affected: In each case, the regime intervenes on the side of the owners, giving capital absolute control over its labor force. Never has the capitalist state acted in such an unconditional, unmediated fashion on behalf of capital.

Thus while the Videla regime represents a unique "break" with Argentine history, the reemergence of the working-class struggle on a massive scale in the face of terror represents a unique breakthrough for the working-class movement in Latin America. Despite the continuing terror, thousands of strikes involving tends of thousands of workers have taken place between November 1978 and January 1981. The Argentine working class has not been immobilized in the same fashion as has occurred in Chile and Uruguay. The explanations for this immobilization, which rely on repression, fail to explain why in Argentina, with similar or greater levels of repression, the struggle has broken out throughout the country and in a variety of industries and regions. Moreover, the level of formal organizations of the working class was higher in Argentina, and the subsequent dismantlement of these organizations was greater, thus leaving few formal institutional forms of expression open. Finally, through the connivance of the great powers (United States, Russia, China), the violations of human rights in Argentina have received far less attention than, say, Chile, and the struggle has certainly received far less outside support. The same can be said for the role of the Church, which has been critical of the regime in Chile but notably acquiescent in Argentina. The question is this: given the massive dismemberment of the formal organization of the working-class movement, the lack of international and internal institutional support, what accounts for the resurgence of working-class mass action?

The Two Faces of the Argentine Left

Attention should be focused on the fundamental division within the Argentine Left, which cuts across the formal political, trade union, and social organizations and ideology that are essential to understanding the process of class struggle emerging in the post-1976 period. There are essentially two Argentine "lefts," or popular movements, each with its distinct political style, social position, and structure. One can be referred to as the "political class" and the other as the "rank and file." The political class is composed of the leaders and organizers within the formal organizations, the professional politicians and trade union bureaucrats, the university intellectuals and professionals, and the spokespeople for the Marxist and nationalist traditions, who, in large part, provide the apparatus for the formal organizations and formulate the program for political action at the national level. The political class has been in charge of organizing the general strikes, the election campaigns, the public demonstrations, the guerrilla raids, the signing of collective agreements, and the publication of journals and manifestos. The political class has also received almost all the attention of the political and social analysts. Most of the writing about the Argentine popular movement refers to the activities and policies of this group and the reactions of the rank and file to the activities organized by the formal organizations.

These analyses seem to be shortsighted and to overlook the fact that the "rank-and-file" working class has its own social, political, and familial networks around which it organizes a good part of its life; that these relations, activities, values, and social position are distinct from those of the political class, even as they share with the "political class" common organizational membership (although different positions in the organization), electoral behavior, and opposition to the military and ruling class. However, there is a common subculture that unites the working class independently of the formal organization, which embraces kinship, neighborhood, work place, and social clubs. These common experiences set off the working class from the political class. The differences manifest themselves in some cases in different forms of verbal expression, but most fundamentally in the notion of compañerismo (comradeship), which comes from sharing the day-to-day hardships, social events, tragedies, sporting events. Moreover, there is even a "racial component," because the rank and file tends to be *cabecita's negras*, while the political class is largely drawn from a "European" background.

In practice, in the pre-1976 period, the two levels, the political class and the rank and file, interacted in general strikes, demonstrations, and elections, but not on a day-to-day basis. There was a separation of class, lifestyle, and language. Thus two sets of class bonds involve the working class: The vertical bonds manifested in its membership and activity in the impersonal national organization (Perónist movement, CGT), linking together the working class on a national level for political struggle; and the horizontal bonds found in the face-to-face relations in the neighborhood and work place, where the struggle is over immediate issues. This distinction within the Argentine popular movement between the "political class" and the "rank and file" is crucial to understanding how and why the Argentine working-class struggle continues, despite the savage repression of the formal organizations and the all-pervasive activities of the secret police and the terroristic paramilitary forces. The capacity of the Argentine working class to sustain collective struggle for class demands is rooted in the distinctive features of the Argentine working class, features found in few other workers' movements in the world in the same degree.

The Argentine Working Class

The most striking feature of the Argentine working class is the extraordinary degree of class solidarity and organization. This is manifested in its unique capacity to execute successfully massive general strikes on a nationwide basis with maximum success. Repeated general strikes of 24, 48, and 72 hours were called and supported by the entire class *voluntarily*, that is, with no effort to "coerce" the diffident class member into participation. Moreover, numerous strikes were called in the middle of workdays—perhaps at 10 A.M.—and in impressive displays of class solidarity hundreds of thousands of workers "downed their tools" in the presence of employers and, at times, in the face of military mobilizations. In 1971 the author witnessed a massive walkout of workers from an autoplant, part of a general strike, in which the workers had to walk through a cordon of heavily armed troops. Not one worker remained in the plant. The class solidarity extended to other strata also, involving small businessmen, teachers, social workers, and so forth. In Córdoba, having my shoes shined, a whistle went off signaling the beginning of a general strike, and the bootblack stopped working, leaving one shoe unpolished. When the strike was called, even the streetwalkers disappeared.

The second feature of the Argentine working class was a general rejection of the state and ruling-class domination and values. This is not to say that the workers did not demand services from the state or did not participate in national pasttimes (soccer matches), but rather it brought its own set of values and interests into play while engaging the adversary. Thus in extracting benefits from the state, the workers did not respond with "gratitude," but as something to which they were entitled and indeed *must receive*. The bourgeoisie was disenchanted with this "prepotencia de clase," as it characterized the self-affirmation of the working class. Even when workers participated in "national events" such as soccer matches, which supposedly bring all classes together, the seating arrangements and form of involvement reflect class differences. Moreover, the "national unity" is somewhat of a surface phenomenon. During the Copa Hemispherica in 1971 in Buenos Aires, a disputed play penalizing the Argentine team led to massive chants of "Argentina"—until the police came onto the field and pointed their riot guns at the vocal, but peaceful, galleries made up overwhelmingly of workers. Immediately, the chant changed to *asesinos*, while the bourgeois Argentines occupying reserved and box seats were silent. The presence of state authorities clearly evoked the underlying class hostilities of the working class, even in this mixed cultural setting.

On a more general level, the notion of class interest is manifested in the intransigent insistence of the working class not to sacrifice its standard of living for an illusory "national development"—capitalist accumulation. The level of mystification in this sense is very low. Even Perón was incapable of imposing any sacrifice of working-class interests in the name of national capitalist growth. On the contrary, his influence was totally dependent on his capacity to secure benefits for the working class and, failing that, his influences began to ebb. From this vantage point, working-class support for Perónist politics was less a product of mystification and more the expression of the search for instrumental goals.

The fourth feature of the Argentine working class was powerful informal bonds, expressed through family, neighborhood, and work place, which reinforced class bonds and links among the working class and against the ruling class. Family and kinship ties have frequently been described as "conservative" forces, limiting class consciousness. This approach assumes what it needs to prove—that the family and kinship groups themselves contain and transmit alien conservative values. In the Argentine case, at least two generations (1940–50 and 1960–70) shared common experiences of class struggle and organization. They shared membership in the same class-anchored social clubs, trade unions, and *asados* (cookouts), and therefore the primary group orientation reinforced class ties. Likewise, working and living associations have been described as inculcating "parochial," "local" outlooks, which are supposedly incompatible with class consciousness. Once again, the argument assumes that the *content* of the local involvement is diffuse or devoid of class content, which is precisely *not* the point: The neighborhoods and work places in Argentina are preeminently class homogeneous, at least to the degree of containing predominantly working and lower-salaried employees and petty vendors. The heavy arms and large contingents of police forces that were mobilized to make arrests in working-class neighborhoods attest to the fear that state authorities had of neighborhood reactions. Likewise, most kidnappings of workers took place after working hours to avoid the collective wrath a the work place.

The fifth feature of the Argentine working class was the high levels of trust, confidence, and mutual support within local working-class communities. This factor is crucial in understanding why the secret police has been hard pressed to break locally organized strikes and protests. It is extremely difficult to crack the tight family, kinship, and neighborhood ties. For a worker to become a police informer would not only label him a traitor to an "abstract" class but an enemy to his most basic and personal relations. It would lead to total ostracism from life-long companions, friends, and, most important, family members. The primary ties provide security for local class organizations and activists that no formal organization can match and to which no police or paramilitary organization has been able to destroy. Within these networks all the prohibited activities take place—and the word hardly ever leaks out. The author viewed a prohibited pro-Perónist film, *"Ni Vencidos ni Vencidors"*, during the Lanusse period, in a Rosario working-class house with thirty or forty other people—essentially three or four families, including grandparents, parents, and children, who had no sense of a security problem. Contrary to more conventional social scientists who speak of a "nonparticipatory," "alienated," or "nonintegrated" working class, the author found a high degree of integration in working-class subculture, which coincides with a rejection or nonparticipation in the dominant or oppresser culture promoted by the ruling class. The working class participated in the formal political and social organization of the class, but it also maintained its class autonomy, exercised through its informal local organizational ties.

State Repression: Political Class and the Rank and File

The central point is that state repression has had a differential effect on the "two faces" of the Argentine Left. Essentially, it was most successful in undermining the formally organized popular movement and least successful in destroying the rank-and-file basis of struggle—even though the latter had borne the brunt of the repression.

The political class has suffered massive destruction. Among the hundreds of thousands of Argentines in the diaspora are many of the intellectual, political, and trade union leaders of the popular movement. The exiles are the relatively more fortunate victims, for the terror has taken a massive toll of victims through innumerous kidnappings and "disappearances." For those few political intellectuals and party people who have remained in Argentina and are not incarcerated, fear has largely paralyzed their public life: The main preoccupation is survival.

Along with the physical decimation of the activist core, the terrorist regime has systematically dismantled the trade union organizations' intervening in the universities and proscribing political parties and destroying all forms of autonomous political and social organization. The end result is that what is left of the formal organization is largely an empty and impotent husk, tightly controlled or totally destroyed by the regime. The traditional political leaders hover together, petitioning and protesting but incapable of defining any new political initiatives or mobilizing any significant popular support. For all intents and purposes, the political class has been incapacitated.

The regime did not confine itself merely to intervening at the apex of the hierarchical order of the political movement; rather, it aimed its principal blows at the middle and lower ranks among the militants of the popular movement. More than any other regime in Argentine history, it acted to *uproot* the mass movement by a frontal assault on the main forces linked to the great mass of the wage-labor force: the factory militants, the shop stewards, the local union leaders. The Videla dictatorship (unlike previous traditional leaders) did not believe that a "handful of foreign-inspired agitators" were stirring up the otherwise complacent working class—nor did they act on that assumption. The dictatorship knew and acted on the assumption that the organized, conscious working class was "responsible" for the strikes, wage demands, and constraints on capital, and therefore it extended a policy that would directly affect the class as a whole: mass terror without constraints against all working class militants, with or without Marxist, Perónist, or syndicalist affiliations. For a brief conjunction, this massive bloody purge did arrest and perhaps intimidate the working class (April 7, 1976 until October 1978).

Many of the known local militants and political cadres were wiped out. The disarticulation of the national networks and formal political structures did temporarily disorient the working class. The result, however, was not permanent atomization or massive paralysis, as the regime had hoped, but a turning inward. The working class turned to the most elementary and secure forms of organization and struggle: to local activity organized around particular industries, factories, or neighborhoods; to limited demands for immediate needs (wage increases). From within each locale, new anonymous leaders emerged, collective spokespersons who negotiated contracts over the phone; the rank and file developed creative forms of action to secure demands and avoid assassination. Local organizations were reconstituted, based on primary and secondary groups; loyalties of kinship and friendship reinforced class ties and ensured security against the terrorist state.

By September 1979 a whole wave of strikes had broken out throughout the metallurgical, transport, and other industries. Hundreds of strikes in large and small plants became everyday occurrences. This massive upsurge occurred despite the continuing terror and in the absence of the formal trade union party and intellectual leadership. This resurgence of rank-and-file action can only be explained by the durability of the underlying class bonds located in the family, neighborhood, and factory, reinforced by the popular culture and provoked by the severe decline in the standard of living.

Explanations that resort to "spontaneity" refuse to look behind the existence of formal organization. The autonomous working-class rank and file of Argentine industrial capitalism activates itself and sustains activity through longstanding association in informal settings and groupings. This informal Argentine Left is today the most vital force in society. Yet it is the least discussed and understood, since communication and interaction is largely within the working class, and few intellectuals, foreign or Argentine, have any substantial relationship with it.

Indeed, for too many years most intellectuals measured class consciousness among workers through questionnaires that evaluated verbal responses in terms of scales derived from abstract ideology. The conclusions usually found an ambiguity or low level of class consciousness—a level that was incomprehensible in terms of the actual levels of struggle. The high level of class consciousness of the Argentine working class was and is manifested through participation in collective class activity and in the day-to-day interaction in places and events that have a specific class character.

In summary, then, despite the massive repression and physical destruction of thousands of local leaders, the Argentine working class has generated new leaders, organizers, and direct action because the neighborhood, the family, and the rank and file in the factories have within themselves the capacity to reproduce themselves. Like Hydra, every time the regime cuts off one head, two take its place.

15

The Nicaraguan Revolution in Historical Perspective

An Overview of the Revolution

The Nicaraguan revolution has great substantive importance for the country and even greater symbolic significance for the continent. For the first time in more than twenty years it was demonstrated that a U.S. armed and trained military dictatorship could be defeated in a popular armed upheaval. The defeats in Chile, Uruguay, Argentine, and other countries throughout the 1960s and 1970s weighed heavily on all popular movements. Now, approaching the 1980s, there is a resurgence of mass popular democratic movements throughout Latin America, of which the Sandinista-led forces were only the most developed and to date the only successful efforts.

Just as the Nicaraguan revolution has a profound symbolic impact on Latin America, so did many Latin Americans contribute with lives and arms to the victory of it. From all over Latin America, volunteers from fifteen to forty years of age joined the FSLN, among them veterans and novices, militants and idealists, to oust Somoza, symbol of tyranny, corruption, and wealth, of U.S. training, support, and subservience. The internationalists included Costa Ricans who, coming to politics, saw the gap between the professions of democracy and the practice of privilege; Chileans, who suffered the defeat of a revolution without a struggle at the hands of the military and the United States and who sought to redeem themselves; Mexicans who came out of the peasant struggles and who saw in Nicaragua a chance to relive the struggles of the past, equalizing the odds. Also included were those from Guatemala, El Salvador, and Honduras, who suffer similar terror and destruction and saw a chance to even the score, ending the reign of the regional gendarme and perhaps opening a new chapter—the first truly sovereign state in Central America governed by the people, not by the oligarchies of a few dozen families, or less. They came from Colombia's occupied universities, the offices and factories of Caracas, from the Chilean and Argentine diaspora, from Zapata country—the Latin American revolutionaries building barricades with the embattled street fighters from Managua, Masaya, Esteli, Leon, cities made famous throughout the world by the thousands of anonymous militants who took the streets and defended their barrios with rifles against Sherman tanks and moved from city to city until they captured the last bunker in Managua.

Nothing ran in Managua except by permission of the Front: factories were closed or in ruins; ports and transport were paralyzed. The workers traded their tools for guns; everywhere, everyone, made a decision to struggle to victory or die. The expression "the final struggle, cost what it may" passed from being a rhetorical exhortation of a guerrilla band to being the living expression of a determined and committed people. The marketplaces are empty: The stalls have been burned, and the vendors have nothing to sell. Weeks earlier, they hid scores of clandestine guerrillas entering the city; even the prostitutes, wielding knives, advised the guard patrols to keep going.

There are several features of the Nicaraguan revolution that bear discussion for their import to the rest of the Third World, especially Latin America. The writings that focus exclusively on the uniqueness of the Somoza dynasty and wealth overlook several historical processes that are operating on a world scale and that found expression in Nicaragua. This chapter will focus on: (1) the historical developments that generated the revolutionary upheaval; (2) the nature of the revolutionary process, the changing patterns, and the configuration of forces, strategies, and alliances; and (3) the contradictory development in the transitional period, i.e., the relationship between the organs of popular power, which were instrumental in the insurrectionary phase, and the governing organs.

Capitalist Development: Autocracy and Revolution

It is important, first, to deal with several misconceptions about the socioeconomic context of the revolutionary struggle. Nicaragua was not a simple "underdeveloped" country wallowing in stagnation and backwardness. From the 1950s to the mid-1970s, the Nicaraguan economy went through a period of rapid growth—large-scale commercialization of agriculture and high-powered expansion of industry, services, and finance. While most observers have noted the private wealth and corruption of Somoza, the fact is that a portion of that wealth took the form of capital investments. The growth of capitalism was accompanied in part by the proletarianization of the peasants in the countryside and the artisan in the city, along with the displacements of others and their incorporation into a large, surplus labor pool, which crowded the central cities in each region.

The state—the Somoza clan—and foreign capital played a decisive role in implanting capitalism and capitalist social relations. The whole process of rapid growth from above was made possible by the autocratic dictatorship and its "free market" and repressive labor policies, a pattern not unknown to other Latin American countries. This configuration of forces displaced many factions and sectors of traditional mercantile society, while they failed to integrate or provide mechanisms of representation for the new classes generated by the new pattern of capitalist development. The very terms for success of the autocratic-development ("from above and outside") model prevented the dominant forces from any sustained and consequential *democratization*. Rather, the pattern was one of selective and time-bound *liberalization*—modification of dictatorial policies—followed by widespread, systematic repression.

While the competitors for power were lodged largely within the two capitalist parties (Liberals and Conservatives), and while the adversaries were mostly capitalist competitors, conflict, including armed and mass activity, was a bargaining weapon to secure a better share of government revenues (subsidies, credit) and led to pacts between Somoza and his bourgeois critics. This pattern began to change only with the massive entry of the Frente Sandinista de Liberación Nacional (FSLN). In fact, parallel to the intransigent opposition of the FSLN, the bourgeois opposition continued to attempt to "deal" with Somoza and the United States in much the traditional pattern; the only difference was that the unsatisfactory results, from the point of view of the masses, gave further sustenance to the Frente and ultimately undermined bourgeois hegemony over the mass movement. Hence, the growth of capitalism and intrabourgeois conflicts provided a gloss of "competitive" politics, limited by the overwhelming concentration of power in the hands of the autocratic dictatorship and the total subordination of the National Guard to his rulership.

Rapid capitalist growth premised on large labor surpluses, labor discipline (no strikes, protests), and extensive as well as intensive exploitation provided a fertile basis for social mobilization in the cities and larger agro-industrial complexes. Unlike the early Sandino-led movement, largely based on peasant recruits, the contemporary Nicaraguan revolution is generally rooted in the *most urbanized, industrialized areas—the most 'advanced' sectors of production and social reproduction*. The revolutionary movement contains the most retrograde forces displaced by dynamic state and foreign capitalist development: the small and medium-size producers, as well as the new industrial working class, middle-class professionals, employees (employed in the modern industrial and service sectors), and the large reserves of underemployed, unemployed, semiproletarianized youth of the cities and countryside, all products of the same process of uprooting that accompanies capitalist development. Generally, the most passive, least rebellious sectors, with some notable exceptions, were the agricultural areas least affected by commercial-capitalist activity, the isolated villages and communities of the South.

The concentration of employed and unemployed workers in the cities, the growth of impersonal wage relations instead of payments in kind, and the decline of personal forms of domination and control in the sprawling urban slums facilitated antagonistic relations. The autocratic state, prime mover of capitalist growth, emasculated legitimate organs of representation and prevented effective articulation of demands for urban services. The social-overhead costs for the reproduction of labor were borne directly and totally by the direct producers. Hence, barrio organizations, initially activated around local and immediate needs, became the vehicles for FSLN mobilization: Only the most radical and determined organizations capable of withstanding the dictatorship could sustain a consequential struggle for incremental gains. The point of habitation became the principal point of organization, the common meeting ground, for employed and unemployed workers, proletarians, and semiproletarians. And the target was the state: the dispenser of social services, controller of social expenditures, the critical agent for urban real-estate speculation and slum eradication.

While the economic boom increased the social weight of the working class and employees in the cities, the economic downturns marginalized the bourgeoisie, especially those medium and small owners without access to state credits and subsidies, pushing them closer to bankruptcy and threatening their property-owning status. The crisis and the lack of access to the Somoza-dominated state pushed the marginalized bourgeoisie into opposition. The convergence of both workers, middle class and bourgeoisie, into a common anti-Somoza struggle and for democracy obscures the fundamentally different interests being pursued and the different concepts of the state. For the bourgeoisie and its petit-bourgeois political representatives, the issue is one of securing access to the state to promote its class interests, financing, credit, protection, subsidies, contracts—and the rapid demobilization and disarming of the masses in order to create a new state apparatus in the most proximate image of itself. For the masses, democracy is the generalization and sustenance of the local organs of popular power—their extension to control of the productive forces to serve barrio needs. *The most crucial issue in the post-Somoza period is political, not economic: reconstruction by whom and for whom?*

The concentration of the insurrectionary struggles in the cities and among the most radicalized working-class forces raises the issue of the *socialist* potentialities inherent in the struggle. The uneven nature of capitalist development, its concentration in certain urban/rural areas, finds expression in the uneven development of the revolutionary struggle. The insurrectionary struggle in the cities developed far in advance of the struggle in general: More important, the tempo and tasks of the revolution are not dictated by the *general* level of the productive forces in the *country as a whole*, but by the level of *class struggle* in the most *advanced* areas.

The Nature of the Revolutionary Process

The revolutionary process in Nicaragua covers a wide array of complementary and combined forms of struggle over a long period. Moreover, the revolutionary movement went through several phases: correcting itself, altering its course, and dividing and converging for the final assault on the Somoza dictatorship. The unquestionable central organization responsible for the overthrow of the autocratic regime is the FSLN, whose origins and development are derived from the Nicaraguan revolutionary experience of the 1920s and 1930s, and from more recent Latin American history.

From Sandino, the guerrilla leader and revolutionary opposed to U.S. occupation in the 1920s and 1930s, the FSLN derived several aspects of its program and orientation: (a) *nationalism* and *anti-imperialism* as the basic tenets of its program, in oppostion to other pro-U.S. oppositionists who presented themselves to the embassy as "democratic alternatives"; (b) *reliance on mass support*, as opposed to efforts mainly by the bourgeoisie to organize elite conspiracies and military coups behind the backs of the masses, thus substituting one elite for another; and (c) *development of armed struggle* as the only effective means of overthrowing the Somoza dictatorship (hence, rejection of all "negotiations," "pacts," and U.S.-sponsored mediations, as ploys to prolong the life of the regime and/or modify it in nonessential ways).

Founded in 1961, FSLN, heavily influenced by the "foco" theory of guerrilla warfare and by the success of the Cuban revolution, launched a series of military actions designed to detonate popular uprisings. These isolated military actions, led largely by students and professionals, were easily put down by the military, inflicting substantial losses but failing to destroy the organization. With the failure of the foco strategy, a complete change in tactics and orientation was introduced and applied beginning in the late 1960s and early 1970s. The decisive shift was toward the organization of mass support in the countryside and cities. The new perspectives envisioned a prolonged, popular war that would combine rural guerrilla activities (to harass the National Guard) and mass struggle in the cities, immediate struggle on local issues and political demands, legal and illegal organization, culminating in the organization of a general strike, the arming of the masses, and a national insurrection. The revolutionary insurrection was seen as a process, not as an event. The process leading to the insurrection can be divided into three phases:

Phase I: Accumulation of Forces in Silence, 1970–74. The FSLN, which generally did not act in its own name, engaged in organizing, mobilizing, and agitating in the barrios, trade unions, and schools through intermediate organizations that projected the basis for the organization of popular power. Through these intermediate organizations, the FSLN began to forge links with the mass movement and establish its legitimacy as a representative of the people. In everyday struggles for light, water, and sewers, combined with its organizational demands for political rights, it began to project itself as a national alternative to Somoza. The Frente's insertion in the strikes and protests following the 1972 earthquake—when the workday for workers was arbitrarily extended, aid funds were pocketed, and businessmen displaced—augmented its importance, especially among the urban working and middle class.

Phase II: Accumulation of Forces with Offensive Tactics: September 1974–August 1978. On September 22, 1974, the FSLN captured a number of high officials in the regime and was able to liberate a substantial number of political prisoners. This action signaled the beginning of a new turn in the struggle, which saw local demands increasingly combined with national political issues: neighborhood issues, with attacks on the dictatorial nature of the state; and trade union rights, with demands for the freeing of political prisoners. A rising wave of mass protests and demonstrations forced the liberal bourgeoisie to augment its pressure on Somoza. With the assassination of *La Prensa* editor Chamorro in January 1978, the bourgeoisie attempted to channel the discontent through a general strike (during which the workers were paid). But the strikes begun by the bourgeoisie passed beyond their control; the incapacity of the bourgeois-led general strike to topple Somoza and their unwillingness to sustain the struggle to the end severely eroded their mass support and hastened the mass exodus toward the FSLN. Throughout this period, mass organization in the cities and guerrilla harassment in the countryside increased.

Phase III: Accumulation of Forces in Strategic Offensive: September 1978–July 1979. The constant mobilization, conflict, and regime repression created the objective conditions for insurrection. Whole neighborhoods and sectors of the city were openly defiant of the regime; the intermediate organizations welded together in the United People's Movement (MPU) openly recognized the FSLN as its representative leader. The FSLN was converted from a guerrilla organization to a mass one. The Somoza regime was increasingly isolated: the bourgeoisie organized in the Broad Opposition Front (FAO); the liberal democrats, calling themselves The Twelve (Los Doce), were openly calling for the overthrow of Somoza, the disbanding of the National Guard, and a coalition including the FSLN; and the MPU increased its organizational network to virtually every area of the country. While politically vulnerable, Somoza was still militarily strong.

The insurrection of September 1978 was partly spontaneous and partly the result of the initiative of a faction of the Sandinistas (the Tercerista, or Insurrectional, wing). A general strike was called by the MPU following the seizure of the Government Palace by the Terceristas and the uprisings in Matagalpa, uprisings in Monimbó, Masaya, León, Chinandega, and the rest of the major cities and towns. The Guard and Air Force destroyed cities, houses, hospitals, and schools in their attempt to drown the insurrection in blood. They failed. The genocidal repression polarized the whole country *against* Somoza and *for* the FSLN. Several strategic tasks faced the FSLN: (1) to unify the three forces; (2) to organize and coordinate the insurrections at the national level; (3) to attack strategic areas affecting the regime; (4) to disperse its forces into several fronts; and (5) to arm the organized local committees in each city.

The strengths and limitations of the September uprising were analyzed. First, within the FSLN there were substantially different conceptions in relation to the political-military strategy—divisions over how to confront the dictatorship—that impeded a unified action. Second, the absence of sufficient arms forced the populace to rely on hunting weapons and handguns; revolvers against tanks. Both issues were resolved first by the unification of the Sandinista tendencies, formally signed in March 1979, and second through a concerted effort to organize and arm popular militias, Comites de Defensa Civil (CDC), and Comites de Defensa de Trabajadores (CDT) throughout the major cities. The positive results of the September insurrection were evidenced in the general recognition of the importance of the masses in the military tasks and the centrality of political organization.

The organizational experience prepared the masses for the political administrative tasks in the subsequent uprising in May-July 1979. Finally, tactically, the FSLN leadership recognized that the armed forces of the regime had to be engaged out of the population centers prior to the mass insurrection, to take some of the pressure off and allow breathing space for the local committees and militia to establish themselves. By the beginning of 1979 a new wave of unrest began to grow. In February there was another uprising in Monimbó (Masaya), continual guerrilla and militia harassment of the Guard, daily barricades, street demonstrations, and takeovers of churches, buildings, and schools. By May the barrios were ready to explode once again, only this time the insurrection was organized, the militants were armed, and the FSLN command was unified. Within a month, twenty cities were in the hands of the people.

From the beginning of the insurrection, the local committees took charge in León, Esteli, Masaya, and Matagalpa, areas of large concentrations of workers and with long traditions of militancy and political struggle, both of which weighing heavily in the level of organization. In León and Masaya, the CDT (Workers Defense Committees) were transformed into military organizations that organized the seizure of the town and took over the factories, continuing production. In the rest of the country, the CDC (Civil Defense Committees) functioned as politico-administrative and defense units, sustaining defense, distributing food, and maintaining sanitary conditions.

The FSLN leadership, especially where the GPP (Prolonged Popular War) and Proletarian Tendency predominated, envisioned the CDC and CDT playing a major role in all aspects of the insurrectionary effort. One document described the functions of the CDC: train the masses in all forms of civil defense; create groups of guards to protect and supply the neighborhoods, preventing the activity of anarchistic groups; create food and provision outlets; collect all types of material that serve to defend the barricades; concentrate all material that could serve for defense against punitive actions by the enemy forces; develop clandestine hospitals and clinics; establish operational barracks; collect medicine; orient the masses to recover food from the regime's supply centers; locate the strategic points through which the enemy might advance; create linkage and supply groups with the Sandinista military groups fighting in the barrios; and provide information to the militia and the military forces about the Somoza forces and their supporters.

The CDT were oriented toward: obtaining control of the principal factories, especially strategic ones in order to make them function in the manner of small war industries; take hold of any and all objects that could be converted into a weapon, making it available to the combatants; maintain the workers concentrated as a class, linking their revolutionary activity with that of the neighborhood masses; create obstacles in the strategic transport lines, impeding the enemies' movement; gain control of the means of communication; paralyze the public sector and call on the technicians to provide aid to the combatants; seizure of the haciendas of the Somozas and their supporters and transform them into refugee centers for noncombatants; and incorporate fighters to the militias or Sandinista army.

The successful insurrection in all the major cities and in eastern Managua reflected the long-term political-organizational work of the FSLN covering the previous decade. Both the formal organizations and the informal networks functioned to bring about complete solidarity between barrio residents and combatants, evidenced in the flood of volunteers, militia units, and the saying that every house was a Sandinista fortress.

Although these mass organizations do not have an explicit class character, the bulk of their membership is drawn from the working class—employees and unemployed. The CDC and the CDT could serve as the basis for a new form of popular representation and government. During the insurrection, the interbarrio committees coordinated defense throughout the municipality and could serve as the instrument for popular control over reconstruction.

Several features of the revolutionary struggle should be underlined because of their importance not only in the Nicaraguan context, but in terms of future revolutionary struggles in the rest of Latin America.

(1) The combined guerrilla movement with mass urban insurrectionary organizations were both necessary ingredients to sustain each other's struggle. The previous debates that counterposed one approach to the other have been surpassed.

(2) The urban mass movements through their organized local power were able to destroy the standing army located in their cities. The notion of the outdatedness of urban insurrections itself has been demonstrated to be outdated. What was clearly in evidence was the high level of political organization, availability of arms, and the broadest organizational unity.

(3) The prolonged nature of the struggle was evidenced in the several stages through which it passed and the concomitant shifts in tactics and strategy. The Nicaraguan experience illustrates the fact that revolution is a process requiring the gradual accumulation of forces, punctured by decisive actions that focus on the essential weaknesses of the regime and mobilize previously uncommitted forces. The flexibility of the revolutionary leadership, reflected in its recognition of the specificities of the issues and problems facing urban/industrial organizations, was necessary in laying the groundwork for mass organization. The fusion of barrio and factory struggles and the dialectical interplay of both clearly demonstrated the critical importance of combining political action at the points of habitation and production. The necessity of combining extralegal and legal struggles provided the military and mass organization necessary to sustain insurrectionary activity. Tactical unity and organizational independence facilitated the maximum application of pressure at critical moments and, at the same time, allowed the revolutionary movement to raise the level of struggle beyond immediate issues to broader systemic problems.

(4) The insurrectionist activities of the Tercerista faction served to detonate action, while the GPP and Proletarian Tendency organizers laid out the mass organization that sustained the struggle. The *audacity* of the former and the organization of the latter were complementary, each requiring the other to make the revolution succeed.

(5) The development of the mass movement passed through a stage of bourgeois hegemony, which was undermined by its incapacity to sustain the struggle once the masses were mobilized. The FSLN displaced the

FAO between February and September 1978, a period in which the struggle increasingly took the form of mass armed struggle. Having been displaced, however, the bourgeoisie has not been eliminated from the scene. The question remains whether it will be able through political manipulation to gain what the masses won militarily.

(6) The self-directed and organized mass organizations evidenced in the uprisings of September 1978 and even more so in May-July 1979 demonstrate that the masses are not looking toward a bourgeois-democratic state dominated by notable personalities, but rather are struggling for a regime that allows direct mass participation in the process of transformation.

(7) The mass organizations that were instruments of struggle against the dictatorship can also be the instruments for "reconstruction." Even before the arrival of the junta, the mass organizations took a leading role in the organization of production and distribution and in the administration of neighborhoods. The Factory Defense Committee, the Civil Defense Committees, and the militia, which were the parallel power to Somoza, could also serve the same function with the junta, *thus ensuring that the revolution continues uninterrupted.*

Conclusion

During the early part of the twentieth century, a number of political economists recognized that the old boundaries of the nation-state were no longer adequate in political-economic analysis. On the capitalist side, such diverse thinkers as Joseph Schumpeter and J. A. Hobson discussed the problems associated with the great transformation of the world into a vast capitalist marketplace, as well as the nature, sources, and consequences of these developments. On the opposite side, in the pre-Stalinist era, among Marxists, Lenin, Trotsky, Luxemburg, Bukharin and numerous others turned to study the growth of capitalism on a world scale—the nature of imperialism, its impact on non-European societies, and the conflictual relationships among expanding productive systems. For a variety of reasons, this global perspective on state and class formation was eclipsed from the early 1930s to the mid-1960s, even as the consequences of the conflictual integration of states in the world capitalist system became catastrophically evident—namely worldwide depressions, wars, and national liberation struggles.

Within the capitalist countries, social studies remained embedded in the national framework, operating within the same units that government policymakers and ruling classes used to legitimate their rule. Nationalist ideology permeated the conceptual apparatuses and the specification of values of consequences, while sophisticated mathematical modeling was based on crude ethnocentric assumptions. In the socialist movement the Stalinist takeover transformed Marxism into an ideology of the state. This ideology, in theory and practice, turned Marxism into a tool of the bureaucratic regime of a single state. Even in those states that broke with the Soviet Union (China and Yugoslavia), the framework of the nation-state took priority in the formulation of policy and subsequently of social analysis. The bureaucratic regime's notion of "building socialism in one country" took hold and initially affirmed in triumphal and exaggerated terms the possibilities of building socialism

275

with the correct leadership and the will of the people. The same willful acts of the bureaucracy that denied the international nature of capitalism, the class struggle, and exploitation later turned around and solemnly proclaimed the absolute necessity to develop trade, technology, and markets with the Western countries, even at the political price of opening up their countries to joint ventures, private farming, expensive licensing agreements, and recognition of spheres of influence. In sum, social science in the East and West, subordinated to the political exigencies of the ruling classes of their respective systems, formulated its problems and analysis within a framework dominated by nineteenth-century ideas of the "autonomous" or independent and self-sustaining nation-states, even as the events of the twentieth century were shattering that framework.

As has been illustrated in these essays, capitalism has become "international" in a number of senses: accumulation is worldwide, the state operates on a global basis, and the class struggles involve political actors across national boundaries. Revolutions and civil wars increasingly become internationalized. Even as the particular locus of class conflict begins at the national level, the protagonists draw sustenance and opposition from a variety of international forces. In this regard, the level of international support between imperialist forces and their collaborator classes is much higher than between revolutionary classes—in part because of the great disparity in technical and economic resources, and in part because of the "national" perspective within which revolutionary forces take power.

Our framework is not an amorphous "world-capitalist system" that dominates states and classes, but rather one that focuses on interstate and interclass relationships set in motion by the processes of international capitalist development and accompanied by class conflict. From the 1940s to the 1970s, the centerpiece of the capitalist interstate system is the U.S. imperial state: Its political and military power was accompanied by the vast growth of its economic holdings. Revolutionary outcomes were directly dependent on the measure of forces between Third World combatants and U.S. military and intelligence organizations. In the 1980s this interstate system will be seriously challenged: European and Japanese capital has increasingly eroded the U.S. economic position; Third World capitalism, dependent and semi-industrialized, has created new centers of conflict and has set in motion radicalized social forces; OPEC countries have increased the competition for energy resources.

The U.S. imperial state continues to operate, but it does so in a world of competitive allies in the West and vulnerable collaborators in the East. The maturing of capitalism on a world scale has not led to greater stability and cooperation, but rather to increasing conflict and competition. The interstate system held together by the imperial state is becoming unglued precisely by the relations engendered by the growth of capitalism within that state framework. And it is in the Third World where the sociopolitical consequences of worldwide capitalist growth are most acutely felt. Proletarianization and unrootedness have been telescoped in a few short decades, aided and abetted by autocratic ruling groups linked to metropolitan classes. Imperial capital's penetration and instrumentalization of all previous forms of production makes a joke of the sterile exercises of academic Marxists who waste their time counting the number of modes of production in a social formation—like scholastics of the Middle Ages enumerating how many angels could dance on the head of a pin.

The existence of a "peasantry" is today a means of capitalizing the economy, of subsidizing the urban or rural wage-labor force, a permanent labor reserve for real-estate capital. The intellectual issue is not only to recognize the variation in the "types of peasants" and the internal differentiation among workers and between wage and salaried strata, but to recognize the common set of conditions imposed by the process of worldwide capital accumulation and the levels of coercion resulting from the emerging neo-fascist dictatorship. The recent revolutions—and the list is growing—have demonstrated the wide array of social classes that have emerged as conscious actors *against* the institutional constraints imposed by the imperial state and its collaborator classes.

While the process of capitalist transformation is worldwide, the process of class resistence begins at the national level: The intersection of internal and international forces finds expression in the "exaggerated" affirmation of national and cultural demands, even as these are combined with social and political programs. The process of imperial-induced capitalist development has created an amalgam of oppositional forces, ranging from petty-commodity producers, salaried consumers, and manual workers to local entrepreneurs and religious figures—each with its own sets of programmatic issues and political perspectives. The processes of transformation of capitalism are thus a problematical phenomena precisely because of the incomplete nature of the capitalist transformation and the absence of any viable international force capable of unifying social forces across national boundaries. The unevenness of imperial-induced capitalist development means that revolutions will include contradictory class forces that resist the full socialization of production, that have no objective interest to counterpose to the market mechanisms, and whose primary basis of conscious solidarity may still be the household.

Thus, while capital is becoming global, and the tendency is toward polarized class societies, the "subjective' element in the social overturn continues to be influenced by past relations of production more than those that are emerging. Collective class action is, in some cases, preceding class consciousness within the labor force as a whole. Recently, industrialized workers and the uprooted rural migrants in the cities are engaging in class warfare in many parts of the Third World. However, the outcomes have not demonstrated a capacity among those classes to institutionalize their power in new forms of governance. The working class in the Third World has challenged the capitalist state, but it has not (as yet) been able to constitute itself as an alternative ruling class. The imperial state has established the basis for worldwide capital expansion, but it has not been able to prevent anticapitalist or anti-imperialist uprisings.

Between the upsurge from labor and the decline of imperial power, there has emerged a series of "national regimes." These regimes attempt to "take up space," capitalizing on the working-class struggles and the deterioration of imperial power. These regimes sustain themselves internally by enlarging the scope and size of the repressive apparatuses and state economic activity, even as they become more integrated into the world-market networks. The all-inclusive state and the immersion in the market, far from being a paradox, result from the unmitigated operations of the market, especially on dependent societies.

The growth of capital engendered by the dictatorial state sets forth a new cycle of conflict and upheaval. However, as the level of productive forces advances, the social demands of the "oppositionists" forces will become more attuned with the increasingly socialized nature of the labor force. The spiraling nature of social and political revolution suggests that, over time, the populist and pseudosocialist revolutionary regimes found in many parts of the Third World—in part a reflection of the underdevelopment of productive forces—will give way to more authentic forms of worker-based socialist societies.

Index

279